IDAHO'S 200 Cities

The North

Learning about Idaho and each of its 200 incorporated cities
– Their Past – Their Present – and Their Future

Volume 1 of 3

IDAHO'S
200 CITIES
The North
Volume 1 of 3

Their Past – Their Present
– and Their Future

Edited by Hal Bunderson

A Project of
The Association of Idaho Cities

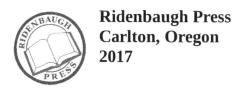

Ridenbaugh Press
Carlton, Oregon
2017

IDAHO'S 200 CITIES: THE NORTH
Copyright ©2017 by the Association of Idaho Cities
All rights reserved. No part of this book may be reproduced or transmitted in any form, by any information storage or retrieval system, without written permission from the publisher, except in case of brief quotations used in critical articles or reviews.
For more information, contact Ridenbaugh Press, P.O. Box 834, Carlton OR 97111.
Printed and bound in the United States of America.
First edition October 2017
10 9 8 7 6 5 4 3 2 1

Library of Congress Cataloging in Publication Data

Association of Idaho Cities.

History – Idaho – cities

Bibliography

1. History. 2. Idaho.

I. Association of Idaho Cities. II. Title.

ISBN-13 978-0-945648-41-3 (softbound)

For more information, or to order more copies of this book, contact:

Ridenbaugh Press
P.O. Box 834, Carlton OR 97111
Phone (503) 852-0010
www.ridenbaugh.com
stapilus@ridenbaugh.com

The Association of Idaho Cities has produced Idaho's 200 Cities or the three-fold purpose of:

- Fostering goodwill, knowledge and understanding of each of Idaho's three Regions and 200 Incorporated Cities
- Helping Idahoans, in fact and at heart, learn of our shared rich heritage
- Promoting economic development and strategic planning in Idaho and in each of its 200 incorporated cities and 44 counties

Proceeds from the sale of Idaho's 200 Cities will finance the not-for-profit purposes of The Association of Idaho Cities.

The Association of Idaho Cities thanks all of the volunteers and staff – too numerous to list – for their contributions to this work.

Table of Contents

Foreword

Idaho's 200 Cities is a six-volume book project that tells the story of Idaho through the history and development of its communities. Three of the books cover history and background about the three north, southwest and east regions of the state; three additional volumes consist of trivia questions and answers.

The project was conceived in 2004 by former Idaho State Senator Hal Bunderson of Meridian who served seven terms in the Idaho Senate and chaired the Senate Local Government & Taxation Committee. During his service in the Legislature, Bunderson was a passionate advocate for local government. He believed policymakers would benefit from a resource that would help them better understand Idaho's communities and their history, opportunities and challenges.

Bunderson presented his novel idea at an Association of Idaho Cities annual conference, generously offering to volunteer his time and expenses to complete this ambitious work if AIC and the cities would do their part. The conference delegates responded with a standing ovation, and the AIC Board unanimously approved the project. Bunderson's late wife, Mary Kay, joined him in his commitment. As Executive Director of AIC, I invited four experts to form a Blue-Ribbon panel of reviewers and editors to read each pre-final draft chapter approved by Senator Bunderson and offer comment:

- Bob Fick, longtime Associated Press Correspondent and Administrative Support Manager for the Idaho Department of Labor;
- Keith Petersen, formerly Idaho State Historian and Associate Director of the Idaho State Historical Society;
- Martin Peterson, former State Budget Director, Executive Director of the Association of Idaho Cities, and Special Assistant to the President of the University of Idaho; and
- Dr. James Weatherby, former Executive Director of the Association of Idaho Cities and Director of the Public Policy Center at Boise State University.

GayDawn Oyler, AIC Administrative Assistant, was designated to manage and control the work on each of the 203 chapters and trivia. In addition to her normal workload, she monitored and managed the progress on hundreds of draft manuscripts and communication between the cities and volunteers, and between Senator Bunderson and the Blue-Ribbon Panel.

As soon as the Board approved the project, Bunderson and AIC staff set about designing the book format and structure as a template for writing the city chapters. The Blue Ribbon Panel and the AIC Board approved the format. Mayors appointed city staff and citizens to help in providing original research and writing their city's chapter using the standard chapter format. Bunderson then led the effort of compiling, editing and writing where necessary, each of the city chapters. He also wrote the regional chapters and trivia books.

Over 100 people contributed several thousand hours of research, writing, proofing and editing for this project. AIC is grateful for the excellent work of these many volunteers. The purposes of this project are five-fold.

1. Promote Economic Development: The books provide valuable information for people considering moving their residence or business to or within Idaho. In a short period of time, people can learn the essential information about a city: its population, elevation, climate, geology, amenities and attractions, economy and major industries, education, health care, transportation, and utilities and services. They can also learn about the history of each city, including the pre-incorporation years, incorporation, turning points and Vision for 2050.

2. Support Long-Term Planning: AIC encourages long-range planning by cities with input from their business leaders and citizens. Over 70 percent of Idaho residents live in incorporated cities and the vast majority of Idaho's jobs and economic activity are located in cities. Idaho's wellbeing depends in large measure on the health and vitality of its cities, which is grounded in long term land use and strategic plans adopted at the local level.

3. Encourage Statewide Unity: Technology has revolutionized the way we live. The geographic, demographic and cultural barriers of the past are losing their significance. The diverse communities of Idaho have much more in common than many people realize. Understanding our shared histories and vision helps us recognize that life is better when we work together for the common good.

4. Education: These volumes are intended to provide a fun, easy way to learn highlights of Idaho history—the warts and the roses. The trivia may also be used to add interest to school history classes, as well as parties and family reunions.

5. Vision for the Future: These volumes offer a projection of what each city may look like in 2050. Going forward, it may assist city officials and candidates for public office with a better opportunity to contemplate, articulate and communicate their vision for their city or political jurisdiction.

While special care has been taken to ensure sound research and accuracy, there may still be errors. AIC invites public comment and additional trivia (with documentation) that may be considered for subsequent editions.

Proceeds from the sale of the books, net of production and publishing costs, will finance nonprofit purposes of the Association of Idaho Cities.

This book project is affectionately dedicated to Senator Hal Bunderson and his wife, Mary Kay. Senator Bunderson's dedicated service to the State of Idaho and its communities is best reflected in these words by Henry Wadsworth Longfellow:

"The heights by great men reached and kept
Were not attained by sudden flight,
But they, while their companions slept,
Were toiling upward in the night."

Ken Harward
AIC Executive Director (1998-2014)

Idaho's Cities: The Basics

Idaho's 200 cities display a wealth of diversity that reflects the social, economic, geographic and political diversity of our state. Despite these differences, Idaho cities have much in common. All look to the Idaho Constitution and state laws governing the creation, form, powers and limitations of city governments. Similarly, all municipal corporations, regardless of population size, operate under the same laws and are referred to as "cities."

About the Association of Idaho Cities

The Association of Idaho Cities (AIC) was founded in 1947 and is a nonpartisan, nonprofit corporation owned, organized and operated by Idaho's city governments. The association's mission is to promote excellence in, and advocate for, city governance, community leadership, and services to citizens to strengthen Idaho cities. AIC provides vital training, technical assistance and advocacy for Idaho's 200 incorporated cities. The organization is governed by a Board of Directors of city elected officials representing seven geographical districts.

Cities by the Numbers

- Idaho has 200 incorporated cities.
- Cities range in population from 218,281 in Boise to a low of 3 in Warm River, a tiny resort community in Fremont County (2016 U.S. Census estimates).
- There are 1,084 elected city mayors and councilors serving their communities.
- 70% of Idahoans choose to live within cities, a percentage that has been steadily increasing over the years.
- To keep Idaho communities safe there are currently 1,300 police officers, 2,700 career fire fighters, and 7,300 volunteer fire fighters responding to emergency service calls.
- Cities are responsible for 2,600 centerline miles of streets and 267 bridges.
- Cities have invested $1 billion in wastewater treatment facilities and treat over 5.84 billion gallons of wastewater each year.
- Cities have invested $475 million in drinking water treatment and delivery facilities.
- Idaho public libraries have 4.3 million print materials in circulation and nearly 1,600 public access Internet terminals.
- Idaho cities have invested $40 million in swimming pools, $90 million in parks and playground equipment, and $35 million in ballparks, tennis courts and skate parks.
- There are over 5,000 acres of city parks and open space, and over 150 miles of developed greenbelts and pathways.

Pre-Statehood

Before Idaho achieved statehood in 1890, the Territorial Legislature granted city charters to three cities: Boise, Lewiston and Bellevue. These charters covered the form of government, powers and responsibilities, taxes and revenue, indebtedness, elections, and the city's ability to grow through annexation.

Lewiston and Boise abandoned their territorial charters in the 1960s when voters approved transitioning the cities to operate under state law.

Bellevue still retains its city charter, which has several distinctive elements relative to other Idaho cities. Members of the city governing body are called aldermen instead of councilors, and the mayor and aldermen are elected to two-year terms (elected officials in cities operating under state law generally serve four-year terms). The Legislature must approve any changes to Bellevue's charter.

Incorporation of New Cities

Any community with a population of 125 or more qualified electors can file a petition for incorporation with the County Commissioners in the County in which it is located. The petition must be signed by 60% of the qualified electors of the proposed city, and must include the name and boundaries of the proposed city. The County Commissioners then have guidelines to follow, including calculating the distance between the petitioning community and any other already incorporated cities in the area, before granting the incorporation request. If the request is granted, a copy of the Articles of Incorporation and the approval are filed with the Secretary of State's Office.

Classification of Cities, Recodification of the Municipal Code

Before 1967, Idaho law provided for three classifications of cities—first class cities, second class cities and villages—with the classifications based on population. Within these three classes of cities, the law provided for four different forms of government: mayor-council, council-manager, commission and village.

Cities in each class operated under different provisions of law concerning the structure, powers and duties of city government, and these laws were amended many times over several decades. The need to modernize and simplify municipal government laws led to a recodification of the municipal code, which was passed by the Idaho Legislature in 1967.

Under the new municipal code, all city classes were abolished and the forms of government were reduced to two: the mayor-council and council-manager. All cities, from the largest in population to the smallest, would operate under the same laws and be called "cities," (except for charter cities). The recodified municipal code was much more streamlined, considerably shorter in length and easier for people to understand.

Forms of City Government

The mayor-council form of government is established by Idaho law as the default form of city government, with a mayor and either four or six councilors. The term of office for mayors and councilors is normally four-years; however, there are occasionally two-year council terms that occur when a vacancy arises in the first two years of the four-year term.

Elections for city mayors and councilors are held in November of odd-numbered years.

At local option, cities may adopt the council-manager form of government, with a five or seven-member council and a professional city manager serving at the pleasure of the council. Currently, only the cities of Lewiston, McCall and Twin Falls operate under the council-manager form of city government.

In council-manager cities, the mayor is selected by the council from among its members at the first meeting in January following a general city election for a two-year term. The mayor's primary role is in chairing council meetings, and the mayor is entitled to vote on all matters before the council, but exercises no tie-breaking or veto power.

The city manager is responsible for overseeing the administration of the city, ensuring that city laws and policies are faithfully executed, appointing department heads, advising the council of the city's financial condition, preparing and submitting a tentative budget for the upcoming fiscal year, and other duties as prescribed by the council.

Roles and Responsibilities

In cities operating under the mayor-council form of government, the mayor is the chief executive and administrative official of the city and has the following powers and responsibilities:

- Breaking tie votes of the council;
- Serving as the presiding officer at council meetings;
- May veto ordinances passed by the council, subject to council override by a majority of the full council;
- Ensuring that city and state laws are enforced;
- Supervising city employees; and
- Performing marriage ceremonies.

The city council is the legislative governing body for the city and has the following powers and responsibilities:

- Adopting local laws (ordinances),
- Determining what services will be provided by the city and the fees for these services,
- Adopting the city budget,
- Setting the city's property tax levy, and
- Receiving financial reports from the city treasurer.

Powers of City Government

Article XII, Section 1 of the Idaho Constitution charges the Idaho Legislature with responsibility to "provide by general laws for the incorporation, organization and classification of the cities and towns, in proportion to the population, which laws may be altered, amended, or repealed by the general laws."

Most of the laws governing cities are found in Title 50 of Idaho Code, titled Municipal Corporations, which defines:

- Forms of city government;
- How to incorporate new cities and disincorporate cities that no longer need to function;
- The process for enlarging the city through annexing adjacent land;
- Roles and responsibilities of the mayor, council, and other city officials;
- How to pass local laws (ordinances);
- City budgeting and finances; and
- Use of urban renewal and tax increment financing to address urban blight and promote economic development.

Cities exercise two distinctly different types of powers: governmental powers and proprietary powers.

- **Governmental Powers:** The most prominent is the police power, which vests cities with authority to pass laws to protect the public health, safety and welfare, provided the laws do not conflict with state or federal law. The police power is derived from Article XII, Section 2 of the Idaho Constitution. Other governmental powers include the powers of taxation, eminent domain and annexation and are derived from laws enacted by the Idaho Legislature.
- **Proprietary Powers:** Cities are empowered to provide certain business-type services for the benefit of citizens and businesses in the city, such as water and sewer service, solid waste collection, street maintenance, parks, airports, etc. Cities derive their proprietary powers from laws enacted by the Idaho Legislature.

How Do Cities Relate to Other Units of Government?

In our federal system of government, the federal government is supreme and cities must comply with federal law and the United States Constitution.

The situation is similar at the state level: the Idaho Legislature and the Idaho Constitution is supreme to all local governments in Idaho and the Legislature exercises considerable control over local governments through policymaking.

Cities are unique among local governments because they are created by their citizens to provide needed services for the community, and cities exercise both governmental and proprietary powers.

In contrast, counties are created by the State of Idaho to perform a mix of state mandated and discretionary functions.

- Counties are empowered by Article XII, Section 2 of the Idaho Constitution to adopt ordinances to protect public health, safety and welfare. County ordinances only apply to the unincorporated territory of the county—cities have police power authority within city limits.
- Counties serve as an arm of the state in administering the property tax system, courts, law enforcement, jails, disaster planning and preparedness, and elections at the local level.

- Other state mandated county services include: indigent medical care, public defenders for indigent criminal defendants, juvenile corrections, planning and zoning, roads and bridges, landfills, and weed control.
- County discretionary functions include: airports, ambulance service, hospitals, parks and recreation, fairs, agricultural extension, and historical societies and museums.

Special districts—highway, cemetery, water/sewer, recreation, library, etc.—are formed by citizen petition to provide necessary and desired services in a specific geographic area and have no regulatory authority.

Cities' Roles in Economic Development

Cities are the engine of Idaho's economy and city officials work in partnership with the Idaho Department of Commerce to attract and retain businesses. The infrastructure cities provide—water, sewer, streets, and stormwater drainage—is an essential factor for businesses deciding where to locate.

Over 40 Idaho communities have urban renewal agencies, which finance infrastructure to make sites ready for new businesses, as well as revitalize deteriorating downtown areas.

An urban renewal plan is adopted by the city council that identifies the work that needs to be done in an area and the funding sources that will pay for the projects. Most urban renewal projects are financed through tax increment financing, which dedicates property tax revenue from development within the area to urban renewal projects.

One of the most powerful economic development incentives in Idaho is the Tax Reimbursement Incentive (TRI), which offers a tax credit of up to 30% on income, payroll and sales taxes for up to 15 years. The incentive is available for a broad range of industries, including aerospace, agriculture, food processing and high-tech, and it is open to existing businesses looking to expand and businesses new to Idaho.

To be eligible for the incentive, the business must:
- Create at least 20 new jobs in rural areas, or at least 50 new jobs in urban areas;
- New jobs must be full-time (30 hours or more) and pay equal to or greater than the average county wage;
- The community must provide a meaningful match, which can be met through in-kind work done by city employees or through the capital investment property tax exemption;
- The company must prove its stability and a significant economic impact to the community and state; and
- The company must provide that the incentive is a critical factor in its decision to locate or expand.

Another economic development incentive often used with the TRI is the capital investment property tax exemption. Businesses that invest a certain amount in new non-retail commercial or industrial facilities can receive a full or partial exemption of property taxes on the new facility and equipment for up to five years. The county commissioners determine the minimum level of capital investment, which must be at least $500,000.

The TRI and capital investment property tax exemption have a proven track record of success in attracting and retaining businesses.

Amy's Kitchen, the nation's leading maker of organic and non-GMO convenience food, purchased the 500,000-square foot facility in Pocatello formerly operated by Heinz. Amy's currently employs approximately 400 employees. When the project is fully staffed over 15 years, the economic impact to the state of Idaho is expected to include new capital investment of $76 million, new total wages of $342 million and new direct state tax revenue of $30 million. Amy's Kitchen received a 26% TRI credit over 15 years and a 75% property tax exemption for capital investment over five years.

Quest Aircraft expanded its existing facility in Sandpoint, adding 75,000 square feet to its production facility that builds KODIAK turboprop airplanes for backcountry and personal use. By the end of the 12-year project term, it is anticipated that there will be 187 new jobs, capital investment of $5.4 million, project wages of $75.8 million and new direct state tax revenue of $4.5 million. Quest received a 25% TRI credit over 12 years. Quest was also granted a 75% property tax exemption for its investment in buildings and structural components, and its exemption for equipment and machinery was 100% in the first two years, 75% in the third year and 50% for the fourth and fifth years.

Cities' Responsibilities in Planning and Zoning

Idahoans are fortunate to enjoy a quality of life that is envied by the rest of the country. Each year, thousands of new residents come to Idaho seeking a new way of life. This growth enhances our economy through housing construction and enlarges the local tax base; however, it also results in increased citizen demands for services and infrastructure, and can lead to development that may threaten the qualities that make our communities so special.

The growth and development of our communities is guided by the planning and land use policies of city and county governments. Under the Idaho Local Land Use Planning Act, every city and county is required to adopt a comprehensive plan, a zoning ordinance, a subdivision ordinance and area of city impact ordinances. These policies are the essential tools for growth management, allowing local officials to direct future development and protect the unique features of their community.

- Comprehensive Plan: The foundational document used to guide the growth and development of a city or county. The planning process emphasizes citizen involvement and a careful study of the social, economic, and environmental characteristics of the planning area. The result is a document that represents the community's consensus about where residential, commercial, and industrial growth should occur; ensures that public services and infrastructure are developed in the most cost-efficient way; and protects quality of life for residents.
- Zoning Ordinance: Historically zoning was used to protect residential areas from incompatible industrial uses like rendering plants. Today,

zoning is used to regulate development in floodplains and on hillsides, conserve valuable agricultural land and open space, protect drinking water sources and preserve historic neighborhoods. Zoning exists to provide a regulatory framework to implement the vision defined in the comprehensive plan. The zoning ordinance consists of two main components: the zoning map and the text of the ordinance. The zoning map shows how the city or county is divided into zoning districts. The text of the ordinance defines the zoning districts, which generally fit within the broad categories of residential, commercial, industrial and agricultural, and defines the types of land uses that are permitted, conditionally permitted and prohibited in these districts. Each zoning district also has standards for lot size, lot coverage, building height, number of stories and setbacks.

■ Subdivision Ordinance: The original purpose of subdivision regulations was to provide a simple, secure method of conveying land by requiring property to be surveyed and mapped before the owner could divide and sell the land. While subdivision regulations continue to provide a secure method of conveying land, they also ensure that land is developed consistent with the comprehensive plan and that facilities and infrastructure are constructed to serve the new development that meet minimum standards of health and safety.

■ Area of Impact Ordinance: The area of city impact is the region surrounding a city that will eventually develop and be annexed into the city. The area of city impact serves two main purposes: it defines the area for city growth and establishes the land use regulations governing the urban fringe area. The area of city impact is established by negotiation between city and county officials. These negotiations result in two ordinances: an ordinance establishing the area of city impact map; and an ordinance setting forth the comprehensive plan, zoning and subdivision regulations that will apply in the area of city impact (city, county or some combination of both). Both ordinances must be approved by the city council and the county commissioners.

The Region

This chapter profiles significant historical matters that either apply to Northern Idaho as a whole, multiple cities within the region or conditions and events that significantly influenced the character, culture and heritage of Idaho and the region.

Distinctive Geographic and Geologic Features

Northern Idaho – commonly called the Idaho Panhandle – generally extends about 250 miles south from the Canadian border, more than half of the entire 479 mile length of the state to the Salmon River, the River of No Return, so called because early supply boats could only make one-way trips downriver to their destinations.

At its narrowest point, the panhandle is about 45 miles wide compared to the state's 305 mile width at its widest point. Substantially all of Northern Idaho is in the Pacific Time Zone. Southwestern and Eastern Idaho are on Mountain Time.

The region's topography is characterized by forested mountains interspersed with numerous lakes, many glacially carved in prehistoric times; rivers; streams; wetlands; magnificent national forests; wilderness areas; and fertile farmland.

A variety of fresh water fish, big game animals, migratory waterfowl and non-game wildlife are abundant. Farmland, such as on the Rathdrum Prairie and the fabulous fertile black soil and rolling hills of the Palouse, characterize certain western portions of the region.

The region's elevation ranges from 738 feet at the freshwater seaport in Lewiston to mountain peaks exceeding 8,000 feet. The prehistoric Lake Bonneville flood that started 14,500 years ago in Eastern Idaho cut the Snake River Canyon gorge, which forms part of the border between Idaho and Oregon and Washington and extends through Hells Canyon – the deepest canyon in North America, at one point nearly 8,000 feet from the top to the river below – before reaching Lewiston. (*See Eastern Idaho, The Region, Distinctive Geographic and Geologic Features – Prehistoric Lake Bonneville.*)

The climate in populated areas is relatively mild. Winter temperatures in most cities generally get no lower than in the teens and rarely above 90 degrees in the summer.

The humidity is moderate and annual precipitation in the lower elevations averages 16 inches in the northern part of the region and 13 inches in the southern, providing ample moisture to irrigate farm crops and lush, heavily wooded mountain forests that often receive significantly more precipitation. Located about 400 miles inland, most Northern Idaho cities have more sunshine days than coastal cities on the same parallel.

Lewis and Clark

Meriwether Lewis and William Clark, leaders of a small military expedition named the Corps of Discovery, were the first non-Indians to enter what is now Idaho. President Thomas Jefferson and Congress authorized the expedition to map a route across the northern part of the nation's Louisiana Purchase and then west to the Pacific Ocean to find "the most direct and practicable water communication across this continent" and establish a U.S. presence on the land that, at the time, was also claimed by England.

They started from their base camp near the mouth of the Wood River in Illinois, located across the Missouri River from St. Louis, in May 1804. After traveling up the Missouri River for over a thousand miles, they spent their first winter near a Mandan Indian encampment in what is now North Dakota.

That spring the party divided. Lewis and Clark dispatched a few men to take their accumulated journals, maps, sketches and specimens of newly discovered plant, animal and bird life to President Jefferson.

The main party that moved west consisted of 33 people including Clark's black slave, York; the French interpreter, Charbonneau; his young Shoshone Indian wife, Sacajawea; and their infant son. Among other things, Lewis believed traveling with a woman and child would be an outward sign of their peaceful intentions.

The expedition first entered what is now Idaho from the east in August 1805, coming over Lemhi Pass about 20 miles southeast of what is now Salmon in Eastern Idaho. There they met a tribe of Shoshone Indians, coincidentally led by Sacajawea's brother Cameahwait.

Weippe Camas Prairie.

Four years earlier, a Hidatsa Indian raiding party had kidnapped Sacajawea. Charbonneau won Sacajawea and another young girl gambling with members of the raiding party and took Sacajawea as his wife.

The meeting with her brother was a happy and emotional event for Sacajawea. Largely due to her influence, Lewis and Clark traded for horses, gained valuable information about the next phase of their journey and enlisted an Indian guide they named Old Toby.

They found there was no navigable stream over Idaho's mountains and the downstream Salmon River was impassable. Based on a reconnaissance expedition by Clark and Cameahwait's description of the country and river ahead, Lewis wrote, "vast mountains of rock eternally covered with snow...Perpendicular and even jutting rocks so closely hemned (sic) in the river that there was no possibility of passing along the shore...the whole surface of the river was beat into perfect foam as far as the eye could reach."

Old Toby said they could cross the mountains over a Nez Perce trail further north. He led the expedition more than 100 miles into what is now Montana and then along the eastern side of the Bitterroot Mountains before re-entering Idaho at Lolo Pass.

It was September, early winter weather was upon them and they had not found the Nez Perce trail. Old Toby said they could still cross the mountains – about 60 miles – in four days. But that was not to be the case. They encountered ravines with dense brush, trees and deadfall. Two days into the trip, snow began to fall. The ridges were steep and slick. Their packhorses slipped. Some stumbled and crashed down the mountainsides. Atop one peak, Clark wrote, "...from this mountain I could observe high rugged mountains in every direction as far as I could see."

Eight days later, Clark and a six-man advance party he led to hunt and provide provisions for the main party were near starvation when they finally emerged from the mountains onto the 150-square-mile Weippe (pronounced Wee-ipe) Prairie near what is now Weippe. There they encountered an encampment of Nez Perce Indians harvesting camas lily bulbs.

At this seasonal encampment, Indian women dug large quantities of the camas roots for winter storage. To prepare the bulbs to eat, they cleaned and crushed them to make a kind of bread or cake.

Clark gave the Nez Perce gifts to show their peaceful intentions. The Nez Perce accepted the gifts and, in return, gave them dried salmon and camas lily cake. The seven starving men gorged themselves on the unfamiliar food and became violently ill.

The Nez Perce knew the power of guns and had two antiquated rifles in their village. They were constantly harassed by their enemy, the Blackfoot Indians armed with rifles obtained from Canadian fur traders. The warriors coveted the rifles and knives carried by Clark and his men.

Some of the Nez Perce braves considered killing the debilitated explorers for their weapons. However, one of their women named Watkuweis dissuaded them.

Blackfoot Indians had kidnapped the woman several years earlier, took her to Canada and sold her to a white trapper/trader. She lived among the white traders before finding her way back home. Regarding Clark and his small band in their weakened condition, she told the warriors, "These are the people who helped me. Do them no hurt."

Steven E. Ambrose, in his book *Undaunted Courage,* wrote, "First Sacagawea, now Watkuweis. The expedition owed more to Indian women than either captain ever acknowledged."

When Lewis and the balance of the starving expedition arrived, they failed to follow Clark's admonition to eat only a little at a time. Instead, they also gorged themselves, becoming sick for several days.

Nez Perce Chief Twisted Hair gave Lewis and Clark directions to the coast. At the confluence of the main and north forks of the Clearwater River near what is now Orofino, the Corps of Discovery established Canoe Camp. There they cut long 3 to 4 foot diameter logs and used Indian burning techniques to hollow out six canoes which carried them to the Snake and Columbia Rivers and on to the Pacific Ocean. On the coast, they constructed a fort and spent the winter.

On the return journey in 1806, they camped at a place they called "Camp Chopunnish," on the Middle Fork of the Clearwater River near what is now Kamiah. They waited from May 14 to June 10 for the mountain snows to melt sufficiently for them to cross. The snow was too deep on their first attempt, forcing them to go back to where there were good pastures to wait several more days. They then traded rifles for Nez Perce Indian guides to lead them across the mountains.

Glade Creek Camp near the present Lolo Pass Interpretative Center is largely undisturbed since Lewis and Clark came through. The National Park Service has also acquired land on the Weippe Prairie to preserve as it looked in 1805 when Lewis and Clark first met the Nez Perce.

American Indians

Northern Idaho Tribes Scholar Sven Liljeblad has estimated that when Lewis and Clark passed through Idaho in 1805, the population of the principal American Indian Tribes within Idaho varied from 6,000 to 10,000. The Pend d'Oreille, or Kalispel, could have numbered about 300; the Coeur d'Alene 700; Kutenai 200 or more; and about 3,000 Nez Perce. All were distinct tribes that existed peacefully together. Some Northern Piute could also have been living within the state's boundaries.

Indians on horseback near Hope.

Liljeblad also estimated that there were about 3,000 Shoshone and Bannock, generally in Southwestern and Eastern Idaho.

In Northern Idaho, deadly skirmishes between white settlers and Indians were few until the mid-1800s when white settlements began springing up at an increasingly rapid rate. When conflicts occurred, settlers appealed to the U.S. Army for protection. Under pressure, most Northern Idaho Indians – the Kutenai were not part of the treaty – agreed to the Treaty of 1855 that specified reservation boundaries where they agreed to live and white settlers would not encroach. The treaty was enforced by the U.S. Bureau of Indian Affairs.

Despite the treaty, white encroachment continued. When prospectors surreptitiously entered reservation land and discovered placer gold in 1860 near Pierce, thousands of fortune seekers flooded onto the reservation in search of the precious metal. The federal government, ostensibly seeking to appease the miners and settlers encroaching onto reservation lands, advanced the highly controversial Treaty of 1863 – superseding the 1855 treaty. However, many Nez Perce bands, including one led by Chief Joseph, refused to sign. (*See Gold Mining, and Idaho Territory, Territorial Capitals – Lewiston and Boise below*.)

Nez Perce War Acting under the authority of the 1863 treaty, the U.S. Bureau of Indian Affairs ordered the Nez Perce to the Lapwai Reservation in 1877. Many Nez Perce were, at the time, in the Wallowa Valley in Oregon and were generally accepting of white settlements. Chief Joseph and the other Nez Perce bands that had not signed the 1863 treaty became angry at the forced move. Tribal leaders knew they could not win against the U.S. Army and were resigned to making the move. However, several young Nez Perce warriors went against the council of their elders and attacked white settlers, killing several.

General O.O. Howard interpreted this action as a general revolt and ordered two Calvary companies and a dozen volunteers under the command of Captain David Perry to intercept the Nez Perce. They met at White Bird Hill. The Nez Perce chiefs' hoped-for truce was lost when shots were fired. It is not known who shot first, but the result was that Howard's ill-prepared troops suffered a humiliating defeat.

Howard then took personal charge, regrouped and started a campaign of hot pursuit of the Nez Perce bands of Chiefs Joseph and White Bird to Montana and the Canadian border. Howard's Calvary – never quite able to catch the Nez Perce who were traveling with women, children and equipage – wired ahead to the military in Montana to intercept the Nez Perce. White Bird and his people got across the border; Joseph's band did not.

That October, Chief Joseph rode alone up a hill in Montana to where U.S. military officers were waiting for his surrender. As Chief Joseph offered his rifle to the officers, he made an impassioned statement of surrender that has since become famous as a criticism of war.

Chief Joseph is quoted as saying, "I am tired of fighting. Our chiefs are killed … The old men are all dead … It is cold and we have no blankets...the little children are freezing to death … My people, some of them, have run away to the hills and have no blankets and food … I want to have time to look for my children … Hear me, my chiefs; my heart is sick and sad. From where the sun now stands, I will fight no more forever."

In 1878 many of the Nez Perce, including Chief Joseph's band, were exiled to Oklahoma Indian Territory. In 1885 the Nez Perce that still remained in Oklahoma were sent back to the Pacific Northwest, with 118 returning to the Lapwai Reservation in Idaho and 149 going with Chief Joseph to the Colville Reservation in north central Washington.

Dawes Severalty Act In an attempt to assimilate American Indians into the white mainstream and open reservation land for settlement, Congress passed the General Allotment Act, generally called the Dawes Severalty Act, in 1877.

Under the act, the head of each Indian family received an allotment of 160 acres of reservation land, each single person over 18 years got 80 acres and each minor orphaned child received 40 acres. Indians who did not want to farm could either sell or lease their land. Any land not allotted was deemed "surplus" and made available for non-Indian settlement.

This law resulted in large-scale settlement by non-Indians on former reservation lands and created a checkerboard ownership pattern throughout the reservations. In

1934 Congress replaced the Dawes Severalty Act with the Indian Reorganization Act which restored the remaining surplus land, placing it into tribal trusts.

Today's Reservations There are two Indian reservations and one tribal land grant located in Northern Idaho, one reservation in Eastern Idaho and one in Southwestern Idaho. Four tribes have gaming casinos and resorts on their reservations. The one in Duck Valley is in process. All of the tribes are involved in natural resource conservation efforts and other economic development activities.

The 2000 Census reported that the Nez Perce had a population of 1,962. Their reservation lies east of Lewiston and encompasses about 770,000 acres.

The Coeur d'Alene Tribe numbered 858 in the 2000 Census. Their reservation is south of the city of Coeur d'Alene and comprises about 345,000 acres.

The Kootenai tribal land is near Bonners Ferry overlooking the Kootenai River. It comprises 12.5 acres provided to the tribe in a 1975 federal land grant as settlement of a conflict; the tribe had declared a peaceful but highly publicized war against the United States, seeking just compensation. The 2000 Census reported the reservation had a population of 110.

Members of the Shoshone and Paiute Tribes live on the 289,820-acre Duck Valley Reservation, which the federal government established in 1877 and enlarged in 1886. The reservation straddles the Idaho/Nevada border. About half of the reservation is in Owyhee County. Most of the reservation's population resides in Nevada.

Most members of the Shoshone and Bannock Tribes live on Eastern Idaho's Fort Hall Indian Reservation near Pocatello. The 2000 U.S. Census reported 4,019 of the reservation residents were tribal members.

Early Trappers/Explorers

David Thompson, an explorer, mapmaker and trader, and his associate, Finan McDonald, were the first trappers to come into Northern Idaho. In September 1809 they passed around the north shore of Lake Pend Oreille, noted in their journals the distinctive point of sand, which is now Sandpoint, and moved on to a peninsula on the east side of the lake, which is now East Hope. They built a log trading post, the first in Idaho, which they named the "Kullyspel House" after the Kalispel Indians.

Thompson and McDonald worked for the North West Company, a Canadian business competing in the fur trade with the British Hudson's Bay Company. Thompson planned to establish a chain of trading posts throughout the Inland Northwest.

In 1811 Thompson abandoned Kullyspel House. He found it was too far off the main line of his other trading posts.

For many years, other fur trappers and traders, including Donald McKenzie who later became a prominent leader of fur-trapping expeditions on the Snake River and its tributaries south of what is now Lewiston, worked the streams of Northern Idaho.

Early Christian Missionaries

The first Christian missionaries in Northern Idaho were Presbyterian missionaries Henry and Eliza Spalding. In 1836 this couple set up a successful mission among the Nez Perce near what is now Lapwai. The Spalding Mission became home to numerous firsts in Idaho, including the first potato crop, the first school, the first irrigation system and the first published book.

Two years later, Asa B. Smith, another Presbyterian missionary, started a mission near what is now Kamiah, which soon proved unsuccessful.

Roman Catholic missionaries established a mission among the Coeur d'Alene Indians in 1842 near the southern end of Lake Coeur d'Alene. A few years later, the potential for flooding persuaded them to move. They re-established their mission at what is now Cataldo where, between 1850 and 1853, the missionaries and Coeur d'Alene Indians constructed a church. This historic house of worship is Idaho's oldest standing building and the focal point of Idaho's 18-acre Old Mission State Park.

Church at Old Mission State Park.

Mullan Road In 1858 U.S. Army Lieutenant John Mullan, a topographical engineer with a crew of around 200, began construction of a 624-mile military wagon road between Fort Walla Walla, Washington, and Fort Benton, Montana, completed with final improvements in 1862. The road was 25 feet wide, cutting through forests, grading roadbeds and building bridges and ferries.

Taking a break from road building, Mullan's men celebrated the nation's birthday on July 4, 1860, and carved their initials on a tree that used to stand on I-90 at the top of Fourth of July Pass, which was named for the event.

While the road was under construction, Mullan and his men would lay night after night on the ground with nothing but pine needles for beds and saddles for pillows. "In my imagination," Mullan wrote, "I heard the whistle of the engine … I saw the country thickly populated, thousands pouring over the borders to make homes in this far western land."

Even though built for military purposes, settlers, prospectors and miners were the principal users of Mullan Road. Today, Interstate 90 generally runs on or near the Idaho portion of this historic road. A commemorative statue of Captain John Mullan stands in front of the city of Mullan's fire station and city hall. The road is on the National Register of Historic Places. A memorial commemorating the road is at Fourth of July Pass, a summit with a 3,081-foot elevation near I-90 about 15 miles east of Coeur d'Alene. It is the location where Mullan and his men celebrated Independence Day in 1861.

Idaho Territory

One of the bills debated in Congress creating Idaho Territory had a provision, passed by the House of Representatives on February 12, 1863, that named the developing boomtown of Idaho City the territorial capital. However, that bill failed and on March 4, 1863, President Abraham Lincoln signed the Organic Act, creating the Idaho Territory and appointing William H. Wallace as territorial governor. The law left it up to the territorial governor to name the temporary capital and the Legislature to name the permanent capital city. (*See Territorial Capitals – Lewiston and Boise below.*)

At that time, the territory included all of what are now Idaho and western Montana and Wyoming and had four counties. The Legislature consisted of a seven-member "Council" and an 11-member House of Representatives. Indian reservations were treaty lands and not part of federal territory.

"One of the most intriguing mysteries of Idaho history is the origin and meaning of the name Idaho," wrote historian Merle W. Wells. It was one of the names proffered by promoters of the new (Colorado) territory after they found Congress would reject their first choice of Jefferson because of its opposition to naming territories after former U.S. presidents. They asserted that Idaho – a name they had apparently coined – was an Indian name meaning "Gem of the Mountains," albeit the word "Gem" as well as "Idaho" could not be referenced to a word or term of any Indian language. The U.S. Senate Committee on Territories was favorably disposed toward naming the territory Idaho until members of the Senate discovered at the last minute that Idaho was not an Indian word. When Congress created the territory in 1861, they chose to name it Colorado, the next prominent name under consideration.

However, the name "Idaho" did not lose its appeal and was used to name geographical locations in Colorado and the Northwest. When Idaho Territory was created in 1863, the name "Idaho" beat out "Montana" as the name of the new territory. Once named, leaders of the new Idaho Territory soon adopted the previously asserted meaning of the word, "Gem of the Mountains," and later applied the "Gem State" nickname as the term that ably describes Idaho's natural physical beauty and mineralization. (*See Gem State below.*)

Territorial Capitals Governor Wallace declared the boomtown of Lewiston as the temporary territorial capital and called the first legislative session to begin December 7, 1863. Lewiston was a fresh water port that received steamers coming up the Snake River from the Columbia River and the Pacific Ocean and was the most accessible town in the territory. It was the trailhead for prospectors heading to the gold fields in Pierce, 75 miles east. (*See Gold Mining below.*)

Before the session started, Wallace was elected Territorial Delegate to the U.S. Congress. He resigned as governor and on December 6, 1863, left for Washington, D.C., leaving Territorial Secretary William B. Daniels to serve as acting governor and to give the first governor's address to the Legislature. President Lincoln appointed Caleb Lyon as Wallace's successor. However, Lyon did not arrive until the next August.

Lewiston was legally on Nez Perce Reservation land in 1863 – technically foreign soil. However, most Lewiston residents conducted business, including buying and selling building lots, as though they had legal ownership, essentially disregarding the Nez Perce Tribe's property rights as a sovereign nation. Hoping to avoid armed conflict with the tribe and likely anticipating federal action to reduce the size of the reservation, town residents negotiated a lease for the townsite.

On June 9, 1863, the Bureau of Indian Affairs negotiated a treaty with several bands of the Nez Perce Tribe to reduce the size of its reservation, established under the Treaty of 1855. The Nez Perce bands that refused to sign the highly controversial treaty included those led by Chief Joseph's father and later Chief Joseph himself – an omission that would later lead to war. (*See American Indians – Nez Perce War above.*)

The 1863 treaty moved the reservation boundary east of Lewiston making the town legally part of Idaho Territory. However, Congress did not ratify the treaty until April 20, 1867, thus delaying the treaty's legal effective date. Most settlers disregarded that technicality and proceeded with their affairs as though the 1863 treaty was in effect.

By 1863 the Pierce area goldfields were playing out and most of the miners were moving to the gold discoveries in such places as Elk City, Florence and the Boise Basin. By that time, Lewiston's population had declined to 414.

In contrast, the Boise Basin gold rush was reaching its peak. Over 16,000 prospectors, miners and settlers had converged on the basin and started several boomtowns. At that time, Boise Basin was second only to Portland as the most populous area in the Northwest. With the political power shifting to the Boise Basin and the governor not yet in Lewiston, the 1863 Legislature deferred naming the permanent territorial capital until the next session.

The second session of the Territorial Legislature convened in Lewiston on November 14, 1864, and on December 7 passed landmark legislation, signed by Governor Lyon, that created Ada County and made the 17-month-old Boise City, a charter city, the Ada County seat of government and Idaho's permanent territorial capital.

Even though the Legislature incorporated the town, Boise had no city government. The new law specified that for the incorporation to be final, the town's citizens had to approve the charter in a city election. Most Boise City residents felt the town had too much government oversight already – territory and county – and did not need any more.

Before the matter was resolved, it would take over three years and considerable effort including several elections; a new charter from the Legislature, January 11, 1866, which allowed appointment versus election of the first city officials; and the realization by community leaders that the owners of city lots could not get clear title to their properties without a functioning city government. On November 18, 1867, pragmatic members of the community took charge and carried out the requirements of the 1866 charter by appointing Boise's first mayor and city council. Lewiston, Boise and Bellevue are the only cities chartered by the Territorial Legislature. Lewiston and Boise have since rescinded their charters. (*See Southwestern Idaho, The Region, Idaho Territory, Territorial Capitals – Lewiston and Boise.*)

Loss of the territorial capital to Boise outraged the citizens of Lewiston and Northern Idaho who filed suit, asserting the law was invalid because the Legislature met six weeks before its official term was to have begun.

Lewiston Probate Judge John G. Berry sided with the plaintiffs and issued an injunction against moving the Great Territorial Seal of Idaho and territorial archives from Lewiston and summoned Governor Lyon to appear in court and answer the charges.

Under the guise of a duck hunting trip, Lyon crossed the river into Washington Territory where he could not be arrested and forced to appear in court. The sheriff carried out the balance of the court order by locking the Seal and the archives in the Lewiston Jail.

In Lyon's absence, newly appointed Territorial Secretary DeWitt Smith became acting governor. On March 2, 1865, Smith requested support from federal troops to retrieve the Seal and archives and rendezvous with him outside the city.

Six weeks later, Smith entered Boise with the Seal and archives. However, that did not end the dispute. Lewiston officials appealed the matter to the territorial district judge, who sustained the ruling of the lower court.

Smith appealed the case to the newly created Idaho Territorial Supreme Court in Boise. On June 14, 1866, the Supreme Court overturned the district court, establishing Boise as Idaho's permanent territorial capital.

Boundaries, Suffrage and Statehood Between the time Idaho became a territory in 1863 and a state in 1890, Congress re-drew Idaho's boundaries three times. These changes reduced the size of Idaho Territory to just over a fourth of its original size from 325,000 square miles to 84,439 square miles, land and water area, about 54 million acres.

The 1887 Congress attempted to change Idaho's territorial boundaries a fourth time by approving a bill that split off the Panhandle from Idaho Territory, adding it to Washington Territory. At the same time, certain Nevada politicians had designs on making Southern Idaho part of Nevada. Citizens of Lewiston, chagrined about their loss of the territorial capital to Boise, greeted the news with a brass band and community celebration. Four days later, however, they learned that Idaho Territorial Governor Edward A. Stevenson and Congressional Delegate Fred T. Dubois had persuaded President Grover Cleveland to pocket-veto the bill. That veto put an end to further modification of Idaho's territorial boundaries. The territory was now ready to become a state.

Fred T. Dubois

Fred T. Dubois was one of Idaho's more colorful politicians. Illinois born, he came to Idaho Territory and served as U.S. Marshal from 1882 to 1886, and was an arch antagonist to any man who ran afoul of antipolygamy laws. (*See Suffrage below.*) Leonard Arrington, in his History of Idaho wrote, "...the Dubois juries convicted anyone on a polygamy charge, regardless of evidence."

Dubois was a highly regarded, gifted politician, representing Idaho for fifteen years in Washington, D.C. He is the only Idaho politician who has been elected to the U. S. Congress by two parties and served with three. He was elected and served as a Republican Territorial Delegate from 1887 to 1890 and the U.S. Senate from 1891 to 1897. He was elected and served in the U.S. Senate in 1901 for the Silver Republican Party. The Silver Republicans broke with the Republican Party which supported the Gold Standard. Before the year was out, Dubois announced he would complete his six-year term as a Democrat. Although he tried, he was not re-elected.

Governor Stevenson vetoed a bill making Eagle Rock, now Idaho Falls, the location for Idaho's land grant college in 1887. In an attempt to appease the Northern Idaho faction, the 1889 Territorial Legislature passed the "olive branch" law locating the state's land grant college, now the University of Idaho, in Moscow. (*See Federal Lands – Private Ownership and Preservation Laws – 1862 Morrill Land Grant Act below.*)

Idaho's State Constitutional Convention convened on July 4, 1889. On November 5 of that year, 12,126 or 66 percent of the 18,408 citizens voting approved the constitution. The 1890 census reported Idaho's population at 88,548.

Because of Idaho's restrictive suffrage laws in effect at the time, only a minority of the adult population were allowed to vote. Although now repealed, Idaho Territorial laws that carried over into statehood withheld the basic civil rights of voting, holding public office and serving on juries from people who, if their voice and vote were not silenced, could have shifted political power from the Republican politicians then in control of the governor's office and the Legislature to the Democratic Party.

The largest body of adult citizens denied suffrage rights were women.

Suffrage rights were also denied bigamists or polygamists whose marriages were marked by a formal ceremony and family structure. The law also denied suffrage to adult male members of any organization that taught the acceptability of bigamy, polygamy or celestial (eternal) marriage as a doctrinal rite. The law did not extend to men involved in either informal co-habitation arrangements or extramarital affairs or multiple pre-marital relationships common in society – non-practicing monogamists.

Since most known or suspected polygamists and bigamists were either in prison, in court or had an arrest warrant issued because of their alleged felonious actions, they had, for all practical purposes, already lost their suffrage rights. Any additional laws denying those rights were redundant as it related to them.

Therefore, the primary objective of the law was to disenfranchise monogamous men who were members of an organization that taught the acceptability of bigamy, polygamy or celestial marriage. Under these provisions of the law, any suspected members of such an organization were, under penalties of perjury, required to take a complex test oath of over 200 words before they could exercise their civil rights. If they signed the test oath, they were essentially disavowing any relationship with the suspected organization and were allowed to vote. If they were subsequently found to be a member of the organization, they were subject to arrest and prison. Any suspected organization members who refused to sign the test oath were denied their suffrage rights.

While the law did not name any organizations, the only known organization in Idaho that fit the definition of the law was The Church of Jesus Christ of Latter-day Saints, also known as Mormons, Latter-day Saints or LDS. (*See Eastern Idaho, The Region: Pioneer Settlements.*)

Members of the Church comprised about a fourth of Idaho's population – of which only a small fraction practiced polygamy – but they were perceived by leading politicos to support the Democratic Party and vote as a block. Republican politicians crafted the law so as to disenfranchise this large block of adult male Church members who would not disavow their faith.

In many local elections in Southern Idaho, the test oath resulted in a huge shift of political power from the majority to a minority of citizens with all the potential mischief such undemocratic actions could produce. (*See Eastern Idaho, The Region, Politics, Polygamy and Civil Rights.*)

Also denied suffrage rights were people of Mongolian descent, aimed at disenfranchising Idaho's Chinese populations; American Indians who had not renounced tribal affiliation; adults under guardianship; and felons.

In November 1896 Idaho voters amended the state constitution to give women the right to vote. Idaho was the fourth territory/state to do so, behind Wyoming, 1869; Utah, 1870; and Colorado, 1893. The federal anti-polygamy Edmunds-Tucker Act of 1887 overturned Utah Territory's 1870 women's suffrage law. It was reinstated in Utah's constitution when it became a state in January 1896. Today, Idaho adult suffrage restrictions apply only to felons.

U.S. President Benjamin Harrison signed legislation making Idaho the 43rd state on July 3, 1890.

Gem State Idaho's "Gem State" designation is a carryover from Colorado and Idaho territorial days when the U.S. Congress erroneously believed the name "Idaho" was an Indian name – no tribal language was specified – meaning Gem of the Mountains. (*See Idaho Territory preamble above.*)

What they could not know at the time was that Idaho indeed had numerous and diverse deposits of gems as well as prodigious ore bodies of precious and industrial metals and minerals in each region of the state.

Idaho gems include the rare Star Garnet found only in Northern Idaho and India, which the Legislature named the state gemstone in 1967 – the most prominent Idaho deposit of the Star Garnet is at Emerald Creek Garnet Area, a Unique Natural Feature 10 miles north of Bovill. Other gems include the

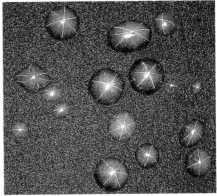
State Gem, the Star Garnet

distinctive Spencer Opal semi-precious stone in Eastern Idaho and quartz, agates, jasper, garnets and geodes in many locations throughout the state.

Today there are numerous publications directing collectors and rockhounds to where they can find old and new mineral deposits and how to beautify the gems, stones and crystals they find. Thousands of hobbyists and professionals make beautiful jewelry and art objects using cut and/or polished Idaho rocks, gemstones and precious metals. Many of these pieces of art are displayed and sold at gem and county fairs held around Idaho and other states as well as in jewelry stores.

By whatever measure – from its diverse natural beauty to mineralization – Idaho is indeed worthy of its designation "Gem of the Mountains".

Federal Lands

Federal land ownership generally began between 1781 and 1802 when the original colonies ceded their western lands between the Appalachian Mountains and the Mississippi River to the new national government.

During the 1800s as the nation moved West, it acquired practical ownership of land previously claimed by France, 1803 Louisiana Purchase; England, Treaty of 1846 (*see below*); Mexico, Treaty of 1848

George Russell homestead cabin near unincorporated Fernwood in Benewah County. Courtesy Marie Russell.

(*see below*); and Russia, 1867 Alaska purchase. Hawaii was annexed into the U.S. as a territory in 1898.

In substantially all cases, Congress, backed by its modern Army, did as other nations and gave limited consideration to the land claims of the Indian tribes – implementing what many termed the nation's Manifest Destiny. The land that Congress did not purchase from the Indians they took by treaty, conquest or passed law that laid claim to the land – actions that the primarily nomadic hunter/gatherer Indians were ill equipped to prevent.

The total land and water surface area of the U.S. now approaches 2.4 billion acres of which nearly 2 billion is in the 48 contiguous states, 0.4 billion in Alaska and 4 million in Hawaii.

Eventually the federal government would transfer ownership of all but about 30 percent of the federal land preserve to private interests and to the states. Today, most of the land under federal jurisdiction is in the 11 contiguous Western states and Alaska. About 64 percent of Idaho is federal land.

Congress transferred land ownership by passing numerous laws designed to encourage settlement, promote timber harvests and metal and mineral extraction and provide land grants to the states to help fund public education and certain infrastructure.

One of the first methods Congress used to dispose of the nation's land was payment of debts in lieu of cash to soldiers – Bounty Land Warrants – which were first issued to Revolutionary War soldiers and, later, to soldiers fighting in the War of 1812. However, the federal government's principal method of disposing of the property from the nation's land and mineral preserve was to use grants or sales at low prices to private parties including farmers, ranchers, railroad companies and miners.

The following is a summary of the more significant laws effecting transfer of federal lands to private and state ownership that may have affected Idaho as well as laws providing for federal management of the remaining land in the nation's preserve.

To encourage settlement and establish an American presence in the West, Congress passed the Preemption Act of 1841, which sanctioned squatters' rights and allowed a person to claim up to 160 acres of a 640-acre section or one square mile of un-surveyed federal land and, later, pay a small fee per acre to the federal government for clear title.

In 1843 non-Indian settlers in Oregon Country's Willamette Valley, mostly U.S. citizens, drafted a constitution for a provisional government that included a provision allowing settlers to claim up to 640 acres of land at no charge. Many of the early Oregon Trail immigrants who began their overland treks in 1841 were motivated by the prospect of this free land in the lush Willamette Valley.

The Treaty of 1846 with England established the boundary between the two countries at the 49th parallel. Congress created Oregon Territory – land between the 49th parallel on the north and the 42nd parallel on the south – on August 14, 1848. The new territory included what are now Oregon, Washington, Idaho, western Montana and western Wyoming. Mexico gave up its land claim south of the 42nd parallel when it lost the war with the U.S. and signed the February 2, 1848, Treaty of Guadalupe Hidalgo. (*See Eastern Idaho, The Region, Idaho/Utah Boundary Resolution.*)

Two years later Congress passed the Donation Land Claim Act of 1850, the forerunner of the Homestead Act. It nullified provisional land grants; created the Office of Surveyor General of Public Lands to provide deeds to property; and granted 320 acres to a white male, or a white male who was 50 percent Indian, over 18 years of age who had resided on the property on or before December 1, 1850, and, if married, an additional 320 acres were deeded to his wife – essentially grandfathering many elements of the provisional government's law. Recipients had to improve the property and live on it for four consecutive years from the time they first settled. This law influenced many marriages.

Male claimants who located on property between December 1, 1850, and December 1, 1853, received 160 acres of land – 320 acres for married couples. In 1854 Congress extended the law for two more years. Thereafter people could purchase up to 320 acres for $1.25 an acre. Subsequently the price was increased and the number of allowable acres decreased. Publication of these liberal land grant laws further spurred the flow of Oregon Trail immigrants crossing Southern Idaho, headed to the Willamette Valley and other locations throughout the West.

The Homestead Act of 1862 superseded the Donation Land Claim Act and provided transfer of 160 acres to a settler, conditional on them improving the property and living on the land for five years. This act was used extensively in Idaho.

Early settlers claimed water rights by diverting irrigation water under the "Doctrine of Prior Appropriation" - first in time-first in right. Later, water rights were administered by the laws of each state as opposed to federal law. In Idaho, these laws were codified in Idaho's Constitution which was approved by the territorial voters on November 5, 1899.

The 1862 Morrill Land Grant Act provided state grants of 30,000 acres for each member of a state's Congressional delegation – Senate and House – for the purpose of providing a source of funds for a state college that taught agriculture, engineering and military tactics. The University of Idaho is Idaho's land grant "college".

The Pacific Railways Acts of 1862, 1863 and 1864 provided massive land grants, including mineral rights and issuance of government bonds, to railroad companies to motivate them to build the first transcontinental railroad – which was completed at Promontory Summit, Utah, in 1869 – and many other railroad lines that would be built throughout the West. Many in Congress expected this land to be sold off in smaller parcels to promote agriculture, harvest of natural resources and building townships. This was done in many cases; however, railroads, needing more cash to finance their enterprises, sold much of their forested land grants in large blocks to lumber manufacturing companies and investors. (*See Forest Products below.*)

The General Mining Laws of 1866 and 1872 generally codified the self-rule methodologies prospectors and miners previously used to govern development of mining districts.

The Timber Culture Act of 1873 allowed homesteaders an additional 160 acres if they planted trees on 40 of those acres. The law's sponsors thought it would have the greatest use

University of Idaho administration building.

in the settlement of the Great Plains. The law had many problems, and Congress repealed it in 1891.

The Desert Land Act of 1877 generally granted farmers ownership of up to 640 acres of arid federal land if they brought it under cultivation and irrigation within three years. This law was of limited use in Northern Idaho but in the mid-twentieth century was actively used in the arid areas of Southern Idaho.

The Timber and Stone Act of 1878, intended to facilitate logging and mining, allowed wooded and other lands unfit for farming to be sold in parcels of 160 acres for $2.50 per acre to those who certified they were buying the land for their own use. This law was principally used in Oregon, Washington, California and Nevada – and heavily abused. It had the practical effect of greatly expanding ownership of forested and mineral lands to large timber companies and syndicates who bought the land through nominal owners. It was repealed in 1891.

In 1905 Congress passed a livestock grazing law under which the federal government sold grazing permits on Forest Reserve land as a means of managing livestock access to public lands. In 1934 Congress passed the Taylor Grazing Act, further clarifying federal grazing laws. The 1976 Federal Land Policy Management Act and the 1978 Public Rangelands Improvement Act provided, among other things, that grazing fees were to be based on market values. Matters relating to livestock grazing on public lands continue to be controversial.

Concurrent with statehood in 1890 and under other federal laws, Idaho received federal grants of about 3.6 million acres to finance public education, the penitentiary and public buildings. Subsequent sales have reduced Idaho's Endowment Trust Lands to approximately 2.5 million surface acres and 3 million mineral acres, all managed by the Department of Lands with oversight from the State Board of Land Commissioners, a five-member board of state-wide elected officeholders chaired by the governor.

At the turn of the twentieth century, Congress passed two other laws that had limited use in Northern Idaho but played crucial roles in the reclamation of Idaho's arid lands in Southern Idaho, turning sagebrush-covered deserts into agricultural oases, the Carey Act in 1894 and the Newlands Reclamation Act in 1902. In Idaho, the Carey Act had its greatest impact in the Magic Valley. The Reclamation Act that authorized creation of the U.S. Reclamation Service – now the Bureau of Reclamation – built irrigation storage, flood control and hydroelectric dams throughout Southern Idaho. (*See Southwestern and Eastern Idaho, The Region, Agriculture and Irrigation.*)

Generally starting with the federal land management laws – Taylor Grazing Act of 1934 and the Federal Land Policy and Management Act in 1976 – the national policy of retaining ownership of the nation's remaining land preserve was established. Legal challenges by "state's rights" advocates seeking management or control of federal lands within a state's borders have proven unsuccessful. (*See Mining and Forest Products – Leading Causes for Loss of Economic Dominance, below.*)

Agriculture and Livestock

In Northern Idaho's early years, farming and ranching generally developed wherever there was a market for agricultural commodities. Following the 1860 gold discoveries near Pierce, farmers began coming into the Lewiston and Weippe areas to raise crops and livestock for sale to the miners. The Homestead Act in 1862 greatly facilitated development of Northern Idaho's agriculture industry. (*See Federal Lands-Private Ownership and Preservation Laws above.*)

Agricultural settlements further developed as Indian reservation lands became available for settlement. The Treaty of 1863 with many Northern Idaho Indians, which replaced the 1855 treaty, significantly reduced the size of the Nez Perce Indian Reservation as did the more complicated and later-occurring development of the Coeur d'Alene Indian Reservation. Both actions had the significant effect of increasing the amount of public land available for farms and settlements by non-Indians. Passage of the Dawes Severalty Act in 1887 further opened large tracts of reservation land for private development. (*See American Indians above.*)

Many settlers also filed homestead claims on forestland that, when cleared of timber, became cultivated farms. In other cases, forest products companies sold cleared forestland to farmers and ranchers. In these settings, the railroad played a dual role of supporting the wood products and agricultural industries.

Agriculture still dominates the economy of several Northern Idaho communities and many ranchers graze their cattle on public lands, albeit the numbers of cattle are significantly less than the herds of Southwestern and Eastern Idaho.

In contrast to the southern part of the state, farms in Northern Idaho generally do not require mechanical irrigation. They receive sufficient rainfall to irrigate their crops. Even though timber covers most of the region, a traveler emerging from lush forests cannot avoid being struck by the productive beauty of the fabulous fertile black soil and rolling hills of the Palouse and its fields of grains and peas or, further north, the bluegrass seed fields of the Rathdrum Prairie.

Agriculture has experienced many changes in both size and efficiency of operation over the past century. Technological innovation and economies of scale have promoted significant farm consolidation. While this consolidation has improved farm productivity and profitability, it did so with significantly fewer employees. This decline in the workforce has had an adverse effect on the economy of most rural cities.

Gold Mining

Following the 1848 discovery of gold in California, hundreds of thousands of prospectors, called forty-niners, streamed into central California where they would ultimately recover from 10 to 20 million troy ounces (tr. oz.) of placer gold. The prospect of finding gold sent thousands of fortune hunters on a search throughout the West for the precious metal.

In 1860 Elias Davidson Pierce and a small party of prospectors surreptitiously trespassed on Nez Perce Reservation land and discovered gold 75 miles east of Lewiston.

Thousands of miners converged on the area that is now Pierce in what was Idaho's first gold rush. Outnumbered and outgunned, the Nez Perce were powerless to keep the prospectors off their reservation. Other prospectors discovered smaller quantities of gold in what is now Latah County in 1860.

As the mines played out, prospectors spread out, making placer gold discoveries in other locations, including Elk City and Florence near the Salmon River and White Bird.

Working in the Florence gold fields, prospector Moses Splawn received information from an Indian, Bannock Louie, about a mountain basin far to the south with yellow colored sands in the streambeds. Following the lead, Splawn and 10 companions found the Boise Basin about 140 miles south and discovered a placer gold bonanza on August 2, 1862, setting off the largest gold rush in Idaho history. (*See Southwestern Idaho, The Region, Mining, Boise Basin-Gold.*)

In 1881 about 80 miles due north of Pierce, A.J. Prichard, who had prospected on the North Fork of the Coeur d'Alene since 1878, found respectable quantities of placer gold near the unincorporated town of Murray.

He wrote to some of his friends and told them of his success. In the spring of 1882 several determined prospectors showed up at his cabin. He reluctantly showed them where he was working.

News of the discovery spread quickly. Influenced largely by the Northern Pacific Railroad's distribution of handbills hyping the discovery in order to sell services to fortune seekers on its line that reached Spokane in 1862, around 10,000 prospectors soon flooded the area of the Coeur d'Alene River and its tributaries searching for the precious metal.

Silver Valley Mines

On May 2, 1884, prospectors discovered an outcropping of galena (lead-sulfide ore) near Burke, a community about five miles due north of Mullan. Their mining claim that would become the Tiger Mine provided further encouragement to prospectors. They now had hard evidence that there were also other metals in the mountains just waiting to be discovered.

Prospectors would eventually establish over 90 mines and 10 mining districts in what would generally become known as the Coeur d'Alene Mining District and, later, the Silver Valley yielding prodigious quantities of silver, lead and zinc – a district that generally began about 30 miles east of Coeur d'Alene and

Rathdrum Prairie

extended to a few miles east of the Idaho/Montana border. Forested mountains and narrow valleys characterize this nearly 40-mile-long and 20-mile-wide area. Other Northern Idaho districts with significant silver and lead production – although very small compared to the Silver Valley mines – include Port Hill, Clark Fork, Pend Oreille, Lakeview and Hoodoo.

These discoveries transformed the Silver Valley. Over the next few decades, thousands of miners would bore and blast under the earth's surface. They would build catacombs of mineshafts and tunnels through the hard rock that would eventually extend over a mile deep and hundreds of miles laterally to hopefully intercept every possible deposit and vein of silver, lead, zinc and copper. The deepest mine, the Star Morning Mine near Burke, is about 8,000 feet deep. The now closed Bunker Hill Mine had over 150 miles of lateral tunnels.

Hard Rock Mines. One of the discoveries that became known as the Sunshine Silver Mine, played a prominent role in Idaho history, including the 1971 mine disaster wherein 91 miners lost their lives, one of the worst mining tragedies ever experienced in the nation. Today a 12-foot-high statue of a solitary miner with his drill pointing skyward stands as a memorial to those who lost their lives. The memorial is located three and a half miles east of Kellogg on Interstate 90 at the Big Creek exit. (*See the city chapter of Kellogg-Sunshine Mine.*)

The most famous ore discovery occurred in September 1885 when Noah S. Kellogg discovered a lead-silver-zinc ore outcropping above what is now Wardner. That discovery would become The Bunker Hill and Sullivan Mining and Concentrating Company (Bunker Hill), the largest mine in the valley.

Fanciful stories describing how Kellogg made his discovery were the chatter in saloons and around campfires. All are hearsay as Kellogg was alone and did not record the events. However, one of Kellogg's partners, James Wardner, wrote a folklore story that has persisted. Wardner said Kellogg and his jackass were on opposite sides of Milo Creek. Kellogg saw the jackass intently looking at an object and went over to investigate. He found the burro staring at a vein of silver-lead ore sparkling in the sun. Area residents often accent this story with the tongue-in-cheek assertion that Kellogg is the only Idaho city founded by a real jackass.

These and later discoveries led to the founding of the mining towns of Kellogg, Mullan, Osburn, Pinehurst, Smelterville, Wallace and Wardner.

At the time Noah Kellogg made his discovery, the closest smelter was in San Francisco. Wardner took ore samples to Selby Smelting Company to seal a sales contract. The first ore shipments were loaded on wagons, transported to the railhead at Rathdrum, then by rail to Portland and by boat to San Francisco.

By 1890 Kellogg, Wardner and their partners had sold their interests in the Bunker Hill Mine to investors headed by a Portland business man, Simeon Reed – founder of Reed College in Portland. Reed hired mining engineers to develop the mine. The new investors also built a concentrator near the mine's main entrance at the town of Wardner. The concentrate was loaded on tramcars and sent two miles down the mountain to the smelter in Kellogg.

Two years later, the company made a critical decision to improve productivity and reduce costs by making a lateral two-mile-long railcar tunnel into the side of the mountain at Kellogg, providing a direct means for loading the ore from the main mineshaft cars onto railcars for transport through the tunnel to the mill. They then moved the concentrator down the mountain to the expanded Kellogg plant site. In 1917 the company would build its own smelter and, in 1928, one of the first electrolytic zinc plants in the country.

Prior to 1920 separating the valuable minerals from the rock was done with mills that pulverized the ore into a powder and then recovered metals from the waste by using inefficient gravity methods. Much of the residue, or tailings, that still contained heavy metals was deposited into the river drainages, principally the South Fork of the Coeur d'Alene River. Subsequently, a new ore-processing technique called "selective flotation" was developed, in part based on research at the University of Idaho. This new method enabled the removal of more metals from the rock, but still left considerable heavy metals in the tailings to be dumped into the river drainages. Spring runoff would often be heavy, scouring the river bottoms and washing the sediments downriver into Coeur d'Alene Lake, soon to be an issue for the mining companies and a lasting problem for the environment. (*See*

Mining and Forest Products-Leading Causes for Loss of Economic Dominance below.)

Labor Union/Mine Owner Conflicts Early mining processes were labor intensive. Most of the mine owners were absent from the mines, employing professional managers to run the operations. Under Reed's management, Bunker Hill cut the miners' pay from $3.50 to $3.00 per day, giving rise to the first secret miners' union in the area. Soon, every major mine in the district had its own union. The mine owners banded together in 1889 and formed the Mine Owners Association to counter the new unions and to deal with another problem – polluting Chain Lakes area farm fields with mill tailings washing into the Coeur d'Alene River.

Three years later, the combative Western Federation of Miners Union was founded in Butte, Montana, and quickly spread to other Western states. By the late 1880s most mineworkers were members of the Western Federation of Miners.

What followed were a sequence of escalating events and maneuvers by both the union and the mine owners that led to violent armed confrontations in 1892 and 1899 and the ultimate 1905 murder of Idaho's former Governor Frank Steunenberg.

Conflict of 1892 As 1892 began metal prices had declined significantly. The owners said the market price was below the cost of production and abruptly announced the immediate closure of the mines.

This dead-of-winter layoff affected about 4,000 workers and sent economic shockwaves through the valley. Five months later, the mines reopened with the owners announcing a lower wage scale. Union officials refused to work for the reduced wages. The owners started hiring non-union employees and armed guards.

The unions responded by asking the mineworkers to arm themselves and take up positions around the mines. In July 1892 the mineworkers blew up the Frisco Mill in the mining town near Gem about four miles northeast of Wallace, because the Gem Union officials discovered that the mine owners had hired a Pinkerton detective, Charles Siringo, to be a spy and infiltrate the union. At that time, Siringo had become the union's secretary.

Pinkerton Detective Charles Siringo

Armed union workers took the non-union crew of a nearby mine captive and threatened to blow up that mill as well. A gun battle ensued, and six men died – three mine-owner guards and three mineworkers. The fight ended when the remaining mine-owner guards surrendered. At the Bunker Hill facility, the mineworkers also took up arms and held the complex for several days.

When the news of the conflict reached Boise, Governor N.B. Willey called in state and federal law enforcement officers and declared martial law. Prosecutors indicted many union leaders and mineworkers. The open conflict ended with the courts dismissing charges against the mineworkers, including those indicted to. killings.

The miners went back to work but the acrimony between the parties only increased. The Western Federation of Miners soon became the lead representative of the smaller unions, and several union leaders successfully ran for election to key local offices.

Conflict of 1899 Seven years later, disagreements again came to a head. On April 24, 1899, many union members working for Bunker Hill marched to the mill offices demanding that all men working underground be paid $3.50 per day and only union men be allowed to work. Albert Burch, the mill superintendent, said that the company wage scale ranging from $3.00 to $3.50 per day would stand and under no circumstances would the company only hire union members. He said that anyone not satisfied could pick up his pay check at the office and leave.

The next day, union members marched on two other mines and made similar demands. These mine owners responded by announcing the shutdown of their operations for an indefinite period. Union leaders and workers were incensed. Union leadership resorted to a plan of destruction and intimidation. As later testified in court, this was a plan similar to the one they had previously used in Colorado.

They cut telegraph lines on April 29 and approximately 1,000 union men, many wearing masks, commandeered the Northern Pacific train at Burke. En route to the Bunker Hill complex, they broke into a mine powder house and loaded one car with 3,000 pounds of dynamite. As the train moved down the canyon, it stopped to pick up more men marching from other mines to meet them.

By some accounts, many mineworkers believed the march was only a show of force to intimidate the mine owners. However, once the march was in progress, union leaders reportedly intimidated mineworkers to elevate the disturbance to violence.

Union leaders had previously posted pickets around the Bunker Hill operation. When the train arrived in Kellogg, they ordered the miners off the train and, in military fashion, marched to the ore concentrator. The union personnel and mineworkers skilled in setting dynamite charges moved in and placed explosives at the ore concentrator's critical structure points. One of these explosive experts was Harry Orchard – an alias for Albert E. Horsley, a long-time union operative who would later confess to other bombings and murders, including the assassination of former Governor Frank Steunenberg. (*See Murder of Former Governor Frank Steunenberg below.*)

With the dynamite charges set, the union leaders ordered the workers back on the train and set off the explosives. The resulting blast destroyed the ore concentrator, which, at that time, was the largest in the world. The leaders left pickets at the mine and drove the train back to Burke, dropping off mineworkers at stops along the way without further incident except for one man who had a fatal accident.

Later, three Bunker Hill employees visited the mill and were captured by mineworker pickets who decided to have some deadly fun. The pickets released the men and told them to run for it. After the three got a short distance away, the pickets opened fire, killing one and wounding the other two.

Even though the mineworkers had cut the telegraph lines, Governor Steunenberg soon learned of the events. He promptly appealed to President William McKinley who sent 600 federal troops to restore order. Steunenberg also had 100 men in Coeur d'Alene sworn in to help the federal troops and declared martial law for the entire mining district. Idaho National Guard troops were unavailable at that time because they were involved in the Spanish-American War and stationed in the Philippines.

The presence of the military brought order and allowed legal processes to proceed. Within a week, law enforcement officers made more than 1,000 arrests, including the Shoshone County sheriff and two county commissioners charged with having prior knowledge of the crimes and failing to intervene.

Affected families lamented the loss of life, property and livelihood. Union leaders seethed over the failure of their plan and the loss of power. According to testimony at the trials, union leaders focused most of their distain and revenge on Steunenberg.

Murder of Frank Steunenberg Five years after leaving office, Steunenberg was returning to his Caldwell home on December 30, 1905. When he opened the picket gate in front of his house, he triggered a bomb that exploded and killed him.

Gov. Frank Steunenberg

With astute detective work, authorities captured Harry Orchard who was living in the Treasure Valley. Orchard would later confess to conspiring with leaders of the Western Federation of Miners in Steunenberg's murder.

Orchard also confessed to participating with members of the union's executive committee in either planning or executing the murder or attempted murder of over 20 people who opposed other union demands made in Colorado, Idaho and California.

Union officials engaged the famous Chicago defense attorney, Clarence Darrow, to lead the defense team. W.E. Borah, later to become a U.S. senator from Idaho, and James H. Hawley, later to become governor of Idaho, served as prosecutors in the case that many believed had overwhelming evidence to convict. At the end of this

Harry Orchard

nationally celebrated trial, the court dismissed all charges against the union officials. However, at the next union election, union members voted the officials out of office.

The court found Harry Orchard guilty and sentenced him to death by hanging. However, because of his cooperation in the trial, the court later commuted his sentence to life in prison.

A statue of Governor Steunenberg stands in a small Boise park across the street facing the Capitol.

Orchard – who died in 1954 after serving 46 years in prison, the longest term ever served by an inmate in the Idaho Penitentiary – is also recognized by placards and the stark cell in which he once lived, now part of the Old Idaho Penitentiary Museum in Boise.

Superfund and Aftermath In 1980 Congress passed the Comprehensive Environmental Response, Compensation and Liberty Act (Superfund) giving federal agencies enforcement and oversight authority and requiring responsible parties to pay for the cleanup of hazardous waste sites. Several Silver Valley areas became Superfund clean-up sites.

In the case of Bunker Hill, the Environmental Protection Agency declared the mill site, including the cities of Kellogg and Wardner, a Superfund site in 1981 and proceeded with the cleanup. With this action, the Bunker Hill operation closed with a loss of over 2.000 jobs. The cleanup included razing almost all of the Bunker Hill structures, removing mill tailings from streams, replacing top soils in about 4,000 residential yards and public places and re-forestation of the surrounding mountains.

Both Kellogg and Wardner now have vibrant non-mining economies. Kellogg is now home to a destination ski and year-round resort and a large national Internet-based automobile dealership. Other Silver Valley cities have also been renovated.

The environmental damage to Lake Coeur d'Alene continues to be problematic. The lake contains an estimated 70 million tons of mine wastes and is now managed under a Lake Management plan supervised by the Coeur d'Alene Tribe, the State of Idaho and EPA.

Historic Mine Production and Ranking The first mining activity in Northern Idaho was placer gold, primarily at Pierce, Elk City-Orogrande and Florence. Idaho's historic gold production of 11 million tr. oz. through 2000 is impressive but pales in comparison to California's total gold production of 40 to 50 million tr. oz. and Nevada's current gold yields of over 1 million tr. oz. per year.

However, when it comes to silver, it is a different story. The Silver Valley alone has produced over 1.2 billion tr. oz., more silver than any other mining "district" in the United States and ranks as one of the most productive mining districts in the world – two other large mining districts are the Potosi District in Bolivia, over 1 billion tr. oz., and the Pachuca-Real del Monte area in Mexico at 1.5 billion tr. oz. Mine production from these countries dates from 1500 to 1875 and is, of necessity, general estimates.

Nevada is the self-proclaimed "Silver State," largely due to silver production from the fabled Comstock Lode near Carson City that yielded 190 million tr. oz. before the mines played out. In contrast, Idaho's largest silver mine, the Sunshine Silver Mine, has already produced over 360 million tr. oz. of silver and is still in operation. One of Idaho's best kept secrets is the prodigious amount of silver it has and is producing. If the right to claim the designation "The Silver State" was based on relative production, Idaho would receive that recognition.

Dr. Virginia Gillerman, Economic Geologist/Associate Research Geologist, Idaho Geological Survey, estimated historical production of precious and industrial metals extracted from Northern Idaho mines from 1862 to 2000, excluding the relatively small amount of gold that was a byproduct of processing lead-silver ore: is as follows:

Gold	Pierce	385,000 tr. oz.
	Murray (Silver Valley)	494,000 tr. oz.
	Elk City	832,000 54 tr. oz.
	Florence	1,000,000 tr. oz.

Total 2,711,000 tr.oz.

Silver	1,208,500,000 tr. oz.
Lead	16,700,000,000 lbs.
Zinc	6,600,000,000 lbs.
Copper	414,500,000 lbs.

In recent years, the price of precious and industrial metals has increased dramatically. This condition is causing a resurgence of mining in Northern Idaho, albeit ore concentrates are now shipped out of state for smelting and refining.

Forest Products

When Henry and Eliza Spalding started Idaho's first sawmill on the Clearwater River in 1836 while on their mission to the Nez Perce Indians, magnificent virgin forests that included trees hundreds of years old covered many parts of Northern Idaho. Forests of Western White Pine – Idaho's state tree, which could exceed 8 feet in diameter at the base and a height of over 200 feet – were common. The largest white pine in the world now stands at 219 feet near the city of Elk River. Most of those giants have been cut over the last century to help satisfy the lumber needs of a growing nation. Others were ravaged by fire. (*See Great Fire of 1910 below.*) Magnificent forests still cover Northern Idaho and parts of Southwestern and Eastern Idaho, but they are generally trees of younger growth.

The first sawmills were generally started to meet local market needs, often agricultural-based settlements or mine owners needing to provide timbers to shore up mineshafts and lumber for buildings at the mines and the burgeoning boomtowns they created. Later, as railroads opened the Northwest, they provided the transportation needed to deliver lumber and other commodities to distant markets and the economic basis for communities to built up around railroad depots, mines and sawmills.

Timberlands and Sawmills For more than a century after becoming a nation, Congress passed laws transferring ownership of public lands to private interests to pay obligations, encourage settlement, build railroads, harvest the nation's timber and mineral wealth, harness water for beneficial uses and grant land to states to fund public schools and infrastructure. (*See Federal Lands – Private Ownership and Preservation Laws above.*)

Beginning in the late 1800s, railroads began extending into timber regions, selling their land grant timberlands and providing transportation services to numerous new sawmills that were harvesting timber off federal and private lands. Farmers and ranchers often purchased cleared forestlands and began agricultural operations. Towns grew up around each significant commercial venture.

In 1891 Congress passed the Forest Reserve Act that allowed the President of the United States to set aside specific areas of public forestlands "to improve and protect the forest...securing favorable conditions for water flows, and to furnish a continuous supply of timber for the use and the necessities of citizens of the United States." At that time, President Benjamin Harrison placed 13 million acres into the reserve. Succeeding presidents increased the reserve's size. In 1905 Congress placed management of the forest reserves under an agency in the U.S. Department of Agriculture – now known as the National Forest System. The U.S. Forest Service now administers 191 million acres.

By 1900 merchantable timber growing in the forests of the Great Lakes states was becoming overcut and lumbermen were looking elsewhere to set up sawmills. Railroads had and were receiving massive federal land grants as an inducement to provide rail service throughout the region.

Largest White Pine Tree in the World. Felled Tuesday Dec. 12th, 1911.

White Pine King—Largest white pine tree in the world—Felled December 12, 1911

Although not a railroad man, Fredrick Weyerhaeuser was one of the largest ultimate beneficiaries of federal forested land grants to the railroads. Already a successful lumber industrialist – buying timberlands, companies and sawmills and harvesting the merchantable pine from Wisconsin and Minnesota forests – Weyerhaeuser set his eye on the Pacific Northwest.

Weyerhaeuser resided in St. Paul, Minnesota, and was neighbor to Jim Hill, head of the Northern Pacific Railroad which received its first federal railroad grants in 1864 that, over the next several years, would exceed 47 million acres for building railroads across the Northern United States. The two men served on each other's boards. One evening Weyerhaeuser learned that Hill had to redeem bonds and was short of cash. On January 3, 1900, Hill sold Weyerhaeuser's syndicate of investors 900,000 acres of timberland in Washington for $5.4 million.

This transaction was one of the first of many ownership transfers of railroad grant timberland to Weyerhaeuser and other lumber industrialists. Later, Weyerhaeuser would form a company to hold certain of his Idaho railroad grant lands, some of which were sold to a predecessor of Boise Cascade Corporation – now consisting of its successors, the privately owned Boise Cascade Holdings L.L.C. and the publically traded and affiliated Boise, Inc., which in 2008 acquired Boise Cascade's Paper Group operations. Both companies are headquartered in Boise. Neither company owns timberlands.

Weyerhaeuser, along with John H. Humbird and other Midwestern sawmill owner-operators and investors, went on to purchase other large tracts of railroad grant and other timberland in Washington, Oregon and Idaho that had not been designated as national forest reserves and built sawmills at optimum locations.

Northern Idaho towns that started or were significantly influenced by timber and wood products include Bonners Ferry, Bovill, Coeur d'Alene, Dover, East Hope, Deary, Elk City, Kootenai, Lewiston, Potlatch, Sandpoint and St. Maries.

The economy of these mill towns was subject to wide economic cycles largely brought on by fluctuating market prices, management/labor conflicts and the continually increasing distance between the mills and available merchantable timber.

Nearly 90 percent of these sawmills have since closed. However, those that remain continue to produce a comparable amount of wood products, albeit most of today's timber is harvested from private and state-owned forestlands. (*See Idaho's Historical Timber Harvest below.*)

Humbird Lumber Company, Kootenai.

Idaho has one pulp and paper mill, the Lewiston facility of Clearwater Paper Corporation, a 2008 spinoff from Potlatch Corporation. The company owns vast tracts of timberlands in Idaho. At its Lewiston facility, the company manufactures lumber, bleached paperboard, pulp and consumer tissue products. (*See the city chapters of Lewiston and Potlatch.*)

Great Fire of 1910 For two terrifying days – August 20 and 21, 1910 – following a summer of drought and high temperatures, a cold front came through bringing fierce winds that whipped smaller fires into raging infernos with flames leaping hundreds of feet high and clouds of smoke rising high into the atmosphere. These conflagrations generated their own blowtorch winds, blowing embers great distances, jumping from tree crowns, igniting other fires in a hopscotch fashion and ravaging Northern Idaho and western Montana.

The fire killed 85 men, mostly firefighters, destroyed several communities in Idaho and Montana and charred others, including much of Wallace – in total burning 3 million acres. Although estimates vary widely on the equivalent board feet destroyed, historian Stephen Payne, in his book *Year of the Fires: The Story of the Great Fires of 1910,* said, "The Forest Service settled on a figure of six billion board feet, about twice the entire national output and that in a year of record production."

The conflagration was so large some credited it with blowing ash halfway around the world. The fire, sometimes termed the Big Burn or the Big Blowup, is the largest fire in U.S. history, greatly influencing future federal forest-management policies.

Fire Aftermath The Great Fire was a catalyst that persuaded Congress to pass the Weeks Act of 1911, named for John W. Weeks of Massachusetts. The Act authorized the federal government to buy private lands within the watersheds of navigable streams and include such lands in the national forest system. While the law was initially used to buy lands in the East, it was also applied in the West. One of the major provisions of the Act was legislating emergency fire fighting funds for aggressive wildfire suppression.

In 1935 the Forest Service adopted the firefighting goal termed the "10 a.m. policy" – all newly detected forest fires were to be put out by 10 o'clock the next morning. The practice of

THE GREAT FIRES OF THE
NORTHERN ROCKIES

Map of "Year of the Fires"—Stephen J. Payne. Courtesy Wallace District Mining Museum and U.S. Forest Service.

parachuting firefighters near hard-to-reach fires – n ow termed Hotshot Crews – began in 1940. The familiar Smoky Bear advertising character and his slogan, "Only you can prevent forest fires," began in 1944.

These aggressive fire suppression programs had the desired effect of reducing forest fires but there were adverse consequences as well. Dr. Jay O'Laughlin, University of Idaho, Forestry and Policy Analysis, said, "Remove fire from the system and over time fuels will accumulate, making the next fire more difficult to control."

The conclusion of World War II started a nationwide housing boom. Providing lumber to build millions of homes for the families of soldiers returning from the war, many going back to school under the G.I. Bill before entering the workforce, was a federal priority. The Forest Service helped satisfy this demand by opening the national forests to increased timber harvests. In just over a decade, the timber harvest from federal lands in Northern Idaho had more than doubled – a high level of timber harvest that would continue for over two decades – all facilitated by improved heavy tractors, equipment, trucks and the 1950s invention of the single person hand-held gasoline-engine chain saw.

At this time, the commercial practice of clear-cutting, generally defined as the removal of all stems in a specified area whether the stems were viable for merchantable timber or not, became a common, but highly controversial, practice of timber harvest – a practice that would continue for more than two decades. Opponents, asserting the practice was tantamount to deforestation and the destruction of natural wildlife habitat, used photos of large clear-cuts to influence public opinion in favor of their preservationist cause.

In 1965 certain federal agencies combined resources to form the National Interagency Coordination Center and National Interagency Fire Center located in Boise. There are now eight participating federal agencies. The center in Boise coordinates resources to fight fires that may occur in any of the 11 geographical areas, called Geographical Area Coordination Centers and headquartered at a city in each of 11 designated areas of the United States, including Alaska.

Beginning in the 1970s Congress passed several laws affecting the protection of the environment, ecosystems, species and riparian areas and access to federal lands for the purpose of mining and harvesting timber. (*See Mining and Forest Products – Leading Causes for Loss of Economic Dominance below*.)

By 1992 there were numerous lawsuits and court injunctions in the Pacific Northwest involving the protection of endangered species and their habitat, including future timber harvests in "old growth" forests. From that time on, as shown in the following chart, timber harvest from federal lands began to fall precipitously.

The next major change in federal forest management law came with the passage of the Healthy Forest Restoration Act of 2003. Under the act, federal agencies were required to work collaboratively with other stakeholders to reduce the risk of large destructive wild fires by thinning dense tree-stands, undergrowth and brush in forested areas; creating fire breaks; improving firefighting practices and insect control, infestations of the pine beetle have killed millions of acres of forests in the West; and requiring communities in affected areas to develop wildfire protection plans. The law also directs the courts to consider the risk of forest fires in deciding cases that could delay thinning projects. Opponents to the law generally asserted it could lead to a return to the open commercial harvest of larger trees of the past with limited positive effect in reducing fire hazards.

Today, the Forest Service employs a mix of fire-fighting policies and tactics including prescribed burning – intentionally set fires designed to achieve specified outcomes – and natural burns' slow to intervene in fires started by natural causes such as lightning.

Dr. O'Laughlin said that during 2000 to 2009, the average number of acres burned each year exceeded 6 million, more than double the average of the preceding two decades.

Opponents to the federal burn practices assert that they waste good timber, and that if the Forest Service employed the mixed-use methodologies used on private and state-owned forestlands, forest fires could be better controlled, habitat preserved and more jobs created.

On August 7, 2007, The Idaho Statesman reported that in the heavy wildfire year of 2003 one private forestland owner of 180,000 acres experienced burns of only 100 acres, contrasted with the burn of 708,000 acres of federal forestlands in Idaho.

Forest Service managers assert their ability to fight wild fires is constrained for multiple reasons including lack of funds, road access and their priority to protect homes that are increasingly being built in forested areas. In addition, Dr. O'Laughlin said, "Forest Service management practices today are designed primarily to modify ecological conditions rather than provide timber supplies. In contrast to federal policies, private and state-owned forestlands are generally managed for a mix of uses that includes timber production."

Today, 36 percent of Idaho's 54 million acres is owned by private, state or local government entities. Federal agencies are responsible for managing the balance of the land – U.S. Forest Service 39 percent, the Bureau of Land Management 21 percent and other federal agencies 4 percent.

Lumber Production History
Researchers at the University of Idaho have estimated that Idaho's statewide lumber production grew from 1.5 million board feet (bf) in 1870 to nearly 1.2 billion in 1925 before falling to around 200 million during the Great Depression of the 1930s. Following the Depression, production rebounded as shown in the chart below, reaching over 1.2 billion bf in 1950.

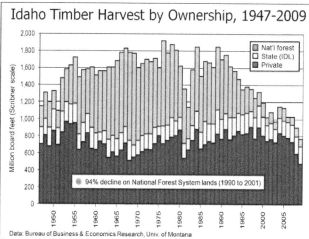

Idaho Timber Harvest by Ownership, 1947-2009

94% decline on National Forest System lands (1990 to 2001)

Data: Bureau of Business & Economics Research, Univ. of Montana
Source: Idaho's Forest Products Industry Current Conditions and 2011Forecast

By the mid-1950s there were over 300 sawmills in Idaho. Within five decades, all of the mills had closed except for 35. However, as shown in the chart above, the remaining mills were producing about the same quantity as the 300 mills were producing decades earlier. Of the 35 remaining mills, 14 each had annual production, prior to the recent recession, generally greater than 50 million board feet of lumber. These mills operate using state-of-the-art computer process control systems including lasers; scanners; mechanized log and lumber handling systems;

and improved saw-blade, edger and trimmer technologies that use substantially fewer – albeit more highly skilled – workers.

As the chart further illustrates, the global economic decline that began in 2007 has had a significant adverse effect on lumber production in Idaho as it has in the industry as a whole. However, as illustrated in previous economic cycles, production will resume as the economy improves.

Timber Harvest by Region As illustrated in the table below, in 2006 about 87 percent of Idaho's timber harvest came from Northern Idaho, 11 percent from Southwestern Idaho and less than 2 percent from Eastern Idaho.

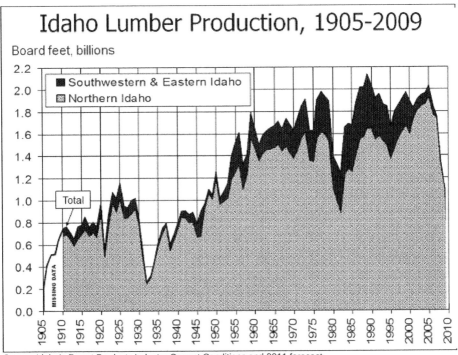

Source: Idaho's Forest Products Industry Current Conditions and 2011 forecast.

The underlying basis for calculating timber harvest by county in the chart below is different than that used to calculate Idaho timber harvest and lumber production used in the table above – largely due to formula inconsistencies in handling the declining size of logs being milled. Dr. O'Laughlin said that many of Idaho's sawmills began to re-tool during the 1980s to handle smaller diameter logs. By 2003 nearly 60 percent of all logs processed in Idaho were less than 10 inches small-end diameter, and some mills were processing logs less than 6 inches small-end diameter.

The U.S. Census Bureau has also reported Idaho lumber production at amounts different than that shown herein. No attempt has been made to reconcile differences as the information disclosed herein is based on methodologies that are generally accepted in the industry to reasonably calculate timber and lumber harvests. The calculations do not include timber used for paper manufacturing and

Table 2—Idaho timber harvest (MMBF Scribner) by county, selected years (sources: Keegan and others 1982, 1988, 1992, 1997, Morgan and others 2004)

County	1979 MMBF Scribner	1979 Percent of Total	1985 MMBF Scribner	1985 Percent of Total	1990 MMBF Scribner	1990 Percent of Total	1995 MMBF Scribner	1995 Percent of Total	2001 MMBF Scribner	2001 Percent of Total	2006 MMBF Scribner	2006 Percent of Total
Northern Idaho												
Clearwater	544	29.0	336	21.0	267	16.0	234	17.0	182	18.0	174	15.6
Shoshone	206	11.0	217	14.0	183	11.0	194	14.0	172	17.0	200	17.8
Idaho	190	10.0	156	10.0	174	10.0	113	8.0	65	6.0	65	5.8
Bonner	142	8.0	175	11.0	197	12.0	139	10.0	124	12.0	93	8.3
Benewah	100	5.0	94	6.0	152	9.0	117	9.0	129	13.0	144	12.9
Boundary	94	5.0	80	5.0	86	5.0	69	5.0	57	6.0	53	4.8
Kootenai	65	4.0	80	5.0	152	9.0	114	8.0	81	8.0	100	8.9
Latah	57	3.0	89	6.0	84	5.0	96	7.0	70	7.0	125	11.2
Nez Perce	8	0.0	12	1.0	17	1.0	8	1.0	4	0.0	10	0.9
Lewis	4	0.0	13	1.0	20	1.0	17	1.0	14	1.0	12	1.1
Northern Idaho	1,410	76.0	1,254	79.0	1,332	79.0	1,100	80.0	855	85.0	976	87.1
Southern Idaho												
Valley	107	6.0	38	6.0	52	3.0	67	5.0	39	4.0	65	5.8
Boise	84	4.0	67	4.0	127	8.0	93	7.0	20	2.0	25	2.2
Adams	52	3.0	66	4.0	87	5.0	28	2.0	25	2.0	30	2.7
Washington	4	a	9	1.0	4	a	6	a	-	a	a	a
Elmore	2.5	a	14	1.0	5	a	38	3.0	7	1.0	a	a
Other Counties	2.0	1.0	3	a	6	a	11	1.0	1	a	6	0.5
Southwestern Idaho	252	16.0	247	16.0	281	17.0	242	18.0	91	9.0	126	11.3
Fremont	76	4.0	43	3.0	20	1.0	2	a	3	a	1	0.1
Lemhi	34	2.0	11	1.0	16	1.0	6	a	1	a	1	0.1
Clark	10	1.0	10	1.0	16	1.0	-	a	1	a	6	0.6
Caribou	4	a	10	1.0	3	a	5	a	5	a	4	0.3
Other Counties	24	1.0	19	1.0	24	1.0	15	1.0	7	1.0	7	0.6
Southeastern Idaho	148	8.0	93	6.0	79	5.0	27	2.0	17	2.0	19	1.7
Southern Idaho	440	24.0	340	21.0	360	21.0	265	20.0	108	11.0	145	12.9
Idaho Total	1850	100.0	1554	100.0	1692	100.0	1,370	100.0	1,007	100.0	1,121	100.0

a Percentage detail may not sum to 100% due to rounding
b Less than 0.05 percent
c Less than 1 MMBF

Source: Idaho's Forest Products Industry and Timber Harvest, 2006 (U.S. Forest Service, in press; compiled from data published periodically by the University of Montana's Bureau of Business and Economic Research.)

unprocessed logs sold to foreign countries.

Loss of Economic Dominance The production of dimensional lumber and silver, lead and zinc ingots were Idaho's largest manufacturing businesses and dominated the economies of Northern Idaho and many cities across the state for nearly a century. Placer gold mining had major economic effects until the mines played out.

Although totally different in operation, raw material, end product and environmental impact of processing, these two natural resource-based industries were subject to many of the same federal laws and regulations including, during recent decades, the almost total loss of access to federal lands.

The following provides leading causes for the decline in economic influence of the mining and wood products industries in Idaho as well as the nation.

Until around 1970 Congressional actions toward railroad companies, settlers and natural resource-based industries were very accommodating. Motivated by a desire to connect the continent with railroad transportation, settle the West and obtain timber and minerals needed for the nation's rapidly growing economy, Congress gave railroad companies over 100 million acres of land grants, including mineral rights, that they could sell to provide cash for the construction of railroads. However, the largest numbers of federal land grants – totaling the most acreage – were to farmers, ranchers, developers and states. (*See Federal Lands – Private Ownership and Preservation Laws above.*)

The federal priority was to encourage private businesses to produce the timber and minerals needed for the nation's rapidly growing economy. There was limited governmental oversight. Business practices generally focused on profitability as opposed to environmental impact and safety of workers until the 1970s.

The use of public lands for mining was, to a great extent, open to all who wished to file mining claims. Claims with proven ore bodies could become patented or deeded to the claim owner. Most of today's mining activity is on such patented land.

The use of public forests was largely unregulated until around 1905 when President Theodore Roosevelt, often described as a conservationist who generally supported sustainable harvest and multiple-use concepts of forest management, helped create the United States Forest Service.

Beginning in 1907 Roosevelt used his executive authority to create scores of national forests, primarily in the Western states. In Idaho, he created 15 – many of which, due to changes in forest management practices and policies, have been combined or consolidated. Idaho's original national forests were the Caribou, Challis, Salmon, Clearwater, Coeur d'Alene, Pend d'Oreille, Weiser, Nez Perce, Idaho, Payette, Boise, Sawtooth, Lemhi, Targhee and Bitterroot.

U.S. Senator Weldon Heyburn from Wallace favored open use and opposed all of Roosevelt's conservation initiatives to protect and manage public lands for public recreation and commercial purposes. On the other side of the debate were the preservationists such as John Muir, founder of the Sierra Club, who wanted to maintain pristine natural environments by banning all development.

In the latter half of the twentieth century, many people across the nation became concerned about the declining quality of air in cities and industrial areas as well as ground and surface water quality, wildlife habitat and the general lack of care government agencies had given to the nation's public lands, environment and worker safety. This motivated Congress to enact laws more closely in accord with preservationist ideology for the management of public lands and the commercial use of natural resources.

In 1970 Congress created the Environmental Protection Agency, the Occupational Safety and Health Administration and the National Institute for Occupational Safety and Health. A few years later, the federal Mine Safety and Health Administration; the Federal Water Pollution Control Act, also known as the Clean Water Act; and the Endangered Species Act of 1973, successor to the Endangered Species Preservation Act of 1966 – laws protecting specific animal species and their habitat – were also enacted.

Idaho created what is now the Department of Environmental Quality and divided Idaho's counties into seven regions, creating public health districts in each. These agencies, in cooperation with federal agencies, have legal oversight of certain environmental matters.

All federal and state agencies, and the regulations they promulgated, established minimum environmental protection and health and safety standards and practices, including those affecting worker safety and the discharge or emission of pollutants into the air as well as total maximum daily loads as required by the CWA, of pollutants in surface water and groundwater contamination. Compliance with these laws required major changes in the operating processes and practices of many businesses.

Certain business activities on public lands were further restricted as environmental groups used these laws to challenge the adequacy of the environmental studies and basis for approvals, aided especially by the National Environmental Policy Act of 1970 and its requirement for a "hard look" at environmental impacts of any significant action involving federal lands or resources before decisions are made.

The National Forest Management Act of 1976 required comprehensive long-range planning. Many private and federal activities became tied up in the courts, with appeals and calls for incorporating new science extending project decisions for years. These lawsuits influenced federal policy and played a significant role in delaying or preventing private access to federal lands for mining and timber harvest purposes. Delays had the practical effect of stopping any business activity that had to work on a return-on-investment timetable.

Decades of aggressive fire suppression and, later, timber harvest restrictions have exacerbated deadfall build up on forest floors with the consequence of potentially more severe and exceptionally hot forest fires that destroy merchantable timber and modify wildlife habitat.

Mining and timber harvests were also adversely affected when Congress acted in 1964 and again in 1980 to protect 4 million acres of Idaho national forests as components of the National Wilderness Preservation System, precluding mining and timber operations as provided by the Wilderness Act of 1964. (*See National Wilderness Areas below*.)

In 2009 Congress also set aside 517,000 acres of Owyhee County in Southwestern Idaho as wilderness, which has limited amounts of merchantable timber and a few mining properties. (*See Southwestern Idaho, The Region, National Wilderness Areas*.)

At the time the wilderness laws were enacted, there were many relatively small parcels of private land in wilderness areas. The laws grandfathered private property rights, allowing people as well as commercial outfitters and guides to use wilderness areas for recreation, hunting and fishing. Private interests, including stock-ownership membership resorts, still own parcels of land in the wilderness. Their members and clients, many of whom are hunters, fly in on small private aircraft or helicopters to backcountry airstrips or float the rivers on rafts or ride horses into their wilderness properties that often have horse stables and modern furnished cabins and lodges with small hydroelectric systems providing electricity and satellite. (*See National Wilderness Areas below*.)

Federal law changes, with attendant increased operating cost requirements to comply with the laws, were only some of the reasons natural resource businesses were not successful. Competitive global market factors, competition from businesses in less or unregulated countries and cost of replacing outdated plants challenged the ability of natural resource-based businesses to achieve profitable operations, forcing many to close.

Many mines, particularly gold mines, closed because the mines simply played out. As new metal recovery technologies became available, old mines were often reopened and even the mine tailings were reprocessed to extract the metals that the old processes failed to remove.

With the closure of mines and sawmills, rural school districts, counties and cities that relied on their share of federal revenues from timber sales and mine production as well as local property taxes from supporting businesses sustained major losses in revenue. Congressional appropriations to make up the revenue shortfall have been inadequate.

During this time, federal agencies also began requiring owners of properties, where their industrial activity had damaged the environment, to pay the cost of cleaning up the hazardous waste called Superfund sites. The ore-processing component of the mining industry was the principal activity affected by these actions. Many companies opted to go out of business, leaving the government – taxpayers – to pay the remaining cleanup costs. (*See Silver Valley Mines – Superfund and Aftermath above.*)

Compared to mining, wood products businesses caused significantly less damage to the environment, albeit staying compliant with CWA regulations requires care to prevent erosion into surface waters, including that caused by road cutting and maintenance and timber harvesting. Compliance with ESA laws protecting rare plants and animals and habitat of endangered species is often problematic for timber harvesting. Although not prohibited by law, the historic practice of clear-cutting remains controversial. Both mining and wood product industries were directly affected by federal health and safety laws.

By the end of the twentieth century, logging and mining on federal lands had almost ceased, albeit, the Forest Service still conducts timber harvests, generally for ecological purposes. Responding to lawsuits, courts have often blocked removing merchantable timber damaged in forest fires and pest infestations. In February 2011 the Forest Service released new rules intended to aid in consensus building and give the Forest Service more flexibility in ecosystem restoration and logging. Mining continues but generally on patented mining claims – concentrated ores are shipped out of state for smelting and refining.

Technological innovation has changed how mining and wood products businesses operate. These once labor-intensive businesses now have much higher productivity with significantly fewer employees, albeit the average educational requirements, skill level and wage of today's natural resource employees has increased substantially. The Idaho Department of Labor published projections of Idaho's total fourth quarter 2010 employment for natural resources businesses – mining, forestry and logging – at 3,251 and wood product manufacturing at 4,526 with average wages of $54,250 and $36,193, respectively. This compared to the state's total employment of 661,334 with an average wage of $34,332.

While lumber manufacturing remains the core business of the wood products industry, changes in the size of logs processed and new technologies and niche businesses that have emerged over the past few decades are changing the industry and, in some cases, broadening the variety of products produced from wood. In addition to expansion of small-log sawmills, there are businesses that press wood mill waste such as sawdust and chips into compressed wood pellets and logs for heating in pellet stoves and fireplaces or for use by paper mills. Bark is processed through large rotating screens producing various sizes of bark used as ground cover in decorative residential and commercial landscapes. Idaho businesses manufacture log homes, wood moldings, laminated beams and trusses and other specialty or niche products.

At the same time, businesses producing and selling competing products – such as steel studs and trusses, extruded plastic moldings and framing, dimensional lumber made from plastic or lumber made from wood fiber combined with resins – are slowly increasing their market shares.

Railroads

Rail service was critical to the development of Northern Idaho's mining, forest products and agriculture industries and in keeping cities vibrant. In several instances, railroad officials platted and named the towns where they built depots or sidings. In some cases, towns bypassed by the railroad literally moved to be near the railroad station and the transportation services it provided.

As a financial inducement to provide rail service, Congress made large grants of federal land to railroads to help pay construction costs. (*See Federal Lands – Private Ownership and Preservation Laws above.*)

The Union Pacific and Central Pacific Railroads completed the first transcontinental railroad at Promontory Point, Utah, in 1869. In 1883 the Northern Pacific Railroad completed a transcontinental railroad across the Northern U.S. The line started at the Wallula, Washington, railhead; proceeded northeast to Spokane; crossed into Idaho near Rathdrum, formerly Westwood; then to the north

Washington and Idaho Railway hauls a load of lumber from Bennett Lumber Products in Princeton through Potlatch on to Palouse. Potlatch is the only city in Latah County served by rail.

shore of Lake Pend Oreille and Sandpoint, where it followed the lake shore to the Clark Fork River before turning east to Missoula, Montana.

As soon as the Northern Pacific completed its transcontinental line, it and other independent railroads began building branch lines to other Northern Idaho communities. They completed a line to Coeur d'Alene and the Silver Valley in 1887. Service came to Moscow in 1890, Lewiston in 1898 and to the farms of the Camas Prairie in 1899.

Great Northern Railway construction crews working east from Puget Sound in 1891 crossed the Pend Oreille River at Newport – now Oldtown – ran through Priest River and along the north side of the Pend Oreille River to Sandpoint. At Sandpoint, the line turned north to Bonners Ferry, where it extended north to Canada and east to connect with the main line in Havre, Montana. Two years later, the Great Northern Railroad – now Burlington Northern – acquired the Northern Pacific.

In 1904 the Potlatch Lumber Company affiliate – the Washington, Idaho and Montana Railway Company, which had originally planned to extend into Montana – built a 45-mile line from Palouse, Washington, through Potlatch and Deary to the western terminus of the Milwaukee Road at Bovill. The railroad would later extend further southeast to Elk River.

With rail transportation available, sawmills began developing around Lake Pend Oreille. In 1906 the Spokane International Railway built a 142-mile line between Spokane and Canada. This line also passed through Sandpoint before continuing on to Bonners Ferry and Eastport where it connected with the Canadian Pacific Railway.

While railroad companies continue to serve many communities for freight and passenger service – Amtrak has a depot in Sandpoint – several of the early lines have been abandoned. Some of the old rail beds are now trails for bicycles and pedestrians that cross over high trestles and terrain with stunning views of some of Northern Idaho's beautiful mountains, lakes and streams.

Frank Church River of No Return Wilderness.

National Wilderness Areas

Northern Idaho is home to all or part of four national wilderness areas. On the Idaho/Montana border south of Lolo Pass is the 1.3-million-acre Selway-Bitterroot Wilderness, 251,000 acres of which are in Montana.

To the south of the Selway-Bitterroot Wilderness is the 2.4-million-acre Frank Church-River of No Return Wilderness Area, which includes part of the Salmon River that had been nicknamed the River of No Return. This wilderness extends south into Valley County in Southwestern, Idaho and Custer and Lemhi Counties in Eastern Idaho.

West of the Frank Church-River of No Return Wilderness is the 206,000-acre Gospel Hump Wilderness. Sixty miles further west is the 215,000-acre Hells Canyon Wilderness Area, 131,000 acres are on the western side of the Snake River in Oregon and 84,000 acres on the eastern side of the river are in Idaho.

Idaho's U.S, Senator Frank Church, who served from 1957 to 1981, is generally recognized as one of the major influencers of passage of the Wilderness Act of

1964 – floor sponsor in the Senate – and establishment of a viable process for designating wilderness areas in the future. He would later co-sponsor other wilderness legislation including The Wild and Scenic Rivers Act of 1968, The Eastern Wilderness Areas Act of 1974 and The Endangered American Wilderness Act of 1978.

Institutions of Higher Learning

The region's principal institutions of higher education are the University of Idaho in Moscow, Lewis-Clark State College in Lewiston and North Idaho College in Coeur d'Alene. Branches of other universities and colleges and Internet-based institutions also operate in the region.

Region's Economic Base

Natural resource-based industries that historically employed large numbers of workers and underpinned Northern Idaho's economy for more than a century began declining in influence in the latter part of the twentieth century. (*See Mining and Forest Products – Leading Causes for Loss of Economic Dominance above*.)

Today's highly automated and efficient logging and wood product businesses continue to produce at the same high levels of the past but with a fraction of the employees and with only about 10 percent of the mills that operated in the 1950s, albeit the mills of today are dramatically more efficient and productive that the mills operating in the mid-twentieth century.

More than 90 percent of the timber harvested in Idaho now comes from private and state-owned lands. The current level of timber harvest will continue to sustain a viable wood products industry in Northern Idaho, but growth is constrained by lack of additional timber, as more than 80 percent of Idaho's standing timber outside of wilderness areas is on National Forest System lands that are largely closed for timber harvest. (*See Forest Products – Idaho's Lumber Production History above*.)

Mining activity is highly regulated and largely limited to the development of ore bodies under previously granted patents. In terms of production and employment, the mining industry is a shadow of what it was. In recent years, however, the price of precious and industrial metals has increased dramatically. This condition is causing a resurgence of mining in the region.

Today, Northern Idaho's population and economy are again growing. The region's economy today is not dominated by any one industry, but is a blend of industries. Hospitality, service, recreation and light manufacturing are leading the way. Many businesses are benefiting from new telecommunication and other high-technology advances that allow them to operate nationally and globally yet live in this stunningly beautiful part of the world. Many retirees, second homeowners and entrepreneurs are moving to Northern Idaho because of its fabulous natural setting and quality of life.

Chatcolet Lake at Heyburn State Park

BENEWAH COUNTY

- Plummer
- St. Maries (County Seat)
- Tensed

Plummer, looking down from the Butte.

Plummer

Statistical Data

Population: 1,026 *
Elevation: 2,722 feet
Precipitation: 24 inches **
Average Snowfall: 8 inches **
County: Benewah

Temperature Range – Fahrenheit: **
Spring: 30 to 67
Summer: 47 to 86
Fall: 30 to 73
Winter: 21 to 41
* U.S. Census Bureau Estimates July 2015
**Historical averages

Plummer lies 35 miles south of Coeur d'Alene and nine miles east of the Idaho/Washington state line. Rolling fields of bluegrass, wheat, oats, lentils and peas interspersed with forested areas surround the city. Most of the farmland is Indian trust land owned by the Coeur d'Alene Tribe.

The city lies in the heart of the Coeur d'Alene Indian Reservation at the junction of U.S. Highway 95 and Idaho Highway 5 which is the west entrance to Heyburn State Park at the base of Lake Coeur d'Alene. It is also the west entrance to the city of St. Maries and the St. Joe River.

Pre-Incorporation Years

In an attempt to assimilate American Indians into the white mainstream, Congress passed the General Allotment Act, or Dawes Severalty Act, in 1887. Under the Act, Indians received an allotment of reservation land. Each head of family received 160 acres. Single persons received a lesser acreage. Any lands not allotted became "surplus" and were made available for non-Indian settlement. This created a checkerboard ownership pattern throughout most reservations in the nation. (*See The Region, American Indians – Dawes Severalty Act.*)

In 1905 the Chicago, Milwaukee, St. Paul and Pacific Railroad, known as the Milwaukee Road, built a rail line through the heavily wooded forests surrounding what are now St. Maries and Plummer. The Oregon-Washington Railroad and Navigation Company (OWR&N) built a line that intersected the Milwaukee Road at Plummer. (*See The Region, Railroads.*)

The federal government completed its survey of the Coeur d'Alene Reservation in 1908 and, under the Dawes Severalty Act, opened the declared surplus land for settlement. As part of the federal surveyors' work, a 640-acre townsite was platted strategically at the junction of the Milwaukee Road and the Oregon-Washington Railroad. Subsequent annexations have increased the townsite to 750 acres.

They named the town Plummer, after Plummer's Camp, a railroad camp located a few miles east. The camp was so named because it was allegedly the one time hideout of the infamous William Henry Plummer who moved to the boomtown of Lewiston in the spring of 1861 following the discovery of gold at Pierce a year earlier.

Plummer was 19 and broke when he came to the California gold fields in 1852. He amazingly soon become prosperous, was elected sheriff, killed a man outside his line of duty, was sentenced to prison, was pardoned by the governor, killed again ostensibly in self defense and fled to Lewiston. There, working in a

Early Plummer

gambling hall, he became a respected citizen; but allegedly led a dual life – he was also the leader of a gang of gold thieves.

In the fall of 1862 possibly sensing people were getting suspicious, he left Lewiston for the newly discovered gold fields in what is now western Montana. There he was again elected sheriff but, allegedly, continued his nefarious business of lawman by day and leader of a band of road agents by night. Several Montana men formed a vigilante committee to stop the numerous gold robberies and murders that the law seemed unable to do. They hung about two dozen suspected criminals – one of whom named Sheriff Plummer as their leader. On the night of January 10, 1864, the vigilantes seized and hung the 31-year-old William Henry Plummer. Many proclaimed Plummer's innocence; but, for whatever reason, after his death, the wave of crime stopped.

The federal government had given the railroad companies land grants as an inducement to build the railroads and encourage settlement. At that time, forest products companies were preparing to build sawmills at locations along the rail lines. (*See The Region, Federal Lands – Private Ownership and Preservation Laws and Forest Products*.)

Incorporation

On July 18, 1910, the first settlers began acquiring lots in Plummer. The town soon had a population of over 200. On August 2, 1910, the settlement became an incorporated village.

Turning Points

Dawes Severalty Act This legislation achieved its intended purpose of converting former Indian reservation land to federal public lands and opening them for settlement. The law played a key role in the founding of Plummer and the development of its

economic base. Congress repealed the Dawes Severalty Act in 1934 and replaced it with the Indian Reorganization Act, placing unsettled reservation land into tribal trusts.

Railroad The railroad played a critical role in the founding of Plummer by providing the site that federal surveyors identified as the best place to plat the new town. The railroad also provided the means for sawmill owners to transport their commodities to market.

Sawmills In the early days there were many small sawmills in and around Plummer. By 1920 as sawmill operators harvested most of the nearby timber, the mills closed. In the 1950s timber interests formed a cooperative which built a sawmill on land leased from the City in the southwestern part of town.

Subsequent owners of the mill, including Pacific Crown and Rayonier, purchased land next to the original site and expanded the mill operations. While under Pacific Crown ownership, the company built an electrical co-generation plant that converted

wood waste to electrical energy. Pacific Crown, in turn, sold all the electricity it generated to Washington Water Power – now Avista Utilities – as an offset to the cost of operating the sawmill. The sawmill, in turn, purchased the power it used from the City of Plummer.

Under Rayonier's ownership, the mill burned down in 1988, causing the loss of 160 jobs. The Coeur d'Alene Tribe purchased the burned-out mill and worked with

Todd Brinkmeyer of Plummer Forest Products to rebuild a state-of-the-art small log mill. In 2006 the Tribe sold the sawmill to Stimson Lumber Company. A significant part of mill operations are still located on property leased from the City of Plummer.

Electricity The Dunkle Brothers operated a sawmill and electrical power plant east of town in 1914 and provided the first electricity to Plummer. However, the availability of electricity was limited to the times the mill was operating.

Two years later, Plummer purchased the power plant and built an electricity distribution system so that the community could have lights into the night. In 1920 Plummer closed the power plant; built power lines to Washington Water Power's Tekoa, Washington, station 13 miles away; and began receiving electrical power from the regulated utility.

The City still operates a distribution system that extends for over 50 miles, including Heyburn State Park. Plummer is one of the smallest municipal power companies and likely the only one in Idaho to extend power so far outside the city limits. Maintaining local control of this utility has provided the community with competitive electric rates. Profits from the utility enable the City to provide additional public services without increasing taxes. **Adapting to a Changing Economy** In the 1980s the Coeur d'Alene Tribe began a major initiative to provide housing and employment opportunities for its members as jobs from the city's natural resource and agriculture-based businesses declined. Private business joined in this construction. The Tribe is now the major employer in the area and has focused on a diverse economic portfolio.

The Benewah Medical Center was built in 1990, a cooperative effort between the Coeur d'Alene Tribe and the City of Plummer. It is a model facility and was the first Tribal Clinic to be open to non-tribal people. Today it serves over 10,000 patients in this city of less than 1,000.

More recently, the Tribe's Casino and Resort complex has come on line nine miles north near Worley. Many Plummer residents work at the complex.

43

Improvements to U.S. Highway 95 have made access to the casino easier for patrons and tourists as well as improved travel conditions for city residents who commute elsewhere to work, shop and do business.

Plummer Today

Amenities and Attractions Plummer has three city parks, comprising 2.7 acres. Park amenities include picnic, children's playground and athletic areas.

Plummer's most significant attraction is Heyburn State Park, located a few miles northeast. The 5,744-acre park is on 2,300 acres of water. Established in 1908, it is the oldest park in the Pacific Northwest.

Coeur d'Alene Tribal Chairman Ernest Stensgar and Mayor Jack Bringman riding in the Plummer Days parade.

Before it was a state park, the area was a gathering place for the Coeur d'Alene Tribe. In the 1930s the park was a Civilian Conservation Corps camp, and many of the park's buildings were constructed by the Corps.

Heyburn State Park is a natural park with a variety of different habitats. The St. Joe River winds its way through the park, and three lakes are located there. Tall Ponderosa Pines tower over grassy hillsides covered in wildflowers. On shadier slopes, cedar trees mix with hemlocks and huge white pines. On the edges of the lakes, the wetland/marsh areas are home to many types of wildflowers and plants. The lake is popular for boating, fishing and other water sports.

Another important attraction is the Coeur d'Alene Tribe's Casino and Resort complex nine miles north near Worley. This destination resort includes a casino, hotel, small conference center, 18-hole professional golf course and facilities that can accommodate concerts as well as boxing matches.

The 73-mile Trail of the Coeur d'Alenes is another prominent Plummer attraction. It is one of the most spectacular paved non-motorized trails in the Western United States. It begins at Plummer and extends east to Mullan. The trail is an abandoned railroad line that passes over high railroad trestles and through national forests and old mining towns. It follows the shoreline of Lake Coeur d'Alene then passes through a chain of lakes and marshland along the scenic Coeur d'Alene River up into the mountains above Mullan.

The 5,300-acre McCroskey State Park is about 20 miles from Plummer. The park contains about 32 miles of multi-purpose trails. An 18-mile drive through the park on unimproved roads with spectacular views of the rolling Palouse country is a high point.

Plummer is in an outdoor paradise. Camping, fishing and hunting can be found in the Coeur d'Alene Forest, 18 miles northeast, and the St. Joe Forest, 25 miles west. Silver Mountain Ski Resort, 35 miles west at Kellogg, offers snow tubing, downhill and cross-country skiing, snowboarding and snowmobiling during the winter and mountain biking, hiking, chairlift rides and other outdoor activities during the summer.

Economy and Major Employers With about 300 employees, the Coeur d'Alene Tribe is the city's largest employer. The Benewah Medical Center employs 150. The Plummer Worley School District and Stimson Lumber Company have approximately 100 employees each. Berg Industries employs nearly 60 at its Plummer plant. The casino employs 1,000 people with seasonal increases, and many Plummer residents work there.

Education The Plummer Worley Joint School District provides most of the city's education. Elementary students attend school at Lakeside Elementary in Worley. Middle school and high school students attend Lakeside Middle School and Lakeside High School in Plummer. The private Coeur d'Alene Tribal school is located 14 miles south in DeSmet. The school teaches kindergarten to eighth grade. It charges no tuition and is open to non-tribal students.

Freedom monument in city park. The American Legion placed it there and it is visited very often each year.

The nearest institutions of higher learning are North Idaho College (NIC) in Coeur d'Alene, 29 miles away, and the University of Idaho in Moscow, 37 miles south. NIC also teaches extension classes in Plummer.

Health Care The Benewah Medical Center is located in the city and provides for most health care needs.

Transportation U.S. Highways 5 and 95 intersect the city.

Spokane International Airport is 49 miles away in Spokane, Washington.

The St. Maries River Railroad provides freight service to spurs in Plummer.

Utilities and Services Private companies provide telephone, cable television and satellite services. The City provides electricity, water and sewer services and police protection. The Gateway Fire Protection District, located in Plummer, provides fire protection.

Vision for 2050

Over the past five decades, Plummer's population has more than tripled but has stabilized in the past 10 years at around 1,000. The city's last annexation occurred in 2006. Plummer's future is linked to actions taken by the Coeur d'Alene Tribe and the need for housing to accommodate the workforce.

As the general economy improves, the Tribe will likely continue development activities centered on tourism. As this occurs, the city's economy will benefit and the population will enjoy moderate growth.

Mayors

1910 Ed Thompson *
1910 R.H. Mercer *
1911 Frank N. McCaslin *
1912 George Mitchell *
1915 Theodore Hill *
1915 Jay D. Parker *
1917 James McCabe *
1919 Henry B. Coplen *
1920 John T. Bush *
1923 H.P. Schmidt *
1924 Charles E. Weinberg *
1927 R.M. Griffith *
1927 Clarence W. Lee *
1929 F.J. Willard *
1935 Howard L. Wiltse *
1935 F.J. Willard *

1937 Louis Dretke *
1937 J.A. Weaver *
1939 John Fothergill *
1941 Douglas Brown *
1942 Pearl S. Taylor *
1947 A.J. Weaver *
1949 Hood Worthington *
1951 Clair Deriford *
1951 Verle D. Bell *
1952 Clair Heriford *
1953 Claude Eikes *
1955 W.C. Anderson *
1957 Warren Shepherd *
1960 Francis Willard *
1964 Claude Eikes *
1968 Edwin Dretke

1969 Austin West
1972 Donald W. Evans
1974 Edwin Dretke
1980 Harold Whitley
1984 Clair Heriford
1992 Jess Marratt
1992 John Wheaton
1993 Harold Whitley
2001 Jack Bringman
2004 Carl Richel
2007 Tim Clark
2012 Terry Allen
2015 Jack Bringman
2016 William Weems
* Village Chairman

Logger memorial, St. Maries

St. Maries

Statistical Data

Population: 2,347 *
Elevation: 2,145 feet
Precipitation: 30 inches **
Average Snowfall: 50 inches **
County: Benewah
Website: www.stmarieschamber.org (Chamber of Commerce)

Temperature Range – Fahrenheit: **
Spring: 30 to 67
Summer: 47 to 84
Fall: 30 to 73
Winter: 23 to 41
* U.S. Census Bureau Estimates July 2015
**Historical averages

St. Maries lies in a beautiful valley carved by the St. Joe River and located about five miles southeast of the lower tip of Lake Coeur d'Alene. Forested hillsides and nearby mountains – rising to nearly 5,000 feet – interspersed by farmland surround the city. The Clearwater Mountains are a few miles south and the St. Joe Mountains, part of the Bitterroot Range, and St. Joe National Forest lie northeast.

The St. Joe River, a tributary to Lake Coeur d'Alene, forms the city's northern border. The St. Maries River, a tributary of the St. Joe River, is on the east. The Coeur d'Alene Indian Reservation lies north, west and southwest of the city, with one-third of the city situated on the reservation.

The cities of Coeur d'Alene and Moscow are 54 road miles northwest and 70 miles southwest, respectively.

Pre-Incorporation Years

Moon over Mount Baldy in winter

When the first trappers/explorers began coming into the lands around Coeur d'Alene Lake in the early 1800s, the Coeur d'Alene Tribe of American Indians were the principal inhabitants of the area. Seeking to benefit from the weaponry, religion, other technology and skills of the white men, many Indians sought white teachers. Fur-trading companies brought the first of these educators, followed in the mid-1830s by Protestant and Catholic missionaries.

Father Pierre Jean DeSmet, a Jesuit Order Priest from Belgium, led the first Roman Catholic mission in the region. After co-founding the St. Mary's Mission among the Flathead Tribe in what is now Montana, he commissioned Father Nicholas Point to expand the work among the Coeur d'Alene Tribe.

Old railroad tracks

In 1842 Father Point established the Mission of the Sacred Heart about one mile from the southern tip of Coeur d'Alene Lake on the north shore of a large river, which he named St. Joseph, later shortened by local residents to St. Joe. Father Point also named the St. Mary's River – later spelled St. Maries. After starting the mission, Father Point found the location was not as favorable as he originally thought. Spring flooding was common and the wetlands were breeding grounds for swarms of mosquitoes.

After four years, Father Point moved the mission about 25 miles north on the Coeur d'Alene River at the western end of what is now Silver Valley. There, priests and Indians built a church building and mission later named Cataldo after Father Joseph M. Cataldo, a Roman Catholic priest prominent in establishing several missions among the Northwest Indian tribes. Today, the Cataldo Church is the oldest public building in Idaho and the location of Old Mission State Park.

In 1860 U.S. Army Lieutenant John Mullan – later promoted to Captain – led 230 soldiers and civilian workers in the construction of a 624-mile military wagon road between Fort Walla Walla, Washington, and Fort Benton, Montana. Interstate

90 generally follows Mullan Road. (*See Northern Idaho, The Region, Mullan Road, The Military Wagon Road That Opened the Region.*)

With the construction of Mullan Road other events followed that brought increased settlement into of the area of Lake Coeur d'Alene, including what is now St. Maries.

In 1877 reacting to concerns about Indian conflicts in the West, General William Tecumseh Sherman, the Union Civil War hero, made an inspection tour of military forts in the Northwest. While traveling over Mullan Road, Sherman passed along the northern shore of Lake Coeur d'Alene. He was so impressed with the setting that he made a recommendation to Congress that they authorize construction of a new military post on the north shore of the lake.

Congress approved Sherman's recommendation and in 1878 authorized construction of Fort Coeur d'Alene on 999 acres of land at the headwaters of the Spokane River. The name of the fort was later changed to Fort Sherman. The military also commissioned Captain C.P. Sorensen, a boat builder from Portland, to build a steamboat to patrol the 30-mile-long lake.

Civilians employed to build the fort and other settlers started a small tent and log cabin village – which they named Coeur d'Alene City – near the fort.

In 1883 A.J. Prichard disclosed his discovery of placer gold near what is now Murray, setting off a major gold rush. Ten thousand people converged on what is now the Silver Valley by the end of 1885, scouring the mountains and streams in search of precious metals.

Old boardwalk

In 1887 in an attempt to assimilate American Indians into the white mainstream, Congress passed the General Allotment Act-Dawes Severalty Act.

Under the Act, Native Americans received an allotment of reservation land. Each head of family received 160 acres; single persons received a lesser acreage. Any lands not allotted became 'surplus" and were made available for non-Indian settlement. This created a checkerboard ownership pattern throughout the reservation. (*See Northern Idaho, Dawes Severalty Act.*)

In 1888 Joseph Fisher filed a claim near the confluence of the St. Joe and St. Maries Rivers, a location where steamers and barges operating on Coeur d'Alene Lake could navigate up the St. Joe River to his property. The following year, Joseph applied for the St. Maries Post Office with himself as postmaster. At the same time, three other members of the Fisher family – brothers William, John and Jesse – built a sawmill. In July 1889 Fisher and two residents, F.W. Haveland and M.A. Phelps, platted the town of St. Maries.

Three years later, the Fisher brothers sold their mill to Fred Grant who enlarged the facility. Joseph Fisher built a hotel.

In 1905 the Chicago, Milwaukee, St. Paul and Pacific Railroad (Milwaukee Road) built a rail line that passed through the heavily wooded forests surrounding what are now St. Maries and Plummer.

The federal government had given the railroad companies land grants as an inducement to build the railroads and encourage settlement. Forest products companies built sawmills at strategic locations along the rail lines. The railroad subdivided some of their land near St. Maries, adding to the size of the city.

In 1908 the federal government completed its survey of the Coeur d'Alene Indian Reservation and designated the surplus land for settlement. As a result, thousands of settlers came onto the former reservation land to settle. Many of these homesteaders settled the land around St. Maries. By 1910 the town's population reached 869.

The 1910 fires bypassed St. Maries, burning within miles of the village. In the 1930s the bodies of 57 of the fallen firefighters were re-interred at Woodlawn Cemetery in St. Maries. The Firefighters Memorial Circle is visited by many visitors each year. (*See Northern Idaho, The Region, Forest Products – The Great Northern Fire of 1910.*)

The first newspaper, the *St. Maries Courier*, a semi-weekly publication, was established February 19, 1901, by E. Deuerslie.

In 1901 Joe Fisher and M.A. Phelps were awarded the franchise to construct, operate and maintain a telegraph and telephone line from St. Maries to Santa, Idaho. By 1905 St. Maries had become a popular summer resort area with three hotels, the largest of which was located on the water front and boasted 80 rooms. Riverboat "steamers" made scheduled trips to Harrison and Coeur d'Alene – some would bring 100 or more visitors on holiday trips to St. Maries. The U.S. mail boats went between St. Maries and the railroad connection at Chatcolet.

Incorporation

On October 16, 1902, St. Maries became an incorporated village. On February 10, 1913, the town met the state requirements and received County approval to change its legal status from village to a city of the second class.

Turning Points

Sawmills The favorable location for a sawmill is the reason Joseph Fisher selected the site of what is now St. Maries. Large stands of timber near the navigable St. Joe River and the smaller St. Maries River were ideal for a new mill and community that his family wanted.

From the beginning, the wood products industry underpinned the city's economy. There are at least two times in the city's history when the citizens of St. Maries took heroic steps to protect their wood products-based economy.

During the Great Depression of the 1930s the remaining and largest sawmill in the city was in the final stages of closure, dismantling and auction by the Reconstruction Finance Administration. Not willing to give up, the citizens rallied to provide the needed capital to save the mill. They reopened the facility as the St. Maries Lumber Company. A few years later, World War II brought increased demand for lumber, and economic prosperity for the city resumed.

In 1961 the mill caught fire and burned. Facing a bleak future, this new generation of citizens showed the same innovation and resilience as their predecessors. Drawing financial support from throughout the county, they formed the Benewah County Development Company (BCDC) and, with federal assistance, built a new plywood mill on the site of the burned facility. The Potlatch Corporation now owns this enlarged facility.

At about the same time, the BCDC financed a mill in Plummer as well as the Regulus Stud Mill in St. Maries – a small-diameter log sawmill now owned by Stimson Lumber Company. (*See Northern Idaho, The Region, Forest Products – Early Sawmills and Towns and Mining and Forest Products – the Decline of Two of Idaho's Signature Industries*.)

Dawes Severalty Act This Act made most former Indian reservation land throughout the nation federal public lands open for settlement. The law played a key role in the development of land around St. Maries. In 1934 Congress repealed the Dawes Severalty Act and replaced it with the Indian Reorganization Act, placing unsettled reservation land into tribal trusts. (*See American Indians, Dawes Severalty Act*.)

Railroad For years tugboats pulled rafts and "brails" of logs to sawmills located on the river and lake. Tugboat and steamer transportation systems also moved lumber and passengers from the St. Maries sawmills to the ports and railheads on northern Coeur d'Alene Lake.

When the railroad came to St. Maries, it largely made the river transportation systems obsolete. Freight, once loaded on rail cars, could generally stay on the rail cars until delivered to its final destination.

No longer do the tugs travel the rivers around St. Maries, except during late winter to break up the ice to prevent flooding during the spring thaws. (*See Northern Idaho, The Region, Railroads*.)

County Seat In 1915 the Idaho Legislature split off the southern part of Kootenai County and created Benewah County with St. Maries as the county seat. This action further added to the prestige and economy of the city.

Floods In years of heavy spring runoff, St. Maries has experienced flooding. The most devastating floods that caused damage in the city occurred in 1933 and 1938, prior to the construction of levees. The most recent flood, occurring in 1997, created Hepton Lake just on the outskirts of the city.

Benewah County courthouse

Domestic Water On October 13, 1936, bids were let out for construction of the Rochat Creek Dam, to provide domestic water for St. Maries. In 1999 the City made improvements to the system by constructing a slow sand filter Water Treatment Plant.

St. Maries Today

Amenities and Attractions City Park, located in the center of town, features an outdoor pool, playground, tennis courts, a baseball diamond and picnic area. Lower City Park has five baseball fields, a soccer field and a skateboard park. Vic Camm Park is a neighborhood park featuring a children's playground and picnic area. Aqua Park, along the St. Joe River, offers picnicking, swimming and boat launching opportunities.

St. Joe River

The historic Hughes House, a log house built in 1902 and located on the corner of 6th and Main, was purchased by the Centennial Committee in 1989 and opened as the Hughes Historical Museum on June 18, 1990.

The third weekend of July is a multi-event celebration that includes art exhibits, cars and snowmobile "grass drags" – the Smart Committee art and music show located at Cherry Bend Boat Park, a county park located on the St. Joe River approximately three miles outside the city; the St. Joe Valley Car Club's annual car show and dance and the St. Joe Snow Rider's grass drag races.

Each Labor Day weekend, the City and local businesses sponsor "Paul Bunyan Days" – a fun-filled four days of logging and pool events, "bed and outhouse" races, Tug of War, street dances, motor cycle cross races, food, crafts, carnival rides, two parades and fireworks.

The third weekend in August brings the annual Benewah County Fair and Jr. Rodeo.

There are several developed forest service campgrounds on the nearby rivers. The closest to St. Maries is the Shadowy St. Joe located 11 miles northeast of town. Other campgrounds include Heyburn State Park, west of town approximately 6 miles, and Misty Meadows Campground and RV Park, 3.5 miles northeast of St. Maries.

There are also miles of groomed snowmobile trails around the city and hundreds of logging trails in the nearby forests. Just outside of town is Christmas Hills Recreation Area, a 600-acre facility devoted to snowmobiling, motorcycling, hiking and mountain biking.

Many outdoor enthusiasts enjoy the excellent hunting, fishing and boating opportunities in and around St. Maries and the nearby forests.

St. Maries plywood mill

St. Maries Golf Course is a nine-hole course located just two miles south of town.

Economy and Major Employers With nearly 400 employees, Potlatch Lumber Company is the city's largest employer. Buell Trucking and Benewah Community Hospital each have around 150 employees. St. Maries School District has over 100 employees. Stimson Lumber Mill and Valley Vista Care Center, a nursing and retirement center, each have around 85 employees.

Shopping is limited to just a few "mom and pop" establishments and two grocery stores. Spokane, Washington, and Coeur d'Alene – both approximately one hour away – offer a larger variety of shopping experiences. The commercial center of St. Maries includes a limited number of retail, financial and service businesses.

Education St. Maries School District operates elementary, middle and high schools in the city. The closest institution of higher learning is North Idaho College in Coeur d'Alene.

Health Care The 35-bed Benewah Community Hospital in St. Maries provides most of the medical care for city residents. St. Joe Valley Clinic, three dentists' offices, an optometrist's office and Valley Vista Nursing Home are also located in the city.

Transportation The north-south Idaho Highway 3 intersects the city. Interstate 90 is 35 miles north on Highway 3. Idaho Highway 5 begins in St. Maries and connects with U.S. 95, 19 miles west. Railroad service is available in the city for freight. The 3,200-foot runway at St. Maries Municipal Airport provides air service for light private and charter aircraft. Air service for larger aircraft is available in Coeur d'Alene and Moscow.

Utilities and Services Private companies provide electricity, telephone, cable and satellite service. The City provides water and sewer services and contracts with a private company for solid waste services. The City also provides police protection. St. Maries Rural Fire Department provides fire protection and St. Maries Ambulance Service serves both the city and the surrounding area.

Vision for 2050

In 1960 St. Maries had a population of 2,435. In the mid-1990s the population grew to around 2,900 before settling back to 2,652 in 2000. Most of the recent growth of the area has happened just outside the city limits. With the decline of the timber industry, fewer young adults are choosing to stay. St. Maries is, however, attracting more and more retirees looking to downsize and simplify their lives in a small, quiet, safe, scenic area with four seasons and abundant opportunities for hunting, fishing, hiking, trail riding and snowmobiling.

Historical population trends of modest growth will continue for many years. By 2050 St. Maries' population will likely approach 3,000. The city will continue to be a wonderful place to live, raise a family and retire in one of the most beautiful locations in Idaho.

Mayors

1902-1913 Unknown *
1913 Henry Mulcahy
1915 O.E. Hailey
1917 J.C. Hunt
1919 Ed Kirk
1921 Fulton Cook
1923 A.B. Annis
1925 Earl Kidder
1927 Lee Carlock
1929 M.H. Donovan
1931 Charles Brebner
1933 A.R. McCabe
1935 Franklin Theriault

1939 Buford E. Lewis
1955 Lee R. Lowry
1957 R.L. Broyler
1959 Charles H. Scribner
1964 Otto Holstein
1974 Everett Anderson
1976 Edwin Mueller, Jr.
1978 Ernest Pendell
2003 Robert Allen
2010 Tami Holdahl
2014 Harry Grubham
* Village Chairman

Tensed

Statistical Data

Population: 121 *
Elevation: 2,557 feet
Precipitation: 24 inches **
Average Snowfall: 8 inches **
County: Benewah

Temperature Range – Fahrenheit: **
Spring: 29 to 65
Summer: 43 to 82
Fall: 28 to 73
Winter: 22 to 42
* U.S. Census Bureau Estimates July 2015
**Historical averages

Tensed lies about 30 miles north of Moscow, six miles east of the Idaho/Washington border. Farmland interspersed with groves of timber and heavily wooded mountains with peaks rising over 4,700 feet surround the city. A high percentage of the land surrounding the city is part of the Coeur d'Alene Indian Reservation.

Pre-Incorporation Years

For centuries, the Coeur d'Alene Indians were the principal inhabitants of the land around what is now Tensed. Unlike many other Native American tribes, the Coeur d'Alene Indians were less nomadic. They had permanent settlements throughout the area.

In 1873 U.S. President Ulysses S. Grant established the Coeur d'Alene Reservation by executive order.

In the same year, the Jesuit's Sacred Heart Mission of the Roman Catholic Church sat up a settlement on the reservation. They named it De Smet – after Father Pierre Jean De Smet, an

Father Pierre Jean De Smet.

early Catholic missionary. Coeur d'Alene Indian members supplied much of the labor in building the Cathedral of the Sacred Heart in De Smet. In 1883 the church built a boys' school in De Smet named the Academy at Sacred Heart.

In 1887 in an attempt to assimilate Indians into the white mainstream, Congress passed the General Allotment Act – also known as the Dawes Severalty Act.

Under the Act, Native Americans received an allotment of reservation land. Generally, each head of family received 160 acres, a single person over 18 received 80 acres and each orphaned child 40 acres. Any lands not allotted became "surplus" and were made available for non-Indian homesteading and settlement.

Indians who did not want to farm could either sell or lease their land. In many parts of the United States, this law encouraged large-scale settlement by non-Indians on reservation lands and created a checkerboard ownership pattern

Early Tensed.

throughout the reservations. (*See Northern Idaho, General Allotment Act and Redistribution of Indian Reservation Lands.*)

To accommodate new sawmills, the railroad constructed a rail line through the reservation with a train depot one mile north of De Smet at what is now the city of Tensed.

Area settlers, primarily people involved in the emerging timber industry began to build a new community around the train depot. They applied to the postal authorities for a post office that they proposed to call Desmet. Postal authorities rejected the name because of potential confusion with the nearby village of De Smet. In apparent frustration, the settlers submitted the name of Temsed – Desmet spelled backward. The

Harvesting grain neat Tensed.

postal authorities accepted the new name; however, when the clerk recorded the name, he or she made a typographical error and spelled the name Tensed.

At the community's peak population there were three lumber mills located nearby on Old Sanders Road. The town had two bars and two gas stations.

Incorporation

Tensed was incorporated on April 14, 1947.

Turning Points

Railroad Tensed owes its origins
to the railroad. As long as there were
timber and wood products to
transport, the railroad and the
community prospered. When the
timber went away, the railroad shut
down and the economy suffered.

Sawmills While the railroad
started the city, the wood products
industry sustained it. By the mid-
1900s the availability of good stands
of nearby timber diminished and
wood market prices were not adequate

Historic photo, bar in Tensed.

to cover increased costs. Sawmills closed, causing the city's economy and
population to contract.

Tensed Today

Amenities and Attractions Tensed has three city parks comprising ten acres.
Park amenities include children's playgrounds and picnic areas.

The Tensed Public Library offers computers and Internet services.

Two state parks are near the city. The 5,300-acre Mary Minerva McCroskey
(memorial) State Park is 12 miles south of Tensed. Heyburn State Park that
comprises 5,744 acres of land and 2,332 acres of water lies at the base of Lake
Coeur d'Alene about 20 miles north of the
city.

Two national forests are near the city.
The St. Joe National Forest lies 12 miles
west across the Coeur d'Alene Indian
Reservation boundary. The Coeur d'Alene
National Forest lies 30 miles north.

Downhill skiing is available at North-
South Ski Bowl, 14 miles due southeast
across the mountains. Following improved
roads, the distance is more than double.

The 73-mile-long Trail of the Coeur
d'Alenes begins about 12 miles north at the city of Plummer. The trail is a paved
non-motorized route built on an abandoned railroad line. It follows the shoreline of
Coeur d'Alene Lake then passes through a chain of lakes and marshland along the
scenic Coeur d'Alene River, over high railroad trestles, through tunnels, national
forests and old mining towns to the mountains of Mullan.

Economy and Major Employers The city's downtown area consists of a few
retail businesses that serve the tourist trade and the nearby farming community.
The largest employer, Cross Key Restaurant, has 18 employees.

Education Tensed is part of the Plummer-Worley Joint School District, which has no facilities in Tensed. Elementary children travel by bus to attend school in Worley. Middle and high school students attend school in Plummer.

The closest institution of higher learning is the University of Idaho in Moscow.

Health Care The closest hospital is Benewah Community Hospital, located about 26 miles northeast in St. Maries. A general medical clinic is located in Plummer.

Transportation U.S. Highway 95 intersects the city. Federal Interstate Freeway 90 can be accessed 45 miles north in Coeur d'Alene.

The closest airport is 32 miles south at the Pullman-Moscow Regional Airport.

Utilities and Services Private companies provide electricity, telephone and satellite services. The City provides water and sewer services and fire protection.

The County provides police protection and solid waste services.

Vision for 2050

In 1960 Tensed had a population of 184. By 1993 the population fell to a low of 85. During the last decade, it has held at about 125. Over the next four decades, the city's growth will follow historical trends. By 2050 the city's population will likely not exceed 200. City and community leaders will continue to provide needed municipal services desired by the town's residents.

Tugboat used by the Hope Lumber Company to tow logs to the mill, circa 1910.

BONNER COUNTY

- Clark Fork
- Dover
- East Hope
- Hope
- Kootenai
- Oldtown
- Ponderay
- Priest River
- Sandpoint (County Seat)

Lightning Creek Bridge, 2009.

Clark Fork

Statistical Data

Population: 540 *
Elevation: 2,090 feet
Precipitation: 31 inches **
Average Snowfall: 30 inches **
County: Bonner

Temperature Range – Fahrenheit: **
Spring: 28 to 64
Summer: 46 to 80
Fall: 29 to 70
Winter: 21 to 37
* U.S. Census Bureau Estimates July 2015
**Historical averages

The city of Clark Fork lies on the northern banks of the Clark Fork River as it begins to broaden into an alluvial delta and wetland on the eastern side of Lake Pend Oreille.

The Kaniksu National Forest lies to the immediate north and south of the city. The Kootenai National Forest begins a few miles east. The Cabinet Mountains punctuate the eastern skyline as the range extends into Montana whose border with Idaho is approximately six miles due east of the city.

The city of Sandpoint is about 25 miles northwest around the top of Lake Pend Oreille via Idaho Highway 200.

Pre-Incorporation Years

For centuries before the arrival of white men in Northern Idaho, the area was inhabited by Kalispel, Flathead and other Indian tribes.

In July 1806 Captains Meriwether Lewis and William Clark and the Corps of Discovery divided their party near what is now the Clark Fork River in Montana to perform several hundred miles of separate explorations on the return trip to St Louis. They separated at a location over 60 miles south of what is now Clark Fork, the city that would bear Captain William Clark's name.

In September 1809 David Thompson and his associate, Finan McDonald, arrived at Lake Pend Oreille on the East Hope peninsula. They worked for the North West Company – a Canadian business in competition in the fur trade with a British concern, the Hudson's Bay Company.

Clarks Fork train station.

Thompson planned to establish a chain of trading posts throughout the Inland Northwest. He built a log trading post at what is now East Hope, seven miles northeast of Clark Fork. He named the post Kullyspel House after the Kalispel Indians. It was the first trading post in what is now Idaho.

In 1811 Thompson abandoned the post. He found it was too far off the main line between his other trading posts. However, trapping for furs and, later, prospecting for gold continued.

As early as 1809, ferries were used to cross the Clark Fork River near what is now Clark Fork. The first makeshift ferries were logs tied together to carry trappers, explorers and miners back and forth.

For several decades, there was little change in the Clark Fork area.

Original Main Street looking north from just north of the railroad station

Then in 1882 the Northern Pacific Railroad (NPR) built a rail line across Idaho's panhandle. The rail line proceeded from Spokane, Washington, to Hauser Junction, then north through Sandpoint and around the top of Lake Pend Oreille through Hope and Clark Fork before turning west to Montana.

61

Clark Fork had its beginnings as a railroad station. The residents of the small Clark Fork rail station, were soon joined by entrepreneurs starting small sawmills and homesteaders.

In 1903 John and Annie Nagel platted the Clark Fork townsite on land for which they obtained a patent from the federal government.

Incorporation

On May 11, 1911, Clark Fork became an incorporated village.

Turning Points

Railroad Clark Fork had its origins as a railroad town. The railroad not only encouraged development of sawmills and provided transportation for mine products, but it provided freight and passenger service that improved the quality of life for area residents. Nearby Sandpoint continues as the only Amtrak rail stop in Idaho.

Whitcomb Store on Railroad Avenue in Clark Fork about1900. In 1909the building was moved to its current location on the corner of Main & Fourth

Sawmills The sawmills located near Clark Fork played a significant role in providing employment until they closed in the mid-1950s.

Mining In the early 1920s prospectors discovered deposits of silver, lead and zinc ore near Spring Creek a few miles northwest of Clark Fork. The Whitedelph Mill and Mine located a few miles northwest of Clark Fork began processing ore in 1926. In 1958 the mine shut down. The closure had a major adverse effect on the city's economy.

Idaho Highway 200 In 1971 the Idaho Department of Transportation built State Highway 200 around the northern and eastern shoreline of Lake Pend Oreille through Clark Fork and on to the Montana Border. The improved transportation corridor has

The Whitedelf Mine,one of three mines that operated in the immediate area. The other two were the Hope and Lawrence Mines.

had a significant positive effect on the city's economy.

Cabinet Gorge Dam In 1952 Avista Corp., formerly Washington Power Company, built the 208-foot-high and 600-foot-long Cabinet Gorge (hydroelectric) Dam on the Clark Fork River located about eight miles southeast of Clark Fork. The dam not only controls flooding but also provides employment for city residents.

Fish Hatcheries In 1938 the federal Work Project Administration built the Clark Fork Hatchery, located on Spring Creek, two miles north of town. In 1985 Avista Corp., the Bonneville Power Administration and the Idaho Department of Fish and Game built the Cabinet Gorge Hatchery located about eight miles southeast of town. These fish hatcheries provide planting stock for game fish such as Kokanee salmon and different species of trout for the region's rivers and lakes as well as employment for many of the

Clark Fork in the early 1900s

city's residents.

Clark Fork Today

Amenities and Attractions The city has two public parks. The parks include ball fields, picnic areas and children's playgrounds.

Idaho Department of Fish and Game manages wildlife preserves and wetlands near the city. These properties allow vantage points for public viewing. Derr Creek is a 240-acre wetland located south of the Clark Fork River, just south of the city.

The 1,750-acre Clark Fork River Delta unit of the Idaho Department of Fish and Game's Pend Oreille Wildlife Management Area is a few miles southeast of the city.

There are also several recreation sites and camping facilities around Lake Pend Oreille and in the surrounding forests.

Many residents travel to nearby Sandpoint – a regional business, medical and retail shopping center – for shopping and services. Sandpoint is also home to the Schweitzer Ski Resort.

Economy and Major Employers Lake Pend Oreille School District is the city's largest employer.

Education Lake Pend Oreille School District, with offices in Ponderay, provides public education to the city's school-age children. Elementary school students attend Hope-Clark Fork Elementary located between Clark Fork and Hope. High school students attend Clark Fork High School located in the city.

The closest institution of higher learning is North Idaho College 73 miles away in Coeur d'Alene. The University of Idaho Clark Fork Field Campus is located in the city. The university offers academic courses and workshops that also accommodates school field trips, overnights and retreats.

The Vogel House was built in the late 1800s and was recently restored as a Bed and Breakfast.

Health Care The closest hospital is Bonner General Hospital in Sandpoint.

Transportation Idaho Highway 200, the Pend Oreille Scenic Byway, begins at Sandpoint where it intersects U.S. Highway 95. To the east, Idaho Highway 200 connects with Montana Highway 200 to Missoula.

Utilities and Services Private companies provide electricity, telephone and satellite services. The City provides water and sewer services as well as fire and police protection.

Vision for 2050

Clark Fork's population has grown moderately over the past 50 years. The city's 1960 population was 452. Historic population trends are likely to continue for

Clark Fork Hatcher station 1937.

the next several decades. The natural beauty and rural attributes of the city – including nearby national forests, the Clark Fork River, other nearby rivers and streams and Lake Pend Oreille – will continue to be the city's greatest attractions. he city's near proximity to larger cities provides residents and visitors with access to excellent urban services and amenities.

In 2050 Clark Fork will continue to be an idyllic place to live and raise a family.

Mayors

Unknown
** Thomas Shields
2010 Jeff Jeffers

2014 Chris Riggins
**Dates Unknown

Dover with the Pend Oreille River in the background

Dover

Statistical Data

Population: 607 *
Elevation: 2,076 feet
Precipitation: 32 inches **
Average Snowfall: 70 inches **
County: Bonner
Website: www.doveridaho.org

Temperature Range – Fahrenheit: **
Spring: 28 to 65
Summer: 47 to 80
Fall: 28 to 70
Winter: 19 to 38
* U.S. Census Bureau Estimates July 2015
**Historical averages

Dover overlooks the northwestern end of Lake Pend Oreille as it blends into the lake's outlet, the Pend Oreille River. The city is elevated because of the reservoir created by the hydroelectric Albeni Falls Dam, located 20 miles downriver between Priest River and Old Town on the Idaho/Washington border.

The Kaniksu National Forest comes within a few miles of Dover except to the east where the city's boundary abuts Sandpoint.

Pre-Incorporation Years

For centuries, the Kalispel Indians hunted and fished in the fast-flowing Pend Oreille River in the area of what is now Dover.

In 1866 a steamboat called the Mary Moody began ferrying trappers, miners and their gear across and around Lake Pend Oreille.

In 1883 the Northern Pacific Railroad completed a rail line from Wallula, Washington, to Missoula, Montana. The railroad passed through the future city of Dover, reaching Sandpoint in 1881. From Sandpoint it continued along the northern and eastern shore of Lake Pend Oreille before turning east near what is now Clark Fork to Montana.

The availability of railroad transportation encouraged development of sawmills around the lake. The Sand Point Lumber Company, and its successor the Humbird Lumber Company, became the largest employer in the area.

In 1907 the Dover Lumber Company opened a sawmill, planer and electrical power plant along the northern banks of the Pend Oreille River, four miles west of Sandpoint. On February 1, 1908, the company president, O.S. Welty, platted a town next to the mill that he initially named Welty. A few years later, to avoid confusion, they changed the town's name to Dover.

In 1921 the A.C. White Lumber Mill in Laclede, 11 miles down river from Dover, burned. The town – consisting of over 40 homes, church and general store – survived. However, without the mill, these structures had little value.

Rather than rebuild at Laclede, A.C. White purchased the Dover Lumber Mill. He then contracted with a local boat company working on Lake Pend Oreille, loaded the Laclede buildings on barges and set them up at Dover.

During the Great Depression of the 1930s, the sawmill avoided shutting down by paying workers with company tokens redeemable at the company's general store.

In 1955 the Army Corps of Engineers completed construction of the 90-foot-high, 775-foot-wide, 200-million-kilowatt-hour hydroelectric Albeni Falls Dam. The reservoir created by the dam raised the water level of the river to that of Lake Pend Oreille.

By the 1980s the town's municipal water system was failing state environmental standards.

In 1987 the City of Sandpoint moved to annex the unincorporated community of Dover. The potential annexation sparked opposition from Dover residents who were fearful they would pay higher taxes without receiving additional services, including an improved water system.

Incorporation

On July 26, 1988, following a door-to-door petition signing campaign, the Bonner County Commissioners approved the incorporation of Dover. The new mayor and city council almost immediately called for a bond election to bring the city's municipal water system into compliance with state environmental rules and law and embarked on an aggressive annexation program of their own.

Turning Points

Sawmill Dover began as a company town built to meet the needs of the sawmill's workers. For decades, the mill underpinned the community's economy. However, in 1989 following multiple changes in ownership and changes in federal regulations restricting timber harvests on federal lands, the sawmill shut down. The mill closure eliminated about 100 jobs. It was a devastating blow to the small community. In 1992 the owners of the mill site cleared the land and built a housing development.

Sandpoint Annexation The risk of annexation is all it took to prompt Dover residents to launch a successful effort to preserve their independent identity as a town.

Dover Today

Amenities and Attractions The Dover city limits consists of 1,864 acres. It has 12 miles of bike and pedestrian trails; 3,300 feet of public beach access; and 10 acres of public parks; as well as many acres devoted to wetland parks.

Dover city hall

The city has several historic buildings. The church, community hall and about 10 of the original homes either moved from Laclede or constructed around 1921 have been preserved and maintained. They are nostalgic witnesses to days when sawmills dominated the area's economy.

Most city residents look to Sandpoint for their employment, shopping, healthcare and urban recreation.

Round Lake State Park is located 14 miles south. This 142-acre forested park surrounds the 58-acre Round Lake. The 4,000-acre Farragut State Park lies 34 miles south at the base of Lake Pend Oreille.

The Wild Horse Trail Scenic Byway starts in Sandpoint and heads north along the eastern side of the Selkirk Mountains. Anciently, the Kootenai Indians followed this historic path to their fishing grounds at Lake Pend Oreille.

The Pend Oreille Scenic Byway begins at the intersection of Highways 95 and 200 on the north end of Sandpoint and follows Highway 200 around the eastern side of the lake and on to the Montana state line.

The Panhandle Historic Rivers Passage begins at the Washington state line and follows the Pend Oreille River through Dover to its end at Sandpoint.

Thirty miles south is Silverwood Theme Park and over 50 amusement rides.

Schweitzer Mountain Ski Resort lies 15 miles north. The ski resort has an average snowfall of 300 inches, 67 ski runs, 2 ski lifts, cross-country ski trails, snowmobiling and sleigh rides. Facilities include a lodge, condominiums and a variety of retail stores.

Many outdoor enthusiasts enjoy boating, water skiing and fishing on the river that forms the city's southern boundary. Hunting, camping, hiking and fishing are available in the nearby Kaniksu National Forest.

Economy and Major Employers The city's commercial areas consist of a few retail and convenience stores and shops. Most of the city's workforce commutes to Sandpoint for work.

Education Lake Pend Oreille School District provides most K-12 education for eastern Bonner County. Dover children commute to elementary, middle, alternative, charter and high schools in Sandpoint. There are also four private schools in Sandpoint.

The closest institution of higher learning, North Idaho College (NIC), is located 40 miles south in Coeur d'Alene. NIC and the University of Idaho offer courses in Sandpoint.

Health Care The closest hospital is Bonner General Hospital in Sandpoint.

Transportation U.S. Highway 2 intersects the city where it merges with U.S. Highway 95 in Sandpoint.

Railroad freight service is available in Sandpoint. Amtrak has a depot in Sandpoint where it provides passenger service to Seattle, Portland and Chicago.

North Idaho Community Express provides public bus transportation between Sandpoint and Coeur d'Alene.

The Sandpoint airport has a 5,500-foot runway and provides service to private, charter and light commercial aircraft. Coeur d'Alene Air Terminal handles heavier aircraft. Spokane International Airport is located 80 miles southwest.

Utilities and Services Private companies provide electricity, telephone, gas, cable and satellite services. The City provides water and sewer services and fire and police protection.

Vision for 2050

Since 2000 Dover's population has grown about one percent annually. Recent historical trends will likely continue.

By 2050 Dover will have a population exceeding 1,000, principally made up of families attracted to Dover's quiet rural setting yet within a short commute to their work and the urban amenities of Sandpoint.

Aerial view of East Hope, about 1996

East Hope

Statistical Data

Population: 214 *
Elevation: 2,062 feet (lakeshore)
Precipitation: 32 inches **
Average Snowfall: 88 inches **
County: Bonner

Temperature Range – Fahrenheit: **
Spring: 34 to 73
Summer: 47 to 82
Fall: 28 to 57
Winter: 20 to 46
* U.S. Census Bureau Estimates July 2015
**Historical averages

Located in eastern Bonner County 50 miles south of the Canadian border, the picturesque Idaho Panhandle city of East Hope is nestled between Idaho's largest lake and the Kaniksu National Forest. The 344-square-mile Lake Pend Oreille (pronounced pon-der-ay), the fifth deepest lake in the United States, lies on the west and the foothills and heavily wooded mountains of the forest are to the east.

The city of Hope borders East Hope on the northwest. Residents often disregard the separate city names and simply refer to the area as the "Community of Hope."

Pre-Incorporation Years

In September 1809 just four years after the Lewis and Clark Corps of Discovery crossed Idaho about 120 miles to the south, two frontiersmen – David Thompson and Finan McDonald – arrived on the East Hope peninsula of Lake Pend Oreille.

Thompson was an explorer, mapmaker and trader. He and McDonald worked for the North West Company – a Canadian business in competition in the fur trade with a British concern, the Hudson's Bay Company.

Thompson planned to establish a chain of trading posts throughout the Inland Northwest. He built a log trading post near what is now East Hope that he named the Kullyspel House after the Kalispel Indians. It was the first trading post in what is now Idaho. In 1811 Thompson abandoned the post because it was too far off the main line of his other trading posts.

Nearly three-quarters of a century later in 1882, the Northern Pacific Railroad built its rail line on the bench area overlooking the east side of the lake. On land deeded from the federal government for building the line, Northern Pacific developed a tourist and resort settlement at what is now East Hope. Within two years, the railroad was promoting tourism with guided fishing and hunting packages. By 1885 it had built a guest facility called Highland House and was selling land to real estate developers, residents and businesses.

Part of East Hope and Strong Creek Drainage, circa 1995.

J.J. Strong, the railroad's superintendent of dining cars and hotels managed the railroad facilities and provided water by piping it from a creek named in his honor.

Among the buyers was real estate developer W.T. Crawford, who would later figure prominently in the history of the city. He moved into the area in 1883 and purchased a tract of land from the railroad for $166.

One of the first businesses in the area was a wood shingle mill named Berry and Benton. This mill, along with many other structures was built near the shoreline at the mouth of Strong Creek.

Krem Kau boatworks, circa 1904.

Strong was a bit of an entrepreneur and opportunist. He purchased a ranch located near the mouth of the creek and opened a guide service that was operated by his two sons, Lewis and Sam. Sam said he and his brother "spent many happy days taking out fishing parties on the lake and hunters into the mountains."

He wrote, "Deer were abundant near Hope, also bear and further back up toward the Canadian border were moose and caribou. Trout were abundant in the lake and brook trout in Strong Creek...(in addition) up on the benches of Hope

Mountain were plenty of grouse and pheasants to be had...we batched in the old log cabin and lived off the fat of the land. The most enjoyable time of my life was spent there and I often wish I were young again and could spend it over."

In 1888 there was a drought at the railroad's division point and depot in Heron, Montana. Because of the abundant springs on the eastern mountainside above Lake Pend Oreille, the railroad moved the Heron facility about a half mile northwest of its lakeshore businesses.

Hope Lumber Company circa 1910.

At that time, the railroad employed a veterinarian named Hope. The railroad named its depot Hope and the community that built up around it took on the same name.

W.F. Sharai came West in 1899 as a railroad employee with the responsibility to hunt wild game for the cooks, but his initial interest was prospecting for precious metals. He found or acquired a silver claim in the mountains above East Hope. Unfortunately for him, his mine was not successful and his financial backers pulled out.

Sharai came from a family of fruit farmers in Michigan. When it became apparent that his mine was a failure, he went back to his agricultural roots. He acquired land and irrigation water rights from a diversion dam across Strong Creek; planted an orchard, vegetables and berries; and began selling produce throughout the area. In 1915 the Hope Herald News described Sharai's strawberry

East Hope circa 1915.

patch as "a wonder." Upon his death, the village of East Hope purchased his water rights. The creek still flows through what is now the western portion of East Hope and supplies the city's domestic water.

In 1890 E. V. Smalley described East Hope in Northwest Magazine as "a handsome and almost level point jutting out into the lake which will afford ample building space for a town of 5,000 people."

In 1901 the Hope Lumber Company built a sawmill in what is now East Hope. It borrowed $75,000 from backers in Michigan to build the mill on lakeshore land purchased from W.T. Crawford for $500. The mill became the economic anchor of the community that, at its peak, had 100 employees.

In 1902 Crawford platted 39 lots on the bench and hillside above the new sawmill. Seeking to differentiate his development from the nearby community of Hope, he named his village East Hope.

It soon became apparent that Crawford's plat had too few lots to meet the residential and commercial demand. Sharai and C.A. Ferguson joined Crawford to enlarge the plat.

Other businesses developed around the mill including retail and service stores, shops and offices, a boat manufacturer and a wood pole mill.

Following Sharai's lead, other settlers planted fruit orchards and a variety of berries. Soon, these East Hope farmers were shipping their fresh produce throughout the region.

Incorporation

On April 13, 1913, East Hope became an incorporated village. The 1920 census reported its population at 223.

Village leaders petitioned the U.S. Postmaster for a post office. While there was already a post office in Hope, East Hope argued that most of the business coming into the Hope Post Office originated in East Hope where "the bulk of the population" lived. The request acknowledged the similarity of the names between the two communities and stated that if their petition was granted, they would change the name of their city from East Hope to Ellisport or some other acceptable name.

However, it never came to that. Postal authorities denied their petition to build a new post office until 1963 when they built a new post office in East Hope, but they retained the name "Hope Post Office."

Turning Points

Sawmill The railroad was the community's first major business. However, the town had limited growth until 1901, when Hope Lumber Company built its sawmill. East Hope became a one company town with the village economy inextricably tied to the mill.

Unfortunately, 19 years later, adverse market forces caused the company to begin cutting back. In 1922 the mill shut down. This business failure had a devastating effect on the local economy and property

Lakefront and state highway 200

values. People had to leave town to find work – including three village trustees, one of whom was the sawmill superintendent, who resigned their positions at the village and left.

Fire. The year before the mill closed, fire broke out in the hotel and spread through the town destroying many homes and businesses. Those who had fire insurance fared much better than those who did not. While the fire spared the mill, it had a devastating effect on the rest of the community. Between the fire and the mill closure, property that was valuable one year became worthless the next. Many properties sold for back taxes. Businesses closed their doors. The mill property became worthless selling for just $100 in 1930.

New Economy The small community languished for the next quarter century until right after World War II when A.L. Pringle, a real estate developer, purchased the old mill property. In 1946 he applied for annexation into the city. Within a few years, marinas, retail businesses and lakeshore homes developed. By 1950 East Hope's population reached 152.

State Highway 200 In 1971 the Idaho Department of Transportation built State Highway 200 along the lakeshore to improve traffic flow. However, it also changed the character of lakefront property, leaving much of it no longer viable for commercial use. Some businesses closed and the land reverted to private residences.

Tourism When the tourist and recreation seasons arrive, the city's population swells. Tourism is now the city's primary commercial activity.

East Hope Today

Amenities and Attractions All of the residents and visitors have one thing in common – they love the beauty and fabulous outdoor amenities of the area. The city rises from 2,062 feet at the lakeshore to 3,120 feet in the terraced foothills. Lush pine and fir forests cover the land. Many homes grace the naturally terraced hillside benches.

East Hope Hotel, circa 1915. It had 25 guest rooms and served as a boarding house for Hope Lumber Company workers. The hotel was destroyed by fire in 1921.

Many residents overlook pristine Lake Pend Oreille where they enjoy boating, fishing and water skiing. They can also go to the nearby national forests with their abundant lakes, streams, wildlife and scenery. Backpacking, fishing and hunting are popular outdoor activities.

The city of Sandpoint – a regional business, medical and retail shopping center and home of Schweitzer Ski Resort – is only a 30-minute drive.

Economy and Major Employers The city's business district consists of two marinas, three eating establishments, a small commercial orchard and vineyard, a marina store and an art gallery. Retirees continue to move into the area and constitute the majority of city residents. Most of the working population commutes to Sandpoint for employment. The rest either own local businesses or work for them.

Education Grade school students attend Hope-Clark Fork Elementary located just east of the city limits. High school students ride buses 10 miles southeast to Clark Fork High School.

The closest institution of higher learning is North Idaho College a two-year community college 50 miles south in Coeur d'Alene.

Health Care The closest hospital is Bonner General Hospital, 20 miles west in Sandpoint.

Transportation State Highway 200 intersects the city, separating the lakeshore from the rest of the community. Highway 200 connects with U.S. Highway 95 in Sandpoint. The closest airport is the Coeur d'Alene Air Terminal.

Utilities and Services Private companies provide electricity, telephone and satellite services. The City provides water and sewer services as well as fire and police protection.

Vision for 2050

The city's population has remained around 200 for several decades. Over the next four decades, this will change as more people come to enjoy its beautiful setting. Most development will be residential, light industrial and commercial and built up along the transportation corridor.

Pats Bay circa 1890

In 2050 the city will have achieved these four city goals: 1. Maintain an overall low density consistent with the existing quality and character of a rural community. 2. Protect and enhance property values and the environment by land use planning that establishes an orderly and predictable pattern of development. 3. Maintain the residential character of East Hope while providing the necessary diversity of housing types. For example, as the value of property escalates, more private residences will be converted into condominium-type developments or service-oriented businesses. The hillside residential area will remain low density. 4. Maintain and promote a healthy economic and social climate.

The common interests of the two communities of East Hope and Hope will continue to bring elected officials of the two communities together to cooperate and find ways to cut costs and consolidate services.

Mayors

1913 W.F. Lutton *	1937 H.N. Berkey *	1970 Stan Sisson
1914 C.A. Ferguson *	1938 E.M. Butler *	1973 Guy Butler
1919 E.I. Boyington *	1945 A.L. Bringle *	1978 Elona Yaryan
1922 F.S. Hayes *	1946 Fred Van Stone *	1994 Bob Harris
1927 Frank Reem *	1949 Pat Rojan *	1999 Lawrence Moon
1931 F.B. Yaryan *	1950 Fred Van Stone *	2008 Jake Both
1932 G.L. Hayes *	1951 Pat Rojan *	2014 Vernon Fleisher
1935 Ralph Henrichs *	1953 Jerry Sherbacker *	* Village Chairman
1936 M.F. Yakley *	1954 Art Petersen	

Hope

Statistical Data

Population: 88 *
Elevation: 2,062 feet
Precipitation: 32 inches **
Average Snowfall: 88 inches **
County: Bonner

Temperature Range – Fahrenheit: **
Spring: 28 to 65
Summer: 47 to 80
Fall: 28 to 70
Winter: 19 to 38
* U.S. Census Bureau Estimates July 2015
**Historical averages

The city of Hope is a hillside community on the eastern shore of the 180-square-mile Lake Pend Oreille, the largest lake in Idaho.

The heavily wooded mountains of the Kaniksu National Forest – part of the 2.5-million-acre Idaho Panhandle National Forests created in 1973 to administer the Kaniksu, Coeur d'Alene and St. Joe National Forests – form the city's eastern boundary. The city of Sandpoint lies 15 miles west. The city's southern boundary is adjacent to East Hope.

Pre-Incorporation Years

For centuries, the Kalispel Indians hunted and fished around Lake Pend Oreille and its tributaries. (*See Northern Idaho, The Region, American Indians.*)

In September 1809 frontiersmen David Thompson and his associate, Finan McDonald, arrived at Lake Pend Oreille near what is now Hope. Thompson was a partner with the North West Company, a Canadian company in competition for the fur trade with the British Hudson's Bay Company.

He built a log trading post he named "Kullyspel House," the first trading post in Idaho. (*See Northern Idaho, The Region, Early Trappers/Explorers*.)

Indians on horseback.

In 1866 the steamboat Mary Moody began ferrying trappers and miners around the lake. Prior to an adequate road system, Hope was a busy port with steamboats carrying passengers, supplies and mail to mining sites around the shoreline and up the Clark Fork River.

Around 1880 the Northern Pacific Railroad began construction of a line from Wallula, Washington, to Missoula, Montana, essentially creating another transcontinental railroad. In 1881 the railroad reached Sandpoint. From there the line continued along the northern and eastern shore of Lake Pend Oreille through Hope and Clark Fork, before proceeding east, reaching Missoula in 1883. The railroad

Hope train depot.

used about 6,000 men, including 4,000 Chinese, to construct the line.

As a financial inducement to build railroads, the federal government granted large tracts of land to the railroads. In 1883 W. T. Crawford, a real estate developer, moved to the area and purchased a parcel of lakefront and foothill land from the railroad.

In 1884 the railroad began building resort facilities on the shoreline near Crawford's property. A year later, a guesthouse named the Highland House had been built, and tourism was being promoted by offering guided fishing and hunting packages.

In 1888 Great Northern Railroad interests acquired the Northern Pacific Railroad. In the same year, there was a drought at the railroad's division point in Heron, Montana. Because of the abundant springs on the eastern mountainside above Lake Pend Oreille, railroad executives decided to move the division point, or depot, from Heron to about one-half mile northwest of its lakeshore businesses. It named the new depot and post office Hope, the name of a veterinarian employed by the railroad.

The railroad built additional tracks and a roundhouse at its Hope facility, as well as housing for workers and a large laundry, servicing rail employees from Portland/Seattle to Saint Paul, Minnesota, and staffed by Chinese workers.

Historic Hope Hotel.

J. J. Strong, superintendent of the railroad's Dining Cars and Hotels, managed the facilities. He provided fresh water to the settlement by piping it from the creek that would later bear his name.

Strong was a bit of an entrepreneur and opportunist. He also purchased a ranch located near the mouth of the creek and opened a guide service operated by his two sons, Lewis and Sam. Sam said he and Lewis, "spent many happy days taking out fishing parties on the lake and hunters into the mountains."

Sam further wrote of the area, "Deer were abundant near Hope, also bear and further back up toward the Canadian border were moose and caribou. Trout were abundant in the lake and brook trout in Strong Creek...up on the benches of Hope Mountain were plenty of grouse and pheasants to be had...we batched in the old log cabin and lived off the fat of the land. The most enjoyable time of my life was spent there and I often wish I were young again and could spend it over."

Old Church.

In 1896 railroad interests filed a plat of the town of Hope with the county.

In 1901 entrepreneurs borrowed $75,000 from backers in Michigan, purchased lakeshore land from Crawford for $500 and built the Hope Lumber Company sawmill. At its peak of 100 employees, the mill was an economic anchor.

In 1902 Crawford platted 39 lots on the bench and hillside above the new sawmill. Rather than keep the name of Hope, he decided to separate his development from the one created by the railroad by naming it East Hope. Adjacent landowners platted their land as East Hope subdivisions.

A commercial district made up of retail and service stores, shops and offices, a boat manufacturer, a wood pole mill, fruit orchards and berry farms developed around the mill. The railroad transported local lumber and agricultural commodities from both Hope and East Hope to distant markets.

Incorporation

In 1903 Hope had a population of around 800 and successfully petitioned the county to become an incorporated village.

The Hope Post Office also served East Hope. When East Hope became incorporated on April 13, 1913, its leaders petitioned postal authorities for their own post office. They argued that East Hope deserved to have its own post office since most of the business coming into the post office originated in East Hope, where "the bulk of the population" lived. Their request acknowledged the similarity of the names between the two communities and stated that if postal authorities granted their petition, they would change the name of their city from East Hope to Ellisport or some other acceptable name.

Part of the Berlin Wall in Hope.

The postal authorities denied their petition. Fifty years later in 1963, postal authorities closed the Hope Post Office facility and built a new one in East Hope. However, they did not change the name. The post office located in East Hope still bears the name "Hope Post Office."

Turning Points

Railroad Hope is a historic railroad town. The railroad established the community and underpinned its economy until 1908 when it moved its divisional office and services several miles west to Kootenai.

W.T. Crawford Crawford's decision to name his subdivision, built next to the Hope Lumber Company sawmill, "East Hope" began a chain of events that resulted in the separation of the cities of Hope and East Hope and had long-lasting effects on relations between the two communities.

Hope Today

Amenities and Attractions The City owns and maintains a cemetery.

With the support from the entire area, the Hope International Film Festival comes to the city each January.

The City manages the 276 acres of timberlands in its watershed. The city has one of the few boat ramps accessible on a year-round basis.

Area residents extensively use Old Highway 200 which runs through the cities of Hope and East Hope for biking and walking.

Nestled between the beautiful Lake Pend Oreille and the Kaniksu National Forest, Hope residents live in one of the most naturally scenic parts of Idaho. Both residents and visitors enjoy boating, water skiing and fishing on the lake and hunting, camping, hiking and fishing in the nearby forest. There are also several recreation sites and camping facilities around Lake Pend Oreille and in the surrounding forests.

Schweitzer Mountain Ski Resort is visible from Hope and lies 25 road miles northwest. The resort has an average snowfall of 300 inches, 92 ski runs, 10 ski lifts, snowboarding terrain park, cross-country ski trails, snowmobiling and other winter activities. Facilities include a lodge, condominiums and a variety of retail stores.

Economy and Major Employers The city's commercial district consists of a pizza shop and a wine bar. Most residents travel to Sandpoint to work, shop and do their business.

Education Lake Pend Oreille School District provides most K-12 education for eastern Bonner County. Primary age children attend school at Hope Elementary located three miles east of the city. Middle and high school students ride buses 11 miles southeast to Clark Fork High School.

The North Idaho College campus is located 65 miles south in Coeur d'Alene. The college offers certain classes at the Bonner Mall 14 miles west.

Health Care Bonner General Hospital in Sandpoint provides most of the medical services needed by Hope's residents.

Transportation State Highway 200 intersects the city and connects with U.S. Highway 95 in Sandpoint.

Railroad freight service is available in Sandpoint. Amtrak has a depot in Sandpoint providing passenger service to Seattle, Portland and Chicago.

The Sandpoint Airport has a 5,500-foot runway and provides service to private, charter and light commercial aircraft. Coeur d'Alene Air Terminal, 60 miles south of Hope, handles heavier aircraft. Spokane International Airport is 95 miles away.

Utilities and Services Private companies provide electricity, telephone, Internet and satellite services. The City provides water. Ellisport Bay Sewer District, an LID, provides sewer services. Hope/East Hope Volunteer Fire District provides fire protection. The Bonner County Sheriff's Office provides police protection.

Vision for 2050

Over the past 50 years, Hope's population has remained somewhat stable at around 100. Over the next four decades, Hope will continue to be a small residential town with a service-oriented business district located in some of the most magnificent natural beauty in Idaho. Population growth could increase significantly as retirees and families come to Hope for affordable housing within an easy commute to the jobs and the urban services available in nearby cities.

Mayors

1967 Dale Anglin *
1967 Alfred Williams
1978 Guy Neyman
1997 Larry Keith
2000 Joe Dean
2004 Larry Keith
2010 Joe Dean
2016 Bill Breen
* Village Chairman
**Names prior to 1967 not available

Aerial view, city of Kootenai.

Kootenai

Statistical Data

Population: 770 *
Elevation: 2,116 feet
Precipitation: 33 inches **
Average Snowfall: 80 inches **
County: Bonner
Temperature Range – Fahrenheit: **

Spring: 28 to 65
Summer: 47 to 80
Fall: 28 to 70
Winter: 19 to 38
* U.S. Census Bureau Estimates July 2015
**Historical averages

Kootenai (pronounced Koo-te-nee) lies on the northern shoreline of the beautiful and glacially created Lake Pend Oreille (pronounced pond-uh-ray). The Kaniksu National Forest begins about five miles northeast.

A mile west is the city of Ponderay, strategically located at the intersection of Idaho Highway 200 and U.S. Highway 95. The commercial center of Sandpoint is on the opposite side of Ponderay, three miles southwest of Kootenai. To the east is farmland interspersed with groves of trees.

Pre-Incorporation Years

Canadian explorer, mapmaker and trader David Thompson and his associate, Finan McDonald, of the Canadian North West Company established Idaho's first trading post at East Hope in September 1809. Thompson named his post Kullyspel House after the nomadic Kalispel Tribe of Indians that frequented the area. (*See The Region: American Indians; and Early Trappers/Explorers.*)

Owners of a steamboat called the Mary Moody started a ferry business in 1866, transporting trappers and prospectors around Lake Pend Oreille.

The Northern Pacific Railroad in 1880 surveyed a line that started at Wallula, Washington; proceeded northeast to Spokane; crossed into Idaho near what is now Rathdrum; and then on to the north shore of Lake Pend Oreille and Sandpoint, where it followed the lake shore through what is now Kootenai. It then proceeded around the lake to the Clark Fork River before turning east to Missoula, Montana. Completed in 1883, the railroad was built by 6,000 men – including 4,000 Chinese workers – creating the critical link that formed another transcontinental railroad. (*See The Region, Railroads.*)

Dr. Hendrix started a wagon freighting business in 1885 with a way station near the railroad about a mile east of what is now Kootenai. The wagons carried freight north over a toll road to Bonners Ferry and beyond.

Bonner Trading Company.

Six years later, construction crews of another railroad, the Great Northern Railway, began building a line from Puget Sound; across the Pend Oreille River at Newport, now Oldtown; through Priest River; and along the north side of the Pend Oreille River to Sandpoint. At Sandpoint, the line turned north to Bonners Ferry, making Hendrix's freight wagon business obsolete. At Bonners Ferry, the railroad extended north to Canada and east to connect with its main line in Havre, Montana. In 1893 the Great Northern Railroad – now Burlington Northern – acquired the Northern Pacific Railroad. By 1892 about 75 permanent residents lived near what is now Kootenai, which at that time was called Boyer.

With the availability of rail transportation, timber interests began building sawmills along the railroad routes.

Kootenai Grange.

Entrepreneurs built the Sandpoint Lumber Company in Sandpoint in 1899. Later, the Ellersick family of four brothers, their families and parents sold their sawmill business in Minnesota and built a single-band sawmill at the Greenough's Spur on the rail line near what is now Kootenai. They named their mill the Kootenai Bay Lumber Company (KBLC) and the community that grew up around the mill and company store, Kootenai.

The location for their mill on the lake was ideal. They could float and store logs on the lake and had railroad access for shipping lumber to distant markets.

In constructing and operating the mill, the four brothers divided their responsibilities between general management, logging, electrical power via steam and physical facilities.

A syndicate of Great Lakes States investors, including John A. Humbird and Fredrick Weyerhaeuser, formed the Humbird Lumber Company (HLC) in 1900. In the same year, the company acquired the Sandpoint Lumber Company and other timber properties.

Following the premature death of Henry Ellersick, the family sold the KBLC to HLC. At the time of the sale in September 1903, KBLC had 123 employees who worked six 10-hour days a week. Laborers were paid 20 cents a day and the sawyer, filer and foreman got 60 cents a day. Following the purchase, HLC built a larger sawmill and planer.

In the late 1800s prospectors found deposits of lead-silver ore near Lake Pend Oreille, and in 1903 investors formed the Panhandle Smelting and Refining Company, platted a company town between Sandpoint and Kootenai that would become Ponderay, built a dock on the lake and began concentrating and smelting ore. Steamboats transported ore from the mines to the processing facility. However, the venture proved unsuccessful and in 1909 closed. HLC employed many of the displaced smelting and refining company workers.

4L Hall.

Within a short time the combined HLC sawmill operations in Sandpoint and Kootenai became one of the largest in the Northwest. The storage yard at Kootenai had over 19 miles of railroad track and used three locomotives to move logs and lumber.

In March 1907 while undergoing repairs, the HLC mill in Sandpoint caught fire. The fire raged out of control burning many surrounding structures including several of Kootenai's mill houses. Fortunately, because of a change in wind direction the Kootenai mill escaped the blaze. They rebuilt the Sandpoint facility, and HLC management increased the production capacity of the Kootenai mill by adding a second shift.

The Northern Pacific Railway Company (NPRC) announced in 1908 that it had chosen Kootenai to be the location of its division point terminal between its Sprague, Washington, and Paradise, Montana, facilities. In order to provide housing for the approximately 1,200 railroad employees – many of whom were transferring from Trout Creek, Montana, with their families – the railroad and HLC chose a 70-acre parcel for a new townsite and formed the Kootenai Townsite Company (KTC) to manage the town's expansion.

HLC owned the townsite land which was, at that time, a dense forest of pine, fir, tamarack and cedar. Within two months, an army of men had cleared the townsite of trees and stumps. KTC then platted the town with 80-foot-wide streets and commercial lots reserved for a school, public park and church.

At the sides of the streets, KTC built 10-foot-wide boardwalks and installed wooden water mains. Sandpoint Water and Light Co. provided electrical power and water.

To discourage speculators, KTC imposed covenants that specified a deadline when owners must complete their buildings and the minimum cost or value of the structures.

The terminal had a 20-stall roundhouse, depot and stockyards used to unload and reload livestock for feed and water.

The Painter Hotel.

By December 1908 Kootenai was emerging as the largest community in the area. Its business district included a drug store, two hotels, a theatre, three restaurants, a blacksmith shop, a livery stable, a pool hall, two barber shops, a dry goods store, a bakery, a roller rink, a tea shop, two bars and an ice house filled in the winter with ice from Lake Pend Oreille.

F.S. Bonner, from Missoula, opened a general merchandise store in 1909 to compete with the Humbird Company Store and HLC began work on a brick bank building. The bank failed in 1916. Subsequently, the building was used for other purposes until on May 18, 1973, the city council began holding meetings in the historic building.

The Congregational Church – now Kootenai Community Church – built a new church on land donated by the Kootenai Townsite Company in 1909. In addition, the Kootenai School opened its four-room brick school house, which was razed in 1986 for a new school building. Residents commuted between Kootenai and Sandpoint via a trolley line that was discontinued in 1917.

Kootenai public school.

Incorporation

On June 30, 1910, Kootenai became an incorporated village. On December 13, 1968, it became an incorporated city to conform to change in Idaho municipal law.

Turning Points

Sawmills Kootenai owes its origins to the wood products industry. The Ellersick family's decision to build their Kootenai Bay Lumber Company at Kootenai was the basis for founding the town. After Humbird Lumber Company acquired the business, it expanded the operation, which in turn strengthened the town's economy.

In June 1930 Humbird ended further participation in the venture. The Weyerhaeuser conglomerate ceased operating the mill and razed the facilities. With no work, the mill workers sold their homes and small ranches for a pittance and left town. The Northern Pacific Hotel built next to the roundhouse in 1920 lasted until 1950, when it was razed by its owners.

With the closure of the mill, Kootenai's business district died out. Many of the wood-framed buildings burned or were demolished.

Railroad The railroad became particularly important to the economy of Kootenai in 1908 when the Northern Pacific Railroad Company announced it would build a division point, or terminal, at Kootenai. That event made Kootenai the dominant economic center in the area. Conversely, when the railroad moved the terminal from Kootenai to Paradise, Montana, in the late 1920s, it had a devastating effect on the town's economy. Today, the Montana Rail Link Railroad passes through town without stopping.

4L Union The Legions of Loyal Loggers and Lumbermen – a government organization of union workers (loggers) and sawmill owners (lumbermen), nicknamed "4L" – joined forces in 1917 to support the troops fighting in World War I. These loyal loggers moved into tall stands of trees to find and harvest spruce trees, a type of wood needed by the military. They built a large 4L Hall in Kootenai for the use of union members and for the community's social events. It burned in the 1940s.

Kootenai Today

Amenities and Attractions The city has a park adjoining city hall. The property was deeded to the city by Matt Schmitt in memory of his father and known as the Matt Schmitt Memorial Park. Coldwater Creek has also donated a lot to the park and planted most of the trees. The Kiwanis of Sandpoint donated the new children's playground equipment.

Kootenai's close proximity to Sandpoint allows its residents to enjoy the amenities and attractions of the larger community – including "Lost in the 50s," a classic automobile show and parade, and the Festival of Sandpoint. The city's residents shop at the large retail complexes located in Ponderay.

The 142-acre forested Round Lake State Park, surrounding the 58-acre Round Lake, is 15 miles south.

Farragut State Park, at the southern end of Lake Pend Oreille, has 4,000 acres devoted to outdoor activities and historical artifacts from the days of World War II when it was a U.S. Naval installation.

Three nearby Idaho Scenic Byways further display the area's beauty. The Pend Oreille Scenic Byway that begins at the intersection of U.S. Highway 95 and State

Highway 200 in Ponderay and passes through Kootenai follows Highway 200 around the eastern side of the lake before proceeding east to the Montana border.

The Wild Horse Trail Scenic Byway starts in Sandpoint, passes on the western side of Ponderay on Highway 95 and heads north along the eastern side of the Selkirk Mountains. It marks the historic path that the Kootenai Tribe followed to its fishing grounds at Lake Pend Oreille.

The Panhandle Historic Rivers Passage Byway begins at the Washington state line on U.S. Highway 2 and follows the Pend Oreille River to its end at Sandpoint.

Schweitzer Mountain Ski Resort is 12 miles north of Kootenai. With an average annual snowfall of 300 inches, the resort has 67 ski runs, ski lifts, cross-country ski trails, snowmobiling and sleigh rides. During the summer, the mountain resort is available for hiking, mountain biking and horseback riding. Resort facilities include a lodge; condominiums; and a variety of retail stores, restaurants and pubs.

Silverwood Amusement and Water Park, 30 miles south of the city, has over 50 amusement rides.

Lake Pend Oreille and the nearby national forest with its mountains, rivers and streams offer a wide variety of outdoor activities. Summer or winter, people can enjoy the outdoors by boating, water skiing, fishing, hunting and cross-country skiing as well as the many trails for hiking, biking, horseback riding and riding ATVs and snowmobiles.

Economy and Major Employers Because the Sandpoint Post Office serves the city of Kootenai, its residents and businesses do not have Kootenai addresses – they have Sandpoint addresses. Coldwater Creek – a direct mail retailer of women's clothing, jewelry and accessories – is headquartered in Kootenai where it has about 550 employees. It is Kootenai's largest employer.

The city's other major employers that in the aggregate employ over 250 include Lignetics, a manufacturer of wood pellet fuel, fire starts and Prest-o-Logs; Idaho Wood Industries, Inc., which produces and markets via direct mail wooden lighting fixtures and bathroom accessories; and Swift Systems, Inc., which designs and builds industrial tanks used in the heating systems of large buildings. The Bonner County Road and Bridge Department and Emergency Medical Services are located in Kootenai. There are several other retail shops and small businesses operating in the city's commercial district.

Some of the city's workforce commute to businesses in Ponderay and Sandpoint for work.

Education The Lake Pend Oreille School District provides most of the primary and secondary education in the county. The school district's administrative offices are located in Ponderay. Kootenai's kindergarten through sixth grade children attend Kootenai Elementary School. The older children attend the middle school, high school, alternative high school or charter school in Sandpoint. Private schools in both Ponderay and Sandpoint also offer kindergarten through high school education.

The closest institutions of higher learning are North Idaho College (NIC) and the University of Idaho on the NIC campus, both 47 miles south in Coeur d'Alene. NIC also has a satellite facility in Ponderay's Bonner Mall.

Health Care The 62-bed Bonner General Hospital in Sandpoint plus general clinics, dental offices, a 55-unit assisted-living center and a 60-bed nursing home provide most of the community's health care services.

Transportation State Highway 200 and U.S. Highway 95 intersect nearby in Ponderay. The Pend Oreille Scenic Byway is a 33-mile segment of Highway 200 that hugs the north shore of Lake Pend Oreille between Sandpoint and Clark Fork. The Byway provides stunning views of the lake.

Dave Wall Field in Sandpoint has a 5,500-foot runway and handles private, charter and light commercial aircraft. Spokane International Airport is 86 miles southwest.

While trains no longer stop in Kootenai, railroad freight services are available nearby on one of three rail lines – the Burlington Northern, Montana Rail Link and Union Pacific. Railroad passenger service is available at the Amtrak station in Sandpoint. The Sandpoint station is the only Amtrak stop in Idaho.

The North Idaho Community Express serves Kootenai and provides public transportation on a fixed route between Sandpoint and Coeur d'Alene.

Utilities and Services Private companies provide electricity, natural gas, telephone, cable and satellite services. The City of Sandpoint provides water services. The Kootenai-Ponderay Sewer District provides sewer services. The Bonner County Sheriff's Department provides police protection. Northside Fire District provides fire protection. Bonner County provides emergency medical services. A private company has the contract to provide garbage collection services.

Vision for 2050

In 1960 Kootenai's population was 180. By 2000 it had grown to 441. In recent years, the population has held at around 500. However, this is about to change.

The city has two new subdivisions under construction – Kootenai Heights and Seven Sisters. These two subdivisions have over 160 home sites.

By 2050 there will also be other major improvements. The Bonner County Museum, which is presently located in Sandpoint, has land in Kootenai on which it plans to build a new museum. The planned Rail and Timber Interpretive Center featuring the importance of these industries to the area will also be a reality.

Mayors

* Unknown	1988 Ruth Lang	2011 Mike Keough
1984 Lew Mulligan	1990 Margaret Gendel-Mjelde	2015 Nancy Lewis

Aerial view of Oldtown

Oldtown

Statistical Data

Population: 181 *
Elevation: 2,180 feet
Precipitation: 31 inches **
Average Snowfall: 60 inches **
County: Bonner

Temperature Range – Fahrenheit: **
Spring: 27 to 69
Summer: 45 to 84
Fall: 28 to 74
Winter: 20 to 40
* U.S. Census Bureau Estimates July 2015
**Historical averages

Oldtown lies on the western shores of the Pend Oreille River as it turns northwest into the state of Washington. The Kaniksu National Forest lies a few miles north of the city.

The cities of Newport, Washington, and Oldtown abut. Stateline Road separates the two cities. Sandpoint is 24 miles east.

Newport's population is 11 times that of Oldtown. Oldtown residents shop and do most of their non-governmental business in Newport.

Pre-Incorporation Years

In September 1809 Canadian explorer, map maker and trader David Thompson and his associate Finan McDonald of the Canadian North West Company established Idaho's first trading post at East Hope. Other trappers and, later, prospectors came into the land that had been the exclusive domain of American Indians.

In 1866 a steamboat called the Mary Moody began ferrying trappers, miners and their gear across and around Lake Pend Oreille. Around this time, steamers – riverboats – began bringing passengers up the Pend Oreille River to Albeni Falls, which is now the location of Albeni Falls Dam.

A riverboat port town named Newport built up on the west banks of the river on the Idaho side of the Idaho/Washington territorial line, about two miles west of the falls. Within a few years, the town had public docks, a post office, a ferry that crossed the river, a general store, a dry goods store, a hotel and several saloons.

In 1883 the Northern Pacific Railroad completed a rail line from Wallula, Washington, to Missoula, Montana. The railroad crossed the Pend Oreille River at Sandpoint. From Sandpoint it continued along the northern and eastern shore of Lake Pend Oreille before turning east to Montana at the Clark Fork River. With the availability of railroad transportation, sawmills began developing along the rail line. In 1906 the Spokane International Railway built a 142-mile rail line between Spokane, Washington, and Canada. This line passed through Sandpoint, Bonners Ferry and Eastport where it connected with the Canadian Pacific Railway.

In 1891 the Great Northern Railway's intercontinental rail line linking Puget Sound near Seattle to Canada and Havre, Montana, reached Newport. This rail line crossed to the north side

Diamond Match Company, Oldtown/Newport

of the Pend Oreille River near Newport and continued east to Sandpoint before turning north to Bonners Ferry. At Bonners Ferry, it extended north to Canada and east to connect with its main line in Havre.

When the railroad reached Newport, it established a train depot with railroad personnel operating out of a converted boxcar. In 1896 the boxcar burned down. Rather than rebuild on the Idaho side of town, railroad officials built a new depot on the Washington side.

The depot agent, Charles Talmadge, purchased 40 acres of railroad property located adjacent to the new depot. He platted the town of Newport, Washington, and began selling lots. Wanting to be near the train depot, businesses on the Idaho

Club Rio

side of the line, including the Newport Post Office, moved to the Washington side of town.

Having lost favor and lacking a municipal structure, the Idaho side of town went into decline with bars, gambling and houses of ill repute dominating the business community. The Idaho side of town was essentially lawless. Law enforcement on the Washington side had no legal authority in Idaho. Local residents termed the old part of the community, the "wild side of town."

In 1946 the Idaho Legislature passed law governing the sale of liquor by the drink and the licensure of establishments offering those beverages. Under that law, businesses selling alcoholic beverages had to be located within incorporated cities or villages. To keep their liquor licenses, local bar owners organized a campaign to incorporate the Idaho side of Newport as "Oldtown."

Incorporation

On April 21, 1947, the Bonner County Commissioners in Sandpoint approved Oldtown as an incorporated village.

Turning Points

Railroad While what is now Oldtown existed as a community before the railroad arrived, the railroad was the catalyst that brought about significant changes to the town, including the movement of the downtown business community from the Idaho to the Washington side of Newport.

Even though the Great Northern Railroad was the only train passing through town, Oldtown benefited from the increased traffic brought by Northern Pacific in Sandpoint and, 15 years later, the Spokane International Railway. Great Northern and Northern Pacific Railroads are both now part of Burlington Northern.

Change in Idaho's Alcohol Beverage Code The 1947 change in state law governing licensure of establishments serving liquor by the drink precipitated incorporation of the village.

Albeni Falls Dam In 1955 the Army Corps of Engineers completed construction of the hydroelectric Albeni Falls Dam located about two miles east of the city. The 200-million-kilowatt dam is 90 feet high and 775 feet wide. The facility and nearby Albeni Falls Dam Recreation Areas provide employment and significant recreation opportunities for city residents.

Oldtown Today

Amenities and Attractions Oldtown residents enjoy the numerous outdoor experiences – including boating, fishing, hunting and camping – available nearby at the Albeni Falls Dam and Recreation Areas and the Kaniksu National Forest.

Most city residents go to Newport for their employment, shopping, healthcare and urban recreation.

The Panhandle Historic Rivers Passage begins at the Washington state line and follows the Pend Oreille River to its end at Sandpoint.

Economy and Major Employers The city's commercial areas include a grocery store, Family Foods, which is also an Idaho State Liquor Dispensary (ISLD) contract liquor store – a major business attraction for Washingtonians. Both Idaho and Washington are alcohol control states, as opposed to license states. As such, customers must buy spirits through state-owned or controlled liquor stores at prices set by the respective states. Prices for bottled spirits are higher in Washington than in Idaho. Many Washingtonians drive to Oldtown and other Northern Idaho cities to buy their spirits. To illustrate the effect: Oldtown sells 17 percent of the spirits sold in the county by ISLD liquor stores.

The balance of the city's employment base includes several small businesses. Many of the city's residents commute to Newport for employment.

Education Lake Pend Oreille School District provides most public K-12 education for eastern Bonner County. Oldtown primary school children attend Idaho Hill Elementary School. Older children commute to Priest River for their middle and high school education.

There are also private elementary and high schools in or near the city.

The closest institution of higher learning, North Idaho College (NIC), is located 55 miles south in Coeur d'Alene. NIC and the University of Idaho offer courses in Sandpoint.

Health Care The closest hospital is the Newport Community Hospital.

Transportation U.S. Highway 2 intersects the city.

Railroad freight service is available in Sandpoint. Amtrak has a depot in Sandpoint, providing passenger service to Seattle, Washington; Portland, Oregon; and Chicago, Illinois. The Sandpoint Airport has a 5,500-foot runway and provides service to private, charter and light commercial aircraft. Spokane International Airport is south of the city.

Utilities and Services Private companies provide electricity, telephone, gas, cable and satellite services. The City provides water and sewer services and fire and police protection.

Vision for 2050

For over 50 years, Oldtown's population has remained at around 200. Historical trends will likely continue. By 2050 Oldtown will continue to be a quaint residential community economically and socially tied to its bordering sister city of Newport, Washington. However, the Newport-Oldtown Chamber of Commerce is actively pursuing economic development opportunities. These efforts and those of other community leaders will have a positive effect on job creation and quality of life for both communities.

Ponderay

Statistical Data

Population: 1,136 *
Elevation: 2,120 feet
Precipitation: 33 inches **
Average Snowfall: 80 inches **
County: Bonner
Website: www.ponderay.org

Temperature Range – Fahrenheit: **
Spring: 30 to 67
Summer: 48 to 80
Fall: 30 to 66
Winter: 19 to 37
* U.S. Census Bureau Estimates July 2015
**Historical averages

The city of Ponderay lies on the northern shoreline of the pristine Lake Pend Oreille (pronounced "Pond-uh-ray," the same pronunciation as the city). The name of the lake is a French word meaning ear (shape of) or earring. It is Idaho's largest lake.

Ponderay is located on the Purcell Trench, a glacially created valley that begins in Canada and continues in a south/southwesterly direction to Rathdrum and Post Falls. On the southeast of the valley, prehistoric glaciers cut the 1,100-foot-deep Lake Pend Oreille before dissipating.

In Idaho, the valley lies between the forested Selkirk and Cabinet Mountain Ranges of the Kaniksu National Forest. The highest mountain in the Selkirk Mountains is the 6,400-foot-high Schweitzer Mountain, home to a local ski resort. The highest mountain in the Cabinet range is Scotchman Peak at 7,009 feet. (*See The Region, Distinctive Geographic and Geologic Features.*)

Ponderay's city center lies about a mile north of Sandpoint. Ponderay has become Bonner County's commercial hub. Many new retail and other businesses have moved to Ponderay to take advantage of its strategic location where two major highways intersect.

Pre-Incorporation Years

In September 1809 Canadian explorer, map maker and trader David Thompson and his associate Finan McDonald of the Canadian North West Company established Idaho's first trading post 15 miles east of Ponderay at East Hope. They named the post after the local tribe of Kalispel Indians. (*See The Region, American Indians; and Early Trappers/Explorers.*)

Owners of a steamboat named the Mary Moody started a ferry business on Lake Pend Oreille in 1866 – the first commercial travel on the lake. Most of the steamboat's business was transporting miners and supplies headed to the gold fields in Canada and Montana Territory across the lake.

In 1881 the Northern Pacific Railroad used 6,000 men – including 4,000 Chinese workers – to start construction of a railroad line from Sandpoint through what is now Ponderay and Kootenai and around the east side of the lake to the Clark Fork River. The rail line then followed the river into Montana. The railroad built its roundhouse – where locomotives are maintained and repaired – two miles east of Ponderay in Kootenai. (*See The Region, Railroads; and Federal Lands – Private Ownership and Preservation Laws.*)

Bay at Volkswalk

Prospectors working around the lake in the late 1800s found placer gold and deposits of lead-silver ore with traces of copper and gold. However, the ability to develop their lead-silver claims was frustrated because they had no way to process the ore. (*See The Region, Gold Mining.*)

Around 1903 a group of private investors formed the Panhandle Smelting and Refining Company. They built a town around an ore processor, smelter and dock on the north end of Lake Pend Oreille. Steamboats brought the ore from the mines to the dock where it was transported to the ore processor.

The ore-processing activity produced large quantities of tailings and slag that they dumped in a pile, slowly creating a small grey-black mountain that is still visible from across the lake. Local residents have named this mountain of slag "Black Rock."

Investors formed the Panhandle Development Company to plat and develop the new town which they initially named "Panhandle." They then proceeded to build a hotel, office buildings, a school and homes in the village.

Apparently the town's name was reconsidered, because on May 5, 1904, the name on the plat filed with Kootenai County in Coeur d'Alene was Ponderay. In

1903 Ponderay was part of Kootenai County. Four years later, the town became part of the newly created Bonner County with its county seat in Sandpoint.

The operations of the Panhandle Smelting and Refining Company were marginally profitable at best. In 1909 financial and legal problems led to its closure.

At that time, the Humbird Lumber Company, Sandpoint's largest employer, operated facilities near Ponderay. Displaced workers at the smelter found employment at Humbird and with the railroad. In 1910 Ponderay's population was 250. (*See The Region, Forest Products.*)

Child walking along lake

Even though the smelting operation failed, steamboats continued using the docks. The Ponderay Transportation Company had two steamboats – a heavy tug called the Ponderay and a smaller steamboat named the Belle. Among other things, these boats carried mail to the post offices in the towns around the lake.

Around 1910 the First State Bank of Ponderay occupied a two-story building of white brick with granite trim. This historic building now contains apartments. Other wood-frame structures built during that period are still standing, some being used as private homes.

Incorporation

On May 27, 1947, Ponderay became an incorporated village. On November 26, 1967, its legal status changed to an incorporated city due to a change in state law.

Turning Points

Panhandle Smelting and Refining Ponderay started as a company town built on mining. Though the smelting business lasted only a few years, it was the basis for creating the city and setting it on the path for more diverse economic growth.

Humbird Lumber Mill The Humbird Lumber Mill began acquiring smaller lumber mills in the area around Ponderay in 1901. When the Panhandle Smelting and Refining Company closed, Humbird was the city's primary economic shock absorber.

The mill was the dominant employer in the area and underpinned the local economy until it closed in 1931.

Transformation into a Retail Center The owners of Bonner Mall owned land between Sandpoint and Ponderay. They needed City services and originally requested annexation into the City of Sandpoint. After Sandpoint turned them down, they made application to Ponderay, which gratefully accepted. The mall, strong traffic patterns, available space and the city's business-friendly attitude were the catalyst that brought many other retail businesses to the city.

Ponderay City Hall.

Ponderay Today

Amenities and Attractions Due to its proximity to Sandpoint, Ponderay residents enjoy the amenities and attractions available there. However, Ponderay has several parks in the planning stages. The city is working on a ommunity walking/biking trail called the Pend d'Oreille Bay Trail that runs along the northern shoreline of the beautiful Lake Pend Oreille.

Each August, Ponderay celebrates "Ponderay Days." Attractions include a car show and business-sponsored activities at the Bonner Mall and other participating stores.

Round Lake State Park is located 13 miles south of Ponderay. This 142-acre forested park surrounds the 58-acre Round Lake.

Farragut State Park has 4,000 acres and lies 35 miles south of Ponderay at the base of Lake Pend Oreille.

Three Idaho Scenic Byways further display the beauty of the area. The Pend Oreille Scenic Byway begins at the intersection of the combined U.S. Highways 95 and 2 and State Highway 200 in Ponderay, passes through the city and follows Highway 200 around the eastern side of the lake then proceeds east to the Montana state line.

The Wild Horse Trail Scenic Byway starts in Sandpoint, passes on the western side of Ponderay on Highway 95 and heads north along the eastern side of the Selkirk Mountains. It marks the historic path that the Kootenai Tribe followed to their fishing grounds at Lake Pend Oreille.

The Panhandle Historic Rivers Passage Byway begins at the Washington state line on U.S. Highway 2 and follows the Pend Oreille River to its end at Sandpoint.

Schweitzer Mountain Ski Resort lies 10 miles north of Ponderay. With an average annual snowfall of 300 inches, the resort has 67 ski runs, ski lifts, cross-country ski trails, snowmobiling and sleigh rides. During the summer, the mountain resort is available for hiking, mountain biking and horseback riding. Resort facilities include a lodge; condominiums; and a variety of retail stores, restaurants and pubs.

Silverwood Amusement and Water Park has over 50 amusement rides. It is located 28 miles south of the city.

Lake Pend Oreille and the nearby national forest with its mountains, rivers and streams offer a wide variety of outdoor activities. Summer or winter, people can enjoy the outdoors by boating, water skiing, fishing, hiking, biking, riding ATV and snowmobile trails, horseback riding, hunting and cross-country snow skiing.

Economy and Major Employers Ponderay's location north of Sandpoint at the junction of two transportation corridors, the combined U.S. Highways 95 and 2 and Idaho Highway 200 and the availability of land at affordable prices have attracted many new businesses and jobs. Nearly 300 businesses – including the Bonner Mall, J.C. Penney, Wal-Mart, Home Depot, smaller retail businesses, restaurants and motels – are located in the city.

Education The Lake Pend Oreille School District provides most of the primary and secondary education for Ponderay's children. The school district's administrative offices are located in Ponderay. The district's three elementary schools, a middle school, a high school, an alternative high school and a charter school are located in Sandpoint. Private schools in both Ponderay and Sandpoint also offer primary and secondary education.

The closest institutions of higher learning are North Idaho College (NIC) and the University of Idaho program on the NIC campus, both of which are located 45 miles south in Coeur d'Alene. NIC also has a satellite facility in Bonner Mall.

Health Care The 62-bed Bonner General Hospital in Sandpoint plus general clinics, dental offices, a 55-unit assisted-living center and a 60-bed nursing home provide most of the community's health care services.

Transportation State Highway 200 and the combined U.S. Highways 95 and 2 intersect Ponderay. Pend Oreille Scenic Byway is a 33-mile segment of Highway 200 that passes through the city. Hugging the north shore of Lake Pend Oreille between Sandpoint and Clark Fork, the Byway provides stunning views of the lake.

The closest airport is Dave Wall Field in Sandpoint. It has a 5,500-foot runway and handles private, charter and light commercial aircraft. Spokane International Airport is located 84 miles southwest.

Railroad freight services are available on one of three rail lines – the Burlington Northern, Montana Rail Link and Union Pacific. Railroad passenger service is available at the Amtrak station in Sandpoint. The Sandpoint station is the only Amtrak stop in Idaho.

The North Idaho Community Express provides public transportation on a fixed route between Ponderay, Sandpoint and Coeur d'Alene.

Utilities and Services Private companies provide electricity, natural gas, telephone, cable and satellite services. The City provides water service and police protection. Kootenai-Ponderay Sewer District provides sewer services. Northside Fire District provides fire protection. Bonner County provides emergency medical services. Waste Management of Idaho, a private company, provides garbage collection services.

Vision for 2050

Ponderay's motto is the "Little City with a Big Future." The City's priorities are to preserve the small town feeling, improve infrastructure, balance land use between residential and commercial and maintain the economic stability that ensures a high quality of life.

By 2050 Ponderay's population will approach 20,000 with the majority of the residents living north of Bronx Road. By that time, Ponderay's area of city impact will extend past Selle Road.

All city roads will be paved with streetlights. City leaders will have resolved the storm water drainage issues. The residential parts of the city will have curbs, gutters and sidewalks with trees lining the streets.

Much of the city's growth will come from planned unit developments. Some single-family homes will still be on acreage lots, but most will be in neighborhoods – single-family homes, condominiums and town homes interspersed with retail stores, restaurants and office buildings. These more self-contained mixed-use areas will reduce the need for people to commute long distances to work. People will use technology to work from home, giving the city more of a "small town" feeling.

By 2050 Ponderay will have a town square near its center. The square will have a recreation park with athletic fields, picnic areas, a swimming pool and a children's playground.

Low-maintenance green spaces landscaped with native plants for wildlife habitat will be interspersed between developed areas.

The Pend d'Oreille Bay Trail, bordering the lake, will be a beautiful place to walk and bike in the summer or snowshoe and cross-country ski in the winter.

Black Rock Park will be a beautiful spot on the lakeshore. The adjoining land will be a public park. There will be a public boat dock and small cafe to enjoy the beauty of the surrounding lake and mountains.

By 2050 the city will have an indoor/outdoor ice rink where ice hockey and ice skating can be enjoyed. In addition, an outdoor amphitheater will be used for the performing arts.

In order to eliminate unnecessary costs and improve services, by 2050 the joint planning efforts of Ponderay, Sandpoint, Kootenai and Dover will likely result in a regionalization approach to providing certain services and infrastructure such as domestic water and sewer.

Mayors

Unknown Charles Fontaine	1980 Palmer Fiksdal	2000 Jessie DeMers
1979 James Steinhouse	1988 James Richter	2008 Carol Kunzeman
	1992 James Hunt	2016 Steve Geiger

Beardmore Building at night

Priest River

Statistical Data

Population: 1,751 *
Elevation: 2,077 feet
Precipitation: 33 inches **
Average Snowfall: 94 inches **
County: Bonner
Website: www.priestriver.org

Temperature Range – Fahrenheit: **
Spring: 27 to 69
Summer: 45 to 84
Fall: 28 to 74
Winter: 20 to 40
* U.S. Census Bureau Estimates July 2015
**Historical averages

The city of Priest River lies at the confluence of the river by the same name and the Pend Oreille River. The river is the outlet to the crystal-clear Priest Lake located 20 miles north. The Pend Oreille River is the outlet for Lake Pend Oreille.

Four miles to the west on the Pend Oreille River is the hydroelectric Albeni Falls Dam. The dam, constructed in 1955, elevated the depth of the river about 65 feet at the dam site, creating a beautiful reservoir extending east behind the dam to Lake Pend Oreille.

The Kaniksu National Forest – part of the Panhandle National Forests since 2000 – and Idaho State Lands are located a few miles north of the city. The Kaniksu National Forest also extends south across the Pend Oreille River. The Idaho/Washington state line is six miles west at Oldtown. Sandpoint is situated 24 miles northeast.

Pre-Incorporation Years

In September 1809 David Thompson and his associate, Finan McDonald, of the Canadian North West Company established Idaho's first trading post on the east side of Lake Pend Oreille near what is now East Hope. Other trappers and, later, prospectors came into the land that had been the exclusive domain of American Indians – principally of the Coeur d'Alene, Kutenai (Kootenai) and Pend d'Oreille or Kalispel Tribes.

In 1866 a steamboat called the Mary Moody began ferrying trappers, miners and their gear across and around Lake Pend Oreille. About this time, steamers and riverboats also began bringing passengers up the Pend Oreille River to Albeni Falls – near what is now Albeni Falls Dam. They then portaged around the falls and boarded steamboats operating up river and on the lake.

Early Priest River street.

A riverboat port town named Newport – now Oldtown – built up on the west banks of the river on the Idaho side of the Idaho/Washington territorial line, about two miles west of Albeni Falls.

In 1883 the Northern Pacific Railroad completed a line from Wallula, Washington, to Missoula, Montana. From Wallula the railroad went northeast to Spokane, crossed into Idaho near Rathdrum – then Westwood – and proceeded north to Sandpoint, where it turned east and then south around Lake Pend Oreille to the Clark Fork River before turning east again to Montana.

With the availability of railroad transportation, sawmills began developing around Lake Pend Oreille. In 1906 the Spokane International Railway built a 142-mile line between Spokane and Canada. This line also passed through Sandpoint before continuing on to Bonners Ferry and Eastport where it connected with the Canadian Pacific Railway.

Around 1889 the Great Northern Railway was making surveys needed to complete its transcontinental railroad linking its main line from Havre, Montana, to the Puget Sound area near Seattle, Washington.

In likely anticipation of the railroad, Henry Keyser acquired land from the Kalispel Indians about a mile east of what is now Priest River – on the east side of Priest River – and started a town he named Priest River in honor of a Jesuit Priest, Father John Roothaan. Other settlers soon joined him.

In 1890 the settlers built the town's first schoolhouse. The following year, postal authorities approved the Priest River Post Office with James Judge as postmaster. In 1892 Charles Jackson opened his general store.

In 1891 the Great Northern Railway construction crews working east from Puget Sound, crossed the Pend Oreille River at Newport – now Oldtown – and reached Priest River. The railroad attempted to change the name of the town to Valencia but, finding that name was already in use elsewhere, accepted the name of Priest River.

From Priest River the rail line continued along the north side of the Pend Oreille River to Sandpoint. At Sandpoint the line turned north to Bonners Ferry. At Bonners Ferry, it extended north to Canada and east to connect with its main line in Havre. In 1893 The Great Northern Railroad – now Burlington Northern – acquired the Northern Pacific Railroad.

The railroad depot in Newport – Oldtown – was a converted boxcar. In 1896 the boxcar burned down. Rather than rebuild on the Idaho side of town, railroad officials built a new depot on the Washington side. Wanting to be near the train depot, businesses on the Idaho side of town, including the Newport Post Office, moved to the Washington side.

Local residents began calling the Idaho side "Oldtown" and, later, incorporated the village with that name.

Finding an adequate number of laborers to construct the railroad was a major effort. The railroad companies advertized throughout the United States and foreign countries. For example, a decade earlier the Northern Pacific Railroad brought in 6,000 workers. Not being able to attract enough construction hands from emigrant labor pools in the Dakotas and Utah, the railroad hired 4,000 laborers directly from China.

The Great Northern Railway also had to recruit laborers outside the U.S. One group of construction hands came from southern Italy. Many of these laborers wanted to immigrate to America and bring their families with them. They settled east of town and established their own school and church. When they completed their work on the railroad, they found work in the wood products industry that was already building up in anticipation of the railroad.

Without fail, spring runoff each year would cause the rivers to flood. The spring of 1894 was an exceptionally heavy snowmelt in the surrounding mountains. The Pend Oreille River overflowed its banks, flooding the town. Seeking to avoid a similar problem in the future,

Early Priest River

Priest River community homeowners and businesses moved their town west across Priest River to the higher ground overlooking the Pend Oreille River.

The emerging wood products industry provided an almost immediate demand for railroad freight service. Beginning in the 1890s logging crews began harvesting timber around Priest Lake and floating logs down Priest River during the spring runoff to the sawmills near the town of Priest River.

In 1900 Charles and Lucy Gumaer Beardmore came to Priest River. The Beardmore's built a sawmill, a stagecoach line to Priest Lake and several of the town's commercial buildings. Lucy became an Idaho State legislator.

In 1901 responding to the increased freight demand from wood products businesses, the Great Northern Railway built a depot in Priest River.

Fourth of July

Incorporation

On March 2, 1949, with a population of around 280, Priest River became an incorporated village.

Turning Points

Railroad The railroad was the catalyst that allowed sawmills to move their commodities to market and the city to grow and prosper. It continues to be an important mode of transportation.

Sawmills The first sawmill in Priest River began operation in the late 1880s. The wood products industry underpinned the city's economy throughout the twentieth century.

During the later part of the century, environmental litigation and changes in federal law and timber management policy substantially closed federal forestlands to timber harvest. Those changes and market factors have adversely affected the wood products industry.

In 2008 Riley Creek Lumber, owner of J.D. Lumber, announced closure of the mill – the largest sawmill in the city. J.D. Lumber had over 200 employees. The loss of these jobs has had a significant adverse effect on the city's economy.

Albeni Falls Dam In response to a huge flood that swept over the valleys of the Columbia River basin in 1948, the U.S. Congress passed the Flood Control Act of 1950. The Albeni Falls Dam was one of those authorized for construction under this act. The Army Corps of Engineers began construction on the dam

Sado band

in January 1951 and continued until its completion in December 1955 at a total cost of $34 million. The dam is located about two miles east of the city of Priest River. The 200-million-kilowatt dam is 90 feet high and 775 feet wide. Today, in addition to preventing flooding in the area, the dam produces enough electricity to supply about 15,000 homes. The facility and nearby Albeni Falls Dam Recreation Area provide employment and significant recreation opportunities for city residents.

Fire In the early morning of December 3, 1973, a devastating fire broke out downtown in Phil's Lounge. The fire destroyed or seriously damaged several nearby structures. Most business owners rebuilt, but outside of the downtown area.

Priest River Today

Amenities and Attractions The city has four parks. The Downtown Park is a resting place for downtown visitors with a child's swing, picnic table and historic steam engine. 4H Park, located next to the city tennis and basketball court, has two picnic tables. City Park has a children's playground, restrooms and picnic area. West Bonner County Park is located on the shore of the Pend Oreille River and has a pavilion, BBQ grill pit, children's playground, picnic area and boat launch.

Priest River Timber Days, an annual celebration of its logging heritage, begins the last Saturday of July.

Priest River Recreation Area with campsites, ball field, boat ramp, beach and restrooms is located on the banks of Priest River adjacent to the Priest River Wildlife Area.

When the Corps of Engineers constructed Albeni Falls Dam, they also built Albeni Cove and Riley Creek Recreation Areas behind the dam. These modern campsites have picnic shelters, boat ramps, beaches and trails.

The city of Priest River is the gateway to Priest Lake. Priest Lake is a jewel surrounded by beautiful forests – a paradise for outdoor enthusiasts. Private homes dot portions of the lakefront.

Economy and Major Employers With about 200 employees, the West Bonner County School District is the city's largest employer. Stimson Lumber has over 100 employees and is the city's second largest employer. Several small businesses, including wood products and airplane float manufacturing, lodging and

Beardmore Building in the day

retail stores provide the balance of the city's employment base.

Education West Bonner County School District has its offices and operates an elementary school, junior high school, high school and alternative high school in Priest River. The closest Idaho institution of higher learning, North Idaho College (NIC), is located in Coeur d'Alene. NIC and the University of Idaho also offer courses in Sandpoint.

Health Care The closest hospital is Newport Community Hospital in Newport, Washington.

Transportation U.S. Highway 2, the Panhandle Historic Rivers Passage Scenic Byway, intersects the city. The highway connects Priest River with Newport, Washington, on the west and Sandpoint on the east. Idaho Highway 57 north to Priest Lake and Upper Priest Lake begins in the city.

Capital for a Day at Priest River

Railroad service for freight is available in the city. Amtrak offers passenger service at its station in Sandpoint.

Priest River Municipal Airport's 2,950-foot runway provides service for light private and charter aircraft.

Sandpoint's Dave Wall Field, has a 5,500-foot runway and handles larger aircraft. Spokane International Airport, the largest airport in the region, is southwest in Spokane, Washington.

Utilities and Services Private companies provide electricity, telephone, and satellite services. The City provides water and sewer services and fire and police protection.

Vision for 2050

In 1960 Priest River had a population of 1,749 and in 2000 the population was 1,754. In the current decade, the city has grown about one percent annually.

Even though the city's population is growing, the underlying basis of the city's economy is changing from wood products to outdoor recreation, hospitality and manufacturing.

Loss of access to federal timberlands and market forces have resulted in the decline of the city's wood products businesses. (*See Northern Idaho, Development and Demise of Renewable Natural Resources*.) Technological innovation has allowed wood products businesses to operate more efficiently with fewer workers. These forces have had an adverse effect on the city's population and economy; reducing the city's employment base faster than other new industries can add jobs. The recent closure of J.D. Lumber Company is an example of the changes that have adversely affected the city's economy and population.

City and community leaders are adapting to the city's changing economy.

Even though the underlying economic basis of the city is changing, the quality of life for city residents will continue. In 2050 Priest River will still be a quiet friendly town surrounded by fabulous forests, mountains, lakes, rivers and streams – one of the most beautiful parts of Idaho to live and raise a family.

Mayors

** Arthur Hagman *	1949 Jack Lewis	1976 Arthur Thayer
1929 Edward Dalva *	1950 Ralph Yarroll	1984 Gary Altmaier
1931 E.J. Peterson *	1951 Robert E. Dow	1988 Zeniff "Whitey" Brower
1933 P.H. Redmond *	1951 Lawrence M. Nelson	1993 Rush "Harvey" Balison
1935 A.C. VanValkenburg *	1957 Lester E. Runnels	1998 Allen "Tom" Hartliep
1937 P.H. Redmond *	1959 Michael Vanovich	2002 William M. Mullaley
1939 Maurice D. Lathrop *	1961 Roland C. Naccarato	2006 James L. Martin
1941 Robert E. Dow *	1964 Michael Vanovich	* Village Chairman
1943 Charles Campbell *	1966 Ted Brower	** Date unknown. All records prior to May 6, 1929 were destroyed in a fire in 1929.
1943 W.E. Schultz *	1974 John Caprai	

View of Sandpoint from Pine Crest Cemetery.

Sandpoint

Statistical Data

Population: 7,760 *
Elevation: 2,085 feet
Precipitation: 31 inches **
Average Snowfall: 60 inches **
County: Bonner
Website: www.cityofsandpoint.com

Temperature Range – Fahrenheit: **
Spring: 27 to 60
Summer: 46 to 81
Fall: 28 to 70
Winter: 20 to 38
* U.S. Census Bureau Estimates July 2015
**Historical averages

Early settlers named their town Sandpoint to describe its picturesque setting on the shores of Lake Pend Oreille (pronounced Pon-duh-ray), French for shape of an ear or earring.

The city lies on a large peninsula that slopes into the northwest end of the lake. The lake is 43 miles long, up to six miles wide and 1,158 feet deep. It is Idaho's largest lake, and Sandpoint is the largest city on the lake. (*See Northern Idaho – Land of Pristine Lakes and Rivers*.)

Geologically, the city lies near the base of the prehistoric "Purcell Trench," a glacially created, valley that begins in Canada and broadens into a wide plain as it divides the forested Selkirk and Cabinet Mountain ranges. The glacial effects that created the valley also formed a long depression in the earth's surface that is now Lake Pend Oreille.

The highest peak in the Selkirk Mountains is Schweitzer Mountain at 6,400 feet, home to Schweitzer Mountain Ski Resort. Scotchman Peak, the highest mountain in the Cabinet Mountain Range, rises to over 7,000 feet.

Courtesy of Jim Parsons Jr.

The August 2004 edition of *Outside Towns* described Sandpoint from the view of a traveler approaching the city from the south on Highway 95: "You cross the two-mile bridge over Lake Pend Oreille and drink in the spectacular Selkirk Mountains looming over the downtown – [with its] small-town sense of community – restored Spanish-mission-style Panida Theater and Winter Carnival. Schweitzer, the uncrowded local ski mountain has 2,400 feet of vertical [drop and 2,900] skiable acres and a Nordic trail network. Summers bring huge-scale paddling, sailing and fishing around the lake's 110 miles of shoreline, plus mountain biking.

Pre-Incorporation Years

For centuries, the Kalispell Indians lived in the general area. Canadian explorer, map maker and trader David Thompson and his associate Finan McDonald of the Canadian North West Company established Idaho's first trading post in September 1809 at East Hope, across Lake Pend Oreille from Sandpoint. In his diary, Thompson made the first recorded description of the Sandpoint area with a simple reference to "a point of sand" extending into Lake Pend Oreille.

In 1866 a steamboat called the Mary Moody began ferrying increasing numbers of trappers and miners with their gear across and around the lake.

Around the same time, the Northern Pacific Railroad (NPR) settled on a route along the northern and eastern shore of Lake Pend Oreille to extend its railroad between Washington and Montana. However, actual construction did not start for more than a decade.

Sandpoint was first settled in 1880 when Robert Weeks opened a general store and NPR surveyed their rail line. Settlers established a village on the sandy peninsula near Sand Creek. They first named their community Pend Oreille but soon changed it to Sandpoint.

A year later, the railroad reached Sandpoint. A visitor who came through the town two years later reported that the community had about 300 residents.

Great Northern Railroad interests acquired the NPR in 1888. Four years later, L. D. Farmin came with his family to Sandpoint as the railroad's agent. Farmin, his wife Ella Mae and their son Earl staffed the railroad station around the clock for $1.55 a day.

The year the Farmins arrived, another visitor reported that "Sandpoint is made up of between three and four dozen rude shacks and perhaps a dozen tents."

The Farmins homesteaded 160 acres on the west side of Sand Creek in 1893. Five years later, the Farmins and others engaged a young surveyor, William Ashley, to make a plat of the Sandpoint town site. Farmin filed the plat in the Coeur d'Alene land office. It included eight city blocks that are now near the center of downtown Sandpoint.

The availability of rail transportation encouraged development of sawmills around the lake, including one that became the city's largest employer, the Sand Point Lumber Company, acquired by Humbird Lumber Company in 1901.

Ella Mae Farmin, Amanda Nesbitt and Carrie Le Huquet organized the first church in Sandpoint, the First Methodist Episcopal Church, on August 31, 1897.

Children were generally educated in private homes until school patrons built a new brick school building in 1906.

Incorporation

Sandpoint became an incorporated village on September 7, 1901. About six years later on January 15, 1907, the status was changed to an incorporated city. Two months later on March 18 the legislature divided Kootenai County to create Bonner County with Sandpoint as the county seat.

Turning Points

Railroad The advent of the railroad in 1881 opened Sandpoint for economic development. It encouraged sawmills and, as the timber was harvested, made possible the conversion of timberland to agriculture.

Even President Teddy Roosevelt stopped at Sandpoint's railroad depot during his 1912 Bull Moose presidential campaign.

Sawmills The Humbird Lumber Company was the sawmill that did most to establish the city's economy. In 1910 Humbird built a Power House to produce steam-generated electricity. The water came from Sand Creek. Sawmill wood waste was used for fuel.

At its peak production, Humbird had 350 employees and was the largest sawmill in the region. However, in 1931 market forces turned negative and the company shut down with a devastating effect on the city's economy.

With the advent of World War II in the 1940s, the town's wood products industry began to pick up again when Jim Brown Jr. organized the Pack River Lumber Co. Initially, the company salvaged stray "deadhead" logs from the lake. The next year, Brown opened a mill three miles west at Dover.

Bridge The 1909 construction of the two-mile-long wooden wagon bridge across Lake Pend Oreille at the headwaters of the Pend Oreille River dramatically improved surface transportation and commerce into the city. When constructed, it was the longest wooden bridge known and eventually became part of U.S. Highway 95.

Then in 1956, 22 years after then Governor Ben Ross dedicated a second Long Wagon Bridge across the lake, federal and state transportation departments replaced the wooden structures with a steel and concrete bridge that is still in use.

Farragut Naval Training Station With the Japanese attack at Pearl Harbor in 1941 and the outbreak of World War II, the U.S. Navy built Farragut Naval Training Station on 4,000 acres at the southern end of Lake Pend Oreille. The lake was deep and large enough for the Navy to conduct research and training in a secure setting. The training base also became an encampment for prisoners of war.

During this time, civilian jobs on base and thousands of military personnel on leave provided a significant boost to Sandpoint's economy. The base is now a state park and museum.

County Seat The city's economy got a boost in 1907 when it was selected as the Bonner County seat of government. It not only gave the city added political and economic influence, it was a source of stable employment and attraction to other businesses. As the city became a regional business and shopping center, many residents in the surrounding communities

Bonner County Court House. Residents still use this courthouse located on 1st Ave. in Sandpoint.

commuted to Sandpoint for work.

Four months after Sandpoint became the county seat, Ignatz Weil, Bonner County's first county clerk, built a courthouse on his lot and sold it to the county for $15,000.

Sandpoint Today

Amenities and Attractions

The city has five municipal parks that comprise a total of 51 acres. The focal point of Sandpoint's natural outdoor amenities is its18-acre park and beach on the lake with 180 boat slips. The other parks are sports oriented. Each year, the city hosts amateur soccer, softball, tennis and football events.

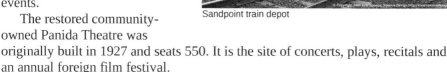
Sandpoint train depot

The restored community-owned Panida Theatre was originally built in 1927 and seats 550. It is the site of concerts, plays, recitals and an annual foreign film festival.

Each year during the first two weeks of August, the city hosts an outdoor music festival that features the Spokane Symphony with nationally known performers and musicians. Spokane is 80 miles southwest of the city.

The Pend Oreille Arts Council produces several other events including the Arts and Crafts Fair, "Sunday Concerts on the Lawn," "Sounds at the Park Place" series and the Winter Carnival.

Two festivals – the North Idaho Timberfest and the Idaho Draft Horse International – are popular events that recount historical celebrations. Each spring and fall, local sponsors also produce two major fishing derbies.

Sand Creek Bridge

Sandpoint architecture blends very old residences with numerous new subdivisions. Many older homes have stood for over a hundred years and have been beautifully preserved and maintained. They stand on tree-lined streets on the northwest shore of the lake, reminiscent of life at a time when timber and railroads were the area's principal industries.

Two Idaho parks are located near the city. Round Lake State Park is 10 miles south, and 142 acres of forest surround the 58-acre Round Lake. The 4,000-acre Farragut State Park is 30 miles south at the base of Lake Pend Oreille.

Three Idaho scenic byways connect with Sandpoint. The Wild Horse Trail Scenic Byway starts in Sandpoint and heads north along the eastern side of the

Selkirk Mountains. The Kootenai Indians followed this historic path to their fishing grounds at Lake Pend Oreille.

The Pend Oreille Scenic Byway begins at the intersection of Highways 95 and 200 in Sandpoint and follows Highway 200 around the eastern side of the lake and on to the Montana state line.

The Panhandle Historic Rivers Passage begins at the Washington state line and follows the Pend Oreille River to its end at Sandpoint.

Commercial attractions include Silverwood Theme Park and its over 50 amusement rides located 25 miles south.

Schweitzer Mountain Ski Resort is just 11 miles north. It has average snowfall of 300 inches, 67 ski runs, 2 ski lifts, cross-country ski trails, snowmobiling and sleigh rides. Facilities include a lodge, condominiums and a variety of retail stores.

Economy and Major Employers

The natural resource industries that once dominated the city's economy are now largely gone. Environmental litigation and federal policy have largely eliminated timber harvest off federal lands. The mining industry in the region, although not a major influence in Sandpoint, suffered a similar fate. In October 2003 Louisiana Pacific Corp, the last sawmill in Sandpoint, closed.

Sandpoint beach

New businesses now underpin the city's economy. The largest is Coldwater Creek, a catalog, Internet and retail store marketer of women's apparel, jewelry, accessories and gifts. One of the key reasons the owners choose to headquarter their operation in Sandpoint is the beauty and outdoor amenities of the area. Starting over 20 years ago from a home-based catalog business, the company has grown to 600 employees in Sandpoint and over 4,000 company-wide.

Litehouse Foods, a family-owned business that produces refrigerated food dressings, dips, sauces and bleu cheese for national distribution, employs 385.

Unicep Packaging, a manufacturer of unit dose medications, employs 125, and Encoder Products Company, a manufacturer of high-precision encoders, has 100 employees.

The largest public employers are the Pend Oreille School District with 500 employees and Bonner County.

Windbag Marina

The Bonner General Hospital and several clinics, dental offices and care centers for seniors are also significant employers.

Schweitzer Mountain Resort and an increasing number of tourism and recreation-based businesses are among the fastest growing employers in or near the city.

Education Lake Pend Oreille School District provides most elementary and secondary education for eastern Bonner County. Three elementary schools, a middle school, high school, alternative high school and charter school are located in Sandpoint. There are also four private schools.

The closest Idaho institution of higher learning is North Idaho College (NIC), a two-year school 45 miles south in Coeur d'Alene. NIC and the University of Idaho both offer courses in Sandpoint.

Health Care Full ranges of medical services are provided at the 62-bed Bonner General Hospital; two general clinics; several dental offices; and, for seniors, a 55 unit assisted-living center and a 60-bed nursing home.

Sandpoint street

Transportation The city is served by three highways. U.S. Highway 95 passes through the city north to south. U.S. Highway 2 extends west to Spokane, and State Highway 200 connects with Missoula, Montana. Several years ago, only one traffic signal was necessary. Now the city has eight signals with an average traffic count of over 25,000 vehicles daily.

Three rail lines converge in the city. The Burlington Northern and Union Pacific provide freight service. Amtrak provides passenger service to Seattle, Portland and Chicago. The Sandpoint station is the only Amtrak stop in the state of Idaho.

North Idaho Community Express provides public transportation in the city and a fixed route between Sandpoint and Coeur d'Alene.

The Sandpoint airport, Dave Wall Field, has a 5,500-foot runway and handles private, charter and light commercial aircraft. Coeur d'Alene Air Terminal handles heavier aircraft. Spokane International Airport, the largest airport in the region, is located 80 miles southwest.

Utilities and Services Private companies provide electricity, natural gas, telephone, cable and satellite services. The city provides water, sewer, fire, police and library services. The county provides garbage collection.

Vision for 2050

Sandpoint's population is growing over 3 percent annually. If current trends continue, by 2050 Sandpoint's population could exceed 20,000. By 2050 the borders of the neighboring communities of the North Shore Metropolitan Area (NSMA) – including Sandpoint, Dover, Ponderay and Kootenai – will have grown so close that, except for legal boundaries, they will appear as a single community.

By 2050 the NSMA will have a shared municipal wastewater plant that will also serve Schweitzer Mountain Ski Resort.

Federal, state and local highway jurisdictions will have improved their roads. U.S. Highway 95 will be a four-lane freeway from Boise to the Canadian border. The Sand Creek Byway will become a reality. U.S. Highway 2 will receive a major upgrade from Montana to Washington as part of the National Parks Service project for the "Lake Missoula Flood Path Route."

The county airport will have full-time commuter service with daily flights to Boise, Seattle and Portland. The city's urban renewal program will provide a major industrial complex at the airport.

The business community – anchored by the headquarter companies of Litehouse Foods, Coldwater Creek, Quest Aircraft and Unicep – will attract many other businesses.

Sandpoint in spring

NIC and the University of Idaho will have expanded satellite programs to support these growing businesses. A convention center and 3,000-seat opera house will support a growing tourist and hospitality industry.

Mayors

1901-1906 Unknown *	1942 L.G. Moon	1988 Ron Chaney
1907 O.F. Page	1946 Don Diehl	1992 Dwight Sheffler
1909 Charles C. Riggs	1948 Floyd Gray	1994 Ron Chaney
1911 Charles Moody	1951 A.R. "Steve" Nelson	1996 David Sawyer
1913 C.F. Ewing	1954 Jim Hunt	2000 Paul Graves
1915 R.B. Himes	1956 Floyd Perks	2002 Ray Miller
1917 C.F. Ewing	1960 Floyd Gray	2008 Gretchen Hellar
1919 E.J. Elliott	1973 Les Brown	2012 Marsha Ogilvie
1921 E.W. Wheelan	1976 Ed Eitzman	2014 Carrie Logan
1927 H.E. Brown	1977 Harold Huff	2016 Shelby Rognstad
1933 Don C. Moore	1979 Gene Holt	* Village Chairman
1935 C.F. Ewing	1980 Sally Cupan	
1937 Malcolm McKinnon	1984 Marian Ebbett	

A Christmas scene in downtown Bonners Ferry.

BOUNDARY COUNTY

- Bonners Ferry (County Seat)
- Moyie Springs

Bonners Ferry

Statistical Data

Population: 2,490 *
Elevation: 1,930 feet
Precipitation: 24 inches **
Average Snowfall: 72 inches **
County: Boundary
Website: www.bonnersferry.id.gov

Temperature Range – Fahrenheit: **
Spring: 29 to 69
Summer: 48 to 83
Fall: 29 to 72
Winter: 20 to 41
* U.S. Census Bureau Estimates July 2015
**Historical averages

Bonners Ferry is located in the spectacularly beautiful and heavily wooded Kaniksu National Forest about 20 miles due south of the Canadian border. Nearby mountain peaks rise nearly 7,000 feet.

The Cabinet Mountain Range is to the east and south of the city, and the Selkirk Mountains lie to the west. Purcell Trench – a prehistoric shearing of the earth's surface along a fault between the Cabinet and Selkirk Mountains – has left a rich fertile agricultural valley.

The Kootenai River passes through the city and valley on its way back into British Columbia, where it joins the Columbia River.

To the south and east are patchworks of alfalfa and pasture intermixed with groves of trees.

Pre-Incorporation Years

When the Lewis and Clark led expedition, the Corps of Discovery, crossed Idaho about 150 miles south in 1805 and 1806, the Kootenai Tribe inhabited the land around what is now Bonners Ferry. The Tribe had formerly lived on the plains east of the Rocky Mountains, but conflicts with the Blackfoot Indians persuaded them to move.

A few years later, explorers and trappers came to the area, followed by Christian missionaries. The most prominent among the Kootenai Indians was Roman Catholic Father Pierre Jean de Smet, a Jesuit missionary.

In 1848 England and the United States negotiated a treaty establishing the boundary between the U.S. and Canada at the 49th parallel. In 1861 federal surveyors built a supply depot near the future town of Bonners Ferry.

The city's origin coincided with the 1863 discovery of gold 120 miles north at Wild Horse Creek in British Columbia. When news of the discovery got out, a gold rush ensued. Prospectors traveling up from the United States called the road to the gold fields "Wild Horse Trail." Where the trail crossed the Kootenai River, it was particularly difficult and dangerous.

Ferry still in operation, early 1900s.

Edwin L. Bonner, a merchant and entrepreneur from Walla Walla, Washington, observed the large number of prospectors and fortune seekers crossing the river and decided to build a ferry and trading post at that location.

He acquired land on each side of the river from Chief Abraham of the Kootenai Tribe and then persuaded the Idaho Territorial Legislature, meeting in Lewiston, to pass a law granting him an exclusive five-year franchise to build and operate a ferry on a seven-mile stretch of river. The law, passed on December 22, 1864, fixed the toll rates at $1.50 per loaded pack animal and 50 cents for a person on foot.

Not all pack animals on the trail were mules and horses. The American Camel Company had sold Arabian camels to miners. Several pack trains of five to six camels each crossed the Kootenai River at Bonners Ferry on the way to the gold fields.

In 1875 Richard Fry, later joined by his brother, took over the ferry and trading post business from Bonner. Fry also

Bonners Ferry early 1900s.

ran a pack train carrying supplies from Walla Walla to the mining camps.

Mrs. Martin Fry taught the first school, which consisted of 10 children from the two families. During the 1870s the settlement grew slowly. Fry's trading post and a few other scattered dwellings on the north side of the river were all that existed. In the outlying areas, a few early pioneers started homesteading.

About 1880 silver and lead mines in the mountains surrounding Kootenai Lake, 50 miles north, were under development. This reinvigorated the traffic of men and materials to the mines and added pressure for developing better transportation systems.

In 1882 the Northern Pacific Railroad reached the north shore of Lake Pend Oreille. Freight wagons and stagecoaches transported freight and passengers from the railhead over a rough toll road between Kootenai and Bonners Ferry.

Steamboat on the Kootenai River, early 1900s.

The Norwegian-built steamboat "Midge" began moving passengers and freight on the Kootenai River and Kootenai Lake in British Columbia between Bonners Ferry and the Canadian mining areas in 1883. The steamboat dock at Bonners Ferry was on the south bank of the river. That same year, property owners platted the town of Bonners Ferry near the dock.

However, building in the floodplain was a problem. Spring runoff often flooded the land. Many early homesteaders and business owners dealt with this problem by building their structures on stilts.

In 1892 the Great Northern Railroad reached Bonners Ferry, bringing economic growth to the new community. Mine, sawmill and agricultural businesses now had an efficient means to move their products to market. S.D. Taylor, editor of the *Kootenai Herald*, relocated his newspaper to the town and renamed it the *Bonners Ferry Herald*.

At that time, Bonners Ferry was still a frontier town with little rule of law. One aspect of the lawless element raised its ugly head in terms of racism and mob rule. When a colony of Chinese began working in the town, a group of whites became angry at the intrusion of the different culture and different-looking settlers and decided they would force them to leave. These white "citizens" incited a mob of whites to march to the Chinese settlements and order them to pack up their possessions and be ready to leave within two hours. At the appointed time, the Chinese settlers were loaded into two empty boxcars and shipped out to unknown destinations.

Incorporation

On April 1, 1899, Bonners Ferry became an incorporated village. By that time, the town had changed considerably. There were new businesses and homes in the city. Settlers had established their ranches and farms in the valley and on bench lands.

Two additional railroad lines crossed the river. Both laid tracks to the Canadian border. The Kootenai Valley Railroad ran along the east side of the valley and the Spokane International Railroad paralleled the Moyie River.

The town built a bridge across the river. However, the ferry still operated during periods of high water.

In 1967 the village became an incorporated city in accordance with a change in state law.

Turning Points

Bonners Ferry Lumber Company, 1915.

Gold Rush and Edwin L. Bonner The discovery of gold in British Columbia was a defining event for the city. The ensuing gold rush established the need for a ferry on the Kootenai River. E.L. Bonner's construction of the ferry and trading post established the city's location and future name.

Railroad When the railroad came 19 years later in 1892, it opened Bonners Ferry and the surrounding area for development by timber and other business interests.

Sawmills A few years after railroad service became available, wood products became the town's dominant industry. Significant commercial sawmill businesses started in 1903 when business interests affiliated with lumber industrialist, Fredrick Weyerhaeuser, established the Bonners Ferry Lumber Company. Although the mill burned down in 1909, it was quickly rebuilt.

Power plant

The Bonners Ferry Lumber Company closed in 1926. Over its 23 years of operation, the mill produced over 733 million board feet of lumber. (*See The Region, Forest Products.*)

The decision to close the Bonners Ferry Lumber Company was based on factors internal to the Weyerhaeuser organization. While closure of the mill had a significant adverse effect on the terminated employees and their families and the town's economy, the mill laid the groundwork for several other wood products companies to flourish into the latter half of the twentieth century when changes in federal law, forest management policies and litigation largely eliminated timber harvests on federal lands. (*See The Region, Mining and Forest Products – Leading Causes for Loss of Economic Influence.*)

Moyie Hydroelectric Dam Built in 1949 to provide electrical power for sawmills and homes in Bonners Ferry, the Moyie Hydroelectric Dam on the Moyie River still provides about a third of the city's electrical power. Bonners Ferry is one of only three cities in Idaho that generates some of its own electrical power from municipally-owned hydroelectric plants. The other two are Idaho Falls and Soda Springs in Eastern Idaho.

Municipal Water and Fire Protection The development of municipal water and fire protection systems provided a major boost to the quality of life for Bonners Ferry residents. The early settlers carried their drinking water from the river and stored it in wooden barrels. The first municipal water system consisted of pumping river water into a holding tank on the hillside with gravity pressuring the water through pipes connected to each home.

After an outbreak of typhoid fever, however, town leaders decided the village needed a safer water supply. In the late 1920s the city piped the pure, crystal-clear mountain water of Myrtle Creek into the town. Myrtle Creek continues as the source of the city's domestic water.

The prevalence of wood stoves, fireplaces and candles posed a constant fire hazard. In 1893 a disastrous fire destroyed half the town's business district. It took several years for the community to recover. In 1905 the town acquired its first gasoline powered fire engine and built a station for the new equipment. The original fire bell now sits atop the firehouse.

Flooding and the Libby Dam The Kootenai River is a beautiful amenity but for many years following heavy snowpack in the mountains and warm spring weather, rapid snowmelt brought damaging floods to the town and valley. In one flood, the post office ended up downstream in Canada.

The river enters the United States from British Columbia in the northwestern corner of Montana, flows south about 50 miles and then turns northwest for 60 miles past Bonners Ferry before turning back north into British Columbia. Ultimately the resolution to the flooding problem would require cooperation from multiple governmental jurisdictions in two states and two countries.

The community's first approach to deal with the flooding was to build on stilts. Later, they created 15 flood districts that built dykes to prevent the water from spreading across the valley. Some of the dykes, such as those built in the mid-1920s around the Kootenai Wildlife Refuge, ranged up to 37 feet above the riverbed. However, the dykes were not foolproof. In 1948 the river rose to a record 35 feet, again flooding the town.

In 1975 the U.S. Army Corps of Engineers, operating under the flood control act of 1962, built the 422-foot-high Libby Dam on the Kootenai River at Libby, Montana, about 60 miles southeast of Bonners Ferry. The dam – which backs up water for 90 miles, 40 miles of which are in Canada – was a joint project between the U.S. and Canada. It put an end to the flooding that had plagued the region.

Kootenai Tribe In 1974 the Kootenai Tribe declared a peaceful, but highly publicized, war against the United States seeking just compensation for this non-treaty signing Indian nation that had not received reservation land. A 1975 federal land grant provided 12.5 acres to the Tribe as settlement of the conflict. Kootenai Tribal land is just outside Bonners Ferry, overlooking the Kootenai River. The

2010 Census reported that the tribe had a population of 82. The tribe now operates the Kootenai River Inn Casino and Spa and a sturgeon and turbot fish hatchery on the river. The casino and spa is a handsome facility that attracts hundreds of people to the resort and the city every week.

Bonners Ferry Today

Amenities and Attractions The city has two municipal parks and a golf course. The Boundary County Museum occupies the former historic Houck Building.

Five miles west of Bonners Ferry is the Kootenai National Wildlife Refuge. This 2,774-acre wetland is an oasis for migrating waterfowl and habitat for other species of wildlife. It is a spectacular

Sunset at Bonners Ferry.

location for bird watching with several miles of walking paths.

Wild Horse Scenic Byway passes through the city. This Byway starts in Sandpoint, passes through Bonners Ferry and then proceeds north on U.S. Highway 95 to British Columbia.

The Scenic Byway follows the trail used by the Kootenai Indians as they traveled to their historic fishing grounds on Lake Pend Oreille. From 1863 to 1880 thousands of prospectors and miners followed the trail north 120 miles to the "Wild Horse Creek" gold fields.

The Kootenai Tribe of Idaho's destination resort – which includes a motel, a restaurant, a casino and a spa – is located nearby and is a major attraction, bringing patrons and tourists from both the U.S. and Canada.

Bonners Ferry has embarked on a revitalization effort. The city has many new streets, curbs, sidewalks, lights, trees and a visitor's center.

The city's most attractive amenity is its spectacular mountain setting. The surrounding mountains, lakes, rivers and streams offer excellent outdoor opportunities for backpacking, hiking, trail riding, fishing, hunting, snowmobiling and cross-country skiing. Downhill skiing is available 30 miles south at Schweitzer

Mountain Resort. Over 300 miles of national forest trails extend deep into the mountains.

Bonners Ferry is the seat of government for Boundary County and was named because it is the only county that crosses the entire state and has a boundary with another country as well as two states – Canada on the north and Washington and Montana on the west and east, respectively. Bonner and Idaho counties also cross the entire state.

Citizens pride themselves on being helpful and accommodating. In May of 2003 Governor Dirk Kempthorne designated the town "the friendliest city in Idaho."

Economy and Major Employers The city has no dominant employers. The Boundary County School District, the Boundary County Community Hospital, the Boundary County government and the U.S. Forest Service are the city's largest public employers. Wood products, hospitality and grocery businesses are the largest private employers.

Agriculture is still an important industry in the valley. Farmers' principal commodities are grain, hay, hops and beef.

Education Boundary County School District provides most of the primary and secondary education. The district operates a high school, alternative and middle schools and an elementary school in town. Four charter and private schools also operate in the city.

The closest Idaho institution of higher education is North Idaho College (NIC), 75 miles south in Coeur d'Alene. NIC has a satellite campus in Bonners Ferry.

Health Care The 62-bed Boundary County Community Hospital, several private clinics, 10 acute-care facilities and a nursing home provide health care services.

Transportation U.S. Highway 95 connects Bonners Ferry with Sandpoint to the south and the Canadian border to the north. In town, a cable-stressed concrete bridge spans the Kootenai River and connects the north and south sides of the city.

Starting just north of town, U.S. Highway 2 cuts southeast along the Kootenai River to Libby, Montana. The closest Interstate is I-90 located 75 miles south in Coeur d'Alene.

Private and charter aircraft use the Boundary County Airport's 4,000-foot-long runway. The closest commercial air service is in Spokane.

The railroad provides freight services in the city.

Utilities and Services Private companies provide electricity, telephone, natural gas, cable, satellite and wireless service. The City owns and operates a hydroelectric dam on the Moyie River that provides about a third of the city's electrical power. The

city also provides water, sewer, law enforcement and a volunteer fire department. The County provides solid waste services.

Vision for 2050

For the past several years, the population of Bonners Ferry has increased from 1 to 2 percent annually. If this moderate growth continues, by 2050 the city's population will exceed 4,000.

Bonners Ferry has generally designed its municipal systems and infrastructure to accommodate moderate growth. However, in the future, there will be additional costs directly attributed to growth. City leaders will continue to seek balance and equity in funding any improvements in municipal systems. The new tax base coming from growth and growth impact fees will pay the incremental cost associated with growth.

In 2050 Bonners Ferry will retain the attributes that make it a great city – hometown charm; cohesion; and a spirit of friendliness, kindness and generosity.

In 2050 it will still be worthy of the gubernatorial recognition it received in 2003 as "the friendliest city in Idaho."

Mayors

1893 James C. McRae *
1894 Wm Fred Kaiser *
1895 J.F. Cook *
1897 B.C. Hemminger *
1899 W.L. Kinnear *
1900 William Eaton *
1903 G.R. Gray *
1904 N.B. Williams *
1905 W.A. Alexander *
1909 James Fitzpatrick *
1912 E.E. Fry *

1915 George R. Gray *
1919 E.E. Fry *
1923 F.A. Shultis *
1925 O.F. Howe *
1927 H.I. Monks *
1929 E.E. Fry *
1933 G.B. Kemp *
1935 Frank Speece *
1937 Frank Lenhart *
1947 Meryl Felch *
1951 Wm Nieland *

1953 Meryl Felch *
1960 August Baylon *
1961 Joseph Wombacher *
1967 August Baylon
1974 Harold Sims
2000 Darrell Kerby
2008 David Anderson
2016 David Sims
* Village Chairman

Moyie Springs Post Office.

Moyie Springs

Statistical Data

Population: 702 *
Elevation: 2,204 feet
Precipitation: 24 inches **
Average Snowfall: 72 inches **
County: Boundary
Temperature Range – Fahrenheit: **

Spring: 29 to 69
Summer: 48 to 83
Fall: 29 to 72
Winter: 20 to 39
* U.S. Census Bureau Estimates July 2015
**Historical averages

All pictures in the Moyie Springs chapter courtesy of Drexel Love.

Moyie Springs, the northernmost city in Idaho, is located about eight miles northeast of Bonners Ferry and about 18 miles due south of the Canadian border.

The heavily wooded Kaniksu National Forest, with mountain peaks rising to nearly 7,000 feet, surrounds the city.

The 100-mile-long Moyie River that has its headwaters in British Columbia passes a half mile south of the city before combining with the Kootenai River that flows into British Columbia, Canada, eventually combining with the Columbia River as it enters into the United States in Eastern Washington.

Pre-Incorporation Years

In the early 1800s when European explorers/trappers came into what is now Northern Idaho, American Indians – primarily of the Kootenai Tribe – inhabited the land around what is now Moyie Springs. They had formerly lived on the plains east of the Rocky Mountains, but hostilities with the more numerous Blackfoot Indians caused them to move west. (*See Northern Idaho, The Region, American Indians*.)

Old Red Bridge.

From 1832 to 1850 trappers maintained a camp and trading post at the confluence of the Moyie and Kootenai Rivers near what is now Moyie Springs. (*See Northern Idaho, The Region, Early Trappers/Explorers*.)

The Treaty of 1846 between England and the United States established the boundary between the two countries at the 49th parallel. Non-Indian settlement in what is now Northern Idaho was limited until 1863 when prospectors discovered gold 120 miles north at Wild Horse Creek in British Columbia, Canada. The ensuing gold rush included thousands of fortune seekers coming up from the U.S. The road to the gold fields passed west of what is now Moyie Springs and led to the development of Bonners Ferry.

Edwin L. Bonner – a merchant and entrepreneur from Walla Walla, Washington – observed the large number of prospectors and fortune seekers crossing the treacherous Kootenai River and concluded that he would build a ferry and trading post at that location.

He acquired land on each side of the river from Chief Abraham of the Kootenai Tribe. He then persuaded the Idaho Territorial Legislature, meeting in Lewiston, to pass a law

First mill: the Fogerty Brothers.

granting him an exclusive five-year franchise to build and operate a ferry on a seven-mile stretch of river. The law, passed December 22, 1864, fixed the toll rates at $1.50 per loaded pack animal and 50 cents for a person on foot.

In 1875 Richard Fry, later joined by his brother, took over the ferry and trading post business from Bonner. Fry also ran a pack train carrying supplies from Walla Walla to the mining camps.

Around 1880 silver and lead were discovered in the mountains surrounding Kootenai Lake, 50 miles north in British Columbia. This discovery reinvigorated the traffic of men and materials to the mines, which put pressure for better transportation systems to be developed.

In 1882 the Northern Pacific Railroad reached the north shore of Lake Pend Oreille, about 30 miles south of Bonners Ferry. Freight wagons and stagecoaches then transported freight and passengers over a rough toll road between Kootenai and the ferry.

Moyie Cash Store and school bus.

In 1883 entrepreneurs began offering steamboat service up the Kootenai River between Bonners Ferry and Kootenai Lake in British Columbia. The steamboat dock at Bonners Ferry was on the south bank of the river. That same year, the owners of the land around the steamboat dock platted the Bonners Ferry townsite.

In 1892 the Great Northern Railroad reached Bonners Ferry. Several years later railroad interests extended two rail lines into British Columbia. One followed the Kootenai River and the other turned east at Bonners Ferry to what is now Moyie Springs then north paralleling the Moyie River. (*See Northern Idaho, The Region, Railroads.*)

The railroad company built a station near the confluence of the Moyie and Kootenai Rivers which they named Moyie Springs – attributed by early settlers to mean the "Clear Water" that came from the springs in Moyie.

With rail transportation available, the Fogarty Brothers built a sawmill and postal authorities approved the Moyie Springs Post Office in the 1920s. The Post Office was located in the Moyie Store until 1953 when a new building was built across from the store. That building still serves as the Moyie Springs Post Office.

Drawing of Moyie Store.

Incorporation

On June 4, 1947, Moyie Springs became an incorporated village, with all adult residents of the town signing the incorporation documents. Residents were motivated to incorporate because of a law passed by the Idaho Legislature in 1947 governing the sale of liquor by the drink and the licensure of establishments offering those beverages. A provision of the law required businesses selling alcoholic beverages to be located within incorporated cities or villages.

Following village incorporation, the Moyie Dance Hall became the Moyie Club with a license to serve alcohol. Moyie Springs changed its municipal legal status to a city in 1964.

Turning Points

Moyie Store, 1982.

Railroad The coming of the railroad in 1907 opened Moyie Springs for development as a city and the surrounding area for the development of the wood products industry.

Sawmills Commercial wood products businesses in the area started in Bonners Ferry in 1903 when the Weyerhaeuser Company built the Bonners Ferry Lumber Company. In 1926 the company consolidated certain of its sawmill operations in Lewiston and closed the Bonners Ferry mill.

The Fogarty Brothers – Moyie Springs – mill has changed hands many times since it was built in the 1920s including such owners as Scott French, Elton King, Moyie River Lumber Co., Georgia Pacific, Louisiana-Pacific and Riley Creek. Now Idaho Forest Group operates its mill on the same property.

Lumber mill.

In addition to the Fogarty Brothers' mill, there were several smaller wood product operations including the Tom Moore sawmill as well as pole and railroad tie mills. (*See Northern Idaho, The Region, Forest Products; Mining and Forest Products, the Decline of Two of Idaho's Signature Industries.*)

Municipal Water and Fire Protection Early travelers made it a point to stop at Moyie Springs and fill their wooden barrels and canteens with the crystal-clear water. In the early 1900s Benton R. Teer pumped Moyie Springs water to the side of his store, the Moyie Cash Store, and encouraged people to partake of the beautiful free water and stop in at his store. Eventually, the City of Moyie Springs acquired rights to the spring water and installed its own water system.

In 1989 the City of Moyie Springs started its Volunteer Fire Department. The department took its first major step to improve its efficiency when it purchased a 1961 Freightliner Fire Truck. Ken English was the first Fire Chief and continues to serve to the present time.

Moyie Springs Today

Amenities and Attractions Each summer, Moyie Springs conducts its annual clean up the town day where residents place the stuff they no longer want on the curb, and the City hauls it away for them.

Thirteen miles west of Moyie Springs is the Kootenai National Wildlife Refuge. This 2,774-acre wetland is an oasis for migrating waterfowl and habitat for other species of wildlife. It is a spectacular location for bird watching with several miles of walking paths.

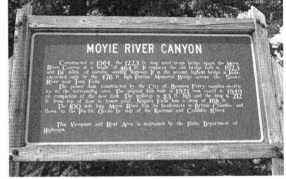

Wild Horse Scenic Byway is the trail used by the Kootenai Indians as they traveled from what is now British Columbia to their historic fishing grounds on Lake Pend Oreille and back. It starts in Sandpoint, passes through Bonners Ferry, and then north on U.S. Highway 95 to British Columbia. Thousands of prospectors and miners followed the same trail as they moved north to British Columbia and the "Wild Horse Creek" gold fields from 1863 to 1880.

The Kootenai Tribe of Idaho operates a motel, restaurant, casino and spa on its 12.5-acre Kootenai Indian Reservation overlooking the Kootenai River in Bonners Ferry. The tribe also operates a white sturgeon hatchery and turbot, flatfish, production program on the river. (*See Northern Idaho, The Region, American Indians – Present-day Reservations.*)

Near Moyie Dam

City residents enjoy the beauty of the surrounding mountains, lakes, rivers and streams. These amenities offer excellent opportunities for backpacking, hiking, boating, trail riding, fishing, hunting, snowmobiling, cross-country skiing and rafting on the Moyie River.

Downhill skiing is available at Schweitzer Mountain Resort, about 40 miles south. Over 300 miles of national forest trails extend deep into the mountains. In the spring, the nearby Moyie Falls offers a spectacular view of the wild river.

The Moyie Bridge was constructed in 1964. The 1,223-foot-long steel truss bridge spans the Moyie River Canyon at a height of 464 feet. It replaced the old bridge built in 1923 and one and a quarter miles of narrow, winding highway. It is Idaho's second tallest bridge – exceeded only by the 486-foot-high Perrine Memorial Bridge across the Snake River near Twin Falls.

The City of Bonners Ferry supplies electricity to the city of Moyie Springs from its hydroelectric dam on the Moyie River. The original dam was built in 1921 and replaced in 1949. It has a drop of 212 feet from the top of the dam to the lower pool, about 39-feet higher than the Horseshoe Falls drop at Niagara Falls.

The Idaho Highway Department maintains the viewpoint and rest area of the falls near Moyie Springs. The best viewing times are during the high runoff period in the spring and early summer. In addition, during daylight hours on weekends in June, July and August, the City bypasses flow around the hydroelectric dams to enhance the visual experience.

Economy and Major Employers Idaho Forest Group has over 100 employees and is the city's largest employer. Several smaller wood products companies, the Moyie Springs Store and the Moyie Club provide most of the other jobs in the city.

Education Boundary County School District provides most of the elementary and secondary education for the city's children. Younger children are transported by bus to Mount Hall Elementary and older children to the schools in Bonners Ferry. Four charter and private schools also operate in Bonners Ferry. The closest institution of higher education is North Idaho College, 85 miles south in Coeur d'Alene. North Idaho College also has a satellite campus in Bonners Ferry.

Health Care The closest hospital is the 62-bed Boundary County Community Hospital in Bonners Ferry.

Transportation U.S. Highway 2 passes near the city and intersects with U.S. Highway 95 to Bonners Ferry or British Columbia about six miles west of town.

Boundary County Airport, with its 4,000-foot runway, is located five miles west of town. The closest commercial air service is in Spokane, Washington.

Moyie Dam and falls

Railroad service for freight is available in the city.

Utilities and Services Private companies provide telephone and satellite services. The City provides water and sewer services and fire protection. The

County Sheriff provides police protection under contract with the City. The City of Bonners Ferry provides electricity from its hydroelectric facility.

Vision for 2050

In 1980 Moyie Springs had a population of 386. During the 1990s the city's population jumped from 415 in 1990 to 659 in 2000, an increase of 59 percent. Since 2000 the population has grown at a more moderate average rate of just over one percent annually. Recent historical trends will likely continue. By 2050 the city's population will approximate 1,200. Existing municipal systems – paid through existing revenue streams, user fees, grants and local improvement bonds approved by the voters – are adequate to manage moderate growth.

Mayors

1947 Loyd Hughes *	1967 Thelma Berger	1996 Joseph Mesenbrink
1949 William Clark *	1972 Travis Youngue	2008 Douglas Evans
1953 Thelma Berger *	1980 Ribert T. Pluid	* Village Chairman

Bridge across the Clearwater River.

CLEARWATER COUNTY

- Elk River
- Orofino (County Seat)
- Pierce
- Weippe

Elk River

Statistical Data

Population: 120 *
Elevation: 2,860 feet
Precipitation: 38 inches **
Average Snowfall: 111 inches **
County: Clearwater
Temperature Range – Fahrenheit: **

Spring: 25 to 63
Summer: 43 to 81
Fall: 26 to 71
Winter: 18 to 39
* U.S. Census Bureau Estimates July 2015
**Historical averages

Elk River is located deep in the pristine scenic backcountry of the Clearwater National Forest at the terminus of Idaho Highway 8. Bovill, the closest city, lies 13 miles to the northwest.

A dam on Elk Creek forms the historic Elk Creek Reservoir, the fishery and former millpond on the east edge of town. Six miles to the south, Elk Creek flows into Dworshak Reservoir at the Dworshak Dam Reservoir Recreation Area.

Pre-Incorporation Years

During the late 1800s sportsmen built a trail into the Elk Creek area. They used it as a rustic hunting and fishing resort.

In 1897 Willard Trumbell filed a homestead claim on the site of what is now the city of Elk River (not to be confused with the historic gold mining town of Elk City, an unincorporated community located in the Nez Perce National Forest about 75 miles due south of Elk River).

A few years later, a small group of homesteaders filed their claims about two miles to the west of Trumbell at Elk Creek Falls.

Beginning in 1900 Frederick Weyerhaeuser and associates began buying up timberland in the Clearwater Mountains east of Moscow. In 1903 Weyerhaeuser created the Potlatch Lumber Company (Potlatch). In the same year, Potlatch acquired a Lewiston sawmill. Weyerhaeuser also formed the Washington, Idaho and Montana Railway Company (WI&M).

In 1906 Potlatch surveyed the timberlands around Elk Creek, which at that time (prior to the 1972 construction of Dworshak Dam) drained into the North Fork of the Clearwater River. Loggers with crosscut saws harvested white pine logs that were skidded by horses and steam donkeys to the river's edge. During spring runoff, the North Fork of the Clearwater River became a waterway used to transport logs to the Lewiston sawmill.

Historic Elk River - note the boardwalk.

In 1907 the WI&M built a line from Palouse, Washington, to Bovill where it connected with the Chicago, Milwaukee and St. Paul Railroad nicknamed the Milwaukee Road. At that time, the Milwaukee Road's branch rail line from St. Maries to Elk River had reached Bovill.

In 1909 Potlatch purchased more than 4,000 acres of area timberland, including Trumbell's homestead.

In 1910, the same year the train arrived, Potlatch began building a millpond to hold the cut logs before processing; an electric powered sawmill, the first known electric powered sawmill in the nation; a planing mill; a dry shed; and a loading platform.

Potlatch changed the community name from Trumbell to Elk River, platted the town, hired hundreds of workers and began building the infrastructure and facilities for their new town.

The town soon grow to over 1,300 residents with hotels, general merchandise stores, hospital, other retail and service businesses, graded streets, waterworks and a boardwalk.

The first school was a tarpaper building located on Front Street. Residents also used the building as a church. Later, Potlatch helped build the first church building.

Incorporation

On October 15, 1910, Elk River had grown sufficiently that the Nez Perce County Commissioners in Lewiston approved the town's application to become an incorporated city.

On February 7, 1911, Elk River became part of the newly created Clearwater County, with the county seat at Orofino, 21 miles southwest.

Turning Points

Potlatch Elk River was a one-company sawmill town. Major Potlatch management decisions had a direct effect on the economic health and vitality of the city.

For nearly two decades, the company's Elk River operations and the city prospered. However, around 1927 Potlatch built a substantially larger wood products manufacturing facility in Lewiston, some of which were duplicative of its

Elk River operations. Potlatch management began to shift work from its Elk River facility to Lewiston.

At the same time, the economies of the nation and the world were going into decline. When the Great Depression hit in the early 1930s, its effects accelerated the closure of the company's Elk River facilities. In 1931 Potlatch shut down the sawmill; in 1933 the planing mill.

By 1933 most businesses had closed. Houses sold for as little as $15 and literally were moved out of town. The population quickly declined to around 400.

To top it off, beginning around 1929, blister rust attacked the white pine trees reducing the sustainable supply of good timber and giving the forest a patchwork look of green and dieing rust-brown trees.

Elk River scenic byway.

In 1936 Potlatch sold its remaining property to the City for a nominal amount. This property included the public water and light systems.

Railroad While ownership of the railroad was independent of Potlatch, its economic fortunes were not. Closure of the railroad coincided with closure of the mills.

Adapting to a New Economy Change in federal forest management policies and environmental litigation has largely shut down federally managed public land to logging. The wood products industry is a shadow of what it was in the mid 1900s and will not likely return.

However, the natural beauty of the greater Elk River area is impressive. City and community leaders are achieving success in promoting these natural amenities and attractions to tourists and outdoor enthusiasts.

Elk River Today

Amenities and Attractions Elk River has two city parks comprising eight acres. The parks have tennis and basketball courts and children's playgrounds.

The city has a library and a museum, the Elk River Historical Society Museum, that has exhibits and artifacts of the city's early history.

There are several campgrounds in the area including the Elk River Recreation District's 64 campground sites around Elk Creek Reservoir. Huckleberry Haven RV Park and the Forest Service offer several full hookups at their campgrounds. Tent campsites are also available.

The Idaho Department of Transportation's 57-mile-long Elk River Back Country Scenic Byway passes through the city. The Byway connects Orofino, Elk

River and Bovill. At Orofino, the byway road climbs up Wells Bench then down to Dworshak Reservoir where it crosses over the reservoir on a suspension bridge named Dent Bridge. The gravel road then winds on to Elk River, where it joins Idaho Highway 8 to Bovill. Travelers often see wildlife of all kinds along this scenic backcountry byway.

Elk Creek Falls is a popular tourist attraction with a parking lot and a walking path through the forest to the falls. The falls is where Elk Creek cascades, pools, then cascades again as it tumbles about 300 feet down the mountain.

Elk River is at the center of breathtaking natural amenities. Elk Creek Reservoir borders the town, while Elk Creek Falls is two miles away. An interpretive trail following the old wagon road between Elk River and Orofino leads to Elk Creek Falls. Three falls cascade over ancient lava flows creating one of Idaho's most picturesque waterfalls.

The reservoir is popular for its fishing and for the swans, ospreys, bald eagles and otters that frequent the area.

Fireworks.

Elk Butte rises to an elevation of 5,824 feet. Accessible on an unimproved road, it is located about five miles northeast of the city and offers a stunning view into two national forests and the Bitterroot Mountains.

Just outside Elk River on Forest Service Road 382 are Perkins Cedar Grove and the oldest and largest tree in Idaho. This tree, a western red cedar, is 177 feet tall and 18 feet in diameter.

The Elk River backcountry has over 300 miles of trails. In the winter months, cross-country skiers and snowmobiles use the trails. In the warmer months, anglers and hunters ride their ATVs to their favorite spots.

Sightseers come just to enjoy nature – to get a glimpse of the elk, deer, moose, bear, bobcat, cougars, grouse, hawks, osprey, mink, pine martin, muskrat, otter, songbirds, wild turkey and other wild species prevalent in the forests. Other visitors come in the spring to pick mushrooms and in the fall to pick huckleberries.

The 850-acre Dworshak State Park is located about 15 miles due southwest from the city, about 40 miles by road.

The entire Dworshak Recreation Area is an exceptional location for boating, fishing, camping, recreational vehicles, swimming, water skiing, hunting, hiking, ATV and snowmobile riding and wildlife viewing.

The Dworshak National Fish Hatchery, located at the confluence of the North Fork and the main Clearwater Rivers near Orofino, captures steelhead trout and Chinook salmon that are returning to spawn. The hatchery spawns the fish and raises them until they are large enough to start their migration to the Pacific Ocean.

Economy and Major Employers A tree nursery, Northwoods, has about 20 employees and is the city's largest employer. The balance of the workforce is primarily employed by the retail businesses serving the tourists and outdoor enthusiasts that come into town.

Education White Pine School District provides elementary and secondary education for Elk River students. Elementary school students attend in Bovill. Secondary students attend school in Deary.

Lewis-Clark State College has a satellite office in Orofino. The closest institution of higher learning is the University of Idaho 54 miles away in Moscow and Lewis-Clark State College 75 miles away in Lewiston.

Health Care The 17-bed Clearwater Valley Hospital in Orofino is the closest medical facility.

Transportation Elk River is located on the Elk River Back Country Scenic Byway at the terminus of Idaho Highway 8.

Elk River airport, completed in 1945, has a 3,000-foot runway used by light private and charter aircraft. The closest commercial airport is the Pullman-Moscow Regional Airport.

Utilities and Services Private companies provide electricity, telephone, cable and satellite services. The homes and businesses in the city have individual sewer and water. The City provides police and fire protection.

Vision for 2050

Following closure of the Potlatch Mill in 1933, the city's population held at around 400. Around 1970, it started on a gradual decline until in 1991 it hit a low of 131. Since that time the city's population has held in a narrow range.

The number of tourists and visitors to Elk River is increasing. We expect this trend to continue as more people come to experience the many beautiful outdoor amenities available around the city. This increasing demand for services can be handled by existing businesses for many years.

Mayors

1912 Andrew Bloom *
1924 Carl Jockheak *
1933 W.T. Marinrau *
1935 Oscar Torgerson *
1936 Axel Anderson *
1947 Frank Currier *
1957 J.E. Hall *

1965 James J. Bakos *
1971 Gene Rouleau
1974 Everet Lovell
1977 Richard Coomer
1978 Jean Dahlky
1982 Bernadine Nordin
1984 James Martin

1992 Tom Tillson
1996 Della Kreisher
2000 James Martin
2008 Mike Walk
2009 John Greenway
2014 James Martin
* Village Chairman

Bridge over the Clearwater into Orofino.

Orofino

Statistical Data

Population: 3,096 *
Elevation: 1,020 feet
Precipitation: 25 inches **
Average Snowfall: 112 inches **
County: Clearwater
Temperature Range – Fahrenheit: **

Spring: 32 to 72
Summer: 50 to 90
Fall: 31 to 79
Winter: 25 to 46
* U.S. Census Bureau Estimates July 2015
**Historical averages

The city of Orofino lies at the confluence of Orofino Creek and the Clearwater River. The city's downtown area lies in a prehistoric forested valley cut by Orofino Creek. The Clearwater River and Highway 12 pass on the southern edge of the city.

Four miles west of the city on the banks of the Clearwater River is the historic Lewis and Clark Canoe Camp. On October 7, 1805, the Lewis and Clark Corps of Discovery, assisted by Nez Perce Indians, completed five large log-hewn canoes used to transport the 33-member party to the Pacific Ocean. (*See Northern Idaho, Lewis and Clark.*)

Three miles over the mountains on the North Fork of the Clearwater River is Dworshak Dam and Recreation Area with its stunningly beautiful reservoir extending 54 miles northeast into the heavily wooded Clearwater National Forest.

The city lies in the northeast corner of the Nez Perce Indian Reservation. The Idaho Correctional Institution-Orofino and State Hospital North are adjacent to the city.

Pre-Incorporation Years

In September 1805 as they emerged cold and starving from the terrible ordeal of crossing the deep snows of the rugged Bitterroot Mountains, the Lewis and Clark Corps of Discovery first encountered the Nez Perce. The Nez Perce were gathering camas bulbs on the Weippe Prairie 15 miles southeast of what is now Orofino.

Nez Perce family camp.

Lewis and Clark stayed with the Nez Perce for several days to recuperate and complete construction of their canoes. They also stayed with the Nez Perce the following year on their return trip to make a report of their expedition to President Thomas Jefferson and Congress.

In 1811 European trappers/explorers began coming into the region. In 1836 Henry and Eliza Spaulding opened their mission to the Nez Perce near what is now Lapwai about 30 miles west of Orofino. In 1838 Asa B. Smith, another Presbyterian missionary, set up an unsuccessful mission to convert the Nez Perce 40 miles south near what is now Kamiah.

Orofino, 1904.

In 1860 Elias Davidson Pierce and a small party of prospectors discovered gold on Nez Perce 1855 Treaty reservation land 22 miles due east of what is now Orofino. The Nez Perce had denied Pierce permission to prospect on their land. However, Pierce's party slipped in anyway and made their discovery. Wilber F. Basset, a member of Pierce's party working on what is now Orofino Creek, dug up a shovelful of sediments that contained small particles of gold called "oro fino," Spanish words for fine gold.

What followed was Idaho's first gold rush. By 1861 about 3,000 miners converged on the area. The Nez Perce were largely powerless to keep the large numbers of prospectors off their reservation. The miners started a boomtown about two miles from the city of Pierce that they named Oro Fino. They also organized the Oro Fino Mining District.

In 1877 the U.S. Bureau of Indian Affairs ordered the Nez Perce, many of whom were at that time in the Wallowa Valley in Washington and friendly to the whites, to move to the Lapwai Reservation in Idaho. Several young Nez Perce warriors were incensed and went against the direction of their chiefs, attacking some white settlements and killing many settlers.

General O.O. Howard interpreted this action as a general revolt and ordered his military to attack the Nez Perce Tribes. What ensued was a running battle where the U.S. Army chased the Nez Perce Tribes of Chiefs Joseph and White Bird to Montana near the Canadian border. White Bird's band escaped across the border but the army captured Joseph's band before they could follow. Several years later, the federal government allowed the remaining Nez Perce to return to their reservation. (*See Northern Idaho – Nez Perce War*.)

Riverside is an important part of Orofino. It is on the south side of the Clearwater River and stretches down river about 4 miles. This shows Riverside in the early days; and the town of Ahsahka. Courtesy Clearwater Historical Museum.

On February 8, 1887, the U.S. Congress passed the Dawes Severalty Act. (*See Northern Idaho – Dawes Severalty Act.*) The Act authorized the survey of American Indian Reservation lands and allotted specific acreages, generally 160 acres per head of household, to tribal members. The Act

Ferry crossing the Clearwater River at Orofino, 1911. Courtesy Clearwater Historical Museum.

specified that land not so allocated be deemed surplus and made available for homesteading. In 1935 Congress repealed the law. However, by that time, a large part of former reservation lands were in the hands of non-Indians.

On November 18, 1895, former Nez Perce Reservation land became open for settlement. At that time, an estimated 5,000 settlers were poised to participate in the land rush allowed by the Dawes Act.

Clifford C. Fuller filed a homestead claim on land where Orofino now stands. Fuller platted a portion of his homestead and set up a trading post. The plat's north boundary was near what is now First Street, where City Hall is located, and ran south to what is known as Canada Hill.

Fuller then organized the Clearwater Improvement Company to sell the lots in the town that he named "Oro Fino."

On May 1, 1897, Fuller was successful in moving the post office from Gilbert, a town located four miles to the south, to his new town. However, postal authorities objected to the two-word name and combined the words into "Orofino."

In 1898 the Northern Pacific Railroad completed its rail line from Lewiston to Orofino and nearby sawmills. The railroad had a major impact in opening the area for settlement and developing its timber resources.

Incorporation

By 1905 Orofino became an incorporated village. By that time, it had a population of 207. In 1906 a major fire destroyed many of the city's buildings. However, residents moved to rebuild their town.

Orofino in 1911, the year Clearwater County was founded and Orofino became its county seat. Far to the left is the State Hospital for the Insane,then Jingle Town and downtown Orofino. The Riverside area is out of view. Courtesy Clearwater Historical Museum.

Turning Points

Dawes Severalty Act The Nez Perce Indian Reservation trust lands now encompass 1,195,102 square miles of land located in parts of Lewis, Nez Perce, Idaho and Clearwater Counties. Orofino owes its existence to the passage of the Dawes Severalty Act. The Act not only induced broad-based settlement by non-Indians, but it allowed Clifford C. Fuller to file a homestead claim that became the village of Orofino.

Railroad and Sawmills In 1898 the Northern Pacific Railroad reached Orofino. The railroad had a major impact in opening the area for settlement and developing its timber resources. Local wood products companies have continued to be an important source of jobs for Orofino residents.

Clearwater County Seat By 1910 the village of Orofino had a population of 384 and was growing rapidly. On February 27, 1911, the Idaho Legislature created

Fishing on Orofino Creek, off Main Street in 1908. Courtesy Clearwater Historical Museum.

Clearwater County with Orofino as the county seat. This action was important to the new village as it established a relatively small but stable employment base and gave prestige to the city as the seat of local government.

By 1918 Orofino's population increased to approximately 800 with a business district that included two banks, two sawmills, a brickyard, lime kilns, electric light and waterworks, two weekly newspapers, several churches, an active commercial club and public schools.

Today, about 40 percent of the county's population resides in the city.

Clearwater National Forest Headquarters On July 1, 1908, the U.S. Forest Service established the Clearwater National Forest with headquarters in Orofino. The new national forest comprised nearly 2.7 million acres from a division of two other national forests. The Forest Service has since remained one of Orofino's largest employers.

First patients and employees, state hospital, 1905.

State Facilities The 1904 Idaho Legislature appropriated funds to build a second Idaho hospital for the mentally ill in Orofino. The hospital – State Hospital North – was to relieve the overcrowded conditions at State Hospital South in Blackfoot and allow patients with families living in Northern Idaho to be closer to their loved ones. Hospital construction began in 1905 with hospital patients providing some of the labor.

Following completion of the new facility, the Idaho Department of Corrections converted the old mental health building into a prison. In 1988 the Department added a new wing. Today, the facility is a standard adult prison designed for male offenders of all custody levels including protective custody, inmate work programs, schooling and counseling.

Operation of these state facilities provides over 200 direct jobs as well as contract employment for many Orofino businesses.

Park by the river

Orofino Today

Amenities and Attractions The city has two city parks comprising 14 acres and one golf course. The parks have picnic and children's play areas and athletic fields. The Clearwater Historical Museum has many artifacts and memorabilia relating to the early life of the region and the city.

The community sponsors annual events that include the "All American Fourth of July" and the three-day Christmas Festival held the first week of December.

Dworshak Dam, Reservoir and Recreation Area is one of Idaho's preeminent areas for outdoor sports and family recreation. Named after Henry Dworshak – a former U. S. Senator from Idaho, who served from 1946 to 1962 – the 400,000-kilowatt hydroelectric dam completed in 1973 is 717 feet high and 3,300 feet long. The reservoir area totals 16,000 acres.

The 850-acre Dworshak State Park is located 24 miles north of the city among the trees and meadows of the reservoir's western shore.

The Idaho Transportation Department's 57-mile Elk River Back Country Byway between Orofino and Elk River offers travelers a memorable

Orofino, 1920

opportunity. The road starts at Orofino and is a no-frills pathway cutting north through the Clearwater Forest, across the Dworshak Reservoir at Dent Bridge and on to Elk River, State Highway 8 and Bovill.

The Dworshak National Fish Hatchery and visitors' center, located at the confluence of the North Fork and the main Clearwater Rivers, captures steelhead trout and Chinook salmon that are returning to spawn. The hatchery spawns the fish and raises them until they are large enough to start their migration to the Pacific Ocean.

The entire Dworshak Recreation Area is an exceptional location for boating, fishing, camping, recreational vehicles, swimming, water skiing, hunting, hiking, ATV and snowmobile riding and wildlife viewing. In spite of its spectacular beauty, this amenity does not receive extensive public use. Local citizens refer to Dworshak Reservoir and Recreation Area as the best-kept secret in the Northwest.

The Nez Perce National Historic Park, managed by the National Parks Service and partially staffed by tribal members, is in Spaulding, 40 miles west on Highway 12. Highway 12 from Lewiston to the Lolo Pass Visitors' Center near the Idaho/Montana border is designated the Northwest Passage National Scenic Byway. The 202-mile byway intersects several parts of the Lewis and Clark trail that passes through Idaho.

The historic Lewis and Clark Canoe Camp is now a state historic site.

Economy and Major Employers The Orofino School District and the Clearwater National Forest have well over 200 employees each and are the city's largest employers. The Idaho Department of Health and Welfare, State Hospital North; Clearwater Valley Hospital; Potlatch Corporation, wood products; and the Idaho Department of Corrections employ well over 100 each. Konkolville Lumber Company and Clearwater Health and Rehabilitation – physical, occupational and speech therapies – have around 75 employees each. The city's downtown business district includes retail, lodging, financial and service businesses.

Education The Orofino School District provides most of the elementary and secondary education for the city and nearby communities. The closest institution of higher learning is Lewis-Clark State College 46 miles west in Lewiston.

Health Care The 17-bed Clearwater Valley Hospital in Orofino and several medical clinics provide for most of the city's healthcare needs.

Orofino, January 1969, looking down Johnson Avenue. Courtesy Clearwater Historical Museum.

Transportation U. S. Highway 12 and State Highway 7 intersect the city.

The 2,500-foot runway at Orofino Municipal Airport serves light private and charter aircraft. The closest commercial airport is in Lewiston.

Railroad service is available for freight.

Utilities and Services Private companies provide electricity, telephone, cable, satellite and natural gas. The City provides water and sewer services and fire and police protection. The County provides solid waste services.

Vision for 2050

For most of the past five decades, Orofino's population has averaged around 3,000. By 2050 employers that presently underpin the city's economy will still play that dominant role. However, by that time the city will have a vibrant segment of its business community serving outdoor recreationists and tourists and the city's population will exceed 4,000.

The city will promote its most prominent amenity, the Dworshak Reservoir and Recreation Area.

Our schools will be providing additional high quality educational opportunities through distance learning and through local programs for both youth and adults.

The city will promote heritage and cultural attractions, and specialized events that people will equate with "Orofino."

Orofino will have all updated infrastructure from improved roads and water and sewer lines to state-of-the-art communication technology while supporting the small town atmosphere to which many people want to escape.

By 2050 Orofino will be a relatively small but premiere resort city whose lifestyle and environment will be revered throughout the Northwest.

Mayors

1906 James Fairley *
1912 Samson Snyder
1914 K.G. Osterhout
1914 J.G. Bullock
1915 Frank Zelenka
1917 A.E. Holmberg
1918 F.A. Jones
1921 N.O. Helgeson
1925 H.R. "Bob" Snider
1931 Fred Luttropp
1943 E.K. Fuller

1947 C.O. Portfors
1951 A.B. Curtis
1974 H.L. "Roy" Clay
1982 Helen Hight
1986 H.L. "Roy" Clay
1990 Paul Decelle
1991 Wayne Shriver
1994 H.L. "Roy" Clay
2000 Joe Pippinger
2008 Ryan Smathers
* Village Chairman

J. Howard Bradbury Memorial Logging Museum, Pierce

Pierce

Statistical Data

Population: 490 *
Elevation: 3,241 feet
Precipitation: 41 inches **
Average Snowfall: 118 inches **
County: Clearwater
Temperature Range – Fahrenheit: **

Spring: 38 to 62
Summer: 51 to 85
Fall: 38 to 60
Winter: 26 to 39
* U.S. Census Bureau Estimates July 2015
**Historical averages

Pierce is nestled deep in the heavily wooded and beautiful Clearwater National Forest, 32 miles east of Orofino. The 4,800-foot-high Bald Mountain Ski Area lays 10 miles north.

Pierce is the location of Idaho's historic first gold rush that in the latter part of 1861 created a population surge of around 6,000 fortune seekers. The gold rush caused a chain of events that profoundly influenced the history of what are now Washington, Idaho and western Montana.

Pre-Incorporation Years

The nomadic Nez Perce Indians inhabited the area when the Lewis and Clark Corps of Discovery first encountered them on the Weippe Prairie in 1805 about 10 miles south of what is now Pierce. (*See Northern Idaho – Lewis and Clark.*)

In 1836 Henry and Eliza Spaulding, Presbyterian missionaries, set up a mission among the Nez Perce near what is now Lapwai where they were successful in converting many to Christianity. (*See Northern Idaho – Early Christian Missionaries.*)

Except for a few trappers and traders, little changed in the Pierce area until 1860 when E.D. Pierce – a former U.S. Army Captain commissioned in the Mexican War, California Gold Rush prospector and later a Hudson's Bay Company trader in Nez Perce country – heard stories of gold showing in the streams flowing through the tribal reservation created by the U.S. Government and the Nez Perce in the Treaty of 1855. He asked Spalding convert and Nez Perce Chief Timothy if his party could prospect for gold on reservation land. Chief Timothy refused. However, Pierce would not accept no for an answer.

A prevailing, albeit disputed, legend is that Pierce persuaded Nez Perce Chief Timothy's 18-year-old daughter Jane to lead his band through the mountains to the promising locations. On September 30, 1860, they dug near a streambed located on Canal Creek one mile north of what is now Pierce. There they found "flour gold" called "oro fino" in Spanish for "fine gold."

Greer Ferry.

Pierce immediately returned to Fort Walla Walla carrying gold dust. There he recruited additional prospectors willing to brave possible armed conflict with the Nez Perce and immediately returned to stake their mining claims.

In November 1860 the larger group of prospectors arrived at the gold fields and staked 71 claims, built sluice boxes for washing gold from the soils, constructed cabins and worked their claims. On December 3, 1860, they founded Pierce City, named after E.D. Pierce.

On January 5, 1861, the prospectors developed an organizational structure similar to that used in other frontier gold rushes by forming a mining district they called Oro Fino, approved a jurisprudence organization with rules of conduct and ownership of claims.

Shoshone County Courthouse.

By June 1 there were about 3,000 persons living in the Pierce area with hundreds more on the way. However, receiving no oversight from the Washington Territorial Capital in Olympia and needing better organization to manage the activities of the new community, the prospectors took matters into their own hands. They held a mass meeting where they voted to create

Shoshone County and elect county officials with Pierce City as the county seat. Shoshone County was formally created by the Washington Territorial Legislature on February 4, 1864, with Pierce as the county seat. They also built a two-story log courthouse that still stands as one of Idaho's oldest public buildings.

Through all of this, the outnumbered Nez Perce were powerless to stop the dramatic population surge that was taking place on their reservation.

The Pierce gold rush not only led to the founding of the city, but it also was the catalyst influencing important political changes in the Northwest.

It was the impetus leading to the founding of Lewiston. Many of the Pierce prospectors came from San Francisco. Beginning in 1860 they traveled north by steamship, then up the Columbia and Snake Rivers to a landing on Nez Perce Reservation land (1855 treaty) at the confluence of the Snake and Clearwater Rivers. Local merchants and settlers in the booming tent city named the landing Lewiston.

Wannigan at Elk Berry Creek.

In 1863 the U.S. government imposed a new treaty on the Nez Perce that superseded the 1855 treaty. In the new treaty, the Nez Perce ceded significant portions of 1855 treaty reservation land, including the land around Pierce and Lewiston, to the federal government. However, Congress did not ratify the 1863 treaty until 1867. Technically the 1855 Treaty was legally in effect until that date. The prospectors and settlers overlooked the technicality and immediately began conducting real estate and other business as though the 1863 treaty was in effect.

The gold rush shifted the territorial population to Pierce. In 1861 the number of ballots cast in the new Shoshone County was greater than any other part of Washington Territory. This population shift forced the hand of Puget Sound interests seeking to keep Olympia as the territorial capital to petition Congress to

Potlatch Forests, Inc., Camp "C" flume in the 1930s.

divide the territory separating the more populous Northern Idaho from Washington. On March 4, 1863, President Abraham Lincoln signed the Organic Act creating Idaho Territory and leaving Washington Territory with boundaries that would remain through its statehood.

As the gold mines began to play out, Pierce prospectors began to fan out for hundreds of miles looking for gold. Certain of these prospectors would go south 60 miles and make discoveries in Elk City. Others went further south to find gold on the Salmon River at Florence.

Some of the Florence prospectors would go further south to find large quantities of gold in the Boise Basin, prompting a gold rush that would lead the Idaho Territorial Legislature meeting in the provisional capital at Lewiston to select Boise as Idaho's permanent capital city.

Other Pierce prospectors would travel east to make major gold discoveries in what is now western Montana. These discoveries prompted railroad interests to build a line from Utah to the Montana gold fields, which, in turn, opened up much

The old Bradbury Memorial Logging Museum.

of Eastern Idaho for settlement.

By 1863 the Pierce area mines had played out and most of the original prospectors had moved on. However, as was often the case in other gold rushes, Chinese miners – who were more meticulous in their mining methodologies and had a lower profit threshold – came in and began working the abandoned claims.

In the 1890s C.D. and Nat Brown, father and son, surveyed the area's timber and were impressed with the large stands of white pine, cedar and other coniferous trees. Congress had passed the Homestead Act in 1862 wherein citizens could receive 160 acres of federal land if they improved the property and lived on it for five years. Many lumber families living in the timber depleted Great Lakes region of the United States moved west. Many of them established homestead claims in the Pierce area and began harvesting the timber.

In 1899 railroad service came to Orofino. In 1925 the railroad extended a line to Pierce. The railroad greatly facilitated the logging and wood products businesses near Pierce.

Incorporation

Although gold miners founded Pierce City on December 3, 1860, and a few months later made the town the county seat of Shoshone County, Pierce did not become an incorporated city until May 17, 1935.

Turning Points

Gold The city of Pierce owes its existence and name to E.D. Pierce and the prospectors that followed him in 1860 to discover and mine for gold.

Timber and Wood Products While gold mining got the city started, the vast surrounding forests of timber and sawmills sustained it. Large logging and milling operations began in 1910.

In 1965 Potlatch constructed its Jaype Plywood plant near Pierce. The plant hired hundreds of workers and was a major economic stimulus to the city. By 1970 the city's population more than doubled to 1,218. The community prospered for nearly three decades until, in 2000, market conditions and change in federal policy restricting timber harvests off federal lands caused Potlatch to close the mill. (*See Northern Idaho – Mining and Forest Products – Effect of Federal Environmental Laws.*) By 2000 the city's population had fallen to 617.

Pierce Today

Amenities and Attractions Pierce has three city parks on 14 acres.

The J. Howard Bradbury Memorial Logging Museum is located in the downtown area. It has many exhibits and artifacts relating to the city's gold mining and logging days.

The historic Shoshone County Courthouse is located behind the museum.

Located on the north end of Main Street is a kiosk that displays

Kiosk on Main Street.

information about local events and attractions as well as exhibits from local artists.

There are many historic mining ruins in and around Pierce including walls made from quartz, remnants of ditches, dams and hydrological erosion that illustrate the techniques used by the old-time miners to extract placer gold from the soils.

Fourteen miles south of the city near Weippe is the National Park Service's Weippe Prairie National Historic Landmark where two trails lead to Lewis and Clark's two campsites – Pleasant Camp and Small Prairie Camp.

About nine miles south of Pierce on the U.S. Forest Service's Browns Creek Road is Musselshell Meadows, the last active spot where the Nez Perce come to gather camas lily bulbs.

The backwaters of Dworshak Reservoir on the North Fork of the Clearwater River are located a about 11 miles northwest of Pierce. Dworshak State Park, 34 miles away, and the Dworshak Recreation Area lie northwest in the Clearwater National Forest.

This Dworshak Recreation Area, reservoir and state park – including the forest lands near Pierce – are exceptional locations for boating, trout fishing, camping, recreational vehicles, swimming, water skiing, big game and turkey hunting, hiking, ATV riding on hundreds of miles of abandoned logging roads and snowmobile riding. In addition to ATV parks, the U.S. Forest Service maintains Walker Park about 10 miles north near Headquarters where there are stands of white pine and red cedar trees 10 to 15 feet in diameter and 200 feet high.

Economy and Major Employers Pierce's economy is heavily dependent on the wood products industry. Several logging and trucking companies, many located at Headquarters, contract with Potlatch Land Corporation to harvest and deliver timber to its Lewiston Mill. Many of its employees live in Pierce.

The Orofino School District is the city's largest public employer. The U.S. Forest Service Work Center in Pierce and the City employ a small number of residents.

The city's downtown area includes a home-health business, the post office, a library, a grocery store, a hardware store, a mercantile, restaurants, bars, an auto parts store and a credit union.

Education The Orofino School District provides most of the K-12 education. K-6 students attend elementary school in Pierce. Junior and senior high school students

Log church.

attend Timberline High School, located halfway between Weippe and Pierce.

The closest institution of higher learning is Lewis-Clark State College (LCSC), located 83 miles west in Lewiston. LCSC also provides night classes in welding and metal fabrication 24 miles south at Kamiah High School.

Health Care The Pierce Pioneer Clinic is a satellite to the 17-bed Clearwater Valley Hospital in Orofino. The clinic provides most of the city's emergency and routine medical care.

Transportation State Highway 11, the Gold Rush Byway that ends at Pierce, is the city's Main Street as it passes through town. U.S. Highway 12 is 30 miles west.

Orofino Municipal Airport's 2,500-foot runway provides air service for light private and commercial aircraft. The Lewiston-Nez Perce County Airport provides commercial airport services.

Utilities and Services Private companies provide electricity, telephone, Wi-Fi Internet and satellite services. The City provides water, sewer, garbage collection and street maintenance services. The Clearwater Sheriff's Office provides police protection The Pierce Rural Volunteer Fire Department provides fire protection services. The County provides EMS services.

Vision for 2050

Since the permanent closure of the Potlatch Jaype Plywood plant in 2000, the city's population has stabilized at just over 500. The city's current economy will likely hold or have moderate growth for many years. The city's existing systems are adequate to handle such growth.

The city seeks to promote entrepreneurship that leverages the area's marvelous natural resources. City leaders want an economy built on the city's heritage and the peaceful and

healthy way of life provided by beautiful national forest surroundings.

Within the next several years, the community will complete the interpretive trail that highlights historic mining sites. By 2050 the much shorter Grangemont Road to Orofino will be improved as an alternative to the more difficult Highway 11 - Greer Grade route.

Mayors

1935 Jacob Gisel	1968 X.E. Durant	2004 Wallace Williams
1938 H.C. Snyder	1978 Robert K. Duffy	2008 Greg Gerot
1939 Chris Johnson	1982 Dan Swan	2012 Carmen Syed
1955 X.E. Durant	1986 Ray Alfrey	2016 Trevor Sparrow
1966 Robert Richel	1990 Robert Brown	

Weippe

Statistical Data

Population: 411 *
Elevation: 3,020 feet
Precipitation: 42 inches **
Average Snowfall: 110 inches **
County: Clearwater
Website: www.weippe.com

Temperature Range – Fahrenheit: **
Spring: 23 to 64
Summer: 41 to 84
Fall: 24 to 72
Winter: 15 to 38
* U.S. Census Bureau Estimates July 2015
**Historical averages

The city of Weippe (pronounced wee-ipe) lies in the Weippe Prairie – made famous as the location where, in 1805, the Lewis and Clark Corps of Discovery first encountered the Nez Perce Indians.

The Clearwater National Forest, including large acreages of state-owned lands, largely surrounds the city and prairie. The Clearwater River lies 12 miles due west of Weippe and about 2,000 feet below the Weippe Prairie plateau. The Nez Perce Indian Reservation begins a few miles due west. Orofino is 27 miles northwest.

Today fertile farms with fields of hay, pasture and some grain now grow on land that previously grew meadow grasses and camas lilies interspersed with forests of pine and fir. Heavily wooded mountains of pine and fir surround the valley.

Pre-Incorporation Years

The Nez Perce were the principal inhabitants of the region when, on September 20, 1805, Clark led the advance party of the Lewis and Clark Corps of Discovery into the Weippe Prairie. Lewis and the main party arrived two days later. At that time, the nomadic Nez Perce

Early Weippe

were at their ancestral encampment on the prairie they named Weippe where expansive fields of camas lily grew.

At these encampments, Indian women dug large quantities of the camas roots from the ground. To prepare the bulbs to eat, they washed and crushed them to make a kind of bread or cake.

When the Lewis and Clark expedition emerged from their several day trip crossing the deep early snows of the rugged Bitterroot and Clearwater Mountain wilderness, they were starving and tired. Early in their trip, Clark stood atop one of the Bitterroot Mountain peaks and said, "from this mountain, I could observe high rugged mountains in every direction as far as the eye could see."

Clark's party met one of the Nez Perce Tribes encamped on the 15-square-mile prairie. He gave the Nez Perce gifts to show their peaceful intentions. The Nez Perce accepted the gifts and gave them food, including dried salmon and camas lily cake. The ravenous travelers

Cardiff mill

gorged themselves on the unfamiliar food and became violently ill.

In their weakened state, some of the Nez Perce considered killing the explorers for their weapons. However, one of the Nez Perce women dissuaded them.

Blackfoot Indians captured the woman several years earlier, took her to Canada and sold her to a white trader. She lived among the white traders before somehow finding her way back home. The white traders apparently treated her much better than the Blackfoot. When Clark and his small band arrived and were in their weakened condition, she told the warriors, "These are the people who helped me. Do them no hurt."

When Lewis and the balance of the expedition staggered out of the mountains, the Nez Perce also provided them with food. They were so hungry, they disregarded Clark's warning and overate. They became so sick, the Corps had to camp on the Weippe Prairie several more days before they could move on to their "Canoe Camp" on the

Chapin Mill Pond

banks of the Clearwater River. At Canoe Camp near what is now Orofino, the Nez Perce assisted them in making five dugout canoes that transported them to the Pacific Ocean.

In June 1806 on the Corps' return trip, they again stayed on the Weippe Prairie where the camas lily was in bloom. Lewis wrote, "The Quawmash (prairie) is now in [bloom] and from the [color] of its bloom at a short distance it resembles lakes of fine clear water."

In 1811 European trappers/explorers began coming into the area. In 1836 Henry and Eliza Spaulding, opened their mission to the Nez Perce near what is now Lapwai.

In 1860 Elias Davidson Pierce and a small party of

Weippe hilltop.

prospectors discovered gold on Nez Perce Reservation land 12 miles northeast of what is now Weippe. By 1861 about 3,000 prospectors converged on the area with more following. The Nez Perce Indians tried to prevent the migration but were outnumbered and unable, absent war, to stop the invasion of prospectors and miners.

The main packhorse and wagon trail to the gold fields was through Weippe. Settlers started farming and raising livestock and crops on the Weippe Prairie to sell to the gold miners.

Wellington Langdon was one of the settlers who began farming and raising cattle and hogs to feed the miners. He also traded with the Nez Perce who treated him as a friend.

However, the flood of white immigrants moving on to the fertile lands where the Nez Perce used to camp and hunt was infuriating the Indians. The matter came to a head in 1875. Many of the Nez Perce were on their reservation at Wallowa in southeastern Washington. Seeking to accommodate the influx of non-Indian settlers into the area, Congress passed law eliminating the reservation and making it part of the public domain.

In 1877 the U.S. Bureau of Indian Affairs ordered the Nez Perce to leave Wallowa and move to the Lapwai Reservation in Idaho. The leadership of the Nez Perce felt wronged but resigned to move as directed. Incensed with the order, however, on June 14 several young Nez Perce warriors went against the direction of their chiefs, attacking nearby white settlements and killing many.

Hutchins and Timberline Lumber.

Nez Perce Chiefs Joseph and White Bird were fearful of what would follow. They moved their people to the base of White Bird Canyon 12 miles southwest of Grangeville.

General O.O. Howard interpreted the raids as a general revolt and ordered his military to attack the Nez Perce Tribes. Two cavalry companies and a force of volunteers discovered the Nez Perce at White Bird Canyon.

The Nez Perce sent messengers under a flag of truce; however, some of the emotionally charged volunteers opened fire. What ensued was the Battle of White Bird Canyon. The battle was a decisive victory for the Nez Perce who inflicted heavy losses but sustained none.

Chiefs Joseph and White Bird knew their bands of a few hundred warriors along with their women

and children were no match against the U.S. Army. They started a tortuous trek to Montana. Their odyssey took them through the Weippe Prairie where they passed by Wellington Langdon's farm.

Langdon was working on his farm when he said that he saw 800 to 1,000 Indians and 2,000 to 3,000 horses coming across the Weippe Prairie. He took refuge in his pigsty and completely covered his body with pig manure. The Nez Perce passed him by.

The U.S. Army chased the Nez Perce bands of Chiefs Joseph and White Bird to Montana near the Canadian border. White Bird's band escaped across the border but the army captured Chief Joseph's band before they could follow. Several years later, the federal government allowed the remaining Nez Perce to return to their reservation. (*See Northern Idaho – Nez Perce War*.)

In 1892 Langdon platted the Weippe townsite on his homestead. Due to changes in county boundaries, Weippe was at one time in Shoshone County, then Nez Perce County and, finally, Clearwater County with Orofino as the county seat.

Weippe dam and mill, circa 1930.

Incorporation

In the mid-1900s citizens were becoming increasingly concerned about the environmental effects of private septic tanks, outdoor privies and inadequate water supply. These concerns were the impetus for Weippe becoming an incorporated city on December 16, 1964. Immediately following incorporation, the City issued bonds to finance construction of municipal water and sewer systems, which they completed in 1968.

Turning Points

Pierce Gold Rush The 1861 gold rush at Pierce persuaded homesteaders to come to the Weippe Prairie to farm, ranch and provide food for the miners. One of these settlers, Wellington Langdon, would become the founder of Weippe.

Sawmills As homesteaders came into the Weippe Prairie, some entrepreneurs built small portable sawmills that they assembled near the homesteads. After they cut the timber needed by the homesteaders in one location, they dismantled their mill and moved to other homesteader locations.

In the early 1900s large sawmill operations came to the Weippe Prairie. In 1920 one of these, Diamond Match Company, built a mill pond on Jim Ford Creek at the northeast corner of Weippe and cut white pine logs into two and a half inch planks that they shipped for the manufacture of wooden matches. Two years later, Diamond sold the mill to Leonard Cardiff who operated the mill for two decades before selling to another operator.

Water tank.

In 1947 Leslie and Lawrence Hutchins built a circle sawmill at Weippe. Their family made innovative improvements to the mill and continued the business until 2005 when they sold it to Empire Lumber Company.

By the 1940s several sawmills were operating in or near Weippe. This caused the village population to swell to about 1,000. Railroad interests had surveyed a spur line to Weippe. However, the increasing availability of lower-cost truck transportation ultimately led to the cancellation of the railroad to Weippe.

In the ensuing years, such factors as cyclical markets, environmental litigation, federal restrictions to forestlands and increasing production costs led to the decline of Weippe's wood products industry. The wood products companies that survived have largely developed niche businesses using timber harvested from private and state-owned lands.

Weippe Today

Amenities and Attractions

The Weippe City Park comprises four acres. Its amenities include picnic tables and children's playground areas, athletic fields and restrooms.

The city's chamber of commerce sponsors the Weippe Camas Festival held at the end of each May. It features a breakfast, Dutch oven cook off, horseshoe tournament, melodrama plays, fun runs/walks, trail rides and dance contests.

Weippe Community Center.

Two and a half miles south of the city, the National Park Service's Weippe Prairie National Historic Landmark marks the area where Lewis and Clark camped. Trails to Lewis and Clark's two campsites – Pleasant Camp and Small Prairie Camp – lie a few miles away on Forest Service roads.

Thirteen miles west of Weippe on the U.S. Forest Service's Lolo Trail Road is Musselshell Meadows, the last active spot where the Nez Perce still gather camas lily bulbs.

Lewis and Clark's Canoe Camp is located 26 miles west near Orofino. The Dworshak Dam on the North Fork of the Clearwater River is located a few miles north of Orofino. The dam forms a 16,000-acre reservoir that extends 54 miles northeast into the heavily wooded Clearwater National Forest.

The entire Dworshak Recreation Area lies several miles northwest of Weippe. This recreation area, including the forest lands near Weippe, has exceptional locations for boating, fishing, camping, recreational vehicles, swimming, water skiing, hunting, hiking, ATV and snowmobile riding and wildlife viewing.

The 850-acre Dworshak State Park is located on the western shore of Dworshak Reservoir north of Orofino, 35 miles from Weippe.

The city of Pierce, Idaho's second oldest city, is located 11 miles northeast of Weippe. It is the location of the historic Pierce Courthouse, the oldest government building in Idaho.

The Northwest Passage Scenic Byway – U.S. Highway 12 – parallels and periodically intersects the general line of travel followed by Lewis and Clark.

The Lewis and Clark National Historic Trail, passing through Weippe, is the actual trail followed by the Lewis and Clark Corps of Discovery – which consisted of 33 men, a woman, her child and Clark's dog.

The Nez Perce Historic Trail follows the line of travel the Nez Perce took when pursued by the U.S. Army during the 1877 Nez Perce War.

Greer Grade begins at the intersection of Highways 11 and 12. As the grade descends 2,000 feet over a series of switchbacks, it provides breathtaking views of the Clearwater River and Valley below.

Downhill skiing is available at the 5,036-foot-high Bald Mountain Ski Area, about 22 miles northeast of Weippe on Highway 11.

Economy and Major Employers The Empire Lumber Company has 35 employees and is the city's largest employer followed by the Orofino School District. Two wood products companies provide about a dozen jobs each.

The city's downtown retail businesses include a small grocery store, two restaurants, a floral-gift shop, an auto repair shop, a taxidermy, a java shop and two bars. The downtown area also has three churches, city hall, a post office, a historical society, a senior citizen center and a library – Discovery Center.

Most of Weippe's residents travel to Pierce or the county seat of Orofino to shop and do business.

Education The Orofino School District provides most of the K-12 education. Weippe junior and senior high school students attend Timberline High School. Elementary students attend Timberline Elementary. The schools are located halfway between Weippe and Pierce. The closest institution of higher learning is Lewis-Clark State College, located 67 miles west in Lewiston.

Health Care The closest health care providers are a medical clinic in Pierce and the 17-bed Clearwater Valley Hospital in Orofino.

Transportation State Highway 11 intersects the city. U.S. Highway 12 is 18 miles west.

Orofino Municipal Airport's 2,500-foot runway provides air service for light private and commercial aircraft. The Lewiston-Nez Perce County Airport provides commercial airport services.

Utilities and Services Private companies provide electricity, telephone, cable and satellite services. The City provides water and sewer services. The Clearwater Sheriff's Office provides police protection. The Weippe Rural Volunteer Fire Department provides fire services. The County provides EMS and solid waste services.

Weippe City Hall.

Vision for 2050

In 1970 Weippe's population was 713. Subsequently, largely due to the decline in the wood products industry, the city's population fell by over 300 residents.

However, during the past several years the city's population has stabilized at around 400. By 2050 the city's population will likely return to the levels experienced in the 1970s and 1980s.

The reasons for this growth include an increased interest in tourism and outdoor recreation, congressional approval of mixed use of federal forestlands and technological innovation that allows families to live in beautiful rural surroundings and work at home.

Weippe's municipal systems and infrastructure are generally adequate to manage the restoration of its former population without making major additions or improvements. New residents have a ready-made peaceful rural community with fabulous scenery and heritage to come and raise their families.

Mayors

1964 William H (Benny) Durant   1968 Norman C. Steadman
1979 Walter D. Steadman

Historic St. Gertrude's.

IDAHO COUNTY

- Cottonwood
- Ferdinand
- Grangeville (*County Seat*)
- Kooskia
- Riggins
- Stites
- White Bird

Cottonwood

Statistical Data

Population: 918 *
Elevation: 3,950 feet
Precipitation: 20 inches **
Average Snowfall: 44 inches **
County: Idaho
Website: www.cottonwoodidaho.org

Temperature Range – Fahrenheit: **
Spring: 30 to 62
Summer: 48 to 79
Fall: 29 to 70
Winter: 23 to 40
* U.S. Census Bureau Estimates July 2015 (chamber of commerce)
**Historical averages

Cottonwood is on the western side of the fertile Camas Prairie at the eastern base of the Clearwater Mountains, about 13 miles northwest of Grangeville.

The Salmon River – the "River of No Return" flows through the mountains about seven miles southwest of the city. Cottonwood Butte Ski Resort, with a summit elevation of 5,565 feet, is seven miles west.

Pre-Incorporation Years

In 1862 a man named Allen opened a way station near what is now Cottonwood at the junction of wagon roads to the gold mining towns of Florence and Elk City. He called it Cottonwood House after the groves of black cottonwood trees growing in the area and where logs were cut to build the station.

During the Nez Perce War in 1877, the U.S. Calvary used Cottonwood House as a field headquarters. (*See The Region, American Indians – Nez Perce War.*)

On June 14, the Nez Perce decisively defeated the U.S. Army at the battle at White Bird Canyon, about 25 miles south. Captain Stephan Whipple received orders to move his detachment to Cottonwood House, dig in and await the arrival of Captain David Perry and his troops, who were bringing supplies from Fort Lapwai.

Whipple knew the Nez Perce were still in the area and sent a reconnaissance party of 12 men to locate them. However, a war party of Nez Perce surprised and killed the cavalrymen. When the reconnaissance party failed to return, Whipple went out in search of the missing men. Finding them dead, he returned

Cottonwood, 1909. Courtesy Michael Peterson.

to his fortifications at Cottonwood House to await Perry and his troops. Meanwhile, the Nez Perce had begun to move up the Clearwater River to Montana but had left a detachment of warriors as a rear guard. At that time, a party of 17 volunteers from Mount Idaho, near Grangeville, was en route to Cottonwood House to join Whipple. The Nez Perce rear-guard warriors intercepted and killed two of the volunteers before moving off the Camas Prairie and joining the rest of the departing tribe.

By 1880 cattle ranchers and farmers had filed homestead claims in the Cottonwood area and were grazing their livestock on the open prairie. Cottonwood soon became an agricultural center. (*See The Region, Federal Lands – Private Ownership and Preservation Laws; and Agriculture.*)

Incorporation

Cottonwood became an incorporated village on October 21, 1901. In 1967 in accordance with a change in state law, Cottonwood became a city.

Turning Points

St. Gertrude's today.

Railroad In 1908 the Northern Pacific Railroad built a branch line from Lewiston to Grangeville, passing through Cottonwood. The coming of the railroad had a significant positive impact on the community. It brought faster passenger and mail service and opened distant markets to farm and wood products commodities produced in the surrounding area. (*See The Region, Railroads.*)

Monastery of St. Gertrude In 1907 the Roman Catholic religious order, serving people throughout the Northwest and known as the Benedictine Sisters, moved from Colton, Washington, to a site three miles west of Cottonwood. They lived in and provided services from a frame house and chapel until the 1920s when they built the Monastery of St. Gertrude from blue porphyry stone quarried nearby. The Sisters also established schools throughout the area that continued until public school consolidation occurred in the 1970s. They added the Historical Museum and Monastery in 1982.

North Idaho Correctional Institution The North Idaho Correctional Institution (NICI) was originally a radar base built by the Air Force in 1954 on 19.28 acres. The current prison site was the enlisted men's quarters. Officers' quarters were located just outside of Cottonwood and currently serve as staff and officers' housing for the Department of Correction and offices for the Bureau of Land Management.

Cottonwood, circa 1910. Courtesy Michael Peterson.

When the Air Force closed the radar site in 1964, the U.S. Forest Service used the property as a Job Corps site until 1973 when it deeded the land to the State of Idaho Department of Correction. The deed stipulated that the department use the facilities primarily for the training and education/rehabilitation of prisoners.

A 1969 Idaho law allowed courts the option of retaining jurisdiction over mainly younger first-time felony offenders for whom the judge determined there was adequate commitment to reform and a high probability the offender could be rehabilitated if they were incarcerated in a facility that taught discipline and provided education designed to help them mainstream back into society when they were discharged months later.

Cottonwood, circa 1930. Courtesy Michael Peterson.

The NICI opened at Cottonwood in 1974. The site was ideal because it provided the courts with a facility where the inmates, "riders" as they are known, can serve their time without living with hardened criminals. It has been an all male facility – except from 1977 to 1984 when women inmates also served time at the prison.

While originally resisted, most city residents now welcome the prison which is one of the town's largest employers.

Cottonwood Today

Amenities and Attractions The city has a park located in the northern part of town on King Street across from the Idaho County Fairgrounds with a cabana, ball field, playground equipment and bathrooms. Also the city has the Wimer Ball Fields in the southwestern part of town on Maple Street with two ball fields used for T-ball, rookie league, Little League and soft ball. The fields have a concession/bathroom facility.

The historic Monastery of St. Gertrude, Historical Museum and Visitors Center are popular tourist and local attractions. The 7,200-square-foot museum has over 70,000 historical artifacts and exhibits, many displaying the early life of the miners, ranchers, farmers, Chinese and Nez Perce Indians who once inhabited the region. The Museum has a Rhoades Emmanuel Memorial Exhibit that has Asian and European artifacts. Some of these Asian items date back to the Ming Dynasty, 1368 to 1644.

Cottonwood milling and flour company, circa 1930.

Also located on the Monastery grounds is the Spirit Center, a 21,800-square-foot conference and retreat center that is available for public rental. In May 2010 the Monastery opened a bed and breakfast to the public.

On the first Sunday of August, the Historical Museum hosts the annual Raspberry Festival.

The Cottonwood Butte Ski Resort averages 45 inches of snow

Cottonwood circa 1950. Courtesy of Michael Peterson.

each year, has seven ski runs with a maximum 845-foot vertical drop and 260 skiable acres.

Many city residents enjoy the numerous outdoor activities available year round in the forests and wilderness areas near Cottonwood. Fishing, river rafting, hunting, camping, hiking, skiing and jet boating are available within a short distance of the city. Four wilderness areas created by Congress are located within a two-hour drive of Cottonwood. To the northeast, U.S. Highway 12 skirts the northern border of the 1.3 million-acre Selway-Bitterroot Wilderness Area of which about 215,000 acres are in Montana.

Idaho Highway 14, which starts a few miles east of Grangeville, leads to the unincorporated but historic sawmill and gold mining town of Elk City. The highway comes close to the 2.5 million-acre Frank Church - River of No Return Wilderness and the 206,000-acre Gospel Hump Wilderness.

The Salmon River joins the Snake River about 25 miles west and then enters the 215,000-acre Hells Canyon Wilderness of which 131,000 acres are in Oregon.

Winchester Lake State Park in Winchester is 26 miles northwest. The park offer campsites, yurts, canoeing, biking, cross-country skiing, snowshoeing and fishing on the lake as well as nearby streams.

Economy and Major Employers With about 170 employees, the regional St. Mary's Hospital is the city's largest employer. Seubert Excavators employs 120 and is the second largest employer. Cottonwood School District has about 90 employees while the NICI has about 70. Several small businesses, government agencies, downtown retail and service businesses provide the balance of the city's employment base.

Education The Cottonwood School District provides most of the city's primary and secondary education. The district operates the Prairie Elementary, Middle and High Schools in the city. The closest institution of higher learning is Lewis-Clark State College, 57 miles north in Lewiston.

Dog Bark Park.

Health Care The 28-bed St. Mary's Hospital provides most of the health care services to city residents. St. Mary's Hospital operates clinics in Cottonwood, Kamiah, Craigmont and Nezperce as well as physical therapy clinics in Kamiah and Grangeville.

Transportation U.S. Highway 95 forms the eastern border of the city.

Cottonwood Municipal Airport is located a mile outside the city and has a 3,100-foot paved runway. The closest commercial airport is in Lewiston.

Utilities and Services Private companies provide electricity, telephone, natural gas, cable and satellite services. The City provides water and sewer services and fire and police protection.

Vision for 2050

In 1960 Cottonwood had a population of 1,081. The 2000 census reported the city's population at 944. In the past decade, the city's population growth has averaged over 1 percent annually. Recent historical trends will continue for several years. By 2050 Cottonwood's population will likely approach 1,500. The city's resources are generally adequate to fund necessary improvements and expansion of municipal services using existing revenue sources or voter-approved bonds.

Mayors

1901 W.L. Brown *	1919 S.J. Peterson *	1961 Felix Hutchins *
1902 W.M. Schiller *	1923 W.W. Flint *	1964 Walt Ruhoff *
1904 J.T. Hale *	1935 E.J. Terhaar *	1972 Francis Arnzen
1905 E.M. Ehrhardt *	1939 John Rooke *	1976 Fred Behler
1907 Stewart Severns *	1947 August Hoene *	1980 Ladd Arnoti
1908 S.J. Peterson *	1947 John Jenny *	1992 Denis Duman
1909 Geo F. McKinney *	1948 W.E. Simon *	1996 Don Hoene
1913 F.S. Wimer *	1949 H.L. Simon *	2000 Dawn Huntley
1915 E.L. Parker *	1949 W.M. Simon *	2004 Denis Duman
1916 John Hoene *	1953 Harold Simon *	2016 Shelli Schumacher
1917 J.V. Baker *	1957 Cletus Uhlorn *	* Village Chairman

Ferdinand City Hall.

Ferdinand

Statistical Data

Population: 160 *
Elevation: 3,730 feet
Precipitation: 20 inches **
Average Snowfall: 44 inches **
County: Idaho

Temperature Range – Fahrenheit: **
Spring: 30 to 62
Summer: 48 to 79
Fall: 29 to 70
Winter: 23 to 40
* U.S. Census Bureau Estimates July 2015
**Historical averages

Ferdinand is located on the northwestern edge of the fertile Camas Prairie about eight miles north of Cottonwood. About 20 miles west are the Craig Mountains, rising to 5,279 feet.

Nez Perce Indian Reservation land and fields of wheat, barley and peas surround the city.

Pre-Incorporation Years

For centuries, the nomadic Nez Perce was the principal tribe of American Indians that frequented the area of what is now Ferdinand, generally passing through on the way to their seasonal encampments.

Following the treaty of 1846 with England that established the boundary between the United States and Canada at the 49th parallel, the federal government created territories and took control of the land. The U.S. Army compelled American Indians to follow the dictates of Congress.

In 1855 the federal government entered into a treaty with the Nez Perce, establishing a reservation that covered a large part of Northern Idaho and Western Washington. However, at the same time the federal government was also promoting settlement of the West and the harvest of its natural resources. On their own initiative, gold prospectors and pioneer settlers knowingly and unknowingly moved onto reservation land.

In 1860 prospectors found gold on reservation land at what is now Pierce. A gold rush ensued with thousands of fortune seekers moving into the area. Most of them came by boat from the coast, up the Columbia and Snake Rivers to the seaport town of Lewiston. Lewiston, which was also on reservation land, became a city of tents, a staging area where people could obtain last minute provisions before moving on to

F.M. Bieker homestead.

the gold fields at Pierce and beyond. The outnumbered Nez Perce were ill equipped to resist.

In 1863 the federal government entered into a new treaty with the Nez Perce that superseded the 1855 treaty. However, not all Nez Perce chiefs signed the new treaty that provided they cede significant portions of 1855 treaty reservation land, including land around Lewiston and the gold mining areas around Pierce, to the federal government. In 1867 Congress ratified the 1863 treaty.

F.M. Bieker

The Nez Perce chiefs who did not sign the treaty were angry about the new restrictions. A military conflict ensued in which the non-treaty signing tribes lost and were forced to comply with congressional and military directives. (*See Northern Idaho, The Region, American Indians*.)

On February 8, 1887, the U.S. Congress further reduced reservation land holdings by passing the Dawes Severalty Act. The Act authorized Native American tribal lands to be surveyed and specific acreages allotted individually to tribal members. Congress deemed land not so allocated as surplus and available for settlement by non-Indians. In 1935 Congress repealed the law placing unclaimed reservation land into a trust for the Indians; however, by that time ownership of most former reservation lands was in the hands of non-Indians.

By November 18, 1895, the federal government completed its surveys of the Nez Perce reservation land and opened it for settlement. An estimated 5,000 people participated in this land rush.

F.M. Bieker was one of those involved. Bieker planned to stake his claim near what is now the unincorporated town of Keuterville. However, upon arrival he found he lacked adequate water.

The next day he happened to find a map of the reservation, which someone had apparently dropped. With the aid of his pocket compass and map, he ran a line five miles from a survey marker and marked his claim. This became his farm, located just west of what is now Ferdinand. Over the following six weeks, he used his claim as a starting point for helping ten other settlers establish their claims.

Bieker constructed a building that included his home and a general store. He then circulated a petition to his neighbors to establish a post office in the store. Initially, he filed the application with the name of St. Anthony. However, postal authorities rejected that name because it was already in use.

In 1898 Bieker successfully reapplied using the name Ferdinand in honor of his mother's hometown of Ferdinand, Indiana.

In 1904 the presidents of Northern Pacific and Union Pacific, co-ventureres in constructing the railroad, visited and approved building a railroad across the Camas Prairie. Construction began in 1905. However, it took several years to complete due to difficult terrain between Culdesac and Cottonwood. Construction of the railroad included a 296-foot-high and 1,500-foot-long steel bridge, four miles west of Ferdinand. The bridge, completed August 20, 1908, was then one of the highest railroad bridges in the nation.

Main Street looking east.

John Vollmer – an officer of the Northern Pacific Railroad – planned to personally profit from the railroad by purchasing land and platting several towns next to the planned railroad depots.

One of these towns was Ferdinand. The railroad tracks passed a quarter mile to the east of the community. Vollmer acquired 40 acres on the opposite side of the tracks where he planned to plat the village of Steunenberg. When Bieker learned of Vollmer's plan, he offered to sell him 40 acres between Ferdinand and the railroad for the new village. Vollmer did not respond to Bieker's offer, so Bieker began selling commercial lots on the land he had offered to Vollmer.

When Vollmer's surveyor arrived to plat Steunenberg, he concluded Vollmer's actions unethical as it would seriously damage the interests of Ferdinand residents and businesses. When Vollmer's agents fired the surveyor, Bieker hired him to plat the expanded Ferdinand townsite on the western side of the tracks.

Determined to move forward with his town of Steunenberg, Vollmer built a hotel, saloon, store and bank. Postal authorities cooperated by approving the Steunenberg post office. However, many of the Ferdinand residents refused to cross the railroad tracks to patronize Steunenberg businesses. The post office closed within a year due to lack of activity. Fire destroyed at least two of Vollmer's buildings and the other businesses ultimately closed, leaving Ferdinand as the surviving community.

Incorporation

On January 15, 1917, Ferdinand's population exceeded the 200 required, and it successfully filed to become an incorporated village.

Turning Points

Railroad The railroad converted a small farming settlement into a small commercial center. It provided freight and passenger transportation to larger cities and allowed local farmers access to distant markets.

Highway 95 When the Idaho Transportation Department (ITD) built the original U.S. Highway 95, Idaho's primary north-south traffic corridor, the road was the city's Main Street.

Ferdinand Public School.

In the 1990s ITD moved the road to the east side of the city to improve traffic flow, essentially allowing thru traffic to bypass the city. This loss of traffic had a significant adverse effect on the city's retail businesses.

Ferdinand Today

Amenities and Attractions Ferdinand has a picnic area as you enter town on Main Street. It has a second picnic area and restroom near the baseball field on 2nd Street and Division. The city also has a swing set, slide, tennis court and basketball court on the north end of 2nd Street next to the Assumption Catholic Church's Parish Hall. The

Downtown Ferdinand.

historic Ferdinand Public School, erected in 1909 and operated until 1960 when the schools consolidated, is still standing and is in wonderful condition.

Ferdinand residents participate in activities of nearby communities. Each June is the "June Picnic," 8 miles north in Craigmont. On the first weekend of August is the Raspberry Festival at St. Gertrude's, 12 miles south of Ferdinand. On the third weekend of August is the Idaho County Fair in Cottonwood.

St. Gertrude's also has a Museum with many wonderful artifacts and exhibits of the area's early inhabitants and settlers.

Winchester Lake State Park in Winchester is 16 miles northwest. The park offers campsites, yurts, canoeing, biking, cross-country skiing, snowshoeing and fishing on the lake as well as nearby streams. Downhill skiing is available at Cottonwood Butte.

Economy and Major Employers Pacific Cabinets Incorporated has around 40 employees and is Ferdinand's largest employer. Other employers include a construction materials business, trucking company, veterinarian, highway district and hospitality industry businesses. Many residents commute to Cottonwood or to nearby farms and ranches for work.

Education The Cottonwood School District provides most of the city's K-12 education. The district operates the Prairie Elementary, Middle and High Schools in Cottonwood where most Ferdinand children attend.

The closest institution of higher learning is Lewis-Clark State College, 57 miles north in Lewiston.

Health Care The 23-bed St. Mary's Hospital/Clinic in Cottonwood provides most of the healthcare needs for city residents.

Transportation U.S. Highway 95 passes on the eastern side of the city.

Cottonwood Municipal Airport, 9 miles southeast, provides service for light private and charter aircraft. The closest commercial airport is 57 miles northwest in Lewiston.

Utilities and Services Private companies provide electricity, telephone and satellite services. The City provides water and sewer services and fire protection. The County Sheriff's Office provides police protection.

Vision for 2050

For the past 40 years, the city's population has ranged around 150. Historical trends are likely to continue.

In 2050 Ferdinand will still be a small peaceful rural agricultural community – a quiet and friendly place to live and raise a family. However, by that time, the community will have completed a number of improvements including the planned installation of children's playground equipment at city picnic areas, removal of the old railroad viaduct and leveling the main road.

Mayors

1917 J.A. Bushue *	1929 J.A. Kuther *	1967 Cecil Uhling
1917 Amil Haener *	1936 E.L. Adkinson *	1968 Rudy Riener
1917 W.J. Adsley *	1937 J.P. Bieker *	1980 Dan Goeckner
1919 F.M. Bieker *	1938 D.S. Morgan *	1988 Eugene Kuther
1921 H.H. Bennett *	1941 Albert T. Zodrow *	1997 Paul Schmidt
1923 A.U. Knutson *	1947 R.H. Demsey *	2008 Gabe Riener
1924 F.M. Bieker *	1948 Joe Aschenbrenner *	* Village Chairman
1925 Tom Hayden *	1949 Cecil Uhling *	

Grangeville today.

Grangeville

Statistical Data

Population: 3,141 *
Elevation: 3,670 feet
Precipitation: 23 inches **
Average Snowfall: 61 inches **
County: Idaho
Website: www.grangeville.us

Temperature Range – Fahrenheit: **
Spring: 30 to 65
Summer: 48 to 83
Fall: 30 to 73
Winter: 24 to 44
* U.S. Census Bureau Estimates July 2015
**Historical averages

Grangeville is a city of multiple gateways. It lies at the northern base of the Clearwater Mountains where U.S. Highway 95 drops into the fertile 200,000-acre Camas Prairie and its beautiful mosaic of wheat, barley and pea fields. The heavily wooded mountains of the Nez Perce National Forest form the city's eastern, southern and western skyline.

Idaho Highway 13, running east out of Grangeville, leads to roads that enter or pass near three wilderness areas. (*See The Region, National Wilderness Areas.*)

To the northeast, U.S. Highway 12 skirts the northern border of the 1.3-million-acre Selway-Bitterroot Wilderness Area – 215,000 acres are in Montana – as it heads to Lolo Pass on the Idaho/Montana border.

Idaho Highway 14 just east of Grangeville leads to the unincorporated but historic sawmill and gold mining town of Elk City and runs near the 2.5-million-acre Frank Church-River of No Return and the 206,000-acre Gospel Hump Wilderness Areas.

The Salmon River, the River of No Return – so named because supply boats could only travel one way – flows several miles to the west and southwest. Thirty miles further west, the Salmon River joins the Snake River as it runs through the 215,000-acre Hells Canyon Wilderness Area – 131,000 acres are in Oregon.

Grangeville is the seat of Idaho County, the largest county in Idaho at 5.4 million acres. Idaho County, Boundary County and Bonner County have the distinction of being the only three counties that cross the entire state, east to west.

Pre-Incorporation Years

In 1860 Elias D. Pierce led a party of prospectors who discovered placer gold near what is now Pierce, located about 70 miles north of Grangeville. The following year, several thousand miners rushed to the area, and by 1863 settlers and ranchers were homesteading on the Camas Prairie, grazing cattle and selling their commodities to the miners. (*See The Region, Gold Mining; and Federal Lands – Private Ownership and Preservation Laws.*)

However, once the gold claims played out, the miners left and the homesteaders lost their market. Further settlement on the Camas Prairie languished for more than a decade.

Then in 1874 the local chapter of a fraternal society called the National Grange of the Patrons of Husbandry wanted to acquire five acres in the community of Mount Idaho for a hall and flour mill. The society's national organization had been founded seven years earlier in Washington, D.C., to advance the interests of farmers. During that time, the national organization had established over 20,000 local granges with 850,000 members nationwide.

At the time, Mount Idaho was the dominant town in the area. A year later, county voters would name it the Idaho County seat, replacing the gold mining boomtown of Florence where the mines were playing out.

Loyal Brown, a leading citizen and founder of Mount Idaho, opposed the Grange

Main Street in Grangeville, 1898.

organization and did not want them in the community. John M. Crooks, an entrepreneur who owned land about two miles north of Mount Idaho, saw the increasingly popular Grange movement as a business opportunity and sought to accommodate the desires of Charity Grange No. 15, the local chapter. In 1875 Crooks platted a townsite on his property, and, to get the town started, he gave a five-acre lot to the Charity Grange. The following year, the Grange built its flour mill and hall with a stockade-type enclosure around its facilities.

However, Crooks did not name the town. Community residents discussed the matter at a Grange Hall meeting. Isabelle Pearson suggested they name their town Grangeville. Others suggested Millville and Wheeling. The residents voted and Grangeville won by one vote. Postal authorities approved the Grangeville Post

Office, and the town began to grow at the expense of Mount Idaho. Twenty-seven years later, voters moved the county seat from Mount Idaho to Grangeville. Today, Mount Idaho is a Grangeville suburb.

It was just months after the Grange completed the stockade walls that the facilities were needed for protection. June 17, 1877, marked the opening battle of the Nez Perce War at White Bird Canyon, about 15 miles southwest of Grangeville – a humiliating defeat for the U.S. Army. Thirty-four soldiers died without the Nez Perce losing one warrior.

As the army regrouped with reinforcements, the Nez Perce moved close to Mount Idaho, and 39 settlers fled to the Grange Hall stockade.

Over the next months the Army relentlessly pursued the bands of Chiefs Joseph and White Bird, covering 1,500 miles – a modern army never quite able to catch the Nez Perce who were traveling with women, children and equipage. Wiring ahead, the pursuing army requested the military in Montana to intercept the Nez

Main Street in Grangeville looking east, 1898.

Perce. They intercepted Chief Joseph and his band 40 miles south of the Canadian border. Chief White Bird escaped into Canada.

On October 5, 1877, Chief Joseph surrendered with a statement against war that would become famous in American history: "I am tired of fighting. Our chiefs are killed. The old men are all dead. It is cold and we have no blankets. The little children are freezing to death. My people, some of them, have run away to the hills and have no blankets and food. I want to have time to look for my children. Hear me, my chiefs; my heart is sick and sad. From where the sun now stands, I will fight no more forever." (*See The Region, American Indians – Nez Perce War.*)

County courthouse. Courtesy Michael Peterson.

With the threat of war past, the Grange Hall became the center of community events. By 1879 several frame homes and businesses dotted the new town site. There was a general merchandise store, a small hotel, a Chinese store, a blacksmith shop and a drugstore operated by the town's medical doctor, a retired army surgeon.

The upstairs of the Grange Hall was used for a school until 1884 when a new school called the Columbia River Conference Academy was built with the Rev. W.A. Hall as principal.

Within six years, the Academy became a public school with a new school building erected on Main Street four years later. The old Academy building became the courthouse.

On December 3, 1885, County Surveyor F.P. Turner made the first official plat of Grangeville. It included nine 200 by 400 foot city blocks bordered by North Second Street, South Street, Mill Street and State Street.

Six months later, A.F. Parker published the first issue of the *Idaho County Free Press*, a newspaper which is still being published. It played a major role in the growth and wellbeing of the community.

Grangeville Arch, circa 1930. Courtesy Michael Peterson.

While the Grange gave the city its name, nearby sawmills and mines bolstered it economy. In 1890 the town was becoming a vibrant regional shopping center. It had three general stores and several other retail businesses along with a hotel, legal and medical offices, a new school and two new Methodist and Episcopal Churches. Within a few years, there were two banks, a second flour mill and a Roman Catholic Church in town.

By 1893 it was clear that the population and economy were shifting from Mount Idaho to Grangeville. However, a ballot initiative to make Grangeville the county seat failed. When the issue resurfaced nine years later, it passed with an overwhelming majority.

Cloudburst, May 23, 1921. Courtesy of Michael Peterson.

Incorporation

Grangeville became an incorporated city on October 15, 1897. Within a year, the town built a domestic water system, and a private utility was providing electricity.

Turning Points

Grange John M. Crooks' grant of a five-acre lot to the Grange for its hall and flour mill provided the anchor that attracted others to the new community. The failure of Loyal Brown and other Mount Idaho leaders to invite the Grange to their town caused Mount Idaho to lose its competitive economic advantage, resulting in the eventual demise of this once vibrant community.

Gold Grangeville was not a gold mining town; however, in 1898 its economy was enhanced when prospectors discovered gold in the Buffalo Hump area, about 11 miles southwest of Elk City. The mining camp purchased supplies from Grangeville businesses for a number of years, providing momentum for Grangeville to become the county seat.

County Seat The county vote to make Grangeville the county seat in 1902 brought jobs and prestige to the town. After the election, the Free Press declared: "We Are the People – Grangeville Easily Wins the County Seat Election – 2,637 to 743 Votes." Grangeville's position as the county seat of government also played a role in securing the Nez Perce National Forest headquarters and airport for the city.

Grangeville Episcopal Church, 1910. Courtesy Michael Peterson.

Fire Grangeville's momentum nearly ended on September 14, 1905, when a devastating fire swept through the business district causing more than $250,000 in damage – the equivalent of over $6 million now. However, leaders responded, and new construction added jobs as the business district rebuilt with new brick structures.

Railroad When the Northern Pacific branch railroad line from Lewiston reached Grangeville in 1908, it brought faster passenger and mail service and opened distant markets to farm and wood products commodities produced in the surrounding area.

Midwest Dust Bowl Grangeville became a haven for farmers caught in the disastrous mid-west "Dust Bowl" of the

Grangeville, circa 1930. Courtesy of Michael Peterson.

1930s. Many of these farm families settled in the Grangeville area causing a dramatic increase in the city's population.

Grangeville Today

Amenities and Attractions Grangeville has three parks on 20 acres, offering athletic fields, picnic areas, children's playgrounds and a public swimming pool. The city also has a golf course, a museum of local history and artifacts, an art gallery and a library.

For three days around July 4th, Grangeville celebrates the nation's independence with its annual "Border Days," a kick-up-your-heels Western celebration that includes parades; street games; dances; and, most importantly, a rodeo that dates back to 1912 and is termed "the oldest rodeo in Idaho."

The nearby Nez Perce National Forest is an outdoor paradise. Located in the forest are approximately 35 campgrounds and stretches of the Selway, Snake, Rapid and Salmon Rivers. Within an hour's drive of the city, opportunities abound for white-water rafting, canoeing, kayaking, hunting, fishing, camping, snowmobiling and skiing.

Downhill skiing and tubing are available at Snowhaven Ski Resort seven miles south of Grangeville, and skiing is available at Cottonwood Butte Ski Resort 18 miles northwest.

Fish Creek Meadows, seven miles south of Grangeville, is a year-round trailhead for a variety of outdoor recreation. There are 11 camp units with parking for large recreational vehicles. A separate parking lot is the trailhead for cross-country skiing and snowmobiling on 90 acres of groomed trails in the winter and mountain biking, ATV riding and horseback riding during the warmer months.

Grangeville Border Days Parade, 2014. Courtesy of Michael Peterson.

Grangeville is located near 600 miles of groomed snowmobile trails running from Winchester to Elk City and Dixie. Parts of the trails reach elevations of 8,000 feet. ATV enthusiasts use the trails in the summertime.

The Highway 13 leg of the Idaho Transportation Department's Northwest Passage Scenic Byway – Highways 13 and 12 – begins in Grangeville. Highway 12 generally parallels the trail that Lewis and Clark's Corps of Discovery followed when it trekked across Idaho in 1805 and on their return trip in 1806.

State Route 14 begins several miles east of the city. It is the only road to the historic sawmill and gold mining town of Elk City and the Idaho Department of Fish and Game's 314-acre Red River Wildlife Management Area.

Economy and Major Employers The city's largest employers are the Grangeville School District with 300 employees; the U.S, Forest Service, the Nez Perce National Forest employs 250; and Idaho County has 150 employees.

Grangeville's private employer base includes a lumber mill, several businesses that serve Camas Prairie farmers and a dynamic downtown center that has over a hundred retail, service and financial businesses serving tourist traffic and other communities in the region.

Education The Grangeville School District provides most of the primary and secondary education. The district has a high school, a middle school and an elementary school in the city. Saints Peter and Paul School is the largest private school with grades one through eight.

The closest institution of higher learning is Lewis-Clark State College, 71 miles northwest in Lewiston.

Health Care The 16-bed Syringa Hospital is the principal health care facility in the city. Also available are two assisted living homes, a long-term care and rehabilitation center and physical therapy clinics.

Frozen Heritage Square, downtown, 2007.

Transportation U.S. Highway 95 and State Route 13 intersect the city. State Route 14 begins 10 miles east of town. U.S. Route 12 is 30 miles north on Route 13.

The Idaho County Airport is located a mile north of the city and has a 5,100-foot runway. It serves forest service, private and charter aircraft.

Utilities and Services Private companies provide electricity, telephone, cable and satellite services. The City provides domestic water, police and fire protection and municipal wastewater services.

Vision for 2050

The 1960 census reported Grangeville's population at 3,642. Primarily due to the loss of jobs in natural resource-based industries, the population declined for the next few decades before stabilizing at around 3,100.

Historical trends are not always indicative of the future. The city's fabulous gateway setting, amenities, attractions and favorable climate will be important factors in changing historical trends by attracting light industrial, tourist and recreation businesses as well as retirees.

Within the next several years, we believe the city will begin experiencing moderate growth. By 2050 Grangeville's population will likely approximate 4,000. Existing municipal systems will generally be able to meet these growth forecasts with routine improvements.

During the next four decades, the city's incorporated area will extend north to the airport to support industrial and commercial development. The city limits will extend approximately one mile to the northwest and east with new residential and light retail businesses. The city's southwestern boundary will extend out only modestly while the southern boundary will remain somewhat constant.

Outside of the city limits, developers will subdivide larger parcels of farmland into five- and 10-acre ranchettes. One historical trend is indicative of the future. In 2050 Grangeville will still be a quiet, peaceful and vibrant hometown where people can work and raise their families.

Mayors

1903 W.W. Brown	1919 W.L. Campbell	1951 R.D. Williams
1905 George M. Robertson	1923 C.H. Wood	1957 Clair C. Inghram
1906 Fen Batty	1925 A.N. Dyer	1959 George M. Klien
1907 F.L. Leonard	1935 Louis E. Bunting	1966 Douglas Adkison
1909 W.W. Brown	1937 C.W. Vincent	1973 Ralph Bos
1913 J Frank Sims	1939 Al J. Wagner	1986 R.D. Workman
1915 R.F. Fulton	1945 G.W. Eimers	1990 Terry Vanderwall
1917 T.E. Edmondson	1947 Joe N. Wagner	2008 Bruce H. Walker

Kooskia City Hall.

Kooskia

Statistical Data

Population: 604 *
Elevation: 1,257 feet
Precipitation: 23 inches **
Average Snowfall: 61 inches **
County: Idaho
Temperature Range – Fahrenheit: **

Spring: 36 to 64
Summer: 49 to 88
Fall: 36 to 664
Winter: 24 to 41
* U.S. Census Bureau Estimates July 2015
**Historical averages

Kooskia (pronounced Koos-kee) lies on an elevated plain at the confluence of the Middle Fork of the Clearwater River as it flows from the east and South Fork of the Clearwater as they merge to form the main Clearwater River. The forks of the rivers and the city wrap around a hogback extension of Mount Stewart.

The Clearwater National Forest begins on the north side of the Middle Fork a few miles northeast of the city. The Nez Perce National Forest begins on the south side of the river. The Selway-Bitterroot Wilderness Area begins about 30 miles east. Grangeville, the Idaho County seat, lies 19 miles south.

The name "Kooskia," is a contraction of the Nez Perce Indian name "Koos-Koos-Kia" recorded in Lewis and Clark's 1805 journals as the name they misunderstood to be the Nez Perce name for the Clearwater River.

Pre-Incorporation Years

On the return trip east from the Pacific Ocean, Lewis, Clark and the Corps of Discovery camped near Kamiah, seven miles north of Kooskia before returning north to the Weippe Prairie and the trail across the Bitterroot Mountains.

Clearwater Ferry across the Middlefork River at Kooskia.

In less than a decade, trappers/explorers began coming into the region. A few Christian missionary groups to the Native American Indians followed two decades later. In 1838 Asa B. Smith, a Presbyterian missionary, started a mission to the Nez Perce near Kamiah. The mission was not successful and soon closed. (*See Northern Idaho – Early Missionaries.*)

In 1855 the Nez Perce signed a treaty with federal representatives that designated their reservation to comprise over a million acres.

Around 1860 gold prospectors came into the area. Elias Davidson Pierce and a small party of prospectors discovered gold on Nez Perce land near what is now Pierce, 25 miles northeast of Kooskia. Thousands of prospectors flooded into the region in what was Idaho's first gold rush. The Nez Perce Indians were substantially fewer in number and largely powerless to keep the prospectors off their reservation. In 1862 prospectors made another gold discovery about 35 miles southeast of Kooskia at Elk City. (*See Northern Idaho – Idaho's First Gold Rush.*)

In 1863 the federal government took note of the increased non-Indian settlement and reduced the Nez Perce Reservation to about 800,000 acres.

Team coming around a bluff on the toll road outside Kooskia.

In 1877 the U.S. Bureau of Indian Affairs ordered the Nez Perce to move to the Lapwai Reservation in Idaho. They refused and a battle termed the Nez Perce War ensued. (*See Northern Idaho – Nez Perce War.*) In one military engagement, the Army attacked and destroyed the village of one of the Nez Perce bands led by Chief Lookingglass. The village site, located five miles east of what is now Kooskia, is today part of the Nez Perce National Historic Park.

In 1887 Congress passed the General Allotment – Dawes Severalty – Act that opened reservation land to settlement. In general, the law allotted 160 acres to each Indian head of household. Land not allocated became surplus and available for white settlement. The Dawes Severalty Act had the long-term effect of further reducing the size of the Nez Perce Reservation to a patchwork of land comprising about 200,000 acres.

In 1895 federal surveyors set aside 104 acres at the confluence of the Middle Fork and South Forks of the Clearwater River for a townsite. A surveyor, James Stewart of the Nez Perce Tribe, platted the town and gave it the name of Stewart. On May 25, 1896, postal authorities approved a post office for the new community. On January 1, 1898, the town's first newspaper, the *Alta Idaho Area Paper*, ran its first issue.

Bird's-eye view of Kooskia.

On March 13, 1899, the Northern Pacific Railroad line reached Stewart where it built a train depot. However, continuing the name of Stewart was problematic. The railroad already served a community named Stewart. At the behest of the railroad, the citizens formally changed the name of their town to Kooskia.

Effective April 14, 1902, the newspaper – with the new name of *Kooskia Mountaineer* – came off the press.

For several decades, agriculture and timber underpinned the Kooskia economy. Much of the agriculture production was on the Camas Prairie to the west. In 1903 the owners of the grain elevators and flourmill in Kooskia designed a mechanized

Dedication of new bridge at Kooskia, 1927.

method of transporting grain from a collection station across the river to the flourmill in Kooskia. They built a one-and-a-quarter-mile-long tram with two cables. Thirty buckets ran on the cable that brought grain into the mill.

Western backcountry outfitters and travelers recognize Kooskia as the home of the Decker Pack Saddle. Around 1900 a blacksmith/packsaddle maker, Oliver B. Robinette, moved to Kooskia. There he perfected the design and construction of a packsaddle known as the Decker Pack Saddle, named after the Decker brothers who developed important aspects of the original design. Robinette's saddles allowed mules and horses to carry heavy loads in relative comfort. The Decker brothers became wholesale purchasers of Robinette's saddles. In addition, the Decker Pack Saddle became the accepted standard approved by the U.S. Forest Service for its backcountry missions.

Incorporation

Kooskia became an incorporated village in 1901, and James Stewart was one of the first five trustees.

Turning Points

Railroad Even though federal surveyors established the town by setting aside land for a townsite, the railroad gave the city its name and underpinned its success. The Kooskia Train Depot became the focal point of passenger, mail and freight traffic. The agricultural and wood products

Kooskia flood, May 22, 1948.

industries prospered because they could now easily move their commodities to distant markets and more promptly receive needed equipment and supplies.

Kooskia Today

Amenities and Attractions Kooskia has four city parks that comprise a total of 25 acres.

The city's most prominent historical building is the Old Victorian Opera Theatre, built in 1912. It is located in the center of town and emulates a splendor of yesteryear. It has a spectacular crystal chandelier, a dessert and sarsaparilla bar and features concerts and melodramas throughout the year.

Kooskia, 1950. Courtesy Michael Peterson.

The city holds its largest celebration, "Kooskia Days," each July. This celebration features a parade, a horse riding contest and a logging competition. Other annual events include the Kooskia City-wide Yard Sale and the Native American Mat – Alyma Root Festival in May, the Lewis and Clark Heritage Days in June, Chief Lookingglass Days in August, a CVRA rodeo in September and the annual "Kiddie" Santa Claus Jingle Parade and Tree Lighting Ceremony in December.

Kooskia offers a wide variety of year-round activities for those who enjoy the natural beauty of mountains, vast forests and crystal-clear rivers. The nearby tributaries to the Clearwater River are fabulous amenities for anglers. These streams are natural habitat for steelhead, cutthroat, Chinook salmon, rainbow trout, bass, whitefish and other popular game fish. Residents can rise early, catch their breakfast trout and still make it to work on time.

Wildlife viewing and hunting are also popular. Large numbers of elk, whitetail deer, moose, bighorn sheep, mountain goats, wild turkey, cougar and black bear roam the vast nearby public lands. Eagles and osprey are common sightings along the rivers.

Other common outdoor activities include hiking, sightseeing, white water rafting, horseback riding, backpacking, bicycling, skiing, snowmobiling, snowboarding and ATVs.

The 850-acre Dworshak State Park on Dworshak Reservoir lies 40 miles north. The 418-acre Winchester State Park with its 103-acre lake is 45 miles west. The U.S. Forest Service offers cabins for rent in the nearby national forests. Several lookout towers that are no longer in use are also an attraction.

Downhill skiing is available at Snowhaven Ski Area a few miles south near Grangeville, Bald Mountain 30 miles north near Pierce and Cottonwood Butte 30 miles west near Cottonwood.

Church at Kooskia.

U.S. Highway 12 and Idaho Highway 13 are part of the Northwest Passage Scenic Byway. The Byway commemorates and frequently parallels or crosses the trail followed in 1805 to 1806 by the Lewis and Clark Corps of Discovery.

The Idaho portion of the Northwest Passage Scenic Byway is 212 miles long. From the western edge of Idaho, the Byway begins at Lewiston and parallels the winding Clearwater River to Kooskia where the Byway forks. The eastern fork continues on Highway 12 along the Wild and Scenic Middle Fork of the Clearwater and Lochsa Rivers before reaching Lolo Pass and the Lewis and Clark Interpretative Center on the Idaho/Montana Border. The southern fork follows Highway 13 to Grangeville and the Camas Prairie.

Five miles east of the city, just off U.S. Highway 12, is Lookingglass Camp – one of 38 sites that comprise the Nez Perce National Historical Park. The U.S. National Park Service manages the park system that follows the trail of the Nez Perce into four states as the U.S. Army pursued them.

Kooskia scenery.

The historic Kooskia Internment Camp, built following Japan's attack on Pearl Harbor in 1941 to imprison American citizens of Japanese descent, is located about 30 miles east of the city in the Lochsa River Canyon at Canyon Creek. The camp is one of two internment camps built in Idaho. The much larger Minidoka War Relocation Center – named Hunt by the Post Office – was located near the city of Eden. The Kooskia Camp inmates volunteered to come to this beautiful location, primarily to work for wages on the construction of U.S. Highway 12.

Economy and Major Employers With nearly 100 employees, Clearwater Forest Industries, a dimensional lumber sawmill, is the city's largest private employer.

The Grangeville School District and the U.S. Forest Service each have about 50 employees and are the city's largest public employers.

The Kooskia business district has a wide range of retail and service businesses. The clientele for these businesses not only includes the citizens of Kooskia but numerous farm families and other citizens living outside the city limits.

Education Grangeville School District provides most of the elementary and secondary education in the area. In Kooskia, district students in grades K-6 attend Clearwater Valley Elementary. Clearwater Valley Middle and High Schools are located on a common campus in the city. Two private schools also operate in the city.

The nearest institution of higher learning is Lewis-Clark State College, located 76 miles northwest in Lewiston.

The Kooskia Technology Learning Center, located on the second floor of city hall, offers public access to several computer stations and the Internet. Lewis-Clark State College offers distance learning and adult education courses at the center.

Kooskia today.

Health Care Two general medical clinics are located in Kooskia. The nearest hospital is the 14-bed Syringa General Hospital in Grangeville.

Transportation Highway 13 passes through Kooskia before intersecting Highway 12 on the north and east of the city just across the South and Middle Forks of the Clearwater River.

The 1,900-foot Kooskia Municipal Airport, with a grass runway, offers service to small private and charter aircraft. The Lewiston-Nez Perce Airport, 73 miles north in Lewiston, is the closest certified carrier airport. Railroad service is available in the city for freight.

Utilities and Services Private companies provide electricity, telephone, cable, CATV and satellite. The City provides water and sewer services and has standby auxiliary power for pumping water from its deep wells and continuous power to sewer lift stations.

The City provides fire protection. The County has a contract with the city to provide police protection. The County also provides solid waste services.

Vision for 2050

The Kooskia population has averaged around 700 for several decades. However, travel and tourism are steadily changing the city's economy. An increasing number of tourists are coming to see the pristine vistas and fabulous scenery along the Northwest Passage Scenic Byway on Highway 12 to the Lewis and Clark Interpretive Center at Lolo Pass on the Idaho/Montana border.

By 2050 the city and its hospitality businesses will have success promoting the city as the gateway to the pristine and fabulously beautiful outdoors; wild and scenic Middle Fork of the Clearwater and Lochsa Rivers, the Clearwater and Nez Perce National Forests, the Selway-Bitterroot Wilderness Area and the rugged trail of the Lewis and Clark expedition over the Bitterroot Mountains. This will lead the city's population to more than double.

The improvements made to the city's infrastructure during the past several years of new main street storm drains, curbs, gutters, sidewalks, paving and street lighting along with a new emergency services building has helped prepare the city for this new growth.

Mayors

1913 Jack Wills *
1913 John T. Quinlan *
1914 Charles H. Gelbach *
1914 C.A. Mulledy *
1915 Jack Wills *
1917 Dale Clark *
1921 O.P. Decker *
1923 W.W. Palmer *
1929 B.P. Stewart *
1935 Asa Clarke *
1937 J.D. Crosby *
1939 C.W. (Carl) Person *

1944 W. Ray Gilroy *
1947 Jeff Lycan *
1949 M. B. Carnefix *
1951 W. Ray Gilroy *
1953 Ned Gibler *
1955 Stanley (S.C.) Potter *
1957 Shirlie Fenn *
1959 Leonard Lee *
1963 Francis E. Wagner
1971 David E. Poncin
1971 Merlyn S. Umphenour
1976 Orvel York

1978 James G. Baylor
1980 Max Thrush
1984 Greg M. Smith
1988 Roberta Joy Lee
1992 Loren Reeves
1993 Don Coffman
1994 Inge Stickney
1998 R. Skipper Brandt
2001 John Schurbon
2007 Charlotte Schilling
* Village Chairman

Riggins in the valley.

Riggins

Statistical Data

Population: 416 *
Elevation: 1,821 feet
Precipitation: 25 inches **
Average Snowfall: 20 inches **
County: Idaho
Website: www.rigginsidaho.org

Temperature Range – Fahrenheit: **
Spring: 35 to 73
Summer: 52 to 91
Fall: 33 to 80
Winter: 27 to 49
* U.S. Census Bureau Estimates July 2015
**Historical averages

Riggins lies in a mountain canyon on a long alluvial bar at the confluence of the Little Salmon and Salmon Rivers 35 miles northwest of McCall and 47 miles south of Grangeville, the county seat.

Idaho County has over 5.4 million acres and is Idaho's largest county. Eighty-five percent of the county is federal lands with high mountains and timbered forests. Given the city's low elevation among high rugged mountains, it has a surprisingly mild winter climate.

The Salmon River is the city's economic lifeblood. From Riggins, the Salmon River – known as the "River of no Return" and the longest free-flowing river in the lower 48 states – makes a ninety degree turn north on its remaining 60-mile course that falls about 900 feet before emptying into the Snake River.

The attraction of rafters, boaters and kayakers to the fast-flowing crystal-clear river has caused residents to name their city "Idaho's Whitewater Capital" and gateway to premier backcountry recreation and adventure.

Thousands of people come each year for exciting but safe whitewater raft excursions on the Salmon River. Some take short trips for a day. Others take customized overnight trips for a longer duration. Trips to the Snake River and Hells Canyon take nearly a week.

Anglers come to fish for steelhead, salmon, trout, bass and sturgeon.

Riggins around the turn of the century.

High-adventure campers pack into the Gospel Hump and Frank Church River of No Return Wilderness that lie to the east or to the Seven Devils Mountains and Hells Canyon National Recreation Area that lie to the west.

Other visitors come to be ferried upriver on jetboats to stay at privately owned wilderness resorts.

Pre-Incorporation Years

For centuries, Nez Perce Indians camped on the alluvial bar that borders the Salmon and Little Salmon Rivers.

During the 1863 gold rush upriver near Florence, prospectors stopped to pan for gold on the bar. Some found small quantities of the precious metal but did not stay.

In 1893 Isaac and Mary Irwin and their five sons purchased a gold mining claim on the bar, filed for a homestead and built the first house in what is now Riggins.

Main Street looking north around the turn of the century.

The Irwins were soon joined by other homesteaders who also began ranching and farming operations. The homesteaders built a schoolhouse on donated land in what is now Riggins. Fourteen students attended the first class.

At that time, John Riggins operated a ferry and blacksmith shop which he later moved to the north end of the bar near the site of the present bridge. In March 1901 John's son, Richard, and his wife, Ethel, came.

In the early years, a vicious saloon fight with obvious results led many local residents to refer to the town as "Gouge Eye."

A few years later, the Northern Pacific Railroad surveyed a line to what is now Riggins. Charley Clay, a principal in the Clay and Irwin Bar, persuaded the survey crew to plat a townsite on the Irwin homestead. In 1908 the railroad extended a branch line to Grangeville but the branch line to Riggins never materialized.

With people acquiring townsite lots, the community petitioned for a post office with Richard Riggins as postmaster. Postal authorities approved the post office

The first high school in Riggins was built about 1940; its first graduating class was in 1941.

but rather than accept the petition name that was already in use by another community, they named it Riggins.

Early settlers followed a narrow, windy north-south wagon road down the Little Salmon Canyon through the community, used the ferry to cross the river and then proceed on to Grangeville. In 1912 the state constructed a bridge across the Salmon River on the north end of town.

In 1926 the federal government established the U.S. highway system, at which time the road became what is now U.S. Highway 95. Around 1937 the federal government funded certain road improvements.

Incorporation

On July 5, 1947, Riggins became an incorporated village.

Turning Points

U.S. Highway 95 In 1926 the treacherous road that came into what is now Riggins became part of the 1,574-mile U.S. Highway 95 from Canada to Mexico – 538 miles of which are in Idaho.

Riggins was geographically isolated until the federal government's 1937 road improvements. In 2000 they

In 1916 the road from Grangeville to New Meadows was improved enough to accommodate cars. These stopped in front of a Riggins store.

reconstructed the highway. However, the high mountains on either side of the city forced the road to remain in the narrow canyon with businesses lined up on each side of the road, causing the Riggins business district to line Main Street through the length of the town.

They also replaced Time Zone Bridge that crosses the Salmon River north of town. The Salmon River divides the state between Pacific time on the north and Mountain time on the south.

Highway 95 is critical to Riggins prosperity and wellbeing.

Outdoor Recreation By the time the sawmill burned in 1982, Riggins was already becoming recognized as a base for exceptional whitewater and back-county recreation. Since that time, residents promoted and gradually developed the outdoor recreation businesses that now underpin the city's economy.

Riggins Today

Amenities and Attractions The city's most significant amenity is the Salmon River. In one way or another, most activities involve the river.

Riggins City Park comprises about five acres and is the location for many local events. The park has facilities for picnicking, children's play area and ball fields.

Riggins is the host to many annual events that are fun for the whole family.

Fishing at the confluence of the Little Salmon and main Salmon River.

The Riggins Sacred Salmon Ceremony and Friendship Feast takes place each May. This event celebrates the return of the salmon to their ancestral waters. Native Americans and non-Indians alike come together in friendship to celebrate this historic event.

In June, the annual Bigwater Blowout River Festival takes place. The event starts in Riggins City Park and includes rafting, fun games and good food.

The 4th of July Freedom Festival takes place each year in Riggins City Park.

The city also holds the Hot Summer Nights celebration in July. This event includes a talent show, kids games, food booths, a beer garden and good music.

Each fall, the city sponsors the

The Riggins Rodeo.

Steelhead Fishing Derby. In October, the city has the annual Regional Art Show and Silent Auction. In December, the city conducts the Community Craft Fair.

During the steelhead run that generally occurs in February and March, the community sponsors the "Women With Bait" steelhead tournament in which over 400 women compete for great prizes.

Economy and Major Employers Many city residents work for the Nez Perce National Forest-Salmon River Ranger District. District offices are located 18 miles north of Riggins.

The Salmon River School District is also a major public employer.

Tourism is Riggins' largest industry. Numerous businesses including river-related outfitter guide operations, motels, grocery and convenience stores, restaurants and RV parks line the Main Street, Highway 95, business district.

Education Salmon River School District provides for the educational needs of children grades K-12. The district offices, elementary, middle and high schools are located in the city.

Health Care Riggins has a medical clinic open four days a week. It also has two assisted living/long-term living facilities and volunteer emergency services. The closest hospitals are Syringa General Hospital in Grangeville and McCall Memorial Hospital.

Transportation U.S. Highway 95 is the transportation corridor connecting Riggins to the cities that lie to the north and south.

Utilities and Services Private companies provide electricity, telephone, DSL and satellite services. The City provides water and sewer services. The City Volunteer Fire and Emergency Services Department provides fire protection and ambulance services. The County Sheriff provides police protection.

Vision for 2050

In 1960 Riggins had a population of 588. Primarily due to the closure of the sawmill in 1982, the 1990 census reported a population of 443. During the past several years, the population has remained around 400.

In order to strengthen the city's economy, in 2006 community leaders preformed a comprehensive study, the "Riggins Area Economic Development Strategy," to evaluate the city's status and develop a long-term vision and strategic plan to achieve their goals.

The study has already obtained community support to begin a revitalization effort. This effort includes improving the municipal wastewater system, developing a public outdoor recreational center on school property and building a health and wellness center and industrial park areas to promote the establishment of small businesses.

Mayors

1968 Cleo H. Patterson
1976 Ward Hall
1982 Ace Barton
1994 Robert Zimmerman
2006 Robert "Bob" Crump
2013 Glenna McClure

Stites Fire Station and City Clerk's office.

Stites

Statistical Data

Population: 221 *
Elevation: 1,306 feet
Precipitation: 23 inches **
Average Snowfall: 61 inches **
County: Idaho
Website: www.stites.communityblogs.us

Temperature Range – Fahrenheit: **
Spring: 33 to 71
Summer: 49 to 88
Fall: 32 to 76
Winter: 26 to 42
* U.S. Census Bureau Estimates July 2015
**Historical averages

The city of Stites is a small, rural community located along the South Fork of the Clearwater River in Idaho County. State Highway 13 – the Northwest Passage Scenic Byway, an All American Road – runs through Stites connecting the city to Kooskia, 4 miles north, and Grangeville, 22 miles south.

Stites lies on the western edge of the Nez Perce National Forest and just south of the Clearwater National Forest. From Stites, people have easy access to rugged peaks, deep canyons, dense forests and remote wilderness.

Pre-Incorporation Years

The Nimiipuu (pronounced nee-mee-poo), the name the Nez Perce Indians call themselves, have resided along the Clearwater River and its tributaries for centuries.

In 1806 on their return trip from their expedition to the Pacific Ocean, the Lewis and Clark Corps of Discovery (Corps) camped at what is now Kamiah from

May 14 to June 9 waiting for the heavy snows in the rugged Bitterroot Mountains to melt sufficiently for them to cross.

While there, Lewis and Clark dispatched members of the Corps to hunt and explore. In early June of 1806 Sergeant John Ordway and two members of the Corps passed near Stites on their return trip from the Salmon River, located about 22 miles southwest. (*See Northern Idaho – Lewis and Clark.*)

Beginning a few years later, white explorers/trappers, Christian missionaries, prospectors and settlers would follow. In 1855 the U.S. Government and the Nez Perce chiefs signed a peace treaty. The treaty acknowledged the ancestral homelands of the Nez Perce and designated a reservation that covered a large part of north central Idaho and western Washington. The treaty prohibited uninvited access onto Indian reservation land.

Timothy James, one of the last survivors of the Nez Perce Indian War of 1877, died in 1958. His Indian name was Hsem-Tsilkin,and he was a member of the band of young Chief Joseph. Courtesy Alexandrea Davis

However, the discovery of gold at what is now Pierce in 1860 brought an uncontrolled influx of miners and settlers onto the reservation. In 1861 prospectors also found gold on reservation land at Elk City. Despite these treaty violations, the Nez Perce remained peaceful.

The miners and white settlers continued to disregard the Treaty of 1855 and move onto reservation land. They appealed to Congress to make more land and natural resources available to white settlement and development. Responding to these pressures, the federal government sought a new treaty with the Nez Perce, the Treaty of 1863. This treaty, which many Nez Perce chiefs refused to sign, greatly reduced the size of the reservation.

In 1877 the U.S Bureau of Indian Affairs ordered all of the Nez Perce to adhere to the 1863 Treaty and move to the Lapwai Reservation in what is now Idaho. The Nez Perce chiefs who had not signed the treaty were angry. However, they planned to avoid a fight by moving east to Montana. Some of the younger warriors disregarded the council of their leaders and attacked some of the settlements, killing many.

Clearwater battlefield. Courtesy Nez Perce National Forest.

General O.O. Howard incorrectly interpreted these forays as a general revolt and sent two cavalry companies to put it down. This escalation ultimately led to the Nez Perce War of 1877. The first major battle occurred June 17, 1877, at White

Bird Canyon, where the Nez Perce soundly defeated the U.S. Cavalry detachment, inflicting heavy losses.

Following the battle, the non-treaty Indians assembled near what is now Stites, where another battle ensued. On July 12, 1877, a fierce battle took place on a broad plateau immediately east and southeast of Stites – now known as the Clearwater Battlefield. Following a fierce battle between the Nez Perce and General Howard's overwhelming force of 600 troops, the Nez Perce combatants along with their families, horses and belongings fled east in hopes of reaching safety in Montana and Canada.

Unable to catch up to the fast moving Nez Perce, Howard wired ahead to General Sherman in Montana to send troops to intercept them. The war finally ended on October 4, 1877, when Chief Joseph surrendered at Bear Paw Mountain, Montana. (*See Northern Idaho, the Nez Perce War.*)

On February 8, 1887, Congress authorized the survey of Native American reservation lands, with specific acreages allotted to tribal members. They ruled any land not so allocated as surplus and available for non-Indian settlement.

The land in the Stites area, a travel corridor used by indigenous peoples in the region for centuries, was on reservation land. It opened for settlement on November 18, 1895. (*See Northern Idaho – Dawes Severalty Act.*)

In 1897 Jacob Stites homesteaded a 160-acre tract at what is now Stites. In 1898 three investors, apparently inspired by the natural transportation-corridor features of the location and the developing commerce created by the Elk City gold mines, acquired 60 acres of Stites – homestead for purposes of platting a new town. Under the terms of the sales contract, Stites retained the right to name the town. The three investors formed the Stites Townsite Company and in May 1899 platted the town named Stites.

Jacob Stites

In 1898 the Northern Pacific Railroad announced plans to build the Clearwater Short Line Railroad through Kooskia to Stites – now the Bountiful Grain and Craig Mountain War of 1877, died in 1958. His Insian name was Hsem-Tsilkin, Railroad (BG&CM).

The first train reached the Stites rail yard in 1902. Virtually all freight destined for Grangeville and Elk City came

Stites Depot. Carl Johnson collection. Courtesy Alexandrea Davis.

through Stites. The community remained a railroad boomtown until 1908 when railroad interests completed the Camas Prairie line from Lewiston to Grangeville. Even with that loss of business, the Stites depot and stockyards remained a shipping point.

The mining activity occurring in the 1860s to 1890s required construction of 53 miles of road over the Clearwater Mountains from the unincorporated town of Harpster, located eight miles south of Stites, to Elk City – the Elk City Wagon Road. Another road, now named Battle Ridge Road, connected Stites to Clearwater, an unincorporated town about 10 miles southeast of Stites. At the turn of the century, two stagecoaches and as many as 40 freight wagons pulled by four to eight mules or horses left Stites each day. For eight years, Mr. Pettibone, one of the town's founders, ran the stage between Stites and Elk City.

Hotel Tremont and a stage to Elk City, circa 1905. Courtesy Alexandrea Davis.

Around 1904 Mr. Pettibone and two other associates formed a telephone company to provide service from Stites to the Bell Telephone system in Grangeville. They installed or connected a continuous wire between the two communities. Where they could use barbed wire fences, company personnel placed strips of insulating rubber inner tube between the wire and fence post. Where there were gaps in the fence line, they installed telephone poles to hang the wire. For allowing the use of their fences, the company gave the farmers free telephone service for one year. P.E. Willis, a Stites entrepreneur and community booster, later acquired the phone line and founded the Stites Telephone Company.

Incorporation

On January 25, 1905, Stites became an incorporated village. At this time, Stites had five saloons, three blacksmith shops, two ice houses, five hotels, four livery barns, three general stores, three warehouses, two assay offices, a bank and a weekly newspaper. On August 25, 1967, Stites became an incorporated city as required by state law.

Pettibone Liveery, circa 1905. Courtesy Alexandrea Davis.

Turning Points

Railroad The decision of railroad executives to build their terminus depot at Stites provided the economic basis that established the town. BG&CM continues to provide freight service to Stites and the few remaining lumber mills along its route.

Fires On September 21, 1908, a blaze destroyed two major businesses. A disastrous fire swept the town in December 1923, destroying half the business district. In August 2003 a fire destroyed two Main Street businesses and the Rebekah/IOOF Lodge.

Floods The South Fork of the Clearwater River inundated the community in 1905, 1911, 1917 and 1948, washing away bridges and generally creating havoc. In 1950 the Army Corps of Engineers improved the dike between the river and the city, thereby eliminating further damaging floods.

Stites Today

Amenities and Attractions The city's location is perhaps its most attractive attribute. The mountains and prairies provide habitat for elk, moose, whitetail and mule deer, black bear, gray wolf, cougar, mountain goats and many smaller mammals. The South Fork of the Clearwater River provides streamside visitors with excellent steelhead and trout fishing, fine camping, picnicking and spectacular scenery.

Stites flood, 1911. Carrie Stadtman Packer collection. Courtesy Alexandrea Davis.

Today, adventurous explorers can start at Stites and retrace portions of the exact routes used as the Nez Perce fled Howard's army in 1877 by following the Nee-Me-Poo National Historic Trail, the Lolo Motorway, the Lolo Trail – all part of the Lolo Trail National Historic Landmark and still sacred to the Nimiipuu – and the historic Elk City Wagon Road.

Superb whitewater recreation is available on the Lochsa and Selway Rivers that merge to form the Middle Fork of the Clearwater River about 20 miles west of Stites.

Downhill skiing is available at Snowhaven Ski Area near Grangeville and Cottonwood Butte near Cottonwood.

An interpretive roadside pullout marks the location of the Clearwater Battlefield, one of the Nez Perce National Historic Park sites. It is on the west side of State Highway 13, approximately two miles south of Stites.

Stites South Fork Bridge, lost in the 1917 flood. Courtesy Alexandrea Davis.

The Nez Perce occupied the ravines above the plateau. The stone rifle pits and barricades raised by the Nez Perce are still present.

The Northwest Scenic Byway parallels or crosses the trail used by Lewis and Clark and the Corps of Discovery when they crossed Northern Idaho in 1805 and again in 1806. The Byway has two segments. The longest segment, Idaho Highway 12, extends from Lewiston, southeast to Kooskia, then east to Lolo Pass and the Lewis and Clark Interpretative Center on the Idaho/ Montana border. The southern segment, Idaho Highway 13, extends from Kooskia south through Stites to Grangeville.

Economy and Major Employers Stites business district consists of nine motels, a convenience store, a hardware store and an automotive/machine repair business. A few small wood-based manufacturing businesses are located near the city limits, including one remaining sawmill. Some residents commute to other cities for work.

Floods, fires, and economic changes caused by reduced access to federal lands for timber harvest and mining, technological innovation that decreaces the need for labor and encourages farm consolidation has slowly reduced the area's workforce and the business mix of the community.

Greving Mercantile, east corner of Main and Bridge Streets, circa 1904. Courtesy Alexandrea Davis.

Education Mountain View School District, with district offices in Grangeville, provides most of the elementary and secondary education in Idaho County. Stites youth attend elementary, junior and senior high schools in Kooskia or are home schooled.

The nearest institution of higher learning is Lewis-Clark State College (LCSC), located 82 miles northwest in Lewiston. LCSC offers distance learning and adult education courses at the LCSC Outreach Center in Grangeville.

The Kooskia Technology Learning Center and Kooskia Library, located in the Kooskia City Center, offer public access to computer stations and the Internet.

Health Care Two family practice medical clinics in Kooskia provide medical care for most of the Stites residents. Syringa Hospital & Clinics, headquartered in Grangeville, operates one of the clinics. The other clinic is a partnership between Clearwater Valley Hospital and Clinics of Orofino and St. Maries Hospital and Clinics in Cottonwood.

Chatterbox Coffee House, 2008. Photo courtesy of Hanna Pierson.

Transportation Idaho Highway 13 connects with Grangeville to the south and Kooskia to the north. Paved and gravel county roads reach east and west from Stites into the surrounding prairies and mountains.

The municipal airport at Kooskia offers grass runway service to small private and charter aircraft. The Idaho County Airport at Grangeville, also used by the U. S. Forest Service, has a 5,101-foot runway. The nearest commercial carrier airport is the Lewiston-Nez Perce Airport in Lewiston.

Railroad service is available for freight.

Utilities and Services Electricity, telephone, satellite and wireless services are available from private businesses. The City provides water and sewer services. The

Stites Volunteer Firefighters Association provides fire protection. The Idaho County Sheriff's Department has a contract with the City to deliver police protection. Idaho County also supplies solid waste pickup services.

Vision for 2050

City officials and community leaders have an ongoing volunteer effort to find better ways to achieve and maintain sustainable prosperity. To this end, a steering committee, composed of local volunteers and facilitated by University of Idaho staff and

Stites Grocery, 2008. Photo courtesy of Hanna Pierson.

private consultants, has recently conducted community hearings, workshops, and projects that have built on past successes and strategically looked for new opportunities.

Increased tourism has infused new money into the local economy and helped local businesses continue in business. The Steering Committee does not see tourism as a complete solution to all economic woes. However, it is an important industry that many Stites businesses will continue to pursue. Tourists and outdoor enthusiasts will

continue to come through Stites to experience the area's wilderness, outdoor sports and activities as well as the area's rich heritage, history, local craftsmen, art and culture. Many local entrepreneurs will continue to seek opportunities to access and develop the area's abundant natural resources.

In 2050 Stites will resemble what it is today – a rural community that is not only safe, close-knit and compassionate but also celebrates its rich heritage and culture and takes pride in its "small town" feel.

Mayors

1905 D.A. Smith *
1905 George Robertson *
1967 Gordon Biesecker
1970 Bernie Owens
1972 Lyle Hendren

1975 Howard Arlt
1985 Thomas Johnson
1988 Howard Arlt
2004 Deborah Vopat
2008 Rey Mireles

2014 Leslie Wilson
2016 Gerald Cathey
* Village Chairman

White Bird today. Courtesy Sheryl Clark.

White Bird

Statistical Data

Population: 93 *
Elevation: 1,560 feet
Precipitation: 23 inches **
Average Snowfall: 61 inches **
County: Idaho
Temperature Range – Fahrenheit: **

Spring: 35 to 73
Summer: 52 to 91
Fall: 33 to 80
Winter: 27 to 49
* U.S. Census Bureau Estimates July 2015
**Historical averages

White Bird lies a few miles from the southern base of the 4,488-foot-high White Bird Hill in a narrow canyon created by White Bird Creek, a tributary of the Salmon River.

The Salmon River, the River of No Return, flows about a mile west of the city. The Nez Perce National Forest begins a few miles east. Grangeville, the Idaho County seat, is 17 miles northeast of White Bird. Riggins is 29 miles south, and Lewiston is 86 miles north.

The city and many nearby geological features bear the name of Chief White Bird, leader of a band of about 300 Nez Perce Indians. Chief White Bird and his followers joined Nez Perce Chief Joseph and Chief Lookingglass in several battles and skirmishes with the U.S. Army in 1877, generally referred to as the Nez Perce War.

The Indians won the first battle of this war about two miles north of the city of White Bird. After that, the Nez Perce had running skirmishes with the army as they fled across Idaho to Montana where other contingents of the U.S. Army intercepted them – killing Chief Lookingglass and capturing Chief Joseph. White Bird and his band, with a few hundred horses, escaped into Canada – avoiding the fate of the other two bands of Nez Perce. (*See American Indians – Nez Perce War.*)

Pre-Incorporation Years

A.D. Chapman and his Umatilla Indian wife built a ferry across the Salmon River near the mouth of what is now White Bird Creek around 1863, about a mile west of what is now White Bird and what is now known as the Jim Kilgore Farm. The ferry was germane to the founding of White Bird.

White Bird circa 1920. Courtesy Mike Peterson.

Chapman and the succeeding owners of the ferry were granted a post office, likely named Chapman as the use of "White Bird" in the naming of geographical locations did not occur until after the 1877 Nez Perce War.

Frontier post offices often consisted of a wooden box in a public location such as a store or office. The postmaster or postmistress was often the store proprietor. People sorted through the box to find their mail. Before wagon roads were available, U.S.

White Bird circa 1925. Courtesy Mike Peterson.

postal carriers transported the mail by horseback or on foot, carrying the mail in their backpacks.

Prospectors discovered gold near Pierce in 1860, prompting Idaho's first gold rush. Most of these prospectors traveled from the coast by steamer up the Columbia and Snake Rivers to Lewiston and then traveled 75 miles east by foot or horseback to Pierce. Use of Chapman's Ferry increased dramatically when prospectors spread out from Pierce to several other placer gold discoveries in the mountains to the south and east. One of the largest was at Florence in 1861.

Initially, the roads were little more than trails used by people on horseback, pack trains and herders driving domestic livestock.

Florence is about 25 miles southeast of what is now White Bird and a similar distance northeast of Riggins. The trail went south of White Bird about 10 miles to Slate Creek, then turned east on Slate Creek Road to the Florence gold fields. Prospectors coming from the south passed through what is now Riggins and either traveled north to take the Slate Creek route or turned east at Riggins for 11 miles up the Salmon River before turning north on the Allison Creek Road to Florence. By 1862 several thousand fortune seekers were panning for gold in the small creeks around Florence.

The community that grew up around Chapman's Ferry became a trailhead and supply station for a steady stream of prospectors and merchants with trains of pack animals carrying food and supplies on the ferry and on to Florence. A small boomtown developed near the ferry where prospectors prepared and equipped themselves for the balance of

The town of White Bird after a big fire, date unknown. Courtesy Mike Peterson.

their journey. Most merchants took their pack trains loaded with food and supplies over the trails to Florence where they sold the goods directly to the miners at prices several times the original cost.

The Florence gold rush reached its peak shortly after it began. By 1863 most of the prospectors had moved on to the bonanza gold discoveries in the Boise Basin and the Owyhee Mountains. (*See Southwestern Idaho, The Region – Mining.*) As placer gold mines at Florence played out, ferry traffic also declined, but service continued for several years. After gold was discovered in the mountains west of Salmon, freighters took supplies from Lewiston – pack trains of mules and horses traveling over 200 miles of rugged mountain trails to Salmon.

The Chapman's sold their ferry to Samuel Benedict and Grat Bernamayon in 1874 and moved into a cabin five miles northeast near a creek now named in their honor.

Benedict and Bernamayon secured a franchise from the Idaho County Commission to operate the ferry. The franchise was originally granted for eight years on condition that the two entrepreneurs build "a good and substantial wire cable ferry." Charges for using their ferry were 75 cents for a horse or mule and rider, 50 cents for a loaded pack animal, 25 cents for a "Horse Light and Loose," 25 cents per head for cattle, 12 cents each for hogs and sheep and 25 cents for a man on foot.

Following Benedict's death, his widow sold the ferry to G.W. Curtis and his partner John Hammer in 1892. The new owners advertised in the Idaho County Free Press on April 5, 1892, "Curtis White Bird Ferry – on the direct route to Joseph and Domecq Plains and [the entire] county situated between the Salmon and Snake Rivers. Our cable is made of the very best Bessemer Steel and the Ferry boat is of the same substantial construction." Curtis's son Fred took over the ferry in 1899.

About 13 miles southwest of White Bird near what is now Pittsburg Landing, Mike Thompson and Albert Kurry built a ferry across the Snake River in 1891. The road between the two ferries – now Forest Road 493, also known as Deer Creek Road – is narrow and steep with many tight switchbacks and breathtaking views. In the early years, the road and ferry provided an important transportation corridor between Oregon and Idaho for the early settlers and river traffic. Today, Pittsburg Landing is a popular developed campground maintained by the U.S. Forest Service with a boat dock and launch for jet boats coming from Lewiston and Cambridge through Hells Canyon, the deepest gorge in North America. (*See The Region, Distinctive Geographic and Geologic Features.*)

Present-day White Bird is near the transportation corridor, U.S. Highway 95, between Lewiston and Boise just east of the Salmon River.

The original road north on the Grangeville side of the mountain had gentle slopes and was relatively easy to travel. However, on the White Bird side it started as a trail that, in part, ran through the long and steep mountain ravine that lies between today's U.S. Highway 95 and the switchback highway built in the 1920s, now the White Bird Hill Grade Historic Site – a 14-mile, 3,000-foot vertical climb. The road was so narrow and steep in places that wagons coming down the gorge often drug logs to slow their speed of descent. A settler built a home and way station a few miles from the bottom of the gulch where travelers could rest and water their animals.

During the 1870s James Baker acquired – likely a homestead claim – the land that would become the future site of White Bird. As reported in Idaho County Voices, a publication written to commemorate Idaho's 1990 centennial celebration, Baker was killed during the brief but difficult times of the Nez Perce War of 1877.

Katherine Kline Clay, another resident of the area, gave an interview in 1911 recounting her experiences near what is now White Bird during the Nez

Catholic Church, built in the early 1900s.
Courtesy of Sheryl Clark.

Perce War when her first husband, Edward Osborn, and other settlers were killed. (*See Southwestern Idaho, New Meadows.*)

After leaving the unincorporated gold mining boomtown of Warren, northeast of McCall, they traveled north through Meadows Valley to a location that consisted of a few log cabins that they called French Bar, presumed to be near what is now White Bird. There is no record that White Bird was ever called French Bar; however, a French Cemetery is about an eighth of a mile from the present-day Salmon Bridge and Old Highway 95.

Although details of accounts vary, Clay said that on June 13, 1877, the men were helping neighbors harvest hay when a messenger rode up with the news that a band of Indians had killed four men, apparently prospectors, working on Slate Creek.

Edward Osborn and those with him hurried to move their families to one of the cabins that had stronger fortifications. They no sooner arrived than a war party led by Chief White Bird attacked the cabin, killing the men and one woman. The other women and children survived by lying flat on the floor as the bullets passed overhead. Clay said that Chief White Bird entered the cabin with some of his warriors. He told the women and children that he intended to spare them, but it was obvious he had great difficulty controlling his warriors who were drunk, apparently from whisky they discovered during an earlier raid.

Clay said Chief White Bird was able to get the women and children out of the cabin and saw them on their way to the home of a family member 12 miles away. The first to arrive at the destination were still in shock. The youngest of the Osborn children, a two-year-old daughter who traveled on the back of an adult, delivered the message of the tragedy. She

IOOF Hall, built in the 1900s. Courtesy of Sheryl Clark.

said, "Pap shot dead, uncle dead, Indians shoot, Momma coming."

Following James Baker's death, the land passed to L.P. Brown, who built a store. He sold the store to Frank and George Fenn around 1889. The Fenn brothers successfully made application to the U.S. postal authorities to open the White Bird Post Office in their store with Frank as postmaster. Steven S. Fenn purchased the remainder of the property from Brown in 1891.

The small community grew slowly until the Fenn's built a stage station in White Bird in 1893. Fenn Station quickly became popular for teamsters and passengers preparing to make the climb up the long wagon road. It was also a welcome rest stop for passengers, teamsters and animals completing the long, stressful, wheel-breaking descent down the road.

As traffic on the road increased, a town began to develop. By 1900 the town had three hotels, a livery stable,

Silver Dollar Bar, built in 1954. Courtesy of Sheryl Clark.

saloons and various small stores and shops. The 1900 census reported a population of 176, and by 1910 the population had increased to 400.

The need for a better road up on the southern slope of White Bird Hill was critical. After the turn of the century, transportation officials began planning for the road but experienced challenges that proved difficult to overcome. The *Salmon River Sun*, a county-wide newspaper, reported on August 21, 1913, "work on the north and south wagon road, under the auspices of the highway commission, is to be started very soon. The courts have upheld the constitutionality of the bond issue and the report seems entirely plausible." Workmen finally began work on grading and graveling the switch-back road up White Bird Hill in 1921.

In an oral history, White Bird resident Virginia Benz Adkison said that around 1936 or 1937 the school was closed for the funeral of a local resident who died working on improving and paving the road.

Incorporation

On September 11, 1956, White Bird became an incorporated village. It became a city in 1967 to conform to the change in Idaho municipal law.

Turning Points

White Bird Hill Roads

The original White Bird Hill Road led to the founding of White Bird. It began as a rest stop for travelers making trips over the White Bird Hill Grade where people going up the hill could get supplies and prepare their rigs for the arduous climb and travelers headed down could rest after making the harrowing trip.

Doc Foskett's, 1900s. Courtesy of Sheryl Clark.

The State used convict labor to help widen the switchback road, built during the 1920s, to two lanes. In 1926 the road became part of U.S. Highway 95. At the time the road was paved in 1938, it had so many switchbacks that, if the arcs were combined, they would constitute 37 full 360-degree circles.

By that time, motor vehicles were replacing horse-drawn wagons and coaches, and the character of the town's business community was changing to less labor-intensive services that catered to car and truck traffic. In 1940 the village population reflected this loss of employment and dropped to 275. By the end of the next decade, it had fallen to 175.

Around 1965 the Idaho Department of Transportation began construction of a new road up White Bird Hill. Contractors took 10 years to complete the complex construction project of massive cuts and fills – now a graceful seven-mile curved road. During this time, the city's population swelled with construction workers, only to fall off when the road was completed.

The new road is elevated as it bypasses White Bird on the west. A frontage road provides access down into the city. From the elevated highway, the landscaped setting below gives the appearance of looking down into a beautiful secluded community nestled in a mountain valley.

White Bird Today

Amenities and Attractions The city has a small downtown park with a memorial to its veterans. The City leases the closed White Bird School from the school district. The school baseball field, playground equipment and stone picnic tables have been donated to the City.

Each June on Father's Day, the community sponsors "White Bird Days," a traditional community reunion that attracts current and former residents and families. The principal event is the White Bird Rodeo.

The nearby Nez Perce National Forest and Salmon River provide a paradise for outdoor enthusiasts. Fishing, boating, hunting, kayaking, ATV riding, snowmobiling and camping are available within a short drive from the city.

Old White Bird Road is on the National Register of Historic Places and is open to traffic. It provides a wonderful opportunity for tourists to take this backcountry drive and relive the area's history.

The nearby White Bird Battlefield Historical Site is part of the Nez Perce National Park system. Unguided walking tours are available at the site.

The historic Dr. Wilson Foskett Home and Drugstore memorializes this dedicated physician who, for 27 years, was the primary medical practitioner and first responder in most of Idaho County. He was known to selflessly put the care of his patients ahead of his own interests. He died in 1924 when the already physically spent doctor, driving from Riggins after responding to the emergency needs of an expectant mother, fell asleep and his car ran off the road into the Salmon River. A roadside monument to this exceptional and beloved man stands near the location of his death.

Pittsburg Landing, a modern 28-unit campground on the Snake River in Hells Canyon, lies across the Salmon River and the 4,300-foot divide between the Salmon and Snake Rivers.

Downhill skiing is available 22 miles northeast at Snowhaven Ski Area, accessed through Grangeville.

Outside of town, there are a couple of camping and RV camps; a couple of boat ramps for boating; lots of fishing, hiking and 4-wheeling where the State

White Bird Veterans Memorial Park. Courtesy Sheryl Clark.

permits; and the Indian Battle Grounds, just north of White Bird.

Economy and Major Employers White Bird's employment base consists of several small businesses and retail stores and shops. Most working residents commute to nearby cities for employment.

Education Grangeville School District provides most of the elementary and secondary education in the area. White Bird children ride the bus to schools in Grangeville or, at the parents' expense, travel to Riggins.

The nearest institution of higher learning is Lewis-Clark State College (LCSC) 55 miles northwest in Lewiston.

Health Care The nearest hospital is the 14-bed Syringa General Hospital in Grangeville.

Transportation U.S. Highway 95 passes on the western edge of the city.

The 5,100-foot runway at Idaho County Airport in Grangeville serves forest service, private and charter aircraft.

The nearest certified commercial airport is in Lewiston.

Utilities and Services Private companies provide electricity, telephone, cable and satellite services. The City provides water and sewer services. Fire protection is provided by the White Bird Volunteer Fire Department. Residents outside the city receive fire protection from the Salmon River Rural Fire Department. The County Sheriff's Office provides police services. A private company provides garbage pickup.

White Bird City Hall. Courtesy Sheryl Clark.

Vision for 2050

Since 1990 the city's population has remained around 100. The population will likely remain somewhat constant.

By 2050 White Bird will continue to be a warm friendly community – a safe and peaceful place to raise a family.

Mayors

1961 Wayne Eller *
1966 Tom Robson *
1967 Tom Robson
1967 Donald Sickels
1982 Wayne Eller

1986 Ben Canaday
1990 Earl Hyghes
1992 Pat Cope
1998 Corby Reid
1993 Keith Ray

2007 Rick Alley
2016 Rodney Pilant
* Village Chairman

Coeur d'Alene Beach.

KOOTENAI COUNTY

- Athol
- Coeur d'Alene (County Seat)
- Dalton Gardens
- Fernan Lake
- Harrison
- Hauser
- Hayden
- Hayden Lake
- Huetter
- Post Falls
- Rathdrum
- Spirit Lake
- Stateline
- Worley

Athol

Statistical Data

Population: 694 *
Elevation: 2,392 feet
Precipitation: 30 inches **
Average Snowfall: 50 inches **
County: Kootenai
Website: www.cityofathol.us

Temperature Range – Fahrenheit: **
Spring: 27 to 66
Summer: 45 to 80
Fall: 28 to 69
Winter: 22 to 39
* U.S. Census Bureau Estimates July 2015
**Historical averages

Athol lies four miles west of Farragut State Park and the southern tip of the beautiful Lake Pend Oreille. The city of Coeur d'Alene is about 16 miles south.

Farmland and forested areas surround the city. Kaniksu National Forest is accessible a few miles east and west of the city.

Pre-Incorporation Years

Until the early 1800s when explorers/trappers began coming into the area, American Indians – primarily of the Coeur d'Alene and Spokane Tribes – had exclusive use of the land as they migrated through the region en route to their encampments near the area's many lakes and streams.

This all changed in 1881 when the Northern Pacific Railway established a depot on its line between Hauser Junction and Sandpoint. They named the train station Athol after a city in Massachusetts, which in turn derived its name from a community in Scotland.

Railroad employees were the town's first residents. Homesteaders soon began filing claims in the general area of the train depot and a small community of a general store and shops was established. In 1895 town residents successfully petitioned postal authorities for a post office.

Athol Train Depot.

However, the location of the new community was on state lands. State surveyors platted the new township but, apparently, did not record the change in ownership. For many years, the town's residents did not have title to their land. However, the state finally corrected the problem.

In 1900 the Methodist congregation built a church that also served as a school until 1902 when school patrons built their first school building. About the same time, the Baptist congregation built their church.

Athol's first water well was dug by hand by Joe Pricsha and his crew. It was 350 plus feet deep. They dug into a large boulder, so they had to dig around it, which made a curve in the shaft. A 5hp pump motor was installed,

Old Athol City Hall.

which supplied the town with water. Later, another shaft with a larger pump was installed in the same hand-dug hole.

In December 1902 Hackett & Wilson opened a sawmill near the city. The mill became the city's largest employer and had the capacity of producing 25,000 board feet of lumber per day. After lumberjacks cleared the timber, farmers brought the land under cultivation.

By 1903 the town had a hotel, a drugstore, a blacksmith, a jewelry store, restaurants, a mercantile store and a saloon.

Incorporation

On August 10, 1909, Athol became an incorporated village. In November 1967 it became an incorporated city in accordance with the requirements of new state law.

Turning Points

Railroad and Sawmill Athol owes its existence and name to the railroad. However, it was the sawmill that provided most of the jobs, allowing the town to grow and prosper.

Athol Today

Amenities and Attractions Two state parks are nearby. The 4,000-acre Farragut State Park is four miles east, and the 142-acre Round Lake State Park is about ten miles north.

Farragut State Park was a World War II naval base that, following the war, the military donated to the state. In 1942 the U.S. Navy built Farragut Naval Training Station on 4,000 acres at the southern end of Lake Pend Oreille. The lake was deep and large enough for the Navy to perform their navel research and training in a secure setting. The training base also became an encampment for prisoners of war.

During this time, civilian jobs on base provided a significant boost to Athol's economy. The park now has a museum commemorating the role of the naval station during the war.

Some of the city's natural amenities include the beautiful surrounding mountains, lakes, rivers and streams. They offer excellent

Methodist Church, built 1900.

opportunities for backpacking, hiking, trail riding, boating, fishing, hunting, snowmobiling and cross-country skiing. Downhill skiing is available at Schweitzer Mountain Resort, about 30 miles north.

About a mile south of town is Silverwood Theme Park. This privately owned park has over 65 rides and attractions including a 12-acre water park. The park draws visitors from throughout the Inland Northwest.

Economy and Major Employers Lakeland School is the city's largest employer. Most residents commute to nearby larger cities to work and shop.

Education Lakeland School District provides the public education in the city. Elementary students attend Athol Elementary. Middle and senior high school students attend school about nine miles east in Spirit Lake.

Farragut Naval Base in World War II.

The closest institution for higher learning is North Idaho College in Coeur d'Alene.

Health Care The closest hospital is Kootenai Medical Center in Coeur d'Alene.

Transportation U.S. Highway 95 to Sandpoint on the north and Coeur d'Alene and Interstate 90 on the south as well as State Highway 58 to Spirit Lake intersect the city.

Local airports provide service for small private and charter aircraft. Airports in Coeur d'Alene and Spokane provide commercial air service.

Rail service is available for freight. Amtrak passenger service is available 26 miles north in Sandpoint.

Athol Elementary School.

Utilities and Services Private companies provide electricity, telephone, gas and satellite services. The city provides water and sewer services as well as police and fire protection.

Silverwood Theme Park.

Vision for 2050

Over the past 50 years, the city's population has grown over 220 percent. The city's 1960 population was 214. However, over the past decade the city's population stabilized at around 700.

While recent population trends will likely continue for the next several years. The city's population will gradually begin to grow at moderate rates of around one percent annually. This growth will primarily come as more young parents see they can raise their families in the peaceful city of Athol where affordable housing is available and still easily commute to work and enjoy the amenities of nearby larger urban centers.

The city's municipal systems are adequate to handle moderate growth within existing tax structures.

Mayors

** Unknown
1994 Lanny Spurlock

2014 Darla Kuhman
2016 Robert Wachter

Aerial view of Coeur d'Alene.

Coeur d'Alene

Statistical Data

Population: 47,912 *
Elevation: 2,187 feet
Precipitation: 30 inches **
Average Snowfall: 50 inches **
County: Kootenai
Website: www.cdaid.org

Temperature Range – Fahrenheit: **
Spring: 27 to 66
Summer: 45 to 80
Fall: 28 to 69
Winter: 22 to 39
* U.S. Census Bureau Estimates July 2015
**Historical averages

Coeur d'Alene (pronounced core-da-lane) is one of Idaho's foremost resort cities and regional business centers. Visitors from around the world come each year for recreation, conferences and meetings in the city's five star hotels. Many hotel rooms have breathtaking views of the vividly blue Coeur d'Alene Lake with forests that come to the water's edge.

Fifteen miles to the west is the Idaho/Washington border. Just a few miles to the east is the Coeur d'Alene National Forest and Mountains as well as the Bitterroot Mountain Range.

Kootenai County is Idaho's third most populous county; and Coeur d'Alene is the state's eighth largest city.

Pre-Incorporation Years

In 1805 to 1806 when the Lewis and Clark expedition crossed what is now Idaho about 120 miles to the south, the Coeur d'Alene Tribe of American Indians inhabited the land of Coeur d'Alene.

In 1809 David Thompson – an employee of the North West Company of Montreal, Canada – led a party into Northern Idaho to explore, map and set up fur trading posts. He drew the first map of North Idaho. He called what would become Coeur d'Alene Lake "Pointed Heart Lake."

In 1841 Roman Catholic missionaries led by Father Pierre Jean de Smet came to teach the Indians their religion and culture.

In 1860 Captain John Mullan led 230 soldiers and civilian workers in the construction of a 624-mile military wagon road from Fort Benton, Montana, through what is now the Silver Valley and the city of Coeur d'Alene, to Fort Walla Walla, Washington. It was the first engineered road in the Inland Northwest. Interstate 90 generally follows Mullan Road.

Fort Sherman.

In 1877 reacting to concerns about Indian conflicts in the West, General William Tecumseh Sherman – the Union Civil War hero – made an inspection tour of military forts in the Northwest. While traveling over Mullan Road, Sherman passed along the northern shore of Lake Coeur d'Alene. He was so impressed with the setting that he made a recommendation to Congress that they authorize construction of a new military post on the north shore of the lake.

Congress approved Sherman's recommendation and in 1878 authorized construction of Fort Coeur d'Alene on 999 acres of land at the headwaters of the Spokane River. The name of the fort was later changed to Fort Sherman. The military also commissioned Captain C.P. Sorensen, a boat builder from Portland, to build a steamboat to patrol the 30-mile-long lake.

Civilians employed to build the fort and other settlers started a small tent and log cabin village near the fort that they called Coeur d'Alene City.

At the same time this was happening, a prospector, A.J. Prichard, made significant placer gold discoveries about 40 miles due east of Coeur d'Alene near what is now Murray. In 1883 he made disclosure of his discoveries to some of his

Steamboat ("steamer") and trolley.

friends, setting off a major gold rush. By the end of 1885 10,000 people converged on Shoshone County, scouring the mountains and streams in search of precious metals. This flow of fortune seekers promoted considerable traffic through the fort and Coeur d'Alene City. The village's economy boomed.

After the discovery of gold in the area, the military allowed use of their steamboat to accommodate the flood of people headed for the gold fields, transporting them across the lake.

Entrepreneurs, seeing business opportunities, immediately began to build and operate additional steamboats – called steamers. Most of the steamers served the practical freight and passenger needs of the miners and, later, the lumber businesses and communities growing up around the lake. However, some steamers also played to the tourist trade by offering upscale accommodations.

Lake Coeur d'Alene.

One of the first settlers near Fort Coeur d'Alene, Tony Tubbs, platted his land into town lots and built the settlement's first hotel, the Hotel d'Landing. A general merchandising store, drug store and law office soon followed. The attorney, Isaac Daily, taught school in the fall of 1884 for the newly formed school district.

In 1884 prospectors in the Coeur d'Alene Mining District, nicknamed the Silver Valley, began to make significant discoveries of silver, lead, zinc and gold ore (silver-lead). In 1885 Noah Kellogg made the largest of these discoveries near what is now Wardner. The mine entrance later moved down the mountain to Kellogg. He and one of his partners named their discovery the Bunker Hill and Sullivan Mine (The Bunker Hill Mine).

While the placer gold mines soon played out, the silver-lead discoveries developed into deep-shaft hard rock mines that operated throughout most of the twentieth century. Some are still in operation.

Finding the silver-lead ore bodies was one thing, but processing the ore was another. Initially, they shipped the ore over an arduous route to a smelter in San Francisco. The Bunker Hill Mine was among the first ore processed. They

Early motel.

transported the ore from the Bunker Hill Mine on freight wagons to Lake Coeur d'Alene, then by steamboat to Coeur d'Alene City, then freight wagon for 13 miles northwest to the Northern Pacific Railway station at Rathdrum where it was loaded on railcars to Portland, then by steamer to San Francisco.

However, use of the difficult overland route would be short lived. In 1896 the Spokane and Idaho Railroad constructed a branch line from the main line south of Rathdrum to Coeur d'Alene. Within the next two years, the railroad would extend to most of the large mines of the Silver Valley.

As the mines developed, they built ore concentrators and smelters in the Silver Valley. The ore freighting business went away; however, the railroad continued playing a central role of transporting heavy metal ingots produced at the smelters as well as moving supplies and passengers.

By 1887 the city had several more retail businesses including shops, hotels, livery stables, a saddle shop and saloons.

Incorporation

On August 22, 1887, the "City" designation was dropped from the name and the Kootenai County Commissioners at Rathdrum, the county seat, made Coeur d'Alene an incorporated village.

Large house in Coeur d'Alene.

Following incorporation, local business leaders set out on an economic development campaign. The most noteworthy of these efforts occurred at Idaho Day during the 1890 Spokane Exposition. Thousands of pamphlets were distributed advertising Coeur d'Alene as the "Switzerland of America."

The pamphlet said the village had a population of 800 and nine steamers operating on the lake. It extolled Fort Sherman and the music of the Fourth Infantry Band. Fort Sherman was officially closed March 9, 1900. The pamphlet listed the village's many businesses, including retail

Coeur d'Alene 1950s.

establishments, a brickyard, a sawmill, a shingle mill, a U.S. Land Office and a newspaper.

In 1906 the city had grown large enough to qualify to change its legal status to an incorporated city. Two years later, the voters approved moving the county seat from Rathdrum to Coeur d'Alene.

Turning Points

Fort Sherman (Coeur d'Alene) Congressional acceptance of General William Tecumseh Sherman's recommendation to build Fort Coeur d'Alene on the north shore of Lake Coeur d'Alene in 1878 led to the formation and name of the city.

Mining in the Silver Valley Coeur d'Alene was not a mining town. However, it was on the early wagon, steamboat and train transportation corridors between the Silver Valley mines to the east and the Washington and Oregon cities to the west. Coeur d'Alene became a supply center and rest stop for thousands of people with business in the mining district. For many years, the Silver Valley mines underpinned the city's growth.

Railroads The coming of the railroad to the city in 1896 established the city as a business center and put it on the course of becoming the most prominent community in Kootenai County.

A few years later, the Oregon Railway & Navigation Company would build a rail line around the southern end of Lake Coeur d'Alene and then on to the Silver Valley. That railroad became a major competitor to the railroad that went through Coeur d'Alene; however, the city was already established and prepared to benefit from the next economic driver in the area sawmills.

In the early 1900s one of the sawmill entrepreneurs, F.A. Blackwell, would also be responsible for building the Coeur d'Alene and Spokane Electric Railroad and the Idaho and Washington & Northern Railroad to Coeur d'Alene.

Steamboats Steamboats were less of a turning point than they were an important player in the development of Coeur d'Alene's economy and the quality of life of its residents and visitors.

In the early years, the steamers were a critical link in moving passengers and freight to and from the mines. For many years thereafter, they played a major role in advancing sawmill interests, facilitating commerce, providing mail and communication to the communities and businesses along the lakeshore and, finally, promoting tourism.

Sawmills In 1900 William Dollar led an investment group that built the Coeur d'Alene Mill. A year later, F.A. Blackwell led another group of investors in a long-range program of purchasing large tracts of timberland and building several sawmills. Dollar, Blackwell and other timber entrepreneurs not only established the wood products industry that replaced mining as the city's economic driver, they invested in other businesses and city infrastructure.

North Idaho College Founded in 1933, this 2-year community college now has about 4,700 students and is one of the city's largest employers. In addition to providing pre-university courses of study, workforce training and housing satellite campuses for Idaho universities, the college makes another significant contribution to the cultural fabric and well-being of the community. It is a center for the performing arts including plays, concerts, lecturers and other activities open to the public.

North Idaho College has made a profound impact on the city of Coeur d'Alene.

Adapting to the New Economy The natural resource based industries that once underpinned the city's economy have declined to a shadow of what they were in the twentieth century. Now, hospitality, tourism, health care and education underpin the city's economy.

The most significant event that elevated the city of Coeur d'Alene as a destination resort and hospitality center occurred in 1986. In that year, the Hagadone Corporation completed the 5-star, 360-room Coeur d'Alene Resort. The resort – with its spectacular views of the lake and wooded mountains, golf course and other amenities – is consistently a major attraction for visitors worldwide. The photograph of the resort, lake and marina has become so well known that it has become a city icon.

Coeur d'Alene Today

Amenities and Attractions The city has 394 acres devoted to 17 developed parks and one natural park. The developed parks offer a wide array of amenities including playgrounds, picnic areas and shelters, an amusement park, baseball and softball diamonds, volleyball and basketball courts,

City park.

soccer fields, a climbing wall, a disc golf course, a skate park, boat ramps and docks, a swimming beach and a band shell.

The natural park, Tubbs Park, is a 120-acre natural area with a 2.2-mile interpretive trail along the shore of Coeur d'Alene Lake.

The city has two golf courses. Both are open to the public. The Coeur d'Alene Resort Golf Course, with its floating green on Coeur d'Alene Lake, is internationally famous.

The North Idaho Centennial Trail is one of the national Millennium Legacy Trails dedicated in 1999. The trail is a paved scenic path used by walkers, runners, bicyclists and the handicapped. The trail meanders for 24 miles from the Idaho/Washington state line along the Spokane River to the 34-acre Coeur d'Alene Parkway State Park, six miles east of the city.

Farragut State Park is 28 miles north. In 1942 at the beginning of World War II, the U.S. Navy built a training station on the southern shore of Lake Pend Oreille.

Tubbs Hill trail.

There were so many Naval personnel living at the station that for two years it was the most populous community in Idaho. While it was a naval station, it provided jobs for hundreds of local residents. After the war, the federal government removed most of the buildings and gave the 4,000-acre facility to the State of Idaho. The park has a military museum and facilities for a variety of activities including boating, swimming, hiking, biking, model airplane flying and a shooting range.

Silverwood Theme Park is 20 miles north near Athol. The park offers numerous rides and attractions including a roller coaster, a steam engine train and various rides on the water.

The Ray and Joan Kroc Corps Community Center is a 109,000-square-foot facility operated by the Salvation Army. It has pools for competitive and leisure swimming, specialized facilities for a variety of indoor athletic games, fitness and exercise equipment and a large hall for church meetings, lectures and the performing arts.

The Kootenai County Fairgrounds and Events Center has interconnected buildings used for the annual county fair each August and numerous other activities including swap meets, shows and exhibits.

Each December, marks the city's Christmas Lighting Ceremony. This large and beautiful display has received national recognition.

The city's closeness to mountains, lakes and forests makesit an extraordinary recreational destination

Coeur d'Alene City Hall.

for almost all types of outdoor sports and activities. It is a place that an increasing number of people call home.

Economy and Major Employers The Hagadone Corporation that owns and operates the Coeur d'Alene Resort has over 1,500 employees and is the city's largest employer. Other major employers in the city include Kootenai Medical Center (1,200); North Idaho College (1,000); Central Partners, a call center (900); Coeur d'Alene School District (900); and the Kootenai Rehabilitation Center (750). Numerous other public and private employers in the city have several hundred employees each.

Coeur d'Alene is a regional shopping and business center. Many of the city's workforces live in nearby communities and commute to the city for work.

Education The Coeur d'Alene School District provides elementary and secondary education to over 10,000 students. The school district includes students in Coeur d'Alene, Dalton Gardens, Hayden, Hayden Lake and part of rural Kootenai

Coeur d'Alene aerial view.

County. Several private schools also provide elementary and secondary education to city students.

While North Idaho College is a two-year community college, the University of Idaho, Lewis-Clark State College, Boise State University and other academic institutions offer educational programs or have outreach programs on campus that offer associate, bachelor, masters and doctoral degrees in a variety of disciplines.

Health Care The 225-bed Kootenai Medical Center is a regional medical center. It is located on a 40 acre, integrated campus of high-tech patient towers, healing gardens, office buildings and public education centers – all connected by green space, bike and walking paths and water features.

Skatepark kiddies parade.

Several general medical clinics, nursing and assisted living homes and other medical providers also provide services for area residents.

Transportation Federal Interstate I-90 and U.S. Highway 95 intersect the city.

The Coeur d'Alene Airport is located nine miles northwest of the city near Hayden. It has two runways – one 7,400 and the other 5,400 feet long. The Spokane International Airport is about 53 miles west of the city.

Rail freight service is available in the city. Amtrak passenger service is available 46 miles north in Sandpoint.

Utilities and Services Private companies provide electricity, telephone, natural gas, cable and satellite services. The City provides water and sewer services as well as fire and police protection.

Vision for 2050

Although the future of the city is subject to unforeseen events that we cannot project, historic demographic and population trends provide useful information for city planning purposes.

Over the past 15 years, the city's population had been growing 3 to 4 percent annually. If those trends continue, by 2050 the city's population will more than double.

City park.

The population growth of the city will likely occur to the north and west. In addition, taller buildings devoted to offices, condominiums, apartments, specialty retail shops, eclectic art galleries and elegant restaurants will likely increase in downtown areas.

Public transportation in the form of light rail, trolley and buses will likely extend their routes to help reduce traffic congestion and mitigate the need to develop additional parking areas in the city.

The city will improve and extend bicycle and pedestrian paths to enable a more fuel-conscious citizenry to get to their destinations safely and efficiently.

The city's infrastructure will develop to meet this growing demand. However, the city will seek to employ impact fees and other approaches to cause growth to pay for itself.

The city will manage its growth in a manner that protects the city's beauty, character and heritage. We anticipate our citizens generous and welcoming spirit will continue to give Coeur d'Alene a special sense of place.

Mayors

1887 Charles D. Warner *
1888 George H. Martin *
1889 James Graham *
1890 George Connors *
1891 H.L. Bancroft *
1892 James H. Harte *
1893 Frank Bustaw *
1894 John Sabin *
1895 Duncan Smith *
1897 George C. Thomson *
1898 John Leurry *
1900 George E. Reynolds *
1901 A.V. Chamberlain *
1904 H.V. Scallon *
1905 Robert Collins *
1907 Hugh V. Scallon

1909 Boyd Hamilton
1911 John T. Wood
1913 R.S. Nelson
1915 S.H. McEuen
1917 C.H. Potts
1919 H.P. Glindeman
1921 J.C. Dwyer
1923 O.W. Edmonds
1927 George Natwick
1931 Jess Ray Simpson
1933 John Knox Coe
1937 A. Grantham
1939 John Knox Coe
1941 P.M. Panabaker
1943 O.W. Edmonds
1945 A.M. Roselund

1947 J.G. Adams
1951 L.L. Gardner
1955 P.A. Christianson
1961 James E. McKinnon
1963 Marc H. Souther
1965 L.L. Gardner
1969 John McHugh
1973 Loren R. Edinger
1977 Don Johnston
1981 Jim Fromm
1985 Raymond L. Stone
1993 A.J. Hassell
1997 Steve Judy
2001 Sandi Bloem
2014 Steve Widmyer
* Village Chairman

Dalton Gardens City Hall.

Dalton Gardens

Statistical Data

Population: 2,370 *
Elevation: 2,264 feet
Precipitation: 30 inches **
Average Snowfall: 50 inches **
County: Kootenai
Website: www.daltongardens.com

Temperature Range – Fahrenheit: **
Spring: 30 to 67
Summer: 50 to 84
Fall: 30 to 74
Winter: 22 to 41
* U.S. Census Bureau Estimates, July 2015
**Historical averages

Located in Idaho's beautiful panhandle, Dalton Gardens sits on the eastern edge of the fertile Rathdrum Prairie. The Coeur d'Alene National Forest lies to the east.

The city of Coeur d'Alene abuts Dalton Garden's southern boundaries. To the north, the cities of Hayden and Hayden Lake border the city.

Pre-Incorporation Years

For millennia, nomadic American Indians lived along the lakes and rivers of northern Idaho. Although the Coeur d'Alene and Spokane Tribes were the most prominent in the Northern Idaho upper panhandle, members of the Kootenai, Flathead and Nez Perce Tribes were frequent inhabitants. Some of the tribes referred to the area as the "Great Road of the Flatheads."

In the early 1800s European explorers came into the upper Idaho panhandle to trap beaver and other fur-bearing animals. Most of these mountain men represented organized businesses such as the Hudson's Bay and Pacific Fur Trading

Companies. Beginning around 1809 they began working the streams in the Rathdrum Prairie. (*See Northern Idaho – Early Trappers/Explorers.*)

Around 1842 Roman Catholic Jesuit missionaries established a mission with the area's Coeur d'Alene Indians. (*See Northern Idaho, Early Christian Missionaries.*)

In 1860 Captain John Mullan led 230 soldiers and civilian workers in the construction of a 624-mile military wagon road from Fort Benton, Montana, through what is now the Silver Valley and city of Coeur d'Alene to Fort Walla Walla, Washington. (*See Northern Idaho, Mullan Road.*)

In 1862 Congress passed the Homestead Act. The Act gave 160 acres of public land to a person who improved the property and lived on it for five years. Many Northern Idaho settlers came into the area traveling on Mullan Road.

The Oscar Canfield Home, believed the first home built in Dalton, was built n 1880. Oscar Canfield had a government contract to furnish beef for soldiers at Ft. Coeur d'Alene.

In 1877 reacting to concerns about Indian conflicts in the West, General William Tecumseh Sherman, the Union Civil War hero, made an inspection tour of military forts in the Northwest. While traveling over Mullan Road, Sherman passed along the northern shore of Lake Coeur d'Alene. He was so impressed with the setting that he made a recommendation to Congress that they authorize construction of a new military post on the north shore of the lake.

Congress approved Sherman's recommendation and in 1878 authorized construction of Fort Coeur d'Alene on 999 acres of land at the headwaters of the Spokane River. In 1887 following Sherman's retirement, the military changed the name of the fort to Fort Sherman. Civilians employed to build and provide services to fort personnel started a tent and log cabin village, which they called Coeur d'Alene City, near the fort.

The need for fresh food for the fort's military personnel and the approximately 100 mules and horses kept at the post as well as the people living in the growing Coeur d'Alene City provided a ready market for fresh agricultural commodities.

One of the first settlers – Oscar F. Canfield, the namesake of Canfield Buttes that lie two miles west of Dalton Gardens – arrived in 1878. He had a contract to supply beef to the fort. Other settlers soon began to stake their homestead claims in the fertile soil north of the fort.

In 1891 settlers locating north of the fort built the first area school in the town of Hayden Lake. Children from what is now the Dalton Gardens area generally walked to that school.

218

In 1903 the settlers in what is now the Dalton Gardens area built a one-room school in their own community that they named Canfield. The school had one teacher who taught grades one through eight.

In 1909 they moved the Canfield School to Hayden Lake and built a new school that they named Dalton. Dalton School had 32 students with two teachers and classrooms. They taught grades one through four in one room and grades five through eight in the other. The school also had two rooms for community use including one room with a stage for live performances.

Many of the early settlers built small irrigation systems and dug wells that ultimately proved inadequate to meet their growing demands as well as the needs of new settlers moving into the area. This prompted the formation of larger private irrigation companies.

On December 4, 1907, the Hayden-Coeur d'Alene Irrigation Company recorded the 979-acre plat that they named Dalton Gardens. The plan was to pump irrigation and domestic water

Old railroad station, circa 1920. The electric train ran between Spokane and Coeur d'Alene; the section between Coeur d'Alene and Hayden (passing through Dalton) was completed in 1906. It ran 4-10 times a day weekdays, hourly on weekends. This station was located where the current city hall now stands.

from Hayden Lake to a high point where the water would gravity-flow at low-pressure through wooden stave and concrete pipes to small farm lots on which settlers raised fruit trees, berries and vegetables.

The project was successful. With irrigation water available, the farmers planted apple, pear, cherry, plum and apricot trees as well as raised superb vegetables and berries.

Originally, the farmers took their produce to Coeur d'Alene and sold it door to door. In 1909 they formed the Dalton Fruit Growers Association to better market their produce.

In 1920 the Association was successful in building an apple packing plant next to the railroad and contracted with another packing plant in Spokane to sell their commodities into the larger market. In addition, they opened a Farmer's Market in Coeur d'Alene. In 1923 a cold snap froze about 50 percent of their fruit trees. The majority of the farmers replanted and

Annual City Picnic at the arena in the early 1990s. The annual picnics are now held at Ward Newcomb Park.

production soon returned to normal. However, on October 31, 1935, there was a hard freeze with temperatures dropping to two degrees below zero. The devastating freeze killed about 90 percent of the apple, pear and cherry trees in the area. Many farmers pulled up their trees and sold portions of their land. The apple packing plant shut down.

At the same time, Dalton Garden residents and farmers were experiencing service delivery problems with their irrigation and domestic water systems. Maintenance problems on the domestic water system became so great that in 1944 they had to replace the entire system. By 1950 farmers were losing so much irrigation water through the leaking irrigation pipes that their crops were suffering. The cost of redoing the system was greater than they could afford. They appealed to Congress and the US Department of Reclamation (Reclamation) for assistance. Congress authorized the system reconstruction. Reclamation – already working on the Rathdrum, Avondale and Hayden Lake projects – oversaw renovation of the entire systems with the final contract completed in 1963.

In 1907 the Coeur d'Alene and Spokane Electric Railroad, later renamed the Spokane and Inland Empire, extended a rail line to Hayden Lake. The railroad built a depot between Coeur d'Alene and Hayden Lake that they named "Dalton." The basis for the name "Dalton" is not known. For the next few decades, the railroad gave the community's economy a major boost.

Incorporation

By 1959 Dalton Gardens had a population of 1,083. Prominent citizens in the town became concerned that Coeur d'Alene would annex the community. On January 13, 1960, they presented signed petitions to the Kootenai County Commissioners requesting incorporation. The commissioners approved incorporation of "Dalton Village" on March 8, 1960.

When Idaho changed its laws in 1967 establishing the legal designation of all incorporated communities as cities, the citizens of Dalton changed the name of their city to "Dalton Gardens."

Rural Dalton Gardens neighborhood.

Turning Points

Fort Sherman The 1878 selection of the north shore of Lake Coeur d'Alene as a military fort had a major effect on the agricultural development of the area north of the fort, including the future city of Dalton Gardens.

Irrigation The 979-acre plat filed by the Hayden-Coeur d'Alene Irrigation Company on December 4, 1907, not only provided the "Dalton Gardens" name of the future city, but it also described the idyllic character of the agricultural community.

Railroad The construction of a rail line through Dalton Gardens in 1907 by the Coeur d'Alene and Spokane Electric Railroad had a profound positive effect. The train provided freight as well as passenger services to the community then named Dalton. Families were able to take advantage of fast and accessible transportation to the larger cities of Coeur d'Alene and Spokane for shopping and cultural experiences. Farmers were able to ship their commodities to larger markets. High school students were able to travel to and from their school in Coeur d'Alene.

Many prominent people traveled on the electric train to tour the beautiful landscapes of the area – the most famous of which was U.S. President William H. Taft who, on September 28, 1909, rode the train through Dalton Gardens.

In 1929 the railroad discontinued passenger service. In 1937 the railroad discontinued its freight service to Dalton. However, freight service remained available in Coeur d'Alene.

Dalton Gardens Today

Amenities and Attractions Dalton Gardens has a two-acre public park called Newcomb Park. The park has picnic and children's play areas, a gazebo and extensive flowerbeds.

The city also has a livestock arena and is in the process of building a pavilion next to the arena.

On the first Saturday following Labor Day, the city sponsors a city-wide picnic in Newcomb Park. The picnic is potluck, with the mayor and city council preparing and serving hamburgers and hotdogs. The Fire Department provides games and educational events. A Dalton Gardens car club provides a car show.

The annual Ironman competition takes place in the area each June. The bike portion of the competition runs from Coeur d'Alene to Hayden, passing through Dalton Gardens.

Perhaps the most significant amenity available to city residents is their close proximity to incredibly beautiful natural surroundings and urban parks and services in the

Wade Newcomb Memorial Park.

neighboring cities of Coeur d'Alene and Hayden Lake. Lake Coeur d'Alene lies three miles south. Hayden Lake is two miles northeast. The Coeur d'Alene National Forest lies just east of the city. The numerous lakes in the area along with the nearby forest lands offer visitors and residents a wide variety of outdoor activities and sports.

Farragut State Park lies about 25 miles north. In 1942 at the beginning of World War II, the U.S. Navy built a training station on the southern shore of Lake Pend Oreille. There were so many Navy personnel living at the station that for two years it was the most populous community in Idaho. While it was a naval station, it provided jobs for hundreds of local residents. After the war, the federal government removed most of the buildings and gave the 4,000-acre facility to the State of Idaho. The park has a military museum and facilities for a variety of activities including boating, swimming, hiking, biking, model airplane flying and a shooting range.

Silverwood Theme Park lies about 18 miles north near Athol. The park offers numerous rides and attractions including a roller coaster, steam engine train and various rides on the water.

Economy and Major Employers Dalton Gardens is a well developed and established community which takes pride in retaining its rural, residential characteristics while being supported by a small commercial district of service and/or retail businesses.

Education The city's school-age children are served by the Coeur d'Alene School District. The district operates an elementary school in Dalton Gardens. Middle and high school students attend schools across the city's boundary in Coeur d'Alene. A church-sponsored school is also located within the city limits.

Health Care City residents travel to Coeur d'Alene for most of their health care needs.

Transportation Highway 95 is approximately a mile west of the city. I-90 is approximately 2 miles south.

Utilities and Services Private companies provide electricity, natural gas, Internet, television and telephone services. Dalton Water Association provides domestic water. Dalton Irrigation District provides irrigation water. Panhandle Health District issues the individual septic system permits. The Kootenai County Sheriff's Department provides police protection. The Kootenai County Fire and Rescue District provides fire protection. Coeur d'Alene Garbage and Waste Management provides solid waste services.

Vision for 2050

In 1960 the city's population was 1,083. Since that time, the population has grown steadily until, in the early 1990s, it stabilized at around 2,300. Recent low-population growth trends will likely continue for the next few decades. Except for normal maintenance and improvements, the city's municipal systems will be adequate to provide needed services.

The City of Dalton Gardens will continue to keep its rural, small town setting.

Mayors

1960 Archie Hunter *	1988 Joseph G. Wark, Jr.	2004 Daniel Franklin
1960 Ward Newcomb *	1992 James C. Howard	2016 Steven Roberge
1977 James C. Howard	1997 A. Ray Tomes	* Village Chairman
1980 Ward Newcomb	2000 R.S. Ron Koontz	

Fernan Lake Village sign.

Fernan Lake Village

Statistical Data

Population: 172 *
Elevation: 2,139 feet
Precipitation: 30 inches **
Average Snowfall: 50 inches **
County: Kootenai

Temperature Range – Fahrenheit: **
Spring: 30 to 67
Summer: 50 to 84
Fall: 30 to 74
Winter: 22 to 41
* U.S. Census Bureau Estimates July 2015
**Historical averages

Fernan Lake Village lies on the eastern shore of the 300-acre Lake Fernan, one of the many lakes that lie in the wooded mountains surrounding the beautiful Coeur d'Alene Lake. The eastern boundaries of the city of Coeur d'Alene virtually surround this residential enclave.

Pre-Incorporation Years

In 1878 Congress authorized construction of Fort Coeur d'Alene on 999 acres of land at the headwaters of the lake's outlet, the Spokane River. The name of the fort was later changed to Fort Sherman. The military also commissioned construction of a steamboat to patrol the 30-mile-long lake.

Civilians employed to build the fort and other settlers built up a tent and log cabin village near the fort and called it Coeur d'Alene City.

In 1883 A.J. Prichard announced his discovery of placer gold about 40 miles due east of Coeur d'Alene near what is now Murray. By the end of 1885 ten thousand people converged on Shoshone County, scouring the mountains and streams in search of precious metals.

These fortune seekers promoted considerable traffic through Fort Coeur d'Alene and Coeur d'Alene City.

In 1884 prospectors in the Coeur d'Alene Mining District – later nicknamed the Silver Valley – began to make significant discoveries of silver, lead, zinc and gold.

While the placer gold mines quickly played out, the silver-lead-zinc discoveries developed into deep-shaft hard rock mines that operated throughout most of the twentieth century. Some are still in operation. (*See North Idaho, Cities of the Silver Valley.*)

Fernan Lake.

Around 1886 a settler named Fernan homesteaded near the site of what is now Fernan Lake Village. Other settlers joined him and called their community Fernan. In 1886 railroad interests built a rail line from Coeur d'Alene to the mines on the western end of the Silver Valley. The following year, the railroad made Fernan Lake Village a way station, and postal authorities authorized a post office by the same name.

Incorporation

On July 15, 1957, Fernan Lake Village became an incorporated village.

Turning Points

Mining The discovery of precious and industrial metals in the Silver Valley induced thousands of fortune seekers, miners, homesteaders and entrepreneurs to settle in what are now Kootenai and Shoshone Counties. Many of the settlers who established Fernan Lake Village were among these pioneers.

Railroad The coming of the railroad and way station provided the important transportation and communication link necessary for the Fernan Lake Village community to prosper.

Fernan Lake Village Today

Amenities and Attractions The most popular attraction for the city is its proximity to Coeur d'Alene. Residents of Fernan Lake Village are able to live in a beautiful uncongested residential area yet be within minutes of the shopping, health care and recreational opportunities offered in Coeur d'Alene.

Fernan Lake is one of north Idaho's popular fisheries. The Idaho Department of Fish and Game reports that anglers harvest nearly 23,000 trout, largemouth bass, catfish, crappie, perch and pike annually. In the winter, the lake is popular for ice fishing. The 4,000-acre Farragut State Park lies 30 miles north. The park has a military museum commemorating its World War II history as a naval training center and facilities for a variety of activities including boating, swimming, hiking, biking, model airplane flying and a shooting range.

Silverwood Theme Park lies 20 miles north near Athol. It offers numerous rides and attractions including a roller coaster, steam engine train and rides on the water.

Nearby mountains, lakes and forests make Fernan Lake Village an extraordinary recreational destination for almost all types of outdoor sports and activities.

Economy and Major Employers Fernan Lake Village is a residential community. Most of its workforce is employed in Coeur d'Alene.

Education Coeur d'Alene School District provides public education for Fernan Lake Village students as well as all students in the greater Coeur d'Alene area. Several private schools also provide elementary and secondary education.

The closest institution of higher learning is North Idaho College (NIC) in Coeur d'Alene. The University of Idaho, Lewis-Clark State College, Boise State University and other academic institutions offer educational programs or have outreach programs on the NIC campus, offering associate, bachelor, master's and doctoral degrees in a variety of disciplines.

Health Care The closest hospital is the 225-bed Kootenai Regional Medical Center in Coeur d'Alene. Several general medical clinics, nursing and assisted living homes and other medical providers are also nearby.

Transportation Federal Interstate I-90 passes on the western edge of the city.

The closest airport is Coeur d'Alene Airport located nine miles northwest of the city near Hayden. It has two runways – 7,400 and 5,400 feet long. The Spokane International Airport is about 53 miles west of the city.

Rail freight service is available in Coeur d'Alene. Amtrak passenger service is available 46 miles north in Sandpoint.

Utilities and Services Private companies provide electricity, telephone, natural gas, cable and satellite services. The City contracts with the City of Coeur d'Alene for water and sewer services as well as fire and police protection.

Vision for 2050

Fernan Lake Village's population has remained constant for over 40 years. The 1970 population was 179. Historical population trends will likely continue.

By 2050 the city will still be a small residential community, offering a great place to unwind, raise families and retire.

Harrison today.

Harrison

Statistical Data

Population: 215 *
Elevation: 2,200 feet
Precipitation: 26 inches **
Average Snowfall: 46 inches **
County: Kootenai
Website: www.harrisonidaho.org (Chamber of Commerce)

Temperature Range – Fahrenheit: **
Spring: 27 to 70
Summer: 50 to 98
Fall: 38 to 98
Winter: 12 to 35
* U.S. Census Bureau Extimates July 2015
**Historical averages

Harrison lies on the shore of a gentle peninsula protruding into the southeast side of Lake Coeur d'Alene at the mouth of the Coeur d'Alene River. It lies 17 miles south of the city of Coeur d'Alene.

Extending over 15 miles to the east and northeast, lies a chain of small lakes linked by the Coeur d'Alene River. These lakes add a beautiful accent to the forested mountain terrain. To the south and southeast lie the St. Joe Mountains and the Coeur d'Alene Indian Reservation. The Coeur d'Alene Forest is 12 miles to the northeast.

Once a bustling town of sawmills and, later, known for its farming, ranching and dairy production, Harrison is now a quiet peaceful resort community that has outstanding recreational opportunities on the lake and the nearby forest and streams.

Pre-Incorporation Years

In 1877 the year of the Nez Perce War (*see North Idaho, Nez Perce War*), U.S. General William Tecumseh Sherman led an expedition west over Mullan Road, a military road constructed seven years earlier. His purpose was to identify possible locations for military forts.

One selected location bordered the northern shore of Lake Coeur d'Alene. A park and North Idaho College now sit on part of the 999 acres selected and set aside by Congress for the fort. When General Sherman retired from the military in 1887, the fort, originally named Fort Coeur d'Alene, was renamed Fort Sherman in his honor.

In 1880 the military commissioned construction of a sternwheeler steamer to carry supplies to the fort and patrol the lake. This became the first of many sternwheelers on Lake Coeur d'Alene.

Harrison's oldest residence: the Crane home, built in 1891.

In 1887 Congress passed the General Allotment Act, also known as the Dawes Severalty Act. The legislation was an attempt to assimilate Native American Indians into the white mainstream. Under the Act, Native Americans received an individual allotment of reservation land. Any lands not allotted became "surplus" and available for non-Indian settlement, primarily under the 1862 Homestead Act. (*See North Idaho, General Allotment Act and Redistribution of Indian Reservation Lands.*)

At that time, the Coeur d'Alene Indian Reservation included what is now the city of Harrison. In 1889 because of the nearby abundance of tall timber and strategic location on the lake and river, influential lumbermen persuaded U.S. President Benjamin Harrison to separate from the reservation a mile-wide strip of land bordering the lake and river for a townsite.

Georgie Oakes at dock.

In 1891 William E. and Edwin S. Crane and George Jones platted the new mill town that they named Harrison in recognition of President Harrison's efforts in getting the land set aside.

Within a short time, several sawmills were operating in the city. The first general store opened in 1892 and the post office in 1893. In order to produce foods for the growing community, farmers began homesteading on an open area to the east of the city that they called Harrison Flats.

By 1899 the town had seven sawmills, four shingle mills, a dozen saloons and a red-light district.

In 1890 the Oregon-Washington Railroad and Navigation Company extended their railroad system through Harrison to connect the mines in Kellogg and Wallace with Spokane.

Harrison dock area, circa 1930s.

Incorporation

On July 24, 1899, Harrison became an incorporated village. By 1902 the community had established schools, churches, fraternal organizations, numerous businesses, banks and a weekly newspaper. In 1904 community leaders were successful in outlawing saloons. The 1911 city directory reported a population of 1,250.

Turning Points

Cutting ice blocks.

Federal Designation of Original Townsite Following the action taken by U.S. President Benjamin Harrison in separating land from the Coeur d'Alene Indian Reservation for a townsite that became the city of Harrison, at least four major turning points came around the same time: sawmills, sternwheelers, Harrison Bridge and the railroad.

Sawmills Harrison started as a sawmill town. During the period from 1890 to 1951, over 30 sawmills, box factories and shingle mills had significant operations in or near the city. The Pacific Northwesterner, Vol. 23 reports that in 1902 there were nine sawmills in Harrison with a daily output of half a million board feet and a monthly payroll of $25,000.

The production from these mills reached an apex in 1917 when, in July, a devastating fire burned through town. When it was over, the fire had destroyed a large part of the business district and many residences.

Some Mills did not recover after the fire. One of the reasons is that extensive logging of the closest available timber stands had significantly reduced the area's supply of logs.

Sternwheeleers When the military built Fort Sherman and built the first sternwheeler in 1880, most roads through the heavily timbered hills were mere trails. Sternwheelers, steam-powered paddlewheel boats, were much better options for moving freight and passengers between the docks and communities around the lake and up river along the lake's two largest tributaries, the Coeur d'Alene and St. Joe Rivers.

In the early 1880s the discovery of precious and industrial metals in the Silver Valley brought a flood of miners and prospectors to the region. These discoveries and, later, demand from the development of the timber industry and tourism on the lake led the Coeur d'Alene Railway and Navigation Company (CR&N) to purchase several sternwheelers.

Because most of the sternwheelers drew less than three feet of water, they could run the twisting, shallow channels of the St. Joe and Coeur d'Alene Rivers. Some sternwheelers had beautifully decorated dining and passenger quarters. Tourists often took a train from Spokane to Coeur d'Alene, boarded one of the sternwheelers and spent a pleasant day on the lake and rivers. At the time, round trip fare from Coeur d'Alene to St. Maries was $1.25.

Lemon homestead, 1902.

The Georgie Oakes was one of the prominent sternwheelers. It was 150 feet long and 24 feet at her beam (widest width) and could carry up to 1,000 passengers. One of the Georgie Oaks cooks was a man named "Tex" Arner. He took great pride in his trade. When passengers did not seem interested in having dinner on the boat, he rubbed onions and a piece of beef across the top of his stove. The aroma penetrated the decks and the guests generally moved to the dining room.

The era of the sternwheelers on Lake Coeur d'Alene was of major importance to the development of Harrison and the industries that underpinned its economy. To accommodate the sternwheelers, piers long enough for multiple sternwheelers to dock at one time bordered the city's shoreline.

The railroad gradually took business away from the sternwheelers until, by the mid-1920s, demand for the sternwheelers substantially ended with many sternwheelers burned and their hulls allowed to sink to the bottom of Lake Coeur d'Alene.

Harrison Bridge Early travelers going north had to cross the Coeur d'Alene River. A ferry-barge pulled through the water with a hand-cranked cable accommodated this crossing.

In 1906 completion of the Post Falls hydroelectric plant raised the water level in Coeur d'Alene Lake and River. As the city grew, the inefficiencies of the ferry became problematic. Martin Gilbertson, a Swede with bridge building experience, was engaged to engineer and construct a wooden trestle bridge across the river and marshlands.

Frank Thompson, grandson of Walter and Sarah Thompson who homesteaded along the lake that bears the family name, recalls the trestle bridge. Born in 1917, Mr. Thompson said it was in use as long as he can remember, describing it as "kind of a rickety thing that carried quite a bit of traffic. It was an essential apparatus in the community. The wooden bridge was constructed on big timber pilings with decking made primarily from planks of fir and larch, four inches wide by eight to 14 feet long and it was tall enough to allow steamboats to pass under."

In 1932 the State replaced the trestle bridge with a new bridge that would last for over seven decades. In October 2007, the State replaced that old structure with a new four-lane 660-foot-long bridge. A plaque that describes the area's history and landscape entitled "Horizons of Harrison" now greets motorists as they cross Harrison Bridge.

McGoldrick Lumber Company near Emida.

Railroad Construction of the railroad in 1890 had a profound impact on Harrison in at least two important ways. On the one hand, Harrison became an important stopping point for the railroad. On the other hand, competition from the railroad was one of the reasons the Lake Coeur d'Alene sternwheelers businesses failed and the Harrison dock business went into decline.

Harrison Today

Amenities and Attractions The city's most attractive feature is its setting. The beautiful, crystal-clear Lake Coeur d'Alene is nearly 30 miles long. The wooded foothills and mountains border the lake shoreline that curves in and out of many inlets and bays.

Harrison's Public Marina, a 72-dock facility is operated in partnership with Kootenai County. The dock and the nearby public swimming beach open the lake to a variety of water sports. Private lodges offer a comfortable place to stay for tourists as well as outdoor enthusiasts.

The Trail of the Coeur d'Alenes, a 72-mile-long non-motorized bike and recreation path, replaces the historic Union Pacific rail line that passes through Harrison. The trail runs from Plummer, 10 miles southwest of Harrison, to Mullan near the Idaho/Montana border. Each year an increasing number of visitors from around the globe come to bike or walk all or part of the trail and enjoy the natural splendor of Northern Idaho and the rich history of the Silver Valley. The fall, with the changing leaf colors of aspen, popular, cottonwood, maples and tamaracks accenting the evergreen forests, is particularly beautiful along the trail. Harrison merchants are expanding their businesses to accommodate the increasing number of travelers who visit the trail.

The city has two municipal parks, an RV Park and tent area. Annual events include the old-fashioned "Pig in the Park Supper." This event occurs each June as a fundraiser for the July 4 Independence Day Celebration. The celebration includes the Old Timer's Picnic, a parade, a yard sale and fireworks.

In August, the Chamber of Commerce sponsors the Jr. Fishing Tournament. In September, there is the "Haul Ass Show and Shine Car Show" with a chili cook off and a pinewood derby for youth and adults. In October, the community sponsors the "Fall Festival in the Park." In December, there is the downtown "Winter Fest Celebration."

Harrison is encouraging preservation of its few remaining historical buildings. One of the success stories is the I.O.O.F. Hall. The private owner of this restored three-story building has renamed it the Harrison Building. Apartments are on the top floor. Businesses rent the lower floors, including the favorite hangout, "One Shot Charlie's."

Harrison today.

Economy and Major Employers The Kootenai School District has 50 employees and is the city's largest employer. Harrison Dock Builders, a construction company, has 27 employees and is the city's largest private employer.

Several lodging, retail and service businesses that serve tourists and residents employ a majority of the remaining workforce.

Education The Kootenai School District provides most of the city's K-12 education. The school district operates the Kootenai JR-SR High School and Harrison Elementary schools.

The closest institution of higher learning is North Idaho College in Coeur d'Alene.

Health Care The closest hospital is the 225-bed Kootenai Medical Center in Coeur d'Alene.

Transportation State Highway 97 intersects the city and connects with State Highway 3, seven miles southeast. Federal Interstate 90 lies 28 miles to the northeast.

The closest air service is the Coeur d'Alene Air Terminal, 22 miles north. The Pullman/Moscow Regional Airport to the south and the Spokane International Airport to the northwest are both about 54 miles away.

Utilities and Services Private companies provide electricity, telephone, gas and satellite services. The City provides water and sewer services and police and fire protection. The County provides solid waste services.

Vision for 2050

Harrison's population has remained constant at around 250 to 300 for nearly five decades. However, historical trends will not likely continue. The population growth in the area and the new Harrison Bridge will have a positive effect on the city's growth.

Community leaders anticipate moderate growth in the future. Since 2002 the City Council has annexed 142-acres for development planned for 156 new homes.

In 2050 the city will continue to have the attributes that make it a beautiful place to visit, start a business, raise a family or retire.

Mayors

1907 Al Fuller	1959 James A. Prudente
1911 A.A. Lerane	1963 Chas A. Phillips
1913 J.A. Pinkerton	1965 Albert Mault
1917 C.A. Packer	1967 Chet Blessing
1921 C.E. Cleveland	1974 Glenn W. Addington
1925 William Honsowetz	1982 George Sorenson
1929 A.L. Greiner	1983 Eugene Stern
1933 L.H. Wheeler	1984 George LaValley
1935 Axel Olson	1988 W. Dean Christensen
1946 S.R. Phillips	1996 David D. LePard
1949 Glenn T. Russell	2004 Barbara Elliott
1953 Roy E. Morgao	2004 Ron JeanBlanc
1955 R.D. Patterson	2006 Josephine Prophet
1956 Ralph W. Cope	2010 Wanda Irish
1957 A.R. Lund	

Hauser Lake.

Hauser

Statistical Data

Population: 680 *
Elevation: 2,220 feet
Precipitation: 30 inches **
Average Snowfall: 50 inches **
County: Kootenai
Website: www.cityofhauser.org

Temperature Range – Fahrenheit: **
Spring: 30 to 67
Summer: 50 to 84
Fall: 30 to 74
Winter: 22 to 41
* U.S. Census Bureau Estimates July 2015
**Historical averages

Hauser has a picturesque setting situated about a mile east of the Washington/Idaho border on the southeastern edge of the Rathdrum Prairie and at the base of the 625-acre Hauser Lake. The Kaniksu National Forest, interspersed by private land, borders the city on the north and west.

The city has distinct upper and lower segments. The largest part of the city wraps around the southern lakeshore.

Idaho Highway 53 intersects the southern part of the city, connected to the upper city by a mile-long city street.

The city of Rathdrum is located about eight miles northwest; Post Falls is about seven miles southeast.

Pre-Incorporation Years

In 1878 Congress authorized construction of Fort Coeur d'Alene on 999 acres of land at the headwaters of the lake's outlet, the Spokane River. The name of the fort was later changed to Fort Sherman. The military also commissioned construction of a steamboat to patrol the 30-mile-long lake.

Civilians employed to build the fort and other settlers built up a tent and log cabin village near the fort and called it Coeur d'Alene City.

First Train Through Hauser, 1886. Picture courtesy of the Museum of North Idaho.

In 1881 the Northern Pacific Railroad constructed a rail line from Wallula, Washington, to Spokane; crossed into Idaho Territory southeast of what is now Hauser; went northeast to Rathdrum, then Westwood; and north to Sandpoint. There the railroad turned east around the top of Lake Pend Oreille to the Clark Fork River before turning east again to Hells Gate near Missoula, Montana. The railroad line was completed in 1883.

In 1883 A.J. Prichard disclosed his discovery of placer gold about 40 miles due east of Coeur d'Alene near what is now Murray. By the end of 1885 over 10,000 people passed through Fort Coeur d'Alene and Coeur d'Alene City as they converged on the area, scouring the mountains and streams in search of precious metals.

In 1884 prospectors in the Coeur d'Alene Mining District – later nicknamed the Silver Valley – began to make significant discoveries of silver, lead, zinc and gold.

While the placer gold mines quickly played out, the silver-lead-zinc discoveries developed into deep-shaft hard rock mines that operated throughout most of the twentieth century. Some are still in operation. (*See Northern Idaho, Cities of the Silver Valley*.)

Hauser Lake Stage Coach, Circa 1900

Hauser Lake Stagecoach
Guy Boston, Owner-Driver

When prospectors made their first discoveries, they had to ship their ore out for processing. In 1885 the owners of the Bunker Hill Mine shipped ore over an arduous route to a smelter in San Francisco. They transported the ore from the Bunker Hill Mine on freight wagons to Lake Coeur d'Alene, then by steamboat to Coeur d'Alene City, then freight wagon to the Northern Pacific Railway station at Rathdrum where it was loaded on railcars to Portland, then by steamer to San Francisco.

However, use of the difficult overland route would be short lived. In 1886 Jim Wardner, a principal in the Bunker Hill Mine and namesake for the city of Wardner, secured financial help from Samuel Thomas Hauser, the governor of Montana, and D.C. Corbin from Spokane to build an ore concentrator at the Bunker Hill Mine.

Hauser Lake Resort Club House, 1910. Courtesy Museum of North Idaho.

Corbin formed the Spokane Falls and Idaho Railroad that in 1886 built a rail connection on the main Northern Pacific rail line about six miles southwest of Rathdrum and constructed a 13-mile branch line to Coeur d'Alene. He named the railroad connection Hauser Junction in honor of his friend and business associate, Governor S.T. Hauser.

In 1887 Corbin formed the Coeur d'Alene Railway and Navigation Company, which extended the line from Coeur d'Alene to most of the large mines in the Silver Valley.

In 1888 the Northern Pacific acquired Corbin's railroad properties and in the next year connected the railroad to its railroad line in Montana, allowing mine owners to transport their ore to Montana smelters. Hauser Junction became a key location for trains traveling from the East to cities on the West Coast.

The lake, located a mile north and previously called Mud and Sucker, soon took on the name Hauser Lake.

Hauser Lake School, 1917. Courtesy Museum of North Idaho.

Incorporation

On May 12, 1947, the community was incorporated.

Turning Points

Silver Valley Mines and the Railroad The late 1880s development of precious and industrial metal mines in the Silver Valley was the catalyst that persuaded railroad entrepreneurs to provide freight and passenger service to the mines and establish Hauser as an important railroad junction.

Firestorm Hauser Lake Volunteer Fire Department was established in 1954. On October 15, 1991, devastating winds, measuring from 50 mph to the extreme of 92 mph; record high temperatures of 10 to 20 degrees above normal; and 42 days with no rain had intensified fire danger in the area. Power lines and trees were down from the winds. Downed transformers caused power outages throughout the area. Soon fire alarms were being called in too fast to handle. Orders were given to evacuate the area. Many families lost their homes and were traumatized by the fire – the effects are still being felt today.

Hauser Today

Amenities and Attractions
Hauser Lake is the city's most prominent attraction. It not only has a natural beauty, it is an excellent fishery for trout and perch. The lake, owned by the State, is a "trophy lake" for Tiger Muskey with a record 43 pounder caught there. Kootenai County manages the boat ramp and park.

Ice fishing is also enjoyed on the lake during the winter. George, a blue heron, stands 8 to 10 feet from those with successful catches, waiting for his share of fish to be thrown to him. Unlike other heron, he never leaves for the winter.

House in Hauser Lake.

Hauser Days usually take place in August.

The city's proximity to Sandpoint and Spokane allows residents to live in a small community, yet have access to the many urban services and recreations available in larger cities.

The city's location near beautiful forested mountains, lakes, rivers and streams offers excellent opportunities for backpacking, hiking, trail riding, fishing, hunting, snowmobiling and cross-country skiing.

Four state parks lie within 30 miles of the city – Farragut at the base of Lake Pend Oreille, Round Lake located south of Sandpoint, Hayden at the base of Coeur d'Alene Lake and the Old Mission west of Coeur d'Alene.

Economy and Major Employers The city has no dominant employers, though there are 14 small businesses within the city limits and area of impact. The majority of city residents commute to Coeur d'Alene, Post Falls or Spokane for work.

Education Lakeland School District, headquartered in Rathdrum, provides most of the K-12 education. Hauser children commute to Rathdrum for their elementary, junior high school, high school, and alternative high school education.

The closest institution of higher learning is North Idaho College in Coeur d'Alene.

Health Care The closest hospital is Kootenai Medical Center in Coeur d'Alene. Several medical clinics and a physical therapy and immediate care center are also available in Rathdrum.

Transportation In addition to Highway 53, U.S. Highway 95 lies about 10 miles west, and Interstate 90 lies about two miles south of town.

Coeur d'Alene Airport serves private, charter and light commuter aircraft. Spokane International Airport provides access to major carriers.

Utilities and Services Private companies provide electricity, telephone and satellite services. Hauser Water Association provides water services, and residents have private septic systems. Kootenai County Sheriff's Department provides police protection. Northern Lakes Fire District provides fire protection.

Vision for 2050

In 1970 Hauser's population was 349 where it held somewhat steady until in the 1990s the population began to swell dramatically. Within a decade, the population more than doubled as people with jobs in nearby cities moved to enjoy the natural and peaceful setting that surrounds Hauser.

Around 2000 the city's population stabilized at around 800. We expect the city's population to hold steady for several years before resuming growth at a moderate rate. In 2050 Hauser will continue to be a residential community – hometown to families who enjoy nature, yet within a short commute to their workplaces.

Mayors

1947-1975 Unknown *
1975 Albert Auckerman
1976-1991 Unknown
1991 Gary Mallon

1995 Ed Peone
2010 Olita Johnston
2014 Claire Hatfield
* Village Chairman

Stoddard Park, Hayden.

Hayden

Statistical Data

Population: 13,870 *
Elevation: 2,278 feet
Precipitation: 30 inches **
Average Snowfall: 50 inches **
County: Kootenai
Website: www.cityofhaydenid.us

Temperature Range – Fahrenheit: **
Spring: 30 to 67
Summer: 50 to 84
Fall: 30 to 74
Winter: 22 to 41
* U.S. Census Bureau Estimates July 2015
**Historical averages

Hayden lies on the eastern edge of the fertile Rathdrum Prairie. The southeast corner of the city extends to the shores of the beautiful, crystal-clear Hayden Lake. The Coeur d'Alene National Forest begins several miles west. The city's boundaries abut those of the cities of Hayden Lake on the east and Dalton Gardens on the south. The Coeur d'Alene Airport abuts the city's western boundary.

Pre-Incorporation Years

For centuries, nomadic bands of American Indians – principally of the Coeur d'Alene Tribe – occupied the land around Hayden. (*See Northern Idaho, The Region, American Indians.*)

In 1877 reacting to concerns about Indian conflicts, General William Tecumseh Sherman, the Union Civil War hero, made an inspection tour of military forts in the Northwest. He traveled over the 624-mile-long Mullan Road, a military road between Fort Benton, Montana, and Fort Walla Walla, Washington. Captain John Mullan and 230 soldiers and workers completed the road in 1860. Through Idaho, the road generally followed what is now the I-90 corridor. (*See Northern Idaho, The Region, Mullan Road, The Military Wagon Road that Opened the Region.*)

When Sherman passed along the northern shore of Lake Coeur d'Alene, he was so impressed with the setting that he recommended to Congress that they authorize construction of a new military post on the north shore of the lake.

Congress approved Sherman's recommendation and in 1878 authorized construction of Fort Coeur d'Alene on 999 acres at the headwaters of the Spokane River. The name of the fort was later changed to Fort Sherman. The military also commissioned Captain C.P. Sorensen, a boat builder from Portland, Oregon, to build an army steamboat to patrol the 30-mile-long lake.

The Lake City Dairy now is the barn at Stoddard Park. This photo was taken when the Whitesetts owned the property.

Civilians employed to build the fort and other settlers started a small tent and log cabin village near the fort and called it Coeur d'Alene City.

About 1879 four settlers, including Matt Heyden, established homesteads on the southwestern shore of what is now Hayden Lake. Historical accounts describe how Heyden and another settler named John Hager played the "seven-up" card game to determine who would have the honor of naming the lake. Heyden won and named the lake after himself. Years later, the name was misspelled Hayden by government personnel and that spelling stuck.

In 1883 A.J. Prichard disclosed his discovery of placer gold about 40 miles due east of Coeur d'Alene near what is now Murray. Ten thousand fortune seekers converged on what is now the Silver Valley area by the end of 1885, scouring the mountains and streams in search of precious metals. (*See Northern Idaho, The Region, Silver Valley Mines.*)

The flood of miners sharply increased the demand for fresh foods. Area homesteaders planted crops to supply commodities to the fort and the miners. Fruit trees and berries were among the most prominent agricultural commodities produced near what is now Hayden. Historical accounts credit Matt Heyden for planting the area's first fruit orchard.

In 1889 James Casey began operating the first sawmill on Hayden Lake. Soon other sawmills began operations.

Four steamboats would eventually operate on the lake – principally serving the timber businesses and prospectors who had achieved limited success in finding placer gold in the area.

Around 1900 railroad interests built an electric-powered train from Coeur d'Alene north to the community of Bonzanta Tavern and the lumber businesses operating on the west shore of the lake. In 1907 the Spokane and Inland Empire Railroad acquired the railroad properties.

About the same time, a man named Justice built the first store in the area. He named his store "Monahan's," and it housed the community's first post office. The post office name of Monahan only lasted for a few years until it became necessary to move the post office to a new facility. At that time, postal authorities approved changing the name from Monahan to Hayden Lake.

By 1924 the mills began to close as they had exhausted most of the nearby merchantable timber. Recreation and tourism joined agriculture as the dominant industries. The Great Northern, the then owner of the railroad, shut down its rail service and sold its mill property at the lake to the Coeur d'Alene Country Club.

The CC and RC Worst Garage, begun in 1937 on Government Way (old US 95) south of Hayden Avenue.

By that time, motor vehicles were becoming the preferred mode of transportation. Retail businesses and a residential community began developing along Government Way, an arterial road that parallels what is now U.S. Highway 95 and extends north from Coeur d'Alene to Idaho Highway 53.

Incorporation

On June 27, 1955, Hayden Village became incorporated as a village. Postal authorities moved the post office to Hayden in 1959. In 1967 Hayden became a city as required by a change in Idaho municipal law and they dropped the word "Village" from the city's name.

Turning Points

Government Way Road The development of businesses along Government Way Road began in the early 1900s and established the city's present location.

Aerial photo taken after the elementary school was built; the Hayden Historic Preservation Commission dates it in the 1950s.

Change in Economic Base With the change in the underlying base of the city's economy from natural resources to recreation and tourism, the city's population began to swell. To accommodate this growth, the city adopted business-friendly policies, including a willingness to annex and provide services to adjoining developments and properties.

Hayden Today

Amenities and Attractions Hayden has over 57 acres devoted to parks.

Finucane Park, donated by the Finucane family, is a 10-acre park located on the northwest corner of Prairie Avenue and Fourth Street. The park includes three baseball/softball fields, covered gazebos, a concession stand, playground equipment and public restrooms.

City Park is located next to City Hall. Park amenities include playground equipment, horseshoe pits, a gazebo, green space, a baseball field, a bandstand and a basketball court.

Hayden City Hall and Fire Department. Picture is dated to soon after the city's incorporation in 1955.

Croffot Park encompasses 25 acres and includes three little league baseball fields, two softball fields, two soccer fields, two basketball courts, horseshoe pits and a tot lot.

Broadmoore Park is a 10-acre neighborhood park. This park includes a tot lot, a walking path, water fountains and ball field. When completely developed, it will also include gazebos, basketball courts and additional walking paths.

Honeysuckle Beach is a city-owned beach, one of two public accesses to Hayden Lake. The beach is open 11 a.m. to 6 p.m. throughout the summer and has certified lifeguards. Amenities include a volleyball court, picnic areas, public boat access, parking, public restrooms, a concession stand and a public fishing dock.

City Park is the home of many of the community's celebrations including Hayden Days, Concerts in the Park and the annual Hayden Business Fair. Other annual community events include Hayden Chamber of Commerce's H.A.Y.D.E.N. Awards on the third Saturday in March. On the third Saturday in April is the family oriented Hayden City Kite Festival. In early May, the community turns out for the Hayden Boat and Water Sports Show. At the end of June is the Ford Ironman. The Hayden Village Art Festival takes place in July, as does the Hayden Olympic Triathlon. Hayden View Triathlon is on August 1. The Veteran's Day Parade is on the Saturday after Veteran's Day in November. In early December, the community welcomes the holiday season with the Christmas Lights Parade.

Hayden is rapidly moving forward in the development of interlocking bike trails and bicycle lanes throughout the city and surrounding area. Bicyclists preparing or participating in events – such as the Coeur d'Alene Ironman, Hayden View Triathlon and Hayden Olympic Triathlon – or just out for a ride are a common sight on Hayden streets.

Located on Hayden Lake and in close proximity to Lake Coeur d'Alene and Lake Pend Oreille, the Greater Hayden area offers the ultimate in water sports – from simply relaxing cruises to motor boating, waterskiing, wake boarding and more. Public boat launches are located at Sportsmen's Access at the north end of the lake. Tobler Marina is located two miles north of Hayden on U.S. Highway 95.

There are over 50 golf courses within a one hour drive of the city. Hayden is home to the Hayden Lake Country Club and Avondale Golf Course. Avondale is an 18-hole course that is open to the public. The Hayden Lake Country Club is a private club with an 18-hole golf course and driving range.

On Government Way, north of Hayden.

Hayden GEMS Senior Center, located in the heart of downtown Hayden, offers an exciting schedule of activities for the older adult.

Many city residents enjoy the many amenities and events available in the larger city of Coeur d'Alene.

The beautiful nearby forested mountains, lakes, rivers and streams offer excellent opportunities for backpacking, hiking, horseback riding, trail riding, swimming, fishing, hunting, kayaking, sailing, snowmobiling, downhill skiing, snowboarding and cross-country skiing – an extraordinary recreational destination for almost all types of outdoor sports and activities.

Four state parks lie within 30 miles of the city – Farragut at the base of Lake Pend Oreille, Round Lake located south of Sandpoint, Hayden at the base of Coeur d'Alene Lake and the Old Mission west of Coeur d'Alene. Silverwood Theme Park lies 17 miles north near Athol. The park offers numerous rides and attractions including a roller coaster, steam engine train and various rides on the water.

Economy and Major Employers With over 300 employees, Verizon Communications Inc. is the city's largest employer. Several businesses with fewer than 100 employees, including retail food stores, also have operations in the city. The Coeur d'Alene School District is the city's largest public employer.

Education The Coeur d'Alene School District provides elementary and secondary education to students in Coeur d'Alene, Dalton Gardens, Hayden, Hayden Lake and part of rural Kootenai County. The school district has an elementary school, a middle school and a high school in Hayden. Several private schools in the Coeur d'Alene area also provide elementary and secondary education to city students.

The closest institution of higher learning is North Idaho College (NIC) in Coeur d'Alene. The University of Idaho, Lewis-Clark State College and Boise State University have outreach programs on the NIC campus that offer associate, bachelor, masters and doctoral degrees in a variety of disciplines. Other academic institutions have facilities in the area offering educational programs, certificates and degrees.

Health Care The 225-bed Kootenai Medical Center in Coeur d'Alene is a regional medical center. It is located on a 40-acre integrated campus of high-tech patient towers, healing gardens, office buildings and public education centers – all connected by green space, bike and walking paths and water features.

Several general medical clinics, nursing and assisted living homes and other medical providers also provide services for area residents.

Transportation U.S. Highway 95 intersects the city. Interstate 90 can be accessed four miles south in Coeur d'Alene. The Coeur d'Alene Airport is located two miles northwest of Hayden. It has two runways – one 7,400 and the other 5,400 feet long. The Spokane International Airport is 42 miles west of the city.

Rail freight service is available in Coeur d'Alene. Amtrak passenger service is available 42 miles north in Sandpoint.

Utilities and Services Private companies provide electricity, telephone, natural gas, cable and satellite services. The City provides water and sewer services as well as fire and police protection.

Vision for 2050

In 1955 the city's land area was 440 acres. In 1960 Hayden's population was 901. By 2007 the incorporated acreage had grown to 5,212 and the city's population to 12,683. Managing this dramatic growth is a major priority. In 2007 city leaders engaged the community and the Hayden Urban Renewal Agency in developing a comprehensive strategic plan. This roadmap for the next few decades addresses all aspects of the city's future including downtown vitalization, parks, transportation, development and design standards, business development and funding such improvements.

By 2050 the city will have either implemented most of the strategic plan's elements or modified them for changed conditions. By that time, the city of Hayden will be even more beautiful – a vibrant community with a pedestrian-friendly downtown and attractive residential communities with an abundance of parks and greenbelts.

Mayors

1955 George F. Johnson *
1959 Frank Fulton *
1961 George Kilian *
1963 John Freligh *
1965 Lyle Peterson *
1965 Leonard Stewart *
1967 Leonard L. Stewart
1975 Chester Hattneberg
1977 Willard Largent
1977 Wilma Hildreth
1978 Robert Crofford
1978 Daniel A. Jones
1979 Robert Croffoot

1979 Russell Greenfield
1981 Robert Croffoot
1983 Wayne Syth
1983 Robert Croffoot
1984 Frank Canale
1988 Richard Panabaker
1994 Robert Croffoot
1994 Vincent A. Rossi
1996 Mike Sperle
2000 Ronald B. McIntire
2016 Steven Griffitts
* Village Chairman

Hayden Lake City Hall and Recreational Water and Sewer District.

Hayden Lake

Statistical Data

Population: 590 *
Elevation: 2,278 feet
Precipitation: 30 inches **
Average Snowfall: 50 inches **
County: Kootenai
Website: www.cityofhaydenlake.us

Temperature Range – Fahrenheit: **
Spring: 30 to 67
Summer: 50 to 84
Fall: 30 to 74
Winter: 22 to 41
* U.S. Census Bureau Estimates July 2015
**Historical averages

The City of Hayden Lake lies on the western shores of the beautiful, crystal-clear 4,000-acre lake that bears the same name. The Coeur d'Alene National Forest, with heavily wooded mountains rising up to 6,000 feet, overlooks the lake on the north, east and south.

The city boundaries of Hayden Lake abut those of Hayden on the north, west and south. The City of Dalton Gardens lies three miles south and abuts the northern borders of the city of Coeur d'Alene.

Pre-Incorporation Years

For centuries nomadic bands of American Indians, principally of the Coeur d'Alene Tribe, occupied the land around Hayden Lake.

In 1860 Captain John Mullan and 230 soldiers and workers completed a 624-mile-long military road – Mullan Road – between Fort Benton, Montana, and Fort Walla Walla, Washington. The road generally followed what is now the I-90 corridor through Idaho.

In 1877 reacting to concerns about Indian conflicts in the West, General William Tecumseh Sherman, the Union Civil War hero, traveled Mullan Road during an inspection tour of military forts in the Northwest.

When Sherman passed along the northern shore of Lake Coeur d'Alene, he was so impressed with the setting he recommended to Congress that they authorize construction of a new military post on the north shore of the lake.

Congress approved Sherman's recommendation and in 1878 authorized construction of Fort Coeur d'Alene on 999 acres at the headwaters of the Spokane River. The name of the fort was later changed to Fort Sherman. The military also commissioned Captain C.P. Sorensen, a boat builder from Portland, Oregon, to build an army steamboat to patrol the 30-mile-long lake.

Civilians employed to build the fort and other settlers started a small tent and log cabin village near the fort that they called Coeur d'Alene City.

Circa 1879 four settlers, including Matt Heyden, established homesteads on the southwestern shore of what is now Hayden Lake. Historical accounts describe how Heyden and one of the other settlers, John Hager, played the "seven-up" card game to determine who would have the honor of naming the lake. Heyden won and named the lake after himself. Years later when government personnel recorded the Heyden name ,they misspelled it "Hayden."

In 1883 A.J. Prichard disclosed his discovery of placer gold about 40 miles due east of Coeur d'Alene near what is now Murray. Ten thousand fortune seekers converged on what is now the Silver Valley area By the end of 1885, scouring the mountains and streams in search of precious metals.

The flood of miners sharply increased the demand for fresh foods over what was already needed to supply the fort. Area homesteaders planted crops to supply commodities to the fort and the miners. Fruit trees and berries were among the most prominent agricultural commodities produced near what is now Hayden Lake. Historical accounts credit Matt Heyden for planting the area's first fruit orchard.

In 1889 James Casey began operation of the first sawmill on the lake. Other sawmills soon followed.

Four steamboats would eventually operate on the lake, principally serving the timber businesses and prospectors who had achieved limited success in finding placer gold.

Around 1900 railroad interests built an electric-powered train from Coeur d'Alene north to the west shore of the lake at a place called Bozanta Tavern to provide transportation to the new timber businesses.

About that same time, a man named Justice built the first store in the area. He named his store "Monahan's." It housed the community's first post office. The post office name of Monahan only lasted for a few years when it became necessary to move the post office to a new location. At that time, postal authorities approved changing the name from Monahan to Hayden Lake.

Due to the increasing population and activity in the area, developers envisioned a first-class summer resort by Hayden Lake. The resort buildings were designed by Kirtland Cutter of Spokane, and the grounds were planned by J.C. Olmstead.

The resort was named Bozanta Tavern and opened in 1906. Bozanta is an Indian word meaning "meeting place by the lake." The resort was an immediate success. Seven trains a day were bringing visitors to the resort to swim, boat, play tennis, ride horseback and enjoy the majestic view.

In 1907 the Spokane and Inland Empire Railroad acquired the railroad properties.

In 1909 a 9-hole golf course was added to Bozanta Tavern. Golf became the mainstay of the resort. In 1912 the golf course was expanded to the first 18-hole golf course in Idaho.

President Howard Taft stayed overnight at Bozanta Tavern in 1909, and President Teddy Roosevelt visited in 1914.

The Great Northern Railroad Corp. purchased the resort in 1919. In 1923 the Coeur d'Alene Country Club was formed and purchased the resort.

Bozanta Tavern and one of the golf greens, circa 1912. Courtesy Museum of North Idaho.

In 1912 F. Lewis Clark completed construction of a 15,000-square-foot mansion on a 12-acre estate overlooking the south shore of the lake. The renovated historic building is now a prominent country inn named "The Clark House of Hayden Lake."

By1924 the mills began to close as they had exhausted most of the area's merchantable timber. Recreation and tourism joined agriculture as the dominant industries. The Great Northern, the then owner of the railroad, shut down its rail service and sold its base property at the lake to the Coeur d'Alene Country Club.

By that time, motor vehicles were becoming the preferred mode of transportation. Business interests began developing to the west along Government Way, an arterial road that parallels present-day U.S. Highway 95 on the east and extends north from Coeur d'Alene to Idaho Highway 53. A new residential community followed this commercial development.

City Hall and district office under construction.

Incorporation

In order to remain competitive, the owners of the golf course at Bozanta Tavern decided that it needed a liquor license. At that time, a community had to be incorporated in order for its businesses to have a liquor license. Encouraged by the golf course, on March 31, 1947, residents living near the course and the lake petitioned the Kootenai County Board of Commissioners to become an incorporated village named Hayden Lake. The commissioners granted the request. In 1967 the legal status of the village changed to that of a city in conformity with new state law.

In 1959 postal authorities moved the post office to Hayden.

Hayden Lake continues to work closely with its sister city of Hayden on matters of common interest. The local Hayden Chamber of Commerce represents the interests of both cities.

Turning Points

Government Way Road The development of businesses along Government Way Road began in the early 1900s and led to the establishment of the city of Hayden. That event was the catalyst leading to the creation of the city of Hayden Lake.

Aryan Nations During the period of the 1970s to 2001, much to

Mayor John Wilkey and City Clerk Nancy Morris on Clean-Up Day.

the chagrin of Hayden Lake residents, the Aryan Nations, a neo-Nazi white supremacist organization, built a 20-acre compound at Hayden Lake.

Conflicts between the Aryan Nations and law enforcement received national attention. In 1999 Aryan Nation guards shot at a private car that ventured near their compound and held the occupants at gunpoint. In the ensuing civil action, an Idaho court awarded $6.3 million in damages to the plaintiffs (the car occupants).

As part of the settlement, the Aryan Nations turned over ownership of the compound to the plaintiffs who, in turn, sold the property to a philanthropist. The philanthropist donated it to North Idaho College, which now manages the land as "Peace Park."

Hayden Lake Today

Amenities and Attractions The city's location on the lake and the beautiful forested mountains, neighboring lakes, rivers and streams offer excellent opportunities for backpacking, hiking, trail riding, fishing, hunting, snowmobiling and cross-country skiing – an extraordinary recreational destination for almost all types of outdoor sports and activities.

Four state parks lie within 30 miles of the city – Farragut at the base of Lake Pend Oreille, Round Lake located south of Sandpoint, Hayden at the base of Coeur d'Alene Lake and the Old Mission west of Coeur d'Alene.

Silverwood Theme Park lies 17 miles north near Athol. The park offers numerous rides and attractions including a roller coaster, steam engine train and various rides on the water.

Economy and Major Employers The city has no major employers. Most of the city's residents commute to other cities to work, shop and do their business.

Education The Coeur d'Alene School District provides elementary and secondary education to students in Coeur d'Alene, Dalton Gardens, Hayden, Hayden Lake and part of rural Kootenai County. The school district operates an elementary school in the city of Hayden Lake. Older students attend junior high and high school in Hayden.

Several private schools in the Coeur d'Alene area provide elementary and secondary education to city students.

The closest institution of higher learning is North Idaho College (NIC) in Coeur d'Alene. The University of Idaho, Lewis-Clark State College and Boise State University have outreach programs on the NIC campus that offer associate, bachelor, masters and doctoral degrees in a variety of disciplines. Other academic institutions have facilities in the area offering educational programs, certificates and degrees.

Health Care The 225-bed Kootenai Medical Center in Coeur d'Alene is a regional medical center. It is located on a 40-acre integrated campus of high-tech patient towers, healing gardens, office buildings and public education centers – all connected by green space, bike and walking paths and water features.

Several general medical clinics, nursing and assisted living homes and other medical providers also provide services for area residents.

Transportation U.S. Highway 95 is about a mile west of the city. Interstate 90 can be accessed four miles south in Coeur d'Alene.

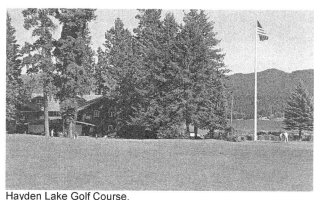

Hayden Lake Golf Course.

The Coeur d'Alene Airport is located two miles northwest of Hayden Lake. It has two runways – one 7,400 and the other also 5,400 feet long. The Spokane International Airport is about 52 miles west of the city.

Rail freight service is available in Coeur d'Alene. Amtrak passenger service is available 42 miles north in Sandpoint.

Utilities and Services Private companies provide electricity, telephone, natural gas, cable and satellite services. The City provides water and sewer services as well as fire and police protection.

Vision for 2050

In 1960 the Hayden Lake population was 247. Since that time the city's population has grown steadily as families have chosen to live in the beautiful lake setting close to their employment and the urban amenities available in nearby cities.

Since 2000 the city's population has grown at just over one percent annually. Recent historical trends will likely continue for decades.

By 2050 Hayden Lake will continue to be a friendly community of over a thousand people who love nature and the fabulous natural beauty of the lake and surrounding forest.

Mayors

1947 Foster Bollinger *
1957 Joseph Grant *
1961 Ben Contrell *
1966 Leonard Morris *
1967 Leonard Morris
1972 Russell Soderling
1976 A.E. Ted Menzel
1984 O.H. Hofmeister

1990 Ralph D. Kizer
1998 John Wilkey
2005 Bob Prince
2007 Todd Walker
2008 Nancy Morris
2012 Chris Beck
* Village Chairman

Sunset on the Spokane River near Huetter.

Huetter

Statistical Data

Population: 101 *
Elevation: 2,133 feet
Precipitation: 30 inches **
Average Snowfall: 50 inches **
County: Kootenai

Temperature Range – Fahrenheit: **
Spring: 30 to 67
Summer: 50 to 86
Fall: 30 to 74
Winter: 21 to 41
* U.S. Census Bureau Estimates July 2015
**Historical averages

Huetter (pronounced hutt-er) lies at the base of Rathdrum Prairie near the northern shore of the Spokane River, the outlet to Coeur d'Alene Lake. The city's land area of 22 acres is bordered by Coeur d'Alene on the east and Post Falls on the west.

Pre-Incorporation Years

In the1890s John T. Huetter – a skilled stonemason and prominent building contractor born in Germany in 1866 and a resident of Spokane in 1892 – built rock quarries, a brick yard and a lumber mill near what is now Huetter. The settlers in the town that grew up around these facilities named the community Huetter.

In 1889 the Northern Pacific Railroad built a rail line along the north shore of the Spokane River to Coeur d'Alene. When the railroad passed through what is now Huetter, it built a fuel and water stop for the steam engines.

In the early 1900s the Spokane and Inland Empire Railroad Company built an interurban electric railroad from Spokane through Post Falls and Huetter to Coeur d'Alene and then north to other Idaho communities.

Incorporation

Huetter first became an incorporated village and then, in 1967 with a change in Idaho law that made all incorporated municipalities cities, Huetter became a city.

Turning Points

Railroad The establishment of a fuel and water stop at what is now Huetter became the catalyst for the construction of other infrastructure that would help characterize the city.

Huetter is now a refueling depot for Burlington Northern Santa Fe Railway and an Idaho Department of Transportation port of entry and visitors" center.

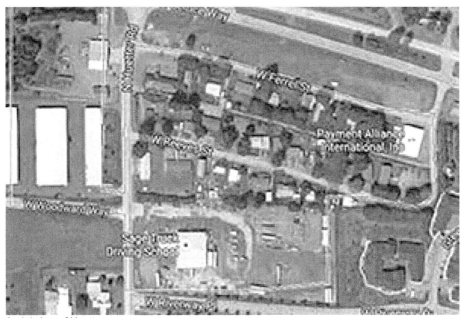
Aerial view of Huetter.

Huetter Today

Amenities and Attractions Four state parks lie within 30 miles of the city – Farragut at the base of Lake Pend Oreille, Round Lake located south of Sandpoint, Hayden at the base of Coeur d'Alene Lake and the Old Mission west of Coeur d'Alene.

Silverwood Theme Park lies 25 miles north near Athol. The park offers numerous rides and attractions including a roller coaster, steam engine train and various rides on the water.

Economy and Major Employers The city's principal employers are a popular bar frequented by residents of nearby cities, the railroad's refueling depot, the port of entry and the visitors' center.

Education Huetter children are bused to Post Falls for their elementary and secondary education.

North Idaho College (NIC) in Coeur d'Alene is the closest institution of higher learning. The University of Idaho also offers courses on the NIC campus.

The University of Idaho Research Park with its Center for Advanced Microelectronics and Biomolecular Research, the North Idaho campus for Workforce Training, Community Education, Small Business Development and Customized Training programs are located in the 300-acre Riverbend Commerce Park in Post Falls.

Health Care The closest hospital is the 225-bed Kootenai Medical Center in Coeur d'Alene. It is located on a 40-acre integrated campus of high-tech patient towers, healing gardens, office buildings and public education centers – all connected by green space, bike and walking paths and water features.

Several general medical clinics, nursing and assisted living homes and other medical providers also provide services for area residents.

I-90 near Huetter.

Transportation East Seltice Way, a divided highway that parallels the south side of I-90, forms the city's northern boundary.

The Coeur d'Alene Airport is located two miles northwest of Huetter. It has two runways – one 7,400 and the other 5,400 feet long. The Spokane International Airport is west of the city.

Rail freight service is available in Coeur d'Alene.

Utilities and Services Private companies provide electricity, telephone, natural gas, cable and satellite services. The City provides water and sewer services. Kootenai County Fire and Rescue provides fire and emergency services. The Kootenai County Sheriff's Office provides police protection under contract with the City.

Vision for 2050

Over the past 50 years, Huetter's population has approximated 100. These historical trends will likely continue for several decades.

Post Falls City Hall.

Post Falls

Statistical Data

Population: 29,896 *
Elevation: 2,150 feet
Precipitation: 30 inches **
Average Snowfall: 50 inches **
County: Kootenai
Website: www.postfallsidaho.org

Temperature Range – Fahrenheit: **
Spring: 30 to 67
Summer: 50 to 86
Fall: 30 to 74
Winter: 21 to 41
* U.S. Census Bureau Estimates July 2015
**Historical averages

Post Falls is the western gateway to Northern Idaho. It is five miles east of the Idaho/Washington border on U.S. Interstate 90. Coeur d'Alene is eight miles east. Spokane, Washington, is 24 miles west.

The Spokane River, the outlet of glacially created Lake Coeur d'Alene, flows on the southern edge of the city. Several glacial lakes surrounded by forested hills and mountains are nearby in the Coeur d'Alene National Forest to the south and east and the Kaniksu National Forest to the north.

The city is at the base of the Rathdrum Prairie, an agricultural oasis of bluegrass seed, mint, hay, wheat, potato seed and livestock. Farmland, interspersed with creeks and outcroppings of granite and native field rock, surrounds the city on the immediate west, north and east.

The Rathdrum Prairie sits atop Idaho's second largest aquifer. The Rathdrum Aquifer provides domestic water for Post Falls and dozens of other communities in Idaho and Washington.

In recent years, the character of Post Falls has changed dramatically. Originally a small mill town, it is now a progressive fast-growing urban community, the tenth largest city in Idaho.

Pre-Incorporation Years

For millennia, the Coeur d'Alene Indians lived along the lakes and rivers of their territorial homeland in Northern Idaho. They called one of their small villages along the Spokane River "Q'emiln" (pronounced Ka-mee'-lin), meaning "throat of the river." This name has carried over to today as Q'emiln Quest, an annual Post Falls festival. (*See The Region, American Indians.*)

Postcard of Chief Andrew Seltice and Frederick Post, depicting their families and historic sites of the region. Courtesy Robert G. Templin.

Early fur traders and explorers followed the Indian trails of the region to interact with the Coeur d'Alene Tribe. (*See The Region, Early Trappers/Explorers.*)

Lieutenant John Mullan and 230 soldiers and civilians completed a 624-mile-long military road between what is now Walla Walla, Washington, and Fort Benton, Montana, in August 1862. Mullan was promoted to Captain after the road was completed. Mullan built the original road that went up the east side of Lake Coeur d'Alene to the Cataldo Mission in 1858 to 1860 using a $130,000 congressional appropriation. With a subsequent appropriation of $100,000, Mullan completed the road through Post Falls in 1861 to 1862. It was the first engineered road in the Inland Northwest. Interstate 90 generally follows the Mullan Road.

When Mullan came through what is now Post Falls, he surveyed the three natural channels, falls and rapids of the Spokane River. He called the spot "Little Falls." Although he built the road for military purposes, the Mullan Road became a thoroughfare for settlers, immigrants and commerce. (*See The Region, Mullan Road, the Military Wagon Road That Opened the Region.*)

Early residents to Post Falls survey the falls, the mill and industrial development along the first channel of the Spokane River. Courtesy of the Museum of North Idaho.

Frederick Post – an experienced millwright from Heyburn, Germany – came to the Inland Northwest in 1871 to find a suitable place to settle. When Post first immigrated to America, he set up a water-powered lumber and grist mill on the Fox River in Illinois. Bypassed by the railroad line, Post dismantled and loaded his machinery on wagons and headed West – initially settling near what is now Rathdrum.

Spokane, Washington, founder James Glover encouraged Post to build a grist mill at the Spokane Falls in Spokane. However, Post was impressed with the water-power potential of Little Falls. He discussed the use of the falls – a trade agreement – with Moses Seltice, son of Chief Andrew Seltice, of the Coeur d'Alene Indians.

Unknown parties chiseled Post's name into the granite outcropping near the falls, now preserved as part of the city's Treaty Rock Park. There are also Indian pictographs on the rock outcropping. Archaeologists believe the pictographs and rock paintings predate Post's arrival. There is no evidence that Post signed a treaty at this location.

Post proceeded to divert water for powering his sawmill and began operations in 1880. The Dart Brothers – one of whom was Post's son-in-law – built a gristmill, and Post built a waterworks to supply domestic water to the developing community.

Frederick Post's lumber mill, circa 1890. Courtesy Post Falls Historical Museum and Museum of North Idaho.

The federal government wrote a new treaty with the Coeur d'Alene Tribe in 1889 that reduced the size of their reservation, placing Post's legal title to the land and water rights he had developed into question. Chief Andrew Seltice signed an abstract of title the same year to help Post defend his claim. The conflict was resolved with Post receiving clear title to the water right and 294 acres. With support from the community, he platted the townsite of Post Falls. That year was also monumental for another reason – the Northern Pacific Railroad reached Post Falls.

Washington Water Power hydroelectric facility, completed 1906. As an Avista facility, it continues to provide power and control of water at Post Falls. Courtesy Museum of North Idaho.

Two years later Congress recognized Chief Seltice's conveyance of title, and President Grover Cleveland signed the legislation.

Post sold a portion of his land and 87 percent of his water rights to R.K. Neill for $25,000 in 1890, retaining the balance of the water rights for the city. Neill wanted to build a hydroelectric dam to supply electricity to the mines in the Silver Valley. However, he was unable to finance the project and sold his property to Washington Water Power Company (WWPC).

WWPC signed contracts with six Silver Valley mining companies and began construction of electric transmission lines from its Spokane facility to the mines.

Chief Andrew Seltice died in 1902. Post died six years later. At Post's funeral, members of the Coeur d'Alene Tribe lined the interior of the church to honor the passing of their friend.

Incorporation

On May 28, 1891, Post Falls became an incorporated village. At that time, the town had a population of about 500. In 1910 the U.S. Census reported a population of 658. In accordance with legislation enacted by the 1967 Idaho Legislature, Post Falls changed its legal status to an incorporated city.

Aerial view of 10-acre farm of Gene and Margie Enders, who raised layer chickens and grains.

Turning Points

Mullan Road and the Homestead Act The 1862 completion of the Mullan Road and the passage of the Homestead Act that same year were key factors in the settlement of Post Falls. The Mullan Road opened the Northwest for travel and commerce, and the Homestead Act of 1862 released public land for private ownership, farming and development. (*See The Region, Federal Lands – Private Ownership and Preservation Laws.*)

Railroad The coming of the Northern Pacific Railroad to Post Falls in 1889 was a major turning point for the city as it opened distant markets for the lumber and agriculture products produced in the area. The railroad continues to be an important option for hauling freight long distances. (*See The Region, Railroads.*)

An interurban electric railroad owned by the Spokane and Inland Empire Railroad Company connected Post Falls with Spokane and Coeur d'Alene in the early 1900s. This was another important step in facilitating local passenger traffic. However, motor vehicles and good roads eventually replaced the electric railroad.

Sawmills Even though ownership of Post's original mill changed hands several times, sawmills underpinned the city's economy for over a century. Sawmill owners brought logs to the mills by floating them down the Spokane River. Later, logs came by rail and finally by truck.

Post Falls High School.

In 1978 under the ownership of Louisiana Pacific Corporation, production in the enlarged mill hit a peak. The company operated the mill three shifts a day and milled 74 million board feet of lumber over the time the mill was under its management.

When the availability of logs declined, the mills gradually shut down. These plant closures had a major adverse effect on the city's economy. (*See The Region, Forest Products.*)

Because of changing market forces, changes in federal forest management policies and regulations and environmental litigation, the mill closed in 1995. The site now awaits a new use for the twenty-first century. (*See The Region, Mining and Forest Products – Leading Causes for loss of Economic Dominance.*)

WWPC Hydroelectric Dam In 1906 when the Post Falls hydroelectric plant came online, it took over delivering electrical power to the Silver Valley mines. The dam also had an important impact on the city's economy and quality of life. It not only provided a stable employment base, but it also brought electrical power to the growing community.

Agriculture Most of the original farmers were homesteaders. Under the Homestead Act, they could file on 160 acres of public land. If they improved the land and lived on it for five years, the land was theirs. Small farms were labor intensive and provided the livelihood for many area families from the turn of the century until the 1970s. (*See The Region, Federal Lands – Private Ownership and Preservation Laws.*)

For many years, Post Falls was home to Seiter's Cannery, a processor of locally produced fruit and vegetables. Before the cannery closed, it provided employment for many area residents.

Farming continues to be a major economic activity in the Post Falls area, albeit most of the farmland is now under the ownership or management of large farm operators. Bluegrass seed has become an important crop while fruit orchards have declined. Poultry and egg production continue as leading agricultural commodities. (*See The Region, Agriculture and Livestock.*)

Old Church, Post Falls' oldest standing building, has been restored to become the city's cultural arts center. The site is listed on the National Register of Historic Places. Courtesy the Post Falls Historical Society.

Interstate 90 Interstate 90 reached Post Falls in 1970. This freeway has had a profound impact on the commercial and residential growth and development of Post Falls. It has not only facilitated city residents commuting to work, but it has also allowed the city to attract tourist traffic to its many amenities and attractions.

Significant residential and business growth has developed on both sides of the interstate as it intersects the city.

City Services – Building a Diversified Economy As the character of the city's economic base has changed, city and community leaders have responded creatively to make the city attractive to a more diversified economy.

Included in these actions was the 1979 construction of a wastewater facility. In 1980 the city completed its first comprehensive plan, designating industrial, commercial and residential zones.

In cooperation with other communities in western Kootenai County, Post Falls has an economic development strategy. Community leaders and area investors are assisting in the development and implementation of this strategy. For example, one private investment, Riverbend Commerce Park, has attracted several private and public tenants. Other leaders were instrumental in attracting businesses to locate in the city. (*See The Region, The Region's Economic Base – Historically and Today.*)

Post Falls Today

Amenities and Attractions The city has 764 acres devoted to 17 individual municipal parks including five under construction. Some of the parks have ball fields, basketball and tennis courts, fishing and boat launch facilities. Many parks have playgrounds, shelters, picnic facilities, scenic views, trails and open space.

Several are near the Spokane River. In both winter and spring, water cascades through the natural gorge of the river which is an excellent trout fishery. Other outdoor enthusiasts use the river for recreational watercraft both upstream and downstream of the city. The river's natural beauty and prominence is the basis for Post Falls' reputation as Idaho's "River City."

The North Idaho Centennial Trail, one of the national Millennium Legacy Trails dedicated in 1999, passes through Post Falls. The trail is a paved scenic path used by walkers, runners, bicyclists and the handicapped. The trail meanders for 24 miles from the Idaho/Washington state line along the Spokane River at Post Falls to the 34-acre Coeur d'Alene Parkway State Park, six miles east of the city of Coeur d'Alene.

Private businesses provide a convention center and motels, a Mississippi sternwheeler that travels east to Lake Coeur d'Alene, a park that offers simulcast dog and horseracing, bingo and a theatre. Thirty golf courses are within 35 miles of the city.

Throughout the year, the Stateline Stadium and Speedway holds such events as the regionally famous Idaho 200 stock car races. On July 3 of each year, the Speedway sponsors a fireworks display commemorating Independence Day and Idaho statehood. (*See The Region, Idaho Territory – Change in Idaho Territorial Boundaries 1863 to 1890, Suffrage and Statehood.*)

Each summer the City sponsors a series of concerts in the park where local artists display their talents. The first weekend of June is Post Falls Days, an annual event that includes a grand parade, a carnival and fiddle-fest. Each October, the Post Falls Historical Society sponsors its Oktoberfest, an annual fall heritage celebration.

In May, the Coeur d'Alene Indians and volunteers sponsor "Q'emiln Quest" (pronounced Ka-mee-lin), an American Indian educational and cultural event. In July, the City and the Coeur d'Alene Tribe sponsor the annual Powwow called "Julyamsh."

Every July the Hot Rod Cafe River City Rod Run produces one of the Northwest's largest car shows.

The city has over thirty churches of various denominations. "Old Church" is the oldest church building in the city. Built in 1890, this historic restored structure now serves as the city's Cultural Arts Center.

Post Falls has several other historic buildings and points of interest listed on the National Register. They include the Washington Water Power Bridge, the Corbin Ditch (Spokane Valley Irrigation Canal), the Samuel and Ann Young Home, Pleasantview School and Treaty Rock.

The city's most alluring attraction is its scenic location next to the Spokane River, Lake Coeur d'Alene and the national forests. The nearby mountains, lakes, rivers and streams offer excellent opportunities for backpacking, hiking and trails for riding horses and ATVs, fishing, hunting, snowmobiling and cross-country skiing.

Farragut State Park is 30 miles north at the base of Lake Pend Oreille and includes 4,000 acres. The 5,744 acres of land and 2,332 acres of water comprising Heyburn State

Official unveiling of three new informational signs at the historical landmark, Treaty Rock, a partnership of the Post Falls Parks Department and thePost Falls Historical Society. Pictured left to right: Post Falls Mayor Clay Larkin; Quanah Matheson, Coeur d'Alene Tribe Cultural Director; KimBrown, Post Falls Historical Society; Felix Aripa, Coeur d'Alene Tribal elder; Judy Meyer, Idaho State Historical Society Trustee; Bob and MaryTemplin, Post Falls Historical Society.

Park are at the base of Lake Coeur d'Alene near Plummer, about 25 miles southeast. The 18-acre Old Mission State Park, home to the oldest building in Idaho, is 35 miles east at Cataldo.

The 73-mile-long Trail of the Coeur d'Alenes, one of the most spectacular paved non-motorized trails in the Western United States, begins in Plummer and extends east on an abandoned railroad line to Mullan, passing through national forests and old mining towns, railroad tunnels and over high railroad trestles.

Round Lake State Park is 40 miles north of the city. This 142-acre forested park surrounds the 58-acre Round Lake.

The historic Washington Water Power Bridge, with its 221-foot-long spandrel arch, was built in 1909 across the natural gorge at Post Falls. It links the city with the hydroelectric dam facilities on the second of the Spokane River's three channels near the water falls where Fredrick Post built his sawmill.

Economy and Major Employers Flexcel-Kimball International, a furniture manufacturer with 500 employees, is the city's largest employer. Center Partners, a call center, and Post Falls School District each employ 400. Red Lion Templin's Hotel and Convention Center has 200 employees. Idaho Veneer, a wood products plant, employs 125. Jacklin Seed, a major bluegrass seed company, has 85 employees.

The city's downtown business district of retail, financial, hospitality and service businesses and public entities makes up the balance of the city's employment base.

Many Post Falls residents commute to other cities for employment.

Education Post Falls School District provides most of the city's primary and secondary education. Several private schools also provide K-12 education.

North Idaho College (NIC) in Coeur d'Alene is the closest institution of higher learning. The University of Idaho also offers courses on the NIC campus.

The 300-acre Riverbend Commerce Park provides space for many businesses and educational institutions including the University of Idaho Research Park with its Center for Advanced Microelectronics and Biomolecular Research. North Idaho College's campus in the park offers Workforce Training and Community Education programs and hosts the Small Business Development and Customized Training programs.

Health Care The 225-bed Kootenai Medical Center in Coeur d'Alene, which operates Post Falls Health Park, is the closest major hospital.

Post Falls has a specialty hospital, day surgery hospital and health care clinics to provide for most of the community's medical and health care needs.

Transportation Interstate 90 intersects the city. State Highway 41, on the east side of the city, connects Post Falls with Rathdrum.

Private, charter and light commuter airline service is available at Coeur d'Alene Airport. Spokane International Airport provides access to large commercial airlines.

Rail transportation for freight is available in the city. Amtrak passenger service is available 53 miles north in Sandpoint.

Utilities and Services Private companies provide electricity, telephone, natural gas, cable and satellite services. The City provides water and sewer services, fire and police protection and road construction and maintenance service within the city boundaries. The County provides solid waste services.

Vision for 2050

In 1960 Post Falls had a population of 1,983. By 2000 the population stood at 17,247. Subsequently, the city's population has grown around 6 percent annually.

Looking long-term, the city's annual growth should decline to a more moderate rate. However, by 2050 even at moderate growth rates, the city's population could still more than double.

City and community leaders have effectively reached out to the citizens of Post Falls in developing the city's comprehensive plans. Citizens want to maintain the area's "small town" friendly attitude. Clean air, clean water, family neighborhoods, green space and preservation of the natural environment are high priorities.

Strategic planning and vision are required to blend these objectives with the citizen's desire for balanced growth and development of the city.

To achieve the desired citizen objectives, city and community leaders are working on building a community that allows its residents to live, work and learn within its boundaries. There must be a blend of culture and commerce. There need to be innovative transportation corridors that involve walking, riding and commuting.

Landowners will likely continue to convert large open tracts surrounding the city into residential subdivisions and commercial developments. To insure protection of the clean environment and high quality of life our citizens have come to expect, city and community leaders will need to work cooperatively to insure municipal systems and infrastructure are adequate and the costs of expansion are born by the growth that created the additional needs.

Mayors

1891 Charles H. Walizer *
1892 C.M. Brown *
1892 C.W. Clark *
1893 Thornton Wheatley *
1894 A.M. Martin *
1899 Samuel Yount *
1900 James A. Fisher *
1903 A.J. Manor *
1905 John Mitchell *
1911 Alf Webster *
1913 Daniel K. Mathews *
1914 J. Whitworth Broadhead *
1916 John Young *
1917 Sherman H. Smith *
1919 Alf Webster *
1920 Eric Johnson *
1920 Sherman H. Smith *
1921 William A. Carter *
1925 John Handy *
1929 Herman H. Eisenhauer *

1935 Ben F. Brigger *
1937 J.A. Munson *
1940 Ben F. Brigger *
1943 Herman Eisenhauer *
1947 Walter J. Stewart *
1951 Winfred C. Staples *
1955 Vincent Grammatica *
1957 Edgar A. Seiter *
1961 W.J. Crowley *
1966 Theodore Snyder *
1968 Cecil Meyer
1972 Don Kamps
1976 Francis Wilhels
1980 Frank Henderson
1983 Kent Helmer
1991 James C. Hammond
1996 Steve "Gus" Johnson
2001 Clay Larkin
2014 Ron Jacobson
* Village Chairman

Rathdrum, 2010.

Rathdrum

Statistical Data

Population: 7,283 *
Elevation: 2,220 feet
Precipitation: 26 inches **
Average Snowfall: 54 inches **
County: Kootenai
Website: www.rathdrum.org

Temperature Range – Fahrenheit: **
Spring: 30 to 67
Summer: 50 to 84
Fall: 30 to 74
Winter: 22 to 41
* U.S. Census Bureau Estimates July 2015
**Historical averages

Rathdrum lies on the western edge of the Idaho Panhandle. Beautiful forested mountains outline the city's northern and western skies. Several crystal-clear mountain lakes and rivers are within a short drive of the city. To the east and south is the Rathdrum Prairie.

Residents enjoy living in this small town with a "neighborhood" atmosphere yet with access to more urban services in nearby cities. The regional shopping and commercial centers of Hayden and Coeur d'Alene are 11 miles southeast. Post Falls is 10 miles south. Shopping centers located southwest in Washington include Liberty Lake, 16 miles; Spokane Valley 22 miles; and the city of Spokane, 29 miles away.

Pre-Incorporation Years

From the beginning, Rathdrum has been a transportation corridor and crossroad. American Indians refer to the area as the "Great Road of the Flatheads." Hunting and gathering groups of the Coeur d'Alene and Spokane Tribes traveled through the area routinely. (*See Northern Idaho, The Region, American Indians.*)

Explorers and trappers representing the Hudson's Bay and Pacific Fur Trading Companies traversed the Rathdrum Prairie in the early 1800s. Roman Catholic Jesuit missionaries came to proselyte the Indians in the 1840s. (*See Northern Idaho, The Region, Early Trappers/Explorers and Early Christian Missionaries.*)

In the late 1860s postal authorities established a pony mail route connecting Walla Walla, Washington, with Missoula, Montana. The route had 21 stations and 25 riders who traveled up to 70 miles per day. The mail route entered Kootenai County near the present town of Stateline and proceeded northeast across the prairie to a relay station at Rathdrum before going on to Steamboat Landing at the south end of Lake Pend Oreille.

Main railroad depot in Rathdrum, circa 1909.

In 1861 a hunter and trapper named Connors built a small cabin where Rathdrum is now located. Ten years later, he sold his "squatter's right" and cabin to Frederick Post. Post traveled to the newly established U.S. Land Office in Lewiston and filed a claim to the property. Eventually, Post transferred his ownership to his son-in-law, Charles Wesley "Wes" Wood. (*See Northern Idaho, The Region, Federal Land Use Laws*.)

Most of the land in the area remained largely unsettled until 1880 when the Great Northern Railroad surveyed for a new rail line. Wood sold half interest in his 60 acres to M.D. Wright. The two of them platted the town, and businesses began to spring up. Frederick Post built a sawmill, Wes Wood a livery barn and Henry Reininger a brewery.

Wes Wood named the new community "Westwood." In 1881 a post office was established by that name with Zach Lewis as postmaster. Lewis received instruction from the postal authorities in Washington, D.C., to give the post office a new name – there were already too many post office towns with names similar to "Westwood."

Old Kootenai County courthouse.

Lewis had difficulty coming up with a name that he felt the postal authorities would accept. He appealed to M.M. Cowley, a former bank president and respected citizen. Cowley provided a number of names, including Rathdrum, the city of his birth in Ireland. Lewis selected Rathdrum and submitted it to the postal authorities. They accepted, and the town of Rathdrum was born.

That year was also pivotal in other respects. In 1881 the railroad reached the town, and the Kootenai County Commission moved the county seat from Seneaquoteen, a trading post near Lake Pend Oreille, to Rathdrum.

The early 1880s marked a time when the town's economy surged. M.D. Wright got the contract to produce railroad ties for the Hauser-to-Coeur d'Alene spur. The lead, zinc and silver mines of the Silver Valley east of Coeur d'Alene were developing. Many of those traveling to the Silver Valley stopped at Rathdrum for supplies. Rathdrum was

Downtown Rathdrum, 1910.

also the railhead for the early freight wagons bringing ore from the Silver Valley mines for shipment to west coast smelters.

The town's commercial district soon boasted a grocery and general merchandise stores, saloons, hotels, restaurants, blacksmiths, liveries, a justice of the peace, a post office, two banks, a creamery, a newspaper called *The Rathdrum Courier*, churches, schools and a fraternal hall.

In 1883 Frederick Post built a domestic water system on the mountain and sold it to a group of stockholders organized by Henry Reininger. At that time, the population had reached about 1,000 – making the town larger than the town of Spokane Falls, now named Spokane.

However, Rathdrum's dramatic growth was fleeting. When the railroad reached Coeur d'Alene in 1886, many of Rathdrum's residents and businesses moved to the new railhead.

Incorporation

Kootenai County completed construction of the county jail and courthouse in 1890. The following year Rathdrum became an incorporated village. During the period of incorporation as many as five passenger trains a day came to the village. The tourists were attracted to the beautiful Hauser Lake, Twin Lakes and Spirit Lake nestled in the nearby mountains.

At that time, Brick became the construction material of choice for many new buildings. One of these buildings was St. Stanislaus Roman Catholic Church. Erected in 1901, it is the oldest brick church in Idaho.

Turning Points

The Railroad Construction of the railroad line to Rathdrum in 1881 was a momentous event. It set the stage for a surge in the city's growth and economic vitality, giving Rathdrum a monopoly as the regional shopping center, railhead and supply depot. (*See Northern Idaho, The Region, Railroads.*)

However, the town's dominant economic status in the region was short lived. When the railroad reached Coeur d'Alene in 1886, Rathdrum's economy collapsed as most of its business community moved to the new regional commercial center.

Old jail.

County Seat For 27 years Rathdrum enjoyed the political prestige of being the seat of government for Kootenai County.

However, when the railroad reached Coeur d'Alene in 1886 most of Rathdrum's commercial and residential base moved. It was only a matter of time until the majority of county voters would also move their county seat of government to Coeur d'Alene; which they did in 1908. Again, Rathdrum experienced an economic blow as county employees moved to the larger city.

Fire In the fall of 1884 while Rathdrum was still a railhead, a disastrous fire consumed 55 buildings located on six city blocks. Because the Silver Valley was booming and there was a growing demand for goods, building owners quickly rebuilt the town.

Fire again broke out in 1924 burning most of the businesses on the south side of Main Street where less water was available for fire suppression. Unlike 40 years earlier, only a few structures were rebuilt.

The New Economy As Rathdrum approached the end of the twentieth century, the city again began experiencing significant growth. The 1990 census reported a population of 2,000. Today it is more than treble that number. Much of the growth comes from younger families finding more affordable housing in Rathdrum and commuting to other cities for work. In addition, an increasing number of retirees are finding their dream homes in this city where they can live near beautiful public forests and lakes but close to urban amenities.

Rathdrum Today

Amenities and Attractions The city has four parks comprising 15 acres – Old City Park, Thayer Park, Stub Meyer Park and Roth Park. Stub Meyer Park offers attractions for people of all ages. The new skate park with the John Brown Playfield for kids is particularly attractive for youth. Two other parks, Heritage and Majestic, are in the planning stages.

As part of the city's revitalization efforts, it has built 12 miles of new asphalt pathways and sidewalks with beautiful landscaping.

Historic attractions include St. Stanislaus Church, the city's old jail and the Methodist Church.

Annual events and festivals that the city's Park and Recreation Department and the Chamber of Commerce join to have a great time organizing are Rathdrum Days in July, the Fishing Derby in the Old City Park in June, December Lights at Christmas time and the Fall Festival.

Ribbon cutting at Splash Park.

Downhill skiing is available at Schweitzer Mountain Resort, 45 miles northeast. Three state parks within 30 miles of the city are Farragut Park near Bayview, Round Lake near Sandpoint and the Old Mission near Coeur d'Alene.

Dominant among the city's natural amenities are the beautiful surrounding mountains, lakes, rivers and streams. They offer excellent opportunities for backpacking, hiking, trail riding, fishing, hunting, snowmobiling and cross-country skiing.

Economy and Major Employers The city has no dominant employers. The majority of residents commute to Coeur d'Alene, Post Falls or Spokane for work.

Rathdrum Fire Station.

The city's largest employer is the Lakeland School District at 320. Steins IGA Grocery Store employs 75. Other employers are Stanford Building, Acme Materials, Dreamwood Cabinets and Rathdrum Power.

Education Lakeland School District provides most of the elementary and secondary education. The district operates a high school, an alternative high school, a junior high school and three elementary schools. The school district also has schools in Spirit Lake and Athol. There are several charter and private schools in the surrounding cities.

The closest institution of higher learning is North Idaho College in Coeur d'Alene.

Health Care Several medical clinics and a physical therapy and immediate care center are located in the city. There is a senior care center with 27 rooms. A residential community for seniors with continued care is under development. The closest hospital is Kootenai Medical Center in Coeur d'Alene.

Transportation Rathdrum is located at the crossroads for State Highways 41 and 53. U.S. Highway 95 is three miles west. Interstate 90 is located 10 miles south of town just outside Post Falls.

Coeur d'Alene airport, located six miles southeast, serves private, charter and light commuter aircraft. Spokane International Airport is 45 miles southwest.

Railroad service for passengers and freight is located 25 miles away in Spokane.

Utilities and Services Private companies provide gas, cable, satellite, electricity and wireless services. The city provides water, sewer and law enforcement. Northern Lakes Fire District provides fire protection.

Vision for 2050

Over the past several years, Rathdrum's population growth has exceeded 5 percent annually. Should that trend continue, by 2050 Rathdrum will have a population approaching 25,000. Even if growth slows, it will still require careful

Rathdrum City Hall, 2012.

planning to insure preservation of the city's heritage and hometown quality of life.

By 2050 the city will have updated all city parks with adequate parking and new equipment. The proposed Heritage and Majestic Parks will be completed. Municipal services will be expanded as necessary to meet citizens' needs.

Rathdrum is one of the oldest towns in Northern Idaho. There is a strong effort on the part of the citizens to keep and learn from the history of the town. Many of the citizens come from families who settled here 100 years ago. The volunteer efforts of these citizens will have resulted in the creation of a historical museum honoring the city's heritage.

Many former residents and retirees will return to enjoy the beauty of this quiet community with close access to the mountains and lakes. They relish having the traditional public access to mountain trails and lakes to hunt and fish enjoyed by them and their families.

To accommodate this growth, the city limits will have spread south into the Rathdrum Prairie.

However, even though Rathdrum will be a larger city, community leaders will make decisions based on the city's comprehensive plan so that Rathdrum's rural culture and heritage is preserved and educational, employment and business needs are met while protecting the environment.

Mayors

1891 A.A. Smith *
1892 John Russell *
1893 M.D. Wright *
1893 Frank Wenz*
1894 W.A. Hart *
1901 Louis Eilbert *
1902 R.C. Thompson *
1903 John Crenshaw *
1904 W.A. Hart *
1905 A. Cook *
1908 W.A. Hart *
1909 Martin Poleson *
1912 F.L. Farnsworth *
1917 A.A. Berger *
1919 George A. Flemming *
1920 C.F. Borrell *
1923 Leo Lentsch *
1927 R.E. Young *
1929 T.L. Quarles *
1930 W.A. Poleson *
1933 O.G. Farnsworth *

1935 Frank Caffrey *
1939 A.B. Nalson *
1947 Murrell Hansen *
1950 C.F. Clark *
1951 Leroy Dixon *
1963 Richard Penman *
1963 Merle Louthan *
1964 William Howell *
1968 Merle Louthan
1972 Williams Banks
1972 Norma Cappell
1973 Robert Jones
1976 Donald Ziegler
1986 James Parker
1991 John Heitstuman
2000 Tawnda Bromley
2002 Joseph Hassell
2004 Brian Steele
2008 Vic Holmes
* Village Chairman

Spirit Lake in December 2012.

Spirit Lake

Statistical Data

Population: 2,040 *
Elevation: 2,567 feet
Precipitation: 46 inches **
Average Snowfall: 163 inches **
County: Kootenai
Website: www.spiritlakeid.gov

Temperature Range – Fahrenheit: **
Spring: 27 to 69
Summer: 45 to 84
Fall: 28 to 74
Winter: 20 to 40
* U.S. Census Bureau Estimates July 2015
**Historical averages

The City of Spirit Lake lies on the terraced eastern shore of a beautiful lake of the same name. Forests surround the city and the lake.

The lake extends west of the city for over four and a half miles. It is a mile wide from north to south and has a maximum depth of 100 feet.

The wooded Selkirk Mountains lie to the north and west of the city. Twin Lakes, two of several other lakes in the area, lie a few miles to the south. The much larger city of Rathdrum, lies 11 miles south. About 10 miles to the west, across the Idaho/Washington border, the 5,878-foot-high Mt. Spokane punctuates the western sky.

Pre-Incorporation Years

Spirit Lake is one of several lakes in Northern Idaho created millions of years ago when glaciers covered the land. (*See Northern Idaho-Glacial Lakes and the*

Purcell Trench.) Native American Indians, who hunted in the area, called the lake "Tesemeni" meaning Lake of Spirits.

Around 1907 F. A. Blackwell led an investment group that purchased 100,000 acres of timberland in the area. He then formed two companies. The first company, the Panhandle Lumber Company, constructed a large sawmill near what is now Spirit Lake. The company also aided in the construction of roads, including a bridge across the narrow lake channel immediately west of the town.

The second company, the Spirit Lake Land Company, platted the company town and built water works, an electric power plant, sewage systems and concrete sidewalks.

Idaho Washington & Northern Railroad station.

By 1910 the town had a vibrant downtown business community that offered a variety of goods and services including retail stores, a bank and a weekly newspaper. The residents built schools and churches and by 1910 the town had a population of 907.

Around 1907 Blackwell also formed a railroad company, the Idaho & Washington Northern Railroad (I&WN), to haul logs to the sawmill and transport finished lumber.

The railroad started at Rathdrum and extended north to the Spirit Lake Sawmill, where it built a roundhouse, then into Washington at Newell – across the border from Old

Mill, early 1930s.

Town – and on to other Washington cities. The Chicago, Milwaukee and St. Paul Railroad acquired the I&WN in 1916.

A high percentage of the timber processed at the Spirit Lake Sawmill came from the forests near Mt. Spokane and were floated across the lake to the sawmill with the use of tugboats.

Incorporation

On January 14, 1908, the Kootenai County Commissioners approved incorporation of the town as the "Village of Spirit Lake."

Turning Points

F.A. Blackwell The City of Spirit Lake owes its origins to Blackwell. His entrepreneurial spirit and unusual set of organization and management skills made the difference. He successfully integrated the business components of sawmill, timber, railroad and tugboats to produce and market wood products. At the same time, he led the effort to build a fully integrated community where

Downtown Spirit Lake, 1930.

company employees had a desirable place to live and raise their families.

Forest Fire In 1939 a terrible forest fire started on the slopes of Mt. Spokane. Pushed by the prevailing western wind, the fire raced toward the Village of Spirit Lake. Town residents were able to save the sawmill but the railroad roundhouse and lumberyard were destroyed. The company, that had produced over a billion board feet of lumber, never recovered.

Over the succeeding decades, the town almost died. Businesses closed. Owners either tore down or abandoned their buildings. Those families who stayed drove to nearby cities for work.

Schools After the fire, public school enrollment declined sharply. In 1961 the Lakeland School District allowed the elementary school to remain open but closed Spirit Lake's middle and high schools. Middle and high school students attended school in Rathdrum. Loss of the schools further disheartened the town's residents.

Beginning in the early 1990s, the city's decline reversed. Families began

Aerial view.

moving into Spirit Lake (*see below*). In 1998 the school district built a school that housed both junior and senior high school students. In 2006 the district built another facility and separated the two schools.

Adapting to the New Economy The population of Spirit Lake held at around 800 until 1992 when it experienced a spillover effect of the economic growth in nearby cities. Families began moving to Spirit Lake and commuting to Rathdrum, Post Falls, Coeur d'Alene and Spokane to work.

This growth has caused new businesses to open. Some restored old buildings or constructed new facilities. Developers have added new subdivisions to accommodate the new residents.

Property values have soared. People are taking pride in the community. Residents were excited about the city's 2008 centennial celebration. Their motto: "Come Look at Us Now."

Spirit Lake Today

Amenities and Attractions The City of Spirit Lake has three municipal parks. One is a small park on Maine St. in the heart of downtown. It provides for a green space and has flower gardens, benches for seating and a flag pole on which the United States flag and the Idaho State Flag fly. Its big park consists of picnic tables, fire pits, playground equipment, and baseball fields. A large gazebo is used for events in the park. The park is located in the center of town. The third park has been used by the Little League for a number of years, and, before that, it was a baseball field for town teams and semi pro teams in the early years.

The lake is the city's most significant amenity. Thousands of tourists come each year for camping, boating and fishing. Attractive homes, many of which are vacation homes owned by people who live outside the area, line the lake's shoreline.

An attraction frequently used by the city's residents is the urban amenities available in other cities within a half hour drive, including shopping, museums, theater and golfing.

The surrounding mountains, lakes, rivers and streams offer excellent opportunities for backpacking, hiking, trail riding, fishing, hunting, snowmobiling and cross-country skiing. Downhill skiing is available at Schweitzer Mountain Resort, 35 miles northeast.

Winterfest 2012.

Two state parks are nearby. The 4,000-acre Farragut State Park is about 15 miles to the east at the base of Lake Pend Oreille. The 142-acre Round Lake State Park is about 10 miles to the north.

Economy and Major Employers The Lakeland School District has about 100 employees and is the city's largest employer. The city's downtown business district, which includes a grocery store and several other retail and service businesses, provides additional employment. Most of the city's residents commute to other cities for employment.

Education Lakeland School District provides elementary and secondary public education in the Spirit Lake/Rathdrum area. Within the city, the district has an elementary school and a junior and senior high school.

The nearest institution of higher learning is North Idaho College in Coeur d'Alene.

Health Care The nearest hospital is Kootenai Medical Center in Coeur d'Alene. There is a doctor's office, a physical therapy office and a dentist in Spirit Lake.

Maine Street now.

Transportation State Highway 41 intersects the city. U.S. Highway 95 lies nine miles to the east on State Highway 54, which begins a mile south of town.

Utilities and Services Public utilities provide electricity, telephone, natural gas and satellite services. The City provides water and sewer services as well as fire and police protection.

Starting in 2007 Avista Utilities brought natural gas to the community. There are two companies come in and haul solid waste out. The County has a refuse point in the Twin Lakes area if residents wish to haul their own household trash.

Water tower at Spirit Lake.

Vision for 2050

By 2050 the City of Spirit Lake will retain its sense of community as a peaceful, family-oriented town. Fewer members of the working population will need to commute to other cities for work. By that time, more workers will be able to use rapidly expanding technologies to work or do business at home.

An increasing number of retirees will choose to live in Spirit Lake because of its beautiful natural setting, yet within a half hour drive of the urban amenities in the larger cities nearby.

The city's population will continue to grow but at slower rates. By 2050 the city's population will likely approximate 5,000.

The city's existing infrastructure will need to expand to give high quality service to existing residents and accommodate growing demands.

The city will continue efforts to control costs and allocate the cost of services and infrastructure to those benefited. Imposing equitable growth impact and user fees will continue to be matters of high priority.

Mayors

1908 W.J. Hireen *
1908 Earle S. Prindle *
1909 J.C.H. Reynolds *
1911 S.A. McCoubrey *
1913 M.E. Kadish *
1915 T.J. Coleman *
1919 E.A. Conlin *
1921 J.H. Gutridge
1922 Barney Smith
1923 Art Webb
1932 Thomas Falkenberg
1935 Robert Jones
1942 Adam Schissler
1942 Walter Lookling
1943 Clifford Holman
1959 J.F. Bacon
1967 Ole W. Nelson
1968 E.A. Bieto

1968 Rex Morehouse
1969 James Beeman
1970 Jack Inman
1976 James Brown, Sr.
1984 Jim Wilson
1985 Joe Cain
1986 Carl Dunbar
1989 Joe Cain
1990 Carl Dunbar
1991 Paul Korman
1995 Robert Street
1995 Cathrine Spadt
1996 Robert Knapp
1999 William Moe
2000 Peter Troglia
2002 Roxy A. Martin
2010 Todd Clary
* Village Chairman

Stateline City Hall.

Stateline

Statistical Data

Population: 44 *
Elevation: 2,120 feet
Precipitation: 30 inches **
Average Snowfall: 50 inches **
County: Kootenai

Temperature Range – Fahrenheit: **
Spring: 30 to 67
Summer: 50 to 84
Fall: 30 to 74
Winter: 22 to 41
* U.S. Census Bureau Estimates July 2015
**Historical averages

Stateline is located on the southeastern edge of the fertile Rathdrum Prairie and the western edge of the Idaho/Washington state line. Residential developments of the unincorporated Washington community of East Farms lie on the city's western border.

Fertile farms extend north and east of the city. Interstate 90 and the Spokane River are less than a mile south.

Pre-Incorporation Years

In 1881 the Northern Pacific Railroad constructed a rail line from Wallula, Washington. to Spokane; crossed into Idaho Territory at what is now Stateline; turned northeast to Rathdrum, then Westwood; then north to Sandpoint. There the railroad turned east around the top of Lake Pend Oreille to the Clark Fork River then turned east again to Hells Gate near Missoula, Montana. The railroad line was completed in 1883.

Incorporation

When Idaho passed a new law in 1947 that allowed slot machines and the selling of liquor by the drink only in incorporated municipalities, Stateline applied for incorporation. On April 14, 1947, Stateline became an incorporated village in order to sell liquor and have slot machines. Its status changed to a city in 1967 as required by the change in Idaho law.

Turning Points

Gambling and Liquor

The passage of Idaho law that required establishments selling liquor by the drink or having slot machines be in incorporated municipalities had a great effect on Stateline. At the time of incorporation, there were six gambling and drinking establishments in the city.

Cruisers at Stateline.

Stateline Today

Amenities and Attractions The city's location near beautiful forested mountains, lakes, rivers and streams offers excellent opportunities for backpacking, hiking, trail riding, fishing, hunting, snowmobiling and cross-country skiing.

Four state parks lie within 30 miles of the city – Farragut at the base of Lake Pend Oreille, Round Lake located south of Sandpoint, Hayden at the base of Coeur d'Alene Lake and the Old Mission west of Coeur d'Alene.

Economy and Major Employers The city's business community consists primarily of the race track, restaurants and bars – some featuring musical jam sessions appealing to their customer base which extends into Washington.

First and Last Chance Tavern, on the border.

Education Lakeland School District, headquartered in Rathdrum, provides most of the K-12 education. Stateline school children commute to Rathdrum for their elementary, junior high, high school and alternative high school education.

The closest institution of higher learning is North Idaho College in Coeur d'Alene.

Health Care The closest hospital is Kootenai Medical Center in Coeur d'Alene.

Medical services and clinics are also available across the state boundary in Washington.

Transportation In addition to Interstate 90, State Highway 53 in Idaho – becoming 290 when it crosses into Washington – lies two miles north of the city.

Stateline Speedway.

Coeur d'Alene airport serves private, charter and light commuter aircraft. Spokane International Airport provides access to major carriers.

Utilities and Services Private companies provide electricity, telephone and satellite services. Homes and businesses in the city have individual wells and septic systems. The County Sheriff's Office provides police protection under contract with the City. The Northern Lakes Fire District provides fire protection.

Vision for 2050

In 1960 Stateline had a population of 33. During the current decade, the city's population has remained constant at around 60.

Worley City Hall.

Worley

Statistical Data

Population: 254 *
Elevation: 2,650 feet
Precipitation: 16 inches **
Average Snowfall: 15 inches **
County: Kootenai

Temperature Range – Fahrenheit: **
Spring: 33 to 57
Summer: 52 to 77
Fall: 37 to 57
Winter: 23 to 36
* U.S. Census Bureau Estimates July 2015
**Historical averages

Worley is located 28 miles south of Coeur d'Alene on a beautiful rolling agricultural plain interspersed by large tracts of forested areas. Fields of bluegrass, wheat, oats, lentils and peas surround the city. This farmland is substantially all tribal trust land of the Coeur d'Alene Indian Reservation.

The incorporated city occupies 127 acres. However, the city's boundaries appear larger because it blends into a suburban community of nearly 100 houses built by the Coeur d'Alene Tribe.

Pre-Incorporation Years

In 1887 in an attempt to assimilate American Indians into the white mainstream, Congress passed the General Allotment Act, also known as the Dawes Severalty Act.

Worley Congregational Church, 1918.

Under the Act, Native Americans received an allotment of reservation land. Each head of family received 160 acres – single persons received a lesser acreage. Any lands not allotted became "surplus" and were made available for non-Indian settlement. This created a checkerboard ownership pattern throughout the reservations. (*See Northern Idaho, Dawes Severalty Act.*)

Charles O. Worley was the area's first Indian agent. Non-Indian settlers first came in 1906. In 1908 in anticipation of an influx of settlers to the area, a new town was platted.

Charles Worley located his office in the new village. As the area's principal federal officer, "Worley" became the described destination of those having business in the growing community.

Martin Walser opened a general store that he named "The Pioneer." He built his store from rough lumber sawn from the trees growing on his lot. He covered the front of his store with tin painted to look like brick.

There were no established roads in the area. Travelers followed trails through grass fields and woods. Walser stocked the shelves of his store with goods he transported about 15 miles by wagon from Fairfield, Washington.

The Bain Wagon Company.

The first post office was located in Walser's store. His daughter was the first postmistress. The Pioneer Store became an informal community center during the early days. The Coeur d'Alene Indians were among the first customers. Walser encouraged them to bring leather-beaded bags for sale at the store. Eventually, Walser displayed these handmade goods in a large glass case. As non-Indian farm and ranch settlers moved into the area, many opened new businesses. In 1910 villagers built the first school – a one-room structure with one teacher.

In 1913 the Chicago, Milwaukee and St. Paul Railroad built its line through Worley. A large construction camp with over 200 workers set up near the Worley town site. They purchased much of their camp food and supplies from the Pioneer Store.

The rail line opened new markets for the area's agricultural and timber products; and, within a very short time, Worley began to develop a thriving business center. By the end of 1913 the village had a new general store, hotel, blacksmith shop and a combination confectionery and pool hall.

In 1916 the hotel burned down and was replaced by a new facility named the Worley Hotel. In that same year, the first sawmill was built on the southwest edge of town. In addition, another general store opened, a telephone line was constructed and the Congregational Church moved into new facilities.

Incorporation

On March 22, 1917, Worley became an incorporated village. The Kootenai County Commissioners appointed trustees to serve until the next election.

Leo's Worley Club.

The next four decades were a period of significant growth. A bank, a butcher shop, a livery stable and a hardware store opened. In 1921 the Roman Catholic and Lutheran churches built their new facilities. In 1923 Washington Water Power brought electricity to the village. In 1924 the school district added a new High School. Construction of U.S. Highway 95 reached Worley in 1926. In 1932 a farmers – cooperative built a large grain elevator near the railroad tracks.

By the 1930s Worley had emerged from a pioneering community of logging and small farms to large wheat and pea farms. In 1956 the village became an incorporated city.

Turning Points

General Allotment or Dawes Severalty Act. The federal law that provided for the allotment of Indian Reservation lands in severalty to Indians prompted an

Grain elevators.

influx of non-Indian families to settle in the area. This was a defining event for the development of Worley.

Railroad. The railroad opened local farm and lumber production to distant markets, accelerated transportation of passengers and mail, as well as added an employment base.

Farm Consolidation. In the 1930s the small farmers, who came to the village to shop and do business, underpinned Worley's economy.

In the decades that followed, increasing technological innovation and costs, market issues and economies of scale made most small farms unprofitable. Larger farm operators gradually acquired or leased the smaller farms. These large operators were able to be more productive with substantially fewer employees.

With the demise of the smaller farms, many of the younger people moved out of the area, leaving Worley more of a bedroom and retirement community.

Changing Economy Within the past several years, two events have had a positive effect on Worley's economy. The most prominent is development of the Coeur d'Alene Tribe's Casino and Resort complex. This destination resort has grown dramatically and is providing employment for Worley residents.

Improvements to Highway 95 have facilitated increased traffic for Casino patrons and tourists as well as improving travel conditions for city residents who commute elsewhere to work, shop and do business.

Worley Grange Hall.

Worley Today

Amenities and Attractions Worley's most significant attraction is the Coeur d'Alene Tribe's Casino and Resort complex. Located four miles north of the city, this destination resort includes a casino, hotel, 18-hole professional golf course and facilities that can accommodate concerts as well as boxing matches.

The 73-mile Trail of the Coeur d'Alenes is one of the most spectacular paved non-motorized trails in the Western United States. It begins five miles south at Plummer and extends east to Mullan. The trail is an abandoned railroad line that passes over high railroad trestles, through railroad tunnels, national forests and old mining towns. It follows the shoreline of Coeur d'Alene Lake then passes through a chain of lakes and marshland along the scenic Coeur d'Alene River up into the mountains of Mullan.

Heyburn State Park, comprising 5,744 acres of land and 2,332 acres of water, lies at the base of Coeur d'Alene Lake six miles southeast of Worley. The lake is popular for boating, fishing and other water sports.

Worley Fire Station.

Economy and Major Employers Most of the city's workforce commutes to the Coeur d'Alene Tribe's Casino and Resort complex or other cities.

The Plummer-Worley School District is the largest public employer within the city. Several other businesses flank U.S. Highway 95 as it intersects the city.

Education The Plummer-Worley School District provides most of the K-12 education for the city's children. Worley Post Office. The elementary school is located in Worley and the middle and high schools are located six miles south in Plummer.

The closest institution of higher learning is North Idaho College in Coeur d'Alene.

Main Street in Worley.

Health Care The 225-bed Kootenai Medical Center in Coeur d'Alene provides most of the city's health care needs.

Transportation U.S. Highway 95 is the area's primary transportation artery.

Citylink, a Kootenai County administered bus system, provides free public transportation throughout the county. The system is funded primarily by a federal grant and matching funds from the Coeur d'Alene Tribe.

The closest airport, generally used for private and charter aircraft, is in Coeur d'Alene. The Spokane International Airport is located 46 miles west.

Utilities and Services Private companies provide electricity, telephone and satellite services. The County provides solid waste services.

Vision for 2050

For the past five decades, Worley's population has remained around 200. The city has a limited amount of land in which it can grow. The adjoining tribal trust land is not available for city annexation.

However, Worley will grow as the Coeur d'Alene Tribe expands its casino and resort complex. There will be a Quad-Park built just south of the city limits. The park will include basketball courts, a football field, tennis courts and a water park. The Casino complex will include several amenities between the resort and Worley. These amenities will include a rodeo arena, an RV park, an airport, an amusement park and a convention center.

Mayor's Oval Office.

By 2050 residential housing and retail businesses will likely line the highway. Within Worley, there will be more housing suitable for seniors and low-income families.

Mayors

1917 A.F. Bayne *
1918-1956 Unknown *
1956 Ernest Lagow
1969 Lloyd Dyer
1972 Paul Follette
1974 Parry Larson
1975 Ed Babbitt

1985 John Teague
1986 Jack Chamberlain
1988 Willis Nigh
1996 Dick Gilbert
1999 Charlene Waddell
* Village Chairman

While automobiles replaced the horse on the road, the "Cat" replaced the horse on the farm.Cat vs horse is shown in this famous picture in 1923 of the first Cat in the Genesee area pulling a combine on the Hampton-Driscoll Farm. The camera captured in an instant the revolution that tractors would bring to farming on the Palouse. Courtesy Wade Hampton Collection.

LATAH COUNTY

- Bovill
- Deary
- Genesee
- Juliaetta
- Kendrick
- Moscow (County Seat)
- Onaway
- Potlatch
- Troy

Bovill Post Office.

Bovill

Statistical Data

Population: 255 *
Elevation: 2,870 feet
Precipitation: 25 inches **
Average Snowfall: 38 inches **
County: Latah
Website: www.bovillidaho.org

Temperature Range – Fahrenheit: **
Spring: 25 to 63
Summer: 43 to 81
Fall: 26 to 71
Winter: 18 to 41
* U.S. Census Bureau Estimates July 2015
**Historical averages

Located 34 miles northeast of Moscow at the junction of Idaho Highways 3 and 8, Bovill is in the center of the beautiful St. Joe National Forest. The Potlatch River runs along the west side of town. The Clearwater Mountains punctuate the city's eastern sky.

The stately western white pine, Idaho's state tree, is prevalent in the surrounding forest. Harvesting these trees for lumber underpinned the city's economy for nearly a century.

Pre-Incorporation Years

Around 1890 Francis Warren, his wife Sylinda and their son Rance filed a homestead claim on a beautiful mountain meadow surrounded by tall timber. They built a log cabin and named the site Warren Meadows. Francis died a decade later and in 1901 Sylinda and Rance sold Warren Meadows to Hugh and Charlotte Robinson Bovill.

Both Hugh and Charlotte came from titled English families and, as such, were well educated. Hugh Bovill also had financial resources. Hugh and Charlotte immigrated separately to America and met and married in Nebraska, where Charlotte worked as a nurse and Hugh had started a horse and cattle ranch.

Hugh had traveled to Montana and Canada purchasing cattle. He was so intrigued with the vast wide-open country that he began a quest to find his paradise in the West, a place to raise his family, prize horses and cattle.

In 1899 he traveled by train to Moscow and began to explore the surrounding area for a suitable ranch. He found his paradise at Warren

Hugh Bovill and horse.

Meadows. After purchasing the Warren property, he returned to Nebraska to bring Charlotte, their two daughters and their livestock back to Idaho.

At the turn of the century, Frederick Weyerhaeuser and his associates purchased timberland in the Palouse-Clearwater drainages from the State and the Northern Pacific Railway. The railroad received land grants from the federal government to help finance building the railroad. (*See The Region, Federal Lands – Private Ownership and Preservation Laws.*)

This undoubtedly influenced others to acquire timberland. Settlers and some "timber cruisers" working in the area – highly skilled professionals that assess and evaluate the quality of timber stands – began filing homestead claims. Many staked their

Bovill Hotel.

claims on the timberland surrounding the meadow, undoubtedly planning to profit by selling off the magnificent stands of timber – described as forests of white pine trees so tall that the only way to see the sky from under them was to lie on your back and look up.

In 1903 Weyerhaeuser and his syndicate of investors formed the Potlatch Lumber Company, named after the Potlatch River. Potlatch is a term used by Northwest Coast Indians to describe certain tribal gatherings. Certain locations in Oregon and Washington also bear the name Potlatch. The company's general manager was William Deary. Weyerhaeuser and Deary appealed unsuccessfully to the Northern Pacific Railroad to build a spur to the Weyerhaeuser timberlands east of the rail terminus at Palouse, Washington. (*See The Region, Railroads.*)

After being rebuffed, the Weyerhaeuser syndicate formed the Washington, Idaho and Montana Railway Company and began construction of a 47-mile rail line from Palouse to Bovill, establishing rail stations along the way. The railroad ran through the town of Potlatch, where in 1905 the Potlatch Lumber Company constructed one of the world's largest sawmills. The railroad's principal purpose was to haul logs to the mill and finished lumber to other railroads with connections to distant markets.

Bovill Depot.

During this time, the Chicago, Milwaukee and St. Paul Railroad (CM&SP) was building a spur from St. Maries through Bovill to Elk River. An affiliate, the Milwaukee Land Company, managed the railroad's grant land and had employed Charlotte Bovill as its land agent. In dealing with her to buy grant land, Deary described her as "confounding" and "contentious."

Settlers near Bovill's property wanted to divert the Potlatch River into a log-holding pond at the end of Warren Meadows. The Bovills decided it was time to accept economic reality and modify Hugh's dream. From 1903 to 1905 they built a larger cabin, a store and a hotel.

In 1907 the Bovills platted the town site and opened a post office with Hugh as postmaster. They immediately began selling building lots, and the new town began to grow.

On May 23, 1910, the community and the officials of the two railroads commemorated the formal joining of the two lines at Bovill. Visitors and dignitaries boarded trains and came great distances to the celebration.

Bovill Main Street.

The ceremony included driving a ceremonial golden spike. However, as they had no railroad spike made of gold, they had to improvise by wrapping an iron spike with gold foil. The Bovill's young daughter, Gwendolyn, was to drive the spike. Unfortunately, when she hit the spike, the foil fell away. Gwendolyn was crushed, but the crowd did not care. It just added to the memory of the event. That evening, Halley's Comet flared across the night sky to finalize the grand celebration.

By 1910 the town of Bovill had a bank, a newspaper and several other businesses under construction. Almost overnight the town had grown to more than 500 people, the third most populous town in the county. The Hotel Bovill was the most prominent building in the community and a welcome attraction for the town's numerous visitors.

In August 1910 a massive forest fire burned north of Bovill, sparing the city but causing terrible destruction throughout Northern Idaho and western Montana. (*See The Region, Forest Products – Great Fire of 1910.*)

Even after selling off much of their platted land, the Bovills still had significant real estate holdings in the town. While Charlotte moved to Coeur d'Alene to provide the children with a better education, Hugh stayed behind to dispose of the real estate. He donated one parcel to the town for a city dump, another for a cemetery and a third for a baseball park. In 1913 he sold his domestic water system to the town for $1,000.

Hugh and Charlotte retained ownership of the hotel until about 1930. The new owners operated the hotel as a boarding house. It later became a private home.

Incorporation

On February 7, 1911, Hugh Bovill and other city leaders petitioned the Latah County Commission to incorporate the town as a village. The commissioners delayed action, apparently awaiting approval from Milwaukee Land Company which owned some of the platted land including the eastern extension of Main Street, the site for City Hall and the city park. On October 12, 1912, the company agreed to the plat and deeded the land to the town.

On May 23, 1913, the Latah County Commission approved the application and Bovill became an incorporated village. In 1967 as part of the change in state law, Bovill became an incorporated city.

Between Bovill and Hog Heaven, 1917.

Turning Points

Railroads and Timber The most significant turning point occurred in 1903 when Weyerhaeuser and his investors formed the railroad and built the 47-mile line from Palouse to Bovill. Once completed, that line and the intersecting CM&SP line opened the area to timber harvest, causing the town to flourish.

The railroads insured prosperity, not only for hauling logs to the sawmills, but also greatly accelerating transport of passengers and the mail.

Town Fire Fire swept through the town in 1914 destroying most of Main Street. Only the Hotel Bovill, the hospital and the opera house were left standing.

The village board of trustees immediately wrote an ordinance requiring brick construction for future business buildings and the town quickly rebuilt. Today many of these brick buildings stand as a reminder of historic Bovill a century ago.

School Consolidation In 1948 the Bovill School District joined with the surrounding school districts to form the Whitepine Joint School District. This consolidation left an elementary school in Bovill that now serves K-3 children.

Paved Roads – Trucks Replacing Trains The State began paving Idaho Highways 3 and 8 in 1955, ending years of traveling over winding dirt and gravel roads. With

Bovill jailhouse, built 1910.

the road improvements, logging trucks began taking market share from the railroads, transporting directly out of the woods to the mills in Lewiston, St. Maries and Potlatch. Good roads and motor vehicles also allowed people living in Bovill to commute to other cities for work. However, as residents began shopping in other cities, local retail businesses suffered and either moved or closed.

Wood Products Industry For more than a century, the wood products industry underpinned Bovill's economy. However, by the end of the twentieth century, federal laws, forest management policies and environmental litigation substantially closed off access to federal lands for timber harvest. (*See The Region, Federal Lands – Private Ownership and Preservation Laws.*)

However, a significant part of Northern Idaho's forests are private or State owned. These forests are managed for mixed use and continue to provide logs for sawmills. (*See The Region, Forest Products – Timberlands and Sawmills.*)

Around 1990 the timber industry found it could cut costs by hiring contract or gyppo loggers, loggers who operate on small budgets and often glean timberlands already cut by larger companies. Bovill area logging companies were forced to cut their payrolls

White Pine King - largest white pine tree in the world - felled December 12, 1911.

and pay rates, placing a financial strain on families, retailers and the city. Jobs became scarce. Property values declined sharply. Homeowners were unable to sell their homes. The best economic options for many were for both parents to work and commute to other cities for employment. This dramatically changed the social fabric of Bovill and many other small rural communities hit by the same phenomenon.

Today around 80 percent of the sawmills that once underpinned the economies of Northern Idaho have closed. Albeit those that remain are highly efficient and more productive with fewer workers and use logs mostly harvested from private and State-owned forests. (*See The Region, Forest Products – Idaho's Lumber Harvest History*.)

Beautifying and Revitalizing the City As the economy continued to erode in the 1990s, city leaders took action to turn Bovill's economy around by improving the city's infrastructure, diversifying its economy and creating jobs. They obtained grants from public and private sources to replace old domestic water lines, built a new recreational vehicle park, acquired the historic St. Joseph Catholic Church to house the City library, built a community center, formed a local improvement district, improved the city streets and constructed bike and walking paths.

Bovill Today

Amenities and Attractions
Bovill has two city parks. Caroline Park has a brick and cobblestone path named "The Billy Walk" after Billy Sanderson – a Bovill resident well-known in Latah County for his "long walks" to Elk River, Clarkia, Deary and Troy. The park also has a war memorial, gazebo and a tall swing.

Village Park, donated by the Potlatch Corporation in 1994, has a baseball field and bleachers. The

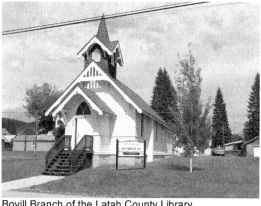

Bovill Branch of the Latah County Library.

park is the location of the annual "Old Timers Picnic" on the third Sunday of July.

The surrounding forest, mountains, streams and reservoirs offer fabulous opportunities for outdoor recreation and activities such as camping, hunting, fishing, hiking and biking. ATV, snowmobile and cross-country ski trails are available in almost every direction.

The closest downhill skiing is 56 miles southeast at Bald Mountain Ski Resort near Pierce.

The 54-mile-long Dworshak Reservoir on the Clearwater River lies 15 miles across the mountains southeast of Bovill. However, hard surfaced road access to this outstanding regional asset and the 650-foot-high Dworshak Dam is 60 miles away at Orofino.

White pine timber and the railroads used to transport the logs spurred the city's early growth. Today logging trucks and automobiles have replaced freight and passenger trains. However, the historic timber heritage of the city is still visible in the rail beds of spur lines used to get the logs out of the woods.

Most of the city's downtown historic buildings still stand but are owned privately and not maintained. Past efforts by the City and community leaders to purchase the buildings have failed.

In 1996 the City purchased the historic St. Joseph Catholic Church from the Catholic Diocese of Boise. With help from the Idaho Historical Society and grants from the White Family Heritage Library, the City has restored the church which now houses the public library.

Many logging and forest service trails near Bovill are available for hiking, ATV and snowmobile use. Some trails connect to Elk River, Avon, Clarkia, Avery and the Potlatch area.

Economy and Major Employers Timber and agriculture continue to underlie the economy. Gyppo loggers employ about 40 residents and in total are the city's largest private employers. The Whitepine School District has 12 employees.

Many residents commute to Moscow for work. The Bovill business community includes two taverns and a Drive In Burgers restaurant. Most citizens travel to Moscow and Deary to shop.

Education The Whitepine School District provides substantially all primary and secondary education for the communities of Bovill, Deary, Helmer and Elk River. The district offices, high school and one elementary school, which serve grades 4-12, are located in Deary. Except for the K-3 children who attend Bovill Elementary, Bovill students travel to school by bus. An Idaho Distance Education Academy (IDEA) school is also located in Bovill.

The closest institution for higher learning is the University of Idaho in Moscow.

Health Care Bovill residents rely on medical clinics located in Troy and Kendrick for most of their health care needs. Bovill has trained EMTs. Ambulance service is available in Deary. The nearest hospital is Gritman Memorial Hospital in Moscow.

Transportation Idaho Highways 3 and 8 intersect the city. Both connect with U.S. Highway 95. The closest connection to the federal highway is via Highway 8 to Moscow.

The nearest airport is the Pullman-Moscow Regional Airport 39 miles southwest.

Utilities and Services Private companies provide electricity, telephone, natural gas and satellite services. The City provides water, sewer and weekly garbage pickup services. The volunteer Bovill Fire District provides fire protection. The County Sheriff's Department provides police protection.

Vision for 2050

By 2050 Bovill will be more of a bedroom community for the Moscow/Pullman area as families choose to locate in Bovill's more affordable and peaceful setting and commute to work. Continued improvement to the highway system will spur growth in and around the city.

The timber industry will likely continue to underpin the city's economy. Potlatch owns large parcels of land near Bovill and is essentially holding the land for future opportunities. The effect on Bovill is uncertain. However, as technologies develop and improve, there could be further significant change in the timber industry.

An increasing number of retirees will come to Bovill to enjoy its peaceful and safe quality of life – a getaway surrounded by undeveloped state, federal and private forestland.

Due to recent improvements to Bovill infrastructure, there should be little need for major improvements to water, sewer or storm drainage systems for several years. The education system will likely remain unchanged.

Bovill is an excellent location for young families wanting to make a difference in their local community. Bovill's population is aging. The city needs new leaders to take on future challenges and develop ideas and plans for its economic growth and community development. The present leaders must be willing to accept new people and ideas.

Working together for a common goal, while keeping open minds to all suggestions, will help bring new people into leadership positions. Change is inevitable and, with the right people and the right attitude, change can be positive and productive.

Mayors

1911 Hugh Bovill *
1911 T.P. Jones *
1913 E.T. Chapin *
1914 L.G. Verdon *
1915 D.C. White *
1923 C.G. Nogle *
1942 J.D. Gilroy *
1943 Chester Yangle *
1947 Alfred Neely *
1949 J.J. Holland *
1949 Donald Candler *
1951 Frank Mallory
1970 George Hays
1974 Lloyd Hall

1979 Gary Egger
1983 Glen Wood
1984 Jimi Kay Mael
1985 Glen Wood
1986 Gary Egger
1990 Dallace Kellom
1991 Ronna Pratt
1992 Becky Kellom
2000 Bradley Dorendorf
2010 Janiece Atkins
2012 Brad Dorendorf
2016 Duane Linderman
* Village Chairman

Deary today.

Deary

Statistical Data

Population: 507*
Elevation: 2,874 feet
Precipitation: 24 inches **
Average Snowfall: 52 inches **
County: Latah
Website: www.deary-id.com

Temperature Range – Fahrenheit: **
Spring: 29 to 65
Summer: 43 to 82
Fall: 28 to 73
Winter: 22 to 42
* U.S. Census Bureau Est. July 2015
**Historical averages

Deary lies at the junctions of Idaho Highways 3, 8 and 9 in the beautiful St. Joe National Forest. It is at the head of the Big Bear and Texas Mountain ridges. Western white pine, Idaho's state tree, is prevalent in the surrounding forest. The Clearwater Mountains lie a few miles east, and the city of Moscow is 21 miles west.

The city lies at the southern base of Potato Hill, known locally as "Spud Hill." This 4,017-foot remnant of a huge volcano derives its name from its shape.

Cold and snowy, winters do not give way to spring until late April after the heavy winter run off. Infrequent rain showers, the prelude to the warm and dry summers, are the only interruption to the sunshine on the Palouse.

Pre-Incorporation Years

Branches of the Nez Perce Indian Tribe inhabited the region for thousands of years before the Corps of Discovery led by Meriwether Lewis and William Clark came down the Clearwater River in 1805.

Although trappers, traders and prospectors subsequently traversed the region, settlement did not begin until the 1880s. Emigrants from the timber-depleted Great Lakes states, mostly Scandinavian, began filing homestead claims. They liked their farmland interspersed with wooded tracts and gradually cleared the timber from parts of their 160-acre homesteads to plant their crops.

Commercial development of the region's timber began in 1900 when Frederick Weyerhaeuser and associates began buying up timberland. In 1903 Weyerhaeuser created the Potlatch Lumber Company to hold some of that property. The company's general manager was William Deary.

Deary worked to increase the company's holdings. In 1907 in the name of the affiliated Washington, Idaho and Montana Railway Company (WI&M), he constructed a 45-mile-long railroad from Palouse, Washington, to Bovill where it connected with the western terminus of the Milwaukee Road.

Blacksmith shop.

The WI&M and Potlatch Lumber Company were responsible for establishing several communities in the area, including Deary, Elk River, Bovill and Potlatch. Potlatch Lumber constructed sawmills at Elk River and Potlatch. Other stations along the WI&M – in addition to the above – Yale, Harvard and Vassar, served as collection points for loading logs for Potlatch mills, mail and supply drop-off points, and depots for passengers riding the WI&M to various other communities along the line.

On February 19, 1906, William Deary and Frederick S. Bell bought a homestead with five acres cleared of timber at the foot of Potato Hill for a future town site. Deary continued to acquire and trade for surrounding land until he felt he was ready to have the town site platted.

Deary discussed the name of the new town with his associates, settling on Yale only to discover that when WI&M Superintendent Theodore Reed platted the town site in 1906, he named the town Deary "in honor of the genial general manager."

A way house was the only building in the new town. When the construction crews left, the way house became the Carlson Hotel.

On September 24, 1907, the Deary Townsite Company began the first sale of lots. Unlike many other towns started by Potlatch Lumber, the company announced that it would clear the land of timber and then sell the land as farmland.

Deary, May 20, 1913.

Two Potlatch Lumber employees, F.C. McGowan and H.P. Henry, were officers in the Townsite Company. The two homes they built for Potlatch still stand and are on the National Register of Historic Places.

Deary school.

The walls of the first business buildings consisted of rough-hewn logs and limbs, the interiors lined with burlap or paper. The Rebekah Hall, one of the early buildings, had flowered tarpaper between the walls.

The Latah County State Bank, an affiliate of the First Bank of Troy, opened its doors September 14, 1908.

Four days later, the local newspaper, the *Deary Enterprise*, began publishing and owner Carl Peterson tried mightily to exact the proper respect for Deary. For example, local residents referred to Potato Hill as Spud Hill, but the Enterprise always referred to the volcanic cone as Mount Deary.

Most families depended on seasonal jobs to augment the production from their farms. Generally, the men would work the seasonal timber harvests for cash while the women stayed at home to run the farm. Being mother, farmer and homemaker in an isolated rural community created strong-willed independent women. The family was an interdependent unit.

The Potlatch Company logged trees year round in some areas and contracted with local logging companies or jobbers. These jobbers hired crews that cut timber along railroad spur lines, where the railroad picked up the logs and brought them to the sawmills.

Joe Wells, a black jobber who emigrated from North Carolina in 1889, was a legendary lumberman in the region. In 1910 Wells held a contract to log 3 million board feet of timber.

Four gangly types in Deary.

With his wife Lou, he operated a lodging house and earned a reputation for hard work and hospitality. Wells dug one of the few water wells in Deary for the lodging house. He and his wife also raised prize livestock – including draft horses and Angora goats. The couple took first place at the Upper Potlatch Fair for their stallions.

Even though Potlatch dominated the Deary economy, other businesses helped diversify the city's business community. In 1909 the Deary Lumber Company, an independent sawmill, was established. The Deary Clay Products Company turned out bricks first used in building the First State Bank at Bovill and the Farmer's Union shipping and warehouse facilities at Deary.

Anton Lee opened his photography studio on July 26, 1909, adding an important historical dimension for the town. Lee photographed people, places and events for postcards and portraits – making a valuable pictorial record of the region.

Incorporation

Deary incorporated as a village on August 27, 1912, six years after platting the town site. The editor of the *Deary Enterprise* newspaper, along with the Deary Commercial Club, promoted Deary and its ventures. They described Deary as "the hub of the upper Potlatch."

Turning Points

Railroad The first major turning point occurred around 1907 when WI&M and Potlatch Lumber completed their rail line and built a train station in Deary, establishing the city as a wood products and railroad town.

Converting Forest Land to Farmland The Potlatch Lumber decision to clear the timber and sell the land for farming brought needed diversity to the city's economy.

Fire In October 1923 fire swept through Deary destroying most of the downtown. It hastened what was likely inevitable. As Potlatch scaled back its activities and roads were paved to the city of Moscow and to the west, Deary settled into its present role as an outlying agricultural community.

Adapting to a New Economy Forest products have been a stabilizing influence on the city's economy. However, in recent years, evolving economic conditions and social preferences have been giving the city a new dimension. Increasing numbers of people choose to live in Deary and commute to work at the University of Idaho in Moscow or Washington State University in Pullman.

Gritman Memorial Hospital, Wal-Mart, Latah County Courthouse and other employers in Moscow have many Deary residents on their payrolls. This change has had the desirable effect of diversifying the city's economy.

Deary Today

Amenities and Attractions The city has a quiet hometown atmosphere. A beautiful city park located on Main Street is the center for community activities. A second park, Nelson Activity Park, is on the east end of town and features a T-Ball field and playground. Another small park is under construction at the site of the Rebekah Hall.

The city's most prominent activity is Deary Day held each year

Deary City Park.

on the first Saturday in August. Activities include food and other booths, a fun run, breakfast, car show, parade, quilt show, BBQ dinner, dunk tank and activities for children.

The surrounding forest, mountains, streams and reservoirs offer unparalleled outdoor recreation opportunities for camping, hunting, fishing, hiking, biking, ATV and snowmobile riding and cross-county ski trails. The nearby St. Joe National Forest largely surrounds the city.

Three state parks – Heyburn, Winchester Lake and Old Mission – are located within an hour's drive of the city. The Latah County Museum in Moscow and the Nez Perce National Historical Park are 25 miles away.

The closest downhill skiing is 70 miles southeast at Bald Mountain Ski Resort in Pierce. The Silver Mountain Ski Resort in Kellogg is 80 miles away.

Fishing and boating are available in the several lakes and rivers that lie within an hour's drive of the city. The 54-mile-long Dworshak Reservoir on the North Fork of the Clearwater River is 16 miles across the mountains southeast of Deary, but road access to the base of the 650-foot-high Dworshak Dam is 50 miles away at Orofino. Lake Coeur d'Alene lies 50 miles north. Other smaller lakes that are popular fisheries include Moose Creek Reservoir seven miles northeast and Spring Valley Reservoir 10 miles southwest.

Economy and Major Employers Timber and agriculture underlie the city's economy. With 20 to 30 employees each, Henderson Logging, Tom Dean Logging, Lawson Logging and Baumgartner Trucking are the city's largest private employers. The Whitepine School District has around 40 employees, and the Idaho Department of Lands employs 15.

The Deary business community includes a beauty salon, grocery store, two restaurants and bars, a saw shop, an automotive business, a car repair shop, a car wash, two gas stations, a mini-market, the Potlatch Corp. office building, the library, several logging companies, the trucking company, a logging consultant, a quilting center and the Idaho Department of Lands office. Moscow is the closest regional shopping center. The Adventist Church has a regional community Service Center, which provides clothing, furniture and a food bank.

Also located in Deary are SHARED Council, the Deary Senior Meal Site, a new recreation building, Boy and Girl Scout Troops, the Deary Recreation District and three churches.

Education The Whitepine School District provides substantially all education from kindergarten through high school. The district offices, high school and an elementary school are located in Deary. Another elementary school is located in Bovill. Other than Bovill Elementary, the students in the neighboring communities of Bovill, Elk River and Helmer attend school in Deary. The Idaho Distance Education Academy (IDEA), a virtual school, is also in Deary.

The closest institution for higher learning is the University of Idaho in Moscow.

Health Care The nearest hospital is in Moscow. There is also a medical clinic 11 miles away in Troy.

Transportation U.S. Highway 95 is the closest major highway. Idaho Highways 3, 8 and 9 all eventually connect with Highway 95.

The nearest airport is the Pullman-Moscow Regional Airport. It is 29 miles east and has a 6,731-foot runway.

Utilities and Services Private carriers provide electricity, telephone and satellite television. The City provides water and sewer services. The volunteer Deary Fire District, formed in 1948, provides fire protection. The Latah County Sheriff's Office provides police protection.

Vision for 2050

In 2050 Deary will still have the same attributes that make it strong today – community pride, excellent schools and a simplified way of life. Its population will have likely increased 50 percent. Most residents will commute to Moscow for work. They will choose to live in Deary because they prefer living in an aesthetically pleasing community away from the hub of activity in the much larger city.

By 2050 the city will have paved its graveled streets. Homes receiving City services, the city's lagoon system and enclaves of unincorporated properties within the city boundaries will all be part of the incorporated city.

The city will have completed construction of its new municipal park with a community Christmas tree and band shell.

The downtown hub currently has two empty commercial buildings. The townspeople have voiced their opinion that, subject to funding, one of the buildings will become a city museum that commemorates Deary's rich heritage.

In 2050 the city's downtown will be vibrant. By that time, the city museum will be a reality. In addition, the city will have led the effort to identify, mark and restore to the extent practicable city and surrounding area historical sites and structures that are of architectural, ecological and educational value.

Mayors

1912 J.A. Harsh *	1955 Norman Nelson *
1917 H.D. Warren *	1959 Orville Slette *
1919 F.S. Curtiss *	1960 Patrick Parsons *
1921 J.A. Harsh *	1963 Eugene Osterberg *
1923 G.H. Wilie *	1965 Thomas Femreite *
1925 L.O. Beyer *	1966 Gerald Lawrence *
1927 J.A. Harsh *	1968 Ray C. Day
1935 Gust Dahl *	1972 Patrick Parsons
1939 George Lawrence *	1973 Leslie Holstine
1941 Joel Burkland *	1977 Robert Hansen
1942 Ira Altag *	1996 Russell L. Foster
1945 Patrick Parsons *	2004 John Henderson
1951 Ira Altag *	* Village Chairman

South Main (Walnut), Genesee.

Genesee

Statistical Data

Population: 956 *
Elevation: 2,675 feet
Precipitation: 24 inches **
Average Snowfall: 48 inches **
County: Latah
Website: www.cityofgenesee.com

Temperature Range – Fahrenheit: **
Spring: 31 to 66
Summer: 45 to 84
Fall: 30 to 74
Winter: 23 to 41
* U.S. Census Bureau Estimates July 2015
**Historical averages

Genesee is encircled by the beautiful and fertile rolling hills and prairie of Idaho's Palouse country. Vast acreages of peas, lentils, wheat, barley and oats interspersed with groves of coniferous trees form a patchwork of color and texture around the city. Genesee is a quiet community nestled half way between Moscow, 17 miles north, and Lewiston, 18 miles south.

Pre-Incorporation Years

Long before explorers and trappers came to the Inland Northwest in the early 1800s, American Indians – principally the Nez Perce and Palouse Tribes – migrated seasonally throughout the region. Each summer many came to the Palouse to harvest Camas bulbs and to fish, hunt and pick huckleberries. (*See The Region, American Indians.*)

In 1805 and 1806 Meriwether Lewis and William Clark led the Corps of Discovery along the Clearwater River several miles south of Genesee. (*See The Region, Lewis and Clark.*)

The first permanent white residents in the area were Henry H. and Eliza Spalding, Presbyterian missionaries, who established a mission near Lapwai in 1836. (*See The Region, Early Christian Missionaries.*)

In 1860 Captain Elias D. Pierce led a party of prospectors onto Nez Perce Reservation land – established by treaty in 1855 – where they found placer gold about 60 miles west of what is now Genesee. The ensuing gold rush attracted thousands of miners, all of whom trespassed on Nez Perce lands.

These fortune seekers came up the Columbia and Snake Rivers to the seaport town of Lewiston, also on reservation land, and then overland to the gold fields near what is now Pierce. (*See The Region, Gold Mining.*)

The prospectors and miners were soon followed by merchants and opportunists. Lewiston became a boomtown, a tent city and a commercial center where those headed for the gold fields obtained provisions before continuing their quests.

President Abraham Lincoln signed the law creating Idaho Territory on March 4, 1863. A few days later he appointed William H. Wallace as territorial governor. Wallace designated Lewiston as the temporary territorial capital and the location for the first session of the Territorial Legislature. (*See The Region, Idaho Territory – Territorial Capitals – Lewiston and Boise.*)

That same year, federal authorities negotiated a new treaty with the Nez Perce, but only some of the Nez Perce signed the document. Failure to get approval of all the Nez Perce would later lead to military conflict. (*See The Region, American Indians – Nez Perce War.*)

The new treaty replaced the 1855 treaty and required that the Nez Perce cede large portions of reservation land, including the areas around Lewiston and Genesee, to the federal government. This action, coupled with the Homestead Act of 1862, brought a wave of settlers onto the fertile prairie of the Palouse. (*See The Region, Federal Lands – Private Ownership and Preservation Laws.*)

John P. Vollmer, a Lewiston businessman and entrepreneur who became the

Soon after the railroad arrived in 1888, new Genesee grew rapidly. Agriculture was everything and it was done with horses and mules. To show off these magnificent animals, the town started "Horse Parades" about 1910; this is how the town looked on parade day a century ago. Courtesy John Luedke Collection.

founder of Genesee, recorded the origins of the town's name. "During the summer of 1870, Alonzo Leland, later editor of the Lewiston Teller; a man named Stone "and myself went for a drive over the high prairie north of the Clearwater River. There was but one habitation in all that vast country then, Caldwell & Rail's cattle ranch at the summit of the Clearwater Bluff. As we drove along, we passed down Cow Creek and through a sequestered little valley still in its natural state, Stone exclaimed: 'This reminds me of my old home, the Genesee Valley in New York State'."

The original town of Genesee, later called Old Town, was built partially on a homestead established by George W. Ashworth in 1878 about one mile east of today's Genesee.

The town was platted on July 10, 1879. Vollmer established the first general store, and by 1887 the town had a post office and 45 inhabitants.

The Spokane and Palouse Railway (S&PR) completed a 112-mile-long rail line from Spokane to Genesee in 1888. One of the four principal officers of the S&PR was John P. Vollmer. Northern Pacific Railroad later acquired S&PR. When S&PR tried to acquire the right-of-way near the original town,

Henry Ford's new invention in 1908 changed the world, andhorses shared Walnut (Main Street) with the "Tin Lizzy" in the parade of 1914. Courtesy Lewiston Tribune.

Jacob Rosenstein, a local merchant, and other citizens who owned the land that S&PR wanted, held out for more money. (*See The Region, Railroads.*)

Rather than pay the higher price, Vollmer bought 40 acres from John H. Evans and platted a "New" Genesee next to the redirected railroad line one mile west of the original community. Residents and businesses of the "Old Town" purchased lots from Vollmer and began their move to the new townsite. Rosenstein also moved his store using skids and horses. The first train arrived in Genesee in July 1888.

As the region's railhead, Genesee thrived until the railroad reached Lewiston in 1898. For 10 years, Genesee was the major shipping point for all agricultural products from Grangeville north. Lured by commerce, rich soil and ample rainfall to irrigate the crops, new citizens flocked to the growing community.

The Genesee Recorder reported in 1888 that the town was booming, boasting six

South Main (Walnut).

mercantile stores, four hotels, two livery stables, three blacksmith shops, three hardware stores, two barber shops, two drug stores, two furniture stores, two tin shops, two millinery shops, two real estate offices, two butcher shops, one newspaper, three grain warehouses, two breweries, schools, churches and many fine residences with 20 more buildings under construction.

About the same time, Genesee residents along with others in Northern Idaho lobbied the U.S. Congress to split Nez Perce County into two counties. Their success resulted in the formation of Latah County, the only known time that Congress created a new county in one of the territories or states. (*See The Region, Idaho Territory, Territorial Capitals – Lewiston and Boise.*)

Incorporation

With a population approaching 300, Genesee became an incorporated village on October 23, 1889. Four years later on June 5, 1893, with a population of over 1,000, Genesee became a city of the second class. In 1967 the Legislature enacted legislation that eliminated classifications of incorporated municipalities, making them all cities.

Turning Points

Agriculture The first settlers coming into Genesee were farmers, and agriculture continues as the area's dominant industry. Recognizing the agricultural potential of the area, the first grain warehouse in Genesee was built by the S&PR in 1888. It was quickly followed by several private grain dealers.

The economic recession leading up to the Panic of 1893 inspired farmers nationwide to band together to ease credit by removing the gold standard and adding silver to our currency, forcing the railroads to lower freight rates and loosening credit controls by Eastern bankers. One such group was the Genesee Farmers Alliance, which began around 1893.

The Genesee Farmers Alliance was replaced by the Genesee Farmers Union in 1909. The Union was the forerunner of the Pacific Northwest (PNW) Farmers Coop. Today, PNW Coop is Genesee's hallmark business and represents some 650 local producers, shipping wheat, peas and lentils throughout the world. (*See The Region, Agriculture and Livestock.*)

Railroad When the S&PR reached Genesee in 1888, it not only built Genesee's first grain elevator and provided transportation needed by area farmers to ship their commodities to market but also provided jobs that helped sustain the town's economy. The 1890 census reported that the town's population was 282, nearly double that of the previous decade. By 1896 Genesee's population had swelled to 1,200.

Completion of the railroad to Lewiston drew business away from Genesee and the town's economy declined. By 1900 the population had dropped to 731.

U.S. Highway 95 In the 1950s the U.S. and Idaho Transportation Departments changed the route of U.S. Highway 95. Old Highway 95 passed through Genesee. The new route passed about two miles to the west. The loss of traffic through town had a significant adverse effect on Genesee businesses serving the traveling public.

On the other hand, construction of the new road over Lewiston Hill in 1977 and widening the road to four lanes in 2007 have dramatically improved safety and travel time for Genesee residents and local farmers trucking agricultural commodities to the Port of Lewiston for barge shipment down the Snake and Columbia Rivers to the ocean-going freighters in Portland, Oregon.

Genesee Today

Amenities and Attractions Genesee has two city parks. One features a picnic pavilion with other facilities. The local high school's athletic field is a center for sports activities.

The town has two buildings on the National Historic Register – the Exchange Bank and the Vollmer Building, now the Volunteer Fire Department. The White Springs Ranch Museum, a few miles north of town, showcases pioneer living on the Palouse.

On the second Saturday in June, the city celebrates Community Day, featuring a parade, trap shoot, the "Cow Creek Run," class reunions, live music, a car show, adult and youth activities and fireworks.

Several religions are represented in the city. In October, St. Mary's Catholic Church, the city's largest denomination, sponsors a dinner benefiting church programs.

In February, the Genesee Volunteer Fire Department puts on its annual "Crab Feed" to raise money for the department.

The Community Center, which houses City Hall and the library, also has public facilities that groups can schedule for their private use through City Hall. The Masonic Lodge, the Genesee Civic Association and the American Legion Post also sponsor activities that are open to the public.

Nearby universities and colleges in Moscow and Lewiston, Idaho, and Pullman and Clarkston, Washington, also offer diverse cultural programs open to the public.

Parts of the Nez Perce National Historic Park, managed by the National Park Service and partially staffed by tribal members, are several miles south in Lapwai and Spalding.

The 960-acre Hells Gate State Park is on the southern edge of Lewiston, part of the 652,488-acre Hells Canyon National Recreation Area that features North

America's deepest river gorge. Cut by the Snake River, the gorge forms the Idaho/Oregon border. The river is more than a mile below the west rim of the gorge. On the Idaho side, the river is 8,000 feet below He Devil Peak of the Seven Devils Mountains. (*See The Region, National Wilderness Areas.*)

Some of Genesee's most popular attractions arise from its location near national forests and rivers. For the outdoor enthusiast, there is fabulous hunting and fishing within a few miles of the city. The Clearwater and Snake Rivers near Lewiston are famous for steelhead and salmon fishing.

The 54-mile-long Dworshak Reservoir State Park and Recreation Area and the National Fish Hatchery that raises steelhead trout and Chinook salmon are about 60 road miles east near Orofino or about 35 miles cross country. A variety of excellent outdoor recreation including boating, water skiing, fishing, camping, swimming, hunting, hiking, ATV and snowmobile riding and wildlife viewing are available at these locations.

Economy and Major Employers The largest employer in town is the Genesee School District with about 50 employees. The Pacific Northwest Farmers Coop is second with about 40 workers. Residents not employed in the several retail, banking and small businesses in the city's commercial district or nearby farms commute to jobs in Moscow and Lewiston.

Education The Genesee School District provides public kindergarten, elementary, middle and high school education.

The closest Idaho institutions of higher learning are the University of Idaho in Moscow and Lewis-Clark State College in Lewiston. (*See The Region, Institutions of Higher Learning.*)

Health Care St. Joseph Regional Medical Center in Lewiston, Gritman Medical Center in Moscow and, in Washington, Clarkston's Tri-State Hospital and Pullman Regional Hospital provide health care for most of the city's residents.

Transportation The city is about two miles east of U.S. Highway 95.

Commercial airline service is available at the Lewiston-Nez Perce County Airport and the Pullman-Moscow Regional Airport, five miles west of Moscow in Washington. Spokane International Airport is a two-hour drive from Genesee.

Utilities and Services Private companies provide electricity, telephone, natural gas, satellite and wireless service. The City provides water and sewer services. The Genesee Volunteer Fire Department provides fire and emergency medical protection. The Latah County Sheriff's Office provides police protection and traffic control under contract with the City.

Vision for 2050

Since 1960 when the city's population was 535, Genesee's population has increased well over 1 percent annually. These trends will likely continue as more families who commute to work in Lewiston and Moscow choose to live in the rural and peaceful city of Genesee. Should these trends continue, the city's population will likely exceed 1,400 by 2050.

There is room for residential and commercial growth within the city limits and surrounding area. The city's infrastructure – sewer and water, streets, parks, fire and police services – and support – through school district, churches and businesses – will expand to accommodate these new residents.

Present and future community leaders will continue emphasizing strategic planning for Genesee's future growth. The cost of needed maintenance and improvements to the city's infrastructure will be paid through normal revenue streams, grants or bonds approved by the voters.

For those who do not miss the hustle and bustle of the big city, Genesee will continue to be a wonderful place to raise a family and enjoy life.

Mayors

1889 J.C. Martin *
1891 Dr. W.C. Cox *
1892 D. Spurbeck *
1893 D.B. Grant
1896 M.A. Means
1898 Dr. P.S. Beck
1902 Dr. J.L. Conant
1903 M.A. Means
1905 Timothy Driscoll
1909 W.M. Thompson
1911 E.E. Oylear
1913 J.T. Nelson
1915 F.E. Lambert
1921 Fred S. Casebolt
1925 John G. Meyer
1937 J.W. Emerson
1947 H.E. Bennett
1949 Charles Schooler
1953 George Anderson
1955 Eli Race

1957 Wayne Roach
1958 Dick Scharnhorst
1974 Larry Sorenson
1980 George Wilson
1986 Mike Martinez
1990 Randy Hall
2000 Tim Sperber
2006 Randy Hall
2010 Steve Odenborg
* Village Chairman
** Genesee was incorporated on October 23, 1889. An article in the Lewiston Tribune (June 5, 1936) noted that Ordinance No. 26 was passed by the town's Board of Trustees in 1893. The ordinance changed the name of the title "Chairman of the Board of Trustees" to "Mayor" and the word "town" to "city" and made the town "Marshall" the "Chief of Police."

Juliaetta Community Library.

Juliaetta

Statistical Data

Population: 578 *
Elevation: 1,155 feet
Precipitation: 25 inches **
Average Snowfall: 25 inches **
County: Latah
Website: www.cityofjuliaetta.com

Temperature Range – Fahrenheit: **
Spring: 36 to 70
Summer: 54 to 88
Fall: 34 to 77
Winter: 28 to 46
* U.S. Census Bureau Estimates July 2015
**Historical averages

Juliaetta lies on the eastern edge of Idaho's fertile Palouse. Fields of wheat, lentils, peas, oats and barley interspersed with tree-covered ravines and forests of coniferous trees surround the city. The Potlatch River flows on the eastern edge of the city where it forms the border between Latah and Nez Perce Counties.

The Nez Perce Indian Reservation lies southeast of Juliaetta. Dworshak Dam, Reservoir and Recreation Area are 20 miles due east of the city. The city of Moscow is 14 miles northwest. Lewiston is 12 miles southwest.

Pre-Incorporation Years

In 1805 to 1806 Lewis, Clark and the Corps of Discovery, assisted by Nez Perce Indians, canoed the Clearwater River five miles south of what is now Juliaetta. Within a few years, explorers/trappers came into the inland northwest in search of beaver pelts.

Feeding chickens on the Schupfer homestead, circa 1900.

In 1836 Henry H. Spalding and his wife Eliza, Presbyterian missionaries, established a mission among the Nez Perce several miles south of what is now Juliaetta near Lapwai.

In 1860 Captain Elias Davidson Pierce led a party of 10 prospectors into the Palouse, passing through what is now Kendrick then heading east for about 50 miles and re-entering Nez Perce Reservation land (1855 Treaty) where they found large quantities of placer gold.

At first Nez Perce tribal chiefs resisted the intrusion of the prospectors but had to relent because within a year 3,000 prospectors flooded into the area of what is now Pierce. Most of the miners came up the Columbia and Snake Rivers to Lewiston on steamers, then overland to Pierce. Even though Lewiston was technically on reservation land, it became a port for the steamers and became a boomtown.

The need for fresh food to feed the swelling numbers of fortune hunters brought the first permanent settlers to the fertile Palouse, which was not on Treaty land.

In 1878 Rupert Schupfer filed a 160-acre homestead claim and platted the town that would become Juliaetta. He named his new town Schupferville.

In 1882 Charles Snyder, another homesteader with property near Schupferville, applied to postal authorities for a post office operated out of his combination home and general store. Snyder's application specified himself as postmaster of the post office that he named Juliaetta after his two daughters Julia and Etta.

Snyder later acquired a lot in Schupferville and built a commercial business that housed the Juliaetta Post Office. In the early years, post offices could be little more than a wood box in which the mail was placed. The mail carrier, riding a horse or buggy, came on a periodic schedule to deliver and pick up the mail. Local residents would thumb through the mailbox to find mail addressed to them. Since all mail addresses specified the name of the post office, Juliaetta became the accepted name of the community.

In the late 1880s the Northern Pacific affiliate, the Spokane and Palouse Railroad (SPR), began construction of a line from Spokane to Lewiston. However, when it reached Genesee, construction had to stop. Building a railroad down the steep and treacherous Lewiston grade was too difficult.

Genesee remained a railroad terminus for a decade while the SPR surveyed and built a new rail line from Moscow to the Potlatch River canyon and then south to Lewiston.

However, in 1890 when the railroad reached Juliaetta, the SPR again had to bring construction to a halt. The Nez Perce Indians would not approve a railroad right-of-way through their reservation. As a result, Juliaetta became a railroad terminus and railhead.

Incorporation

On April 19, 1892, with a population approaching 500, Juliaetta became an incorporated village. By that time Lewiston merchants who desperately wanted the railroad, cured the right-of-way problem by acquiring the rail corridor from the Nez Perce for $75,000.

Unfortunately for the railroad and the Lewiston merchants, the general economic collapse – "the Panic of 1893" – caused the railroad to delay construction for six more years. From 1890 to 1899 Juliaetta was the railroad's terminus.

Bird's eye view of Juliaette, Circa 1911.

During this time, the city prospered as area businesses and farmers brought their livestock and commodities to the railhead for shipment and to pick up freight.

Turning Points

Railroad Even though Juliaetta's early days began as an agricultural-based economy, the coming of the railroad changed the community. For about a decade, Juliaetta was a railhead and business center. Even after it reached Lewiston, the railroad still had a positive influence on Juliaetta's economy until it closed.

Partnership with Kendrick The cities of Juliaetta and Kendrick (the Community) now work cooperatively together in achieving certain educational and municipal objectives. With just over 3 miles separating the two towns, the Community approved educating K-7 students in Juliaetta Elementary and the older students in Kendrick.

In recent years, the Community has developed a joint Comprehensive Plan. This cooperative effort is reducing redundant costs, providing better utilization of scarce resources and improving the quality of life of residents of both cities.

Juliaetta Today

Amenities and Attractions
Juliaetta has two small parks
downtown that comprise a total of
one acre and Centennial Park.
Centennial Park has ball fields,
gazebo and restroom facilities.
Centennial Park is also the Juliaetta
trailhead for the bike/walking path
that connects Juliaetta and
Kendrick along the abandoned rail
right-of-way. Juliaetta has added
trees and park benches along its
section of the trail.

The 850-acre Dworshak State
Park is located 25 miles southeast
of the city on the western shore of
the 16,000 acre Dworshak
Reservoir. The reservoir extends 54
miles northeast of the dam into the
heavily wooded Clearwater National Forest.

Coulter's Creek Vineyard and Winery.

The Dworshak National Fish Hatchery, located at the confluence of the North
Fork and the main Clearwater Rivers about 25 miles southeast near Orofino,
captures steelhead trout and Chinook salmon that are returning to spawn. The
hatchery spawns the fish and raises them until they are large enough to start their
migration to the Pacific Ocean.

The entire Dworshak Recreation Area is an exceptional location for boating,
fishing, camping, recreational vehicles, swimming, water skiing, hunting, hiking,
ATV and snowmobile riding and wildlife viewing.

Hells Gate State Park is located about 30 miles southwest, just south of
Lewiston. This 960-acre park is part of the 652,488-acre Hells Canyon National
Recreation Area. The Area includes North America's deepest river gorge. This
Snake River gorge forms the Idaho/Oregon border. On the Oregon side, the gorge
lies more than a mile below Oregon's west rim. On the Idaho side, the gorge is
more than 8,000 feet below He Devil Peak of the Seven Devils Mountains.

The Nez Perce National Historic Park, managed by the National Park Service
and partially staffed by tribal members, is located in Spalding, 20 miles south.

Economy and Major Employers Browning Cut Stock Company, a millwork
wood products business, has about 30 employees and is the city's largest private
employer. The Kendrick School District also has about 30 employees at Juliaetta
Elementary and is the city's largest public employer.

There are also several small wood products, retail and other businesses located
in the city. Many city residents commute to Moscow and Lewiston for
employment.

Education The Kendrick School District provides K-12 education for the city's children. In 1947 school patrons voted to combine the Juliaetta and Kendrick school districts. K-7 students attend Juliaetta Elementary and the older children attend Kendrick Jr-Sr High School.

Juliaetta Elementary School.

The closest institutions of higher learning are the University of Idaho in Moscow and Lewis-Clark State College in Lewiston.

Health Care The closest hospitals are St. Joseph Regional Medical Center in Lewiston and Gritman Medical Center in Moscow.

Transportation Idaho Highway 3 intersects the city. U.S. Highway 12 is eight miles south.

Commercial airline service is available at the Lewiston-Nez Perce County Airport and the Pullman-Moscow Regional Airport located in Washington, five miles west of Moscow.

Utilities and Services Private companies provide electricity, telephone, satellite and wireless services. The City provides water and sewer services and fire protection. Police protection is provided by the County Sheriff under contract with the City.

Vision for 2050

Juliaetta's population has ranged from 368 in 1960 to as high as 617 in 2000. The population has declined about six percent in recent years. However, we expect earlier growth trends will resume as more families with jobs in Moscow and Lewiston come to the more affordable and peaceful community of Juliaetta to raise their families.

The city's water systems are adequate to handle significant growth. However, within the next few years, the city's municipal wastewater system is due for upgrade. The community will finance these improvements through a combination of user fees and bonds approved by the voters.

Kendrick Post Office on Main Street. Courtesy Juliaetta - Kendrick Heritage Foundation.

Kendrick

Statistical Data

Population: 299 *
Elevation: 1,250 feet
Precipitation: 25.39 inches **
Average Snowfall: 24.6 inches **
County: Latah
Website: www.kendrick-juliaetta.org
Temperature Range – Fahrenheit: **

Spring: 34 to 72
Summer: 52 to 90
Fall: 33 to 80
Winter: 26 to 46
* U.S. Census Bureau Estimates July 2015
**Historical averages

Kendrick is in the fertile and beautiful Palouse region of Northern Idaho. Rolling hills of wheat, lentils, peas, oats and barley interspersed with tree-covered ravines and forests of pine and fir surround the city. The Potlatch River forms the city's eastern and southern borders. Moscow, the Latah County seat, is 18 miles northwest.

Twenty-five miles east is the Clearwater National Forest and the fabulous Dworshak Recreation Area.

Pre-Incorporation Years

For centuries, the Nez Perce and Palouse Indian Tribes would leave their winter camps along the Clearwater and Snake Rivers and come into the land of the Palouse to dig camas and kous roots, fish, hunt and pick huckleberries. (*See The Region, American Indians.*)

Fur traders and trappers first entered the area around 1810. Two decades later, Christian missionaries, seeking Indian converts, came into the area. (*See The Region, Early Trappers/ Explorers and Early Christian Missionaries.*)

As the California gold discoveries that started in 1848 played out, many fortune hunters left California to prospect throughout the Western United States. In 1860 Captain Elias Davidson Pierce led a party of 10 prospectors through what is now Kendrick and then east for about 50 miles near what is now the city of Pierce. There they found large quantities of placer gold. (*See The Region, Gold Mining.*)

Another gold rush ensued. Prospectors swarmed into Northern Idaho looking for gold.

Pack train leaving Kendrick in 1894. Picture courtesy of Juliaetta -Kendrick Heritage Foundation.

Some were impressed with the land and returned. In the late 1860s the first permanent settlers began filing homestead claims in the fertile Palouse.

In 1887 Lon Nichols homesteaded the land that would become the townsite of Kendrick. Nichols sold to Thomas Kirby, and in 1889 Kirby platted the town which he named Latah. He built a drugstore on one of the lots and on May 24, 1889, he received approval from the postal authorities to place the Latah Post Office at the rear of his drugstore with himself as postmaster. (*See The Region, Federal Lands" Private Ownership and Preservation Laws.*)

Bird's eye view of Kendrick. Courtesy Juliaetta - Kendrick Heritage Foundation.

Several months later, Kirby gave land to the Northern Pacific Railroad in exchange for the promise that they would build their line through town. In May 1890 J.P. Kendrick, the railroad's chief engineer, made a new plat for the town. Out of respect for the chief engineer, the community changed the name of the town to Kendrick. (*See The Region, Railroads.*)

One of the early residents of the new town was J.M. Walker, president of the Hardware Implement Company and founder of the town's first bank. Other businesses at the time included a flourmill, a lumber mill and an electric power plant on the Potlatch River.

312

Incorporation

On October 15, 1890, Kendrick became an incorporated village with Kirby and Walker among the five trustees.

The first train arrived in Kendrick on February 4, 1891. The route ran from Pullman, Washington, through Moscow; east to Troy, then called Vollmer; and southeast to Kendrick. The last 14 miles into

Main Street. Photo courtesy of Juliaetta - Kendrick Heritage Foundation.

Kendrick had a 1,525-foot drop in elevation.

A few months later the railroad reached Juliaetta, where it halted construction. The Nez Perce Indians would not approve a railroad right-of-way through their reservation. As a result, Juliaetta became a railroad terminus and the Kendrick rail yard became an operational center on its end of the line. Lewiston merchants, who desperately wanted the railroad, cured the right-of-way problem by acquiring the rail corridor from the Nez Perce for $75,000.

Unfortunately for the railroad and the Lewiston merchants, "the Panic of 1893" and the general economic collapse that occurred caused the railroad to delay construction for six more years.

With the ability to ship commodities to distant markets, the Potlatch River Valley thrived, and area shippers filled the railcars with timber, livestock, various grains, flour, dairy products, nuts, fruits and vegetables.

In accordance with the change in municipal law enacted by the 1967 Idaho Legislature, Kendrick became a city.

Turning Points

Railroad The railroad is responsible for the early economic vitality of the city and giving Kendrick its name. Railroad transportation was the catalyst for the wood products and agriculture industries to flourish. In 1902 the year after the railroad arrived, the town had a population of 600. Two years later, the community's public and commercial district included five churches; five fraternal lodges; two hotels; over 40 businesses; a

Train, 1912, photo courtesy of Juliaetta - Kendrick Heritage Foundation.

bank; an opera house; a telephone company; two newspapers; schools; and nine sawmills, three in town and six further upstream.

Until 1936 when trucks and improved roads made it obsolete, the grain farmers around Potlatch Ridge and a Kendrick grain elevator company developed a novel approach to move grain from atop the bluff to the elevators below.

Their first attempt, a 1,500-foot metal pipe down the slope with a vertical drop of 140 feet, proved problematic because the friction created by the grain falling through the long pipe damaged the grain and wore out the pipe.

They solved the problem with a "bucket tram" which included eight towers ranging in height

Implement Warehouse. Photo courtesy of Juliaetta - Kendrick Heritage Foundation.

from 30 to 40 feet that extended from the top of the bluff to the elevators below. A half-mile-long cable with large buckets every 75 feet ran through a pulley around the cross-arms of the towers. They filled the buckets with sacked grain at the upper warehouse. A brakeman at the top of the tram controlled the tram's speed. At the bottom, workmen filled every fifth bucket with supplies ordered by those on top. Gravity power from the grain-filled buckets coming down lifted the supplies to the top of the bluff.

In 1965 the town was shocked to learn that the railroad was discontinuing passenger service. In 1985 the railroad also ceased freight service.

Fires Kendrick's first big fire occurred on August 16, 1893. During that fire, 31 businesses and the post office burned to the ground. Within three months, however, most business owners rebuilt – this time with brick.

On August 5, 1904, a fire started in the sawdust on the floor of the Palace Hotel Saloon and destroyed five blocks – including 19 homes and 43 businesses. Neighboring communities sent wagonloads of food, bedding and supplies to help the victims.

After this fire, the village trustees passed an ordinance requiring all buildings in the business district to be constructed of brick with firewalls between the structures. The City

After the fire of August 5, 1904. Courtesy of Juliaetta -Kendrick Heritage Foundation

dedicated a city park where the owners of one of the hotels decided not to rebuild.

Another large fire hit the Kendrick area in 1939, destroying 12,000 acres and more than a dozen farm homes and buildings. In 1948 Kendrick residents formed a volunteer fire department.

Telephone The first telephone service came to Kendrick in 1895. It consisted of a one-wire line that connected the towns between Moscow and Lewiston. The local telephone company installed one telephone booth in each town. The Kendrick booth was located in the H.P. Hull General Store.

When a call came in, a store employee ran to find the desired party. Often the messenger ran down Main Street shouting the name of the party who had a call waiting.

The Interstate and Potlatch Telephone Companies began installing business and residential telephones in Kendrick around 1904.

Partnership with Juliaetta The cities of Juliaetta and Kendrick, known as The Community, began to work cooperatively in achieving certain educational and municipal objectives. With just over three miles separating the two towns, The Community approved educating kindergarten through seventh grade students in the Juliaetta Elementary School and the older students in Kendrick.

In recent years, The Community has developed a joint comprehensive plan. This cooperative effort is reducing redundant costs, providing better use of scarce resources and improving the quality of life of the residents of both cities.

Bandstand Gazebo in Kendrick Park. Photo courtesy of Juliaetta - Kendrick Heritage Foundation

Fraternal Temple The magnificent Kendrick Fraternal Temple was constructed in 1905. The building is a showplace of unique architecture. The red brick were manufactured by the local Fructl Brick factory in Kendrick. In order for the building to stand out from the others on Kendrick's Main Street, brick was imported from Mica, Washington. One hundred shares were sold at $800.00 each to fund the building. It has been the home of many fraternal

Magnificent Fraternal Temple in Kendrick, built in 1905. Photos courtesy of Juliaetta - Kendrick Heritage Foundation.

organizations over the years including Odd Fellows, Knights of Pythias, Woodsmen of the World, Rebekah Lodge, Rathbone Sisters, Eastern Star, Masons, and the Grange. One by one these organizations died out and then deeded the property to the surviving organization.

The building had fallen unto extreme disrepair and the community recognized the need for a museum and research center as well as a community center. In 2010 restoration of the magnificent 1905 Fraternal Temple started and now houses the community's museum, research center and community center. Many organizations now have their meetings at this location and nearly every organization in the town contributed to its restoration.

Kendrick Today

Amenities and Attractions Kendrick has three city parks covering two acres. Kendrick Memorial Park is downtown and features children's playground equipment, a gazebo and the Living War Memorial Pool built in 1947 to commemorate area residents who served in the military.

Wallace Park, on the west end of town, is the site of the city's domestic water well and a sign welcoming visitors to Kendrick. Travis Park has RV sanitation facilities.

Locust trees, a few of which were planted in 1910, line Main Street and add beauty to the downtown business district.

The Kendrick museum and research center opened in April 2015 in the magnificent restored

Paved walking trail between Kendrick and Juliaetta in the fall. Courtesy of Milt Patterson.

1905 Fraternal Temple on Main Street. It is a must-see when you visit Kendrick.

A 5.3 mile paved walking trail along the Potlatch River was built on the abandoned railroad bed between Kendrick and Juliaetta in 2002.

The 850-acre Dworshak State Park is located 25 miles southeast of the city on the western shore of the 16,000-acre Dworshak Reservoir. The reservoir extends 54 miles northeast of the dam into the heavily wooded Clearwater National Forest.

The Dworshak National Fish Hatchery, located at the confluence of the North Fork and the main Clearwater Rivers, about 25 miles southeast near Orofino, captures steelhead trout and Chinook salmon that are returning to spawn. The hatchery spawns the fish and raises them until they are large enough to start their migration to the Pacific Ocean.

The entire Dworshak Recreation Area offers exceptional boating, fishing, camping, swimming, water skiing, hunting, hiking, recreational vehicle parks, ATV and snowmobile riding and wildlife viewing.

Hells Gate State Park is about 30 miles southwest just south of Lewiston. This 960-acre park is part of the 652,488-acre Hells Canyon National Recreation Area which includes North America's deepest river gorge. This Snake River gorge forms the Idaho/Oregon border. On the Oregon side, the gorge plunges more than a mile below Oregon's west rim. On the Idaho side, the gorge is more than 8,000 feet deep at He Devil Peak of the Seven Devils Mountains.

The Nez Perce National Historic Park, managed by the National Parks Service and partially staffed by tribal members, is 22 miles south in Spaulding.

Economy and Major Employers The largest employer is the Kendrick Joint School District with 53 employees. Brocke & Sons, a seed and fertilizer supplier, has 35 employees.

Education The Kendrick School District provides

Block 1904 in Kendrick. Courtesy Juliaetta - Kendrick Heritage Foundation.

primary and secondary education for the city's children. The school district buses the elementary school students five miles to Juliaetta. The district's middle and high school students attend school in Kendrick.

The nearest institutions of higher learning are the University of Idaho in Moscow and Lewis-Clark State College, 28 miles south in Lewiston.

Health Care The nearest hospital is Gritman Medical Center in Moscow, which also operates a clinic in Kendrick. There are also a dentist's office and a drug store in town.

Transportation State Highway 3 connects the city with Lewiston to the south and Deary to the north. State Highway 99 to Moscow intersects Highway 3 just south of the city.

Utilities and Services Private companies provide electricity, telephone and satellite services. The City provides water and sewer services and fire protection. The County Sheriff provides police protection.

Vision for 2050

For the past five decades, Kendrick's population has ranged between 325 in 1990 and 443 in 1960. Population trends will increase as the city's economic development efforts prove successful.

Kendrick has joined with Juliaetta in an economic development plan. The cities seek to attract businesses that add value to the area's

Locust Blossom Festival. Photos courtesy of Milt Patterson.

traditional agricultural and resource-based industries, as well as small technology-based businesses and business that promotes tourism.

In order to promote tourist traffic, the City has developed an RV park next to the paved walking trail. The park provides easy access to fishing, hunting and boating.

Success in these initiatives should have a significant positive effect on the city's economy and population.

Mayors

1890 J.M. Walker *
1892 M.S. Freeman *
1894 W.S. Adams *
1894 A.W. Warren *
1895 C.F. Hamlin *
1896 M.X. Freeman *
1897 R.C. Sinclair *
1898 J.J. Mitcham *
1899 Math Jacobs *
1900 W.R. Graham *
1901 D.J. Rowlands *
1903 J.J. Mitcham *
1905 A.C. White *
1905 R.B. Himes *
1907 R.C. Bibb *
1907 G.M. Lewis *
1909 E.D. Bradbury *
1910 D.T.A. Mackintosh *
1911 J.F. Brown *
1916 William Freytag *
1917 L.G. Peterson *
1919 N.E. Walker *
1923 A.V. Dunkle *
1924 E.H. Dammarell *
1925 E.T. Long *
1928 N.E. Walker *

1929 E.T. Long *
1931 W.J. Carroll *
1933 E.A. Deobald *
1939 R.H. Ramey *
1941 G.W. McKeever *
1943 E.A. Deobald *
1945 Walter Brocke *
1947 G.W. McKeever *
1949 L.A. Wallace *
1951 Walter Brocke *
1953 Ed Nelson *
1955 Frank Abrams *
1961 Charles Deobald *
1964 L.A. Wallace *
1966 George Brocke, Jr. *
1968 Donald H Eichner
1970 Robert E. Watts
1978 Wayne G. Harris
1986 Darrel Brocke
1990 Jerry Brown
2002 Dana Magnuson
2006 James Hoogland, Jr.
2008 Dale Lisher
2014 Mark Lapinskas
* Village Chairman

Moscow today.

Moscow

Statistical Data

Population: 24,767 *
Elevation: 2,583 feet
Precipitation: 24 inches **
Average Snowfall: 48 inches **
County: Latah
Website: www.ci.moscow.id.us

Temperature Range – Fahrenheit: **
Spring: 31 to 56
Summer: 54 to 85
Fall: 30 to 74
Winter: 23 to 41
* U.S. Census Bureau Estimates July 2013
**Historical averages

Moscow (pronounced MOSS-coe) is at the base of Idaho's panhandle on the eastern edge of the fertile rolling hill and prairie country called the Palouse. Vast acreages of dry peas, lentils and wheat interspersed by groves of coniferous trees surround the city.

The St. Joe National Forest is 25 miles north and northeast. The western edge of the Clearwater National Forest is 45 miles southeast.

The city is home to the University of Idaho. The influence of the university and the city's picturesque agricultural setting and close proximity to two heavily wooded national forests make Moscow a beautiful and intellectually stimulating place to live and raise a family.

Pre-Incorporation Years

The Nez Perce called the area around the present city of Moscow "Tatkinmah," the place of the young spotted deer. They valued the area for its supply of camas lily bulbs, which they harvested each fall for food.

The first permanent settler, Almon Asbury Lieuallen, staked a homestead claim in the valley in 1871. Other settlers soon followed. Many of these settlers brought hogs that fed on the camas bulbs by digging them out of the ground with their snouts. The settlers were so impressed with the abundance of camas bulbs for their hogs that they gave the area the tongue-in-cheek name of "Hog Heaven."

Moscow Valley.

A year later, postal authorities opened a mail route – carried by horseback – between Lewiston and the settlements to the north.

One of these settlements was Hog Heaven. However, when Lieuallen established the first post office for the little community, he sited it about a mile west of the present city of Moscow and officially gave it the name of Paradise Valley, ostensibly in recognition of Paradise Creek which flowed nearby.

Lieuallen built a small general store on the west side of the future location of Moscow's Main Street in 1875. He moved the post office to the general store where he kept the mail in a shoebox.

Lieuallen stocked his store with goods that he hauled by wagon from Walla Walla, Washington. James H. Hawley – in his book *History of Idaho, The Gem of the Mountains* – recounts that in 1897 W.G. Emery gave an account of the first store in Moscow. He said, "Two ordinary wagon-boxes would have held his (Lieuallen's) entire stock in the store, but the prevailing prices made up in size for the smallness on the stock. Five pounds of flour sold for one dollar, brown sugar was fifty cents a

Historic Moscow Main Street.

pound, common butts and screws were fifty cents per pair and everything else in proportion. But at Lewiston, prices were infinitely worse."

In 1877 more settlers arrived in Paradise Valley. Certain leaders in the town sought to come up with a better name for the town, but they could not reach consensus. Samuel Neff, the new postmaster, filed a postal permit that changed the name of the post office and the community to Moscow.

The reason for choosing the name of Moscow is not clear. However, Neff was born in Moscow, Pennsylvania. Before coming to Idaho, he also lived in Moscow, Iowa. Lieuallen said that he liked the name of Moscow because he believed the community was comparable to Moscow, Russia, in that both sought to be cities of brotherly love.

A visitor to the town in 1880 described Moscow as a lane between two farms, with a flax field on one side and a post office on the other.

By the 1880s settlers on the fertile Palouse were producing increasingly large quantities of farm commodities. However, the lack of transportation to distant markets was problematic.

In 1885 the Palouse and Columbia Railroad – eventually the Union Pacific – extended a rail line to Moscow and built a depot. In the next several years, other railroad companies built rail lines into the city to compete for the growing freight and passenger business.

Historic Moscow City Hall during construction.

The economy of Moscow soon rivaled Lewiston, its sister city and the county seat of Nez Perce County. Many people living in the northern part of the county wanted to divide Nez Perce County into two counties with Moscow and Lewiston as the respective county seats.

Since becoming a territory in 1863, Idaho's territorial boundaries were changed three times. (*See The Region, Idaho Territory – Change in Idaho Territorial Boundaries 1864 to 1890.*)

In the mid-1880s there were political attempts by the U.S. Congress to again divide Idaho among neighboring states and territories. Many in Northern Idaho wanted to become part of Washington Territory. Certain

Main Street, circa 1960.

Nevada politicians had designs on making Southern Idaho part of Nevada. The last of these attempts occurred in1887. Before recessing, Congress had passed a bill splitting off the Panhandle from Idaho Territory and adding it to Washington Territory. However, Idaho Territorial Governor Edward A. Stevenson and Congressional Delegate Fred T. Dubois persuaded President Grover Cleveland to pocket-veto the bill. That veto put an end to further congressional attempts to modify Idaho's territorial boundaries.

The issue of where to site the state's land grant university came before the Idaho Territorial Legislature in 1887. (*See The Region, Federal Land Grant Laws.*) Legislation establishing the school at Eagle Rock – now Idaho Falls – passed the legislature but was vetoed by the governor. A delegate to the Territorial Legislature from Moscow presented an amendment to the bill substituting Moscow for Eagle Rock. That also failed. However, a bill placing the question of dividing Nez Perce

County on the ballot passed the legislature. At the next election, the vote to divide the county failed.

Representatives of Moscow, led by territorial delegate Fred Dubois, appealed to the U.S. Congress. On May 14, 1888, Congress passed an act reducing the size of Nez Perce County and creating Latah County with Moscow as the county seat.

The federal law designated the county commissioners and authorized them to sell bonds to erect a courthouse. This was likely the only time in the nation's history that the U.S. Congress created a new county.

In 1889 the Territorial Legislature approved establishing the University of Idaho (UI) at Moscow. This action, termed the "olive branch" law along with creation of Latah County, persuaded Moscow voters to withdraw support for Northern Idaho becoming part of Washington. Washington became a state on November 11, 1889.

University of Idaho Administration Building.

Incorporation

The new county commissioners and Moscow residents wasted no time in organizing their new governments. On July 12, 1887, Moscow became an incorporated town. On the same day, the new government met at 7:30 p.m., adopted 33 ordinances and designated standing committees to run the town. The community grew rapidly. By 1910 Moscow had a population of 3,670.

Turning Points

Railroad The railroad was a major stimulus to the economy of Moscow. It provided needed transportation for moving large quantities of farm commodities to market as well as passengers and mail.

University of Idaho On January 30, 1889, Idaho Territorial Governor Edward Stevenson signed the bill establishing the UI as Idaho's public land grant university and locating it in Moscow. Commonly known as the university's charter, the act became part of Idaho's state constitution – signed July 3, 1890.

Ghormley Park.

World War I When the United States entered World War I in 1917, Moscow's citizens and UI students made major contributions and sacrifices. The war took the lives of 32 university students. One of the students who lost his life was Lieutenant Dudley Loomis, the namesake of the Moscow Post of the American Legion.

After the war, enrollment at the university surged. This was a period of growth in new construction on the university campus and in the city.

Frank Bruce Robinson The Great Depression and stock market crash of 1929 caused many people to look for psychological peace. Frank Bruce Robinson formed a mail order set of religious teachings and instruction he called "Psychiana." His daily mailings were distributed internationally from his base in Moscow and averaged several thousand pieces per day. The volume of his business brought the Moscow Post Office up to a first class ranking.

Robinson became a major benefactor to the community. He not only expanded his business holdings in the city, but he also provided the city with its first youth center and donated land for the county park named in his honor.

World War II Following World War II, the federal education assistance program called the GI Bill was instrumental in the UI student body nearly doubling. This resulted in another increase in construction on the university campus and in the city.

Moscow Today

Amenities and Attractions Moscow is a quintessential university town. The UI is an integral part of the city's economic, educational, cultural and social fabric.

Moscow is a regional shopping center, also serving the campus community of 12,000 students, over 2,900 faculty and staff and thousands of visitors each year.

The university's beautiful campus and activities are without question the city's most prominent attractions. The campus covers 1,585 acres. The core campus area has over 200 buildings positioned among stately trees, spacious lawns and open areas. The campus has 150 acres devoted to an 18-hole golf course, 63 acres for an arboretum and botanical garden and 860 acres used primarily by the college of Agricultural and Life Sciences for farming and

Friendship Square Main Street, downtown Moscow.

research activities. Municipal wastewater from the city is treated and used to irrigate all of the landscaped areas on campus.

The university sponsors many public events. Prominent among these are indoor NCAA Football Bowl Subdivision (FBS, formerly Division 1-A) football, basketball, track and field events. In addition, the University of Idaho Lionel Hampton International Jazz Festival, a four-day event each February, brings in thousands of students from throughout the U.S. and Canada to meet and receive instruction from some of the world's greatest Jazz artists.

The city's amenities include 16 municipal parks. Park services include developed picnic and activity areas as well as open spaces for passive recreation and viewing wildlife. In addition, there are ball fields, youth sports programs, indoor recreation areas, a skate park and an aquatic center with a swimming pool and water features for patrons of all ages.

The Latah County Historical Society operates a museum in the historic McConnell Mansion, built in 1886. The mansion is the former residence of William J. McConnell, who served as Idaho's governor from1893 to 1897 and was the founder of the McConnell-Maguire Company, Idaho's largest mercantile firm at the time. It failed in the 1890s due to the effects of the depression of 1893.

Moscow has earned its reputation as "Heart of the Arts." The Third Street Gallery, located on the second and third floors of Moscow City Hall, regularly hosts art exhibits as well as the City's permanent art collection. The Prichard Art Gallery is an outreach facility of the University of Idaho in downtown Moscow. That gallery hosts nine to 11 exhibitions annually. Local businesses regularly participate in the annual Art Walk activities that include temporary exhibits around town. In addition, the University of Idaho hosts several exhibits including those in the Reflections Gallery in the Idaho Commons Building on campus.

Farmers Market.

The Appaloosa Museum is located on the Idaho/Washington border. The Appaloosa horse breed is Idaho's state horse – spotted horses were noted amonng the Nez Perce Indians by Lewis and Clark. (*See The Region, Lewis and Clark and American Indians*.)

The city also features three performing arts locations. The Kenworthy Performing Arts Center is in the historic Kenworthy Theater in downtown Moscow. The Hartung Theatre accomodates live performances that include Shakespeare plays performed outdoors next to the main theater building. The Kiva Building on the UI campus was named due to its resemblance to the Pueblo kivas of the Southwest. This Googie-style structure lives up to its name, serving the Theater & Film Department as one of two main venues. The Idaho Repertory Theatre, "the longest running professional repertory theatre in the Inland Northwest," also uses the space for some of its productions. The Kiva Theatre is an intimate 125-seat theater, configured for theater-in-the-round. It also features digital lighting.

East City Park is one of many outdoor venues in the city for community and regional events – such as Rendezvous in the Park, the Renaissance Fair and the city's weekly summer children's entertainment and concert series.

Other annual community activities include the Latah County Fair in September. The Moscow Renaissance Fair takes place each May and features arts, crafts, foods, dancing, storytelling and other festivities. The Mardi Gras is celebrated in the spring. Rendezvous in the Park occurs each July with four evenings of concerts to suit a variety of musical tastes. The classical concert actually takes place in the late afternoon with some related activities for kids occurring separately.

The nearby public lands offer a variety of outdoor recreation options. In the winter, there are telemark and cross-country skiing and snowmobiling. In the warmer months, there are recreational trail and mountain biking, hiking, hunting, fishing, camping, boating, golfing, garnet hunting and white-water rafting.

Fire Station circa 1927.

Economy and Major Employers

With over 2,900 employees, the University of Idaho is by far the city's largest employer. The Moscow School District and the Gritman Medical Center each have approximately 350 employees. Wal-Mart and Latah Health Services each employ about 200. The City of Moscow employs 135. Many Moscow residents commute to Pullman, Washington, to work at Washington State University. The proximity of the University of Idaho and Washington State University led to the region's identity as the Palouse Knowledge Corridor, where a highly educated workforce helps shape the economic climate and employment opportunities.

The city's downtown and commercial areas are vibrant with a broad mix of retail and service businesses including two regional shopping malls and a variety of restaurants, motels, banks and independent businesses.

Historically, production agriculture was a leading component of the city's economy. Vast tracts of farmland still surround the city. However, technological innovation

Fire Station circa 2010.

and farm consolidation have increased farm productivity with substantially fewer workers. The research and development work of the University of Idaho College of Agricultural and Life Sciences continues to be of major importance to the local agriculture industry.

Education With four elementary schools, one junior high and two high schools, the Moscow School District provides most of the city's public education. There are also eight private schools and two charter schools in Moscow.

The University of Idaho is Idaho's land grant and primary research institution. Washington State University, Washington's land grant institution is eight miles west. The University of Idaho and Washington State University collaborate on many projects and issues. Other higher education and technical schools in or near the city are New St. Andrews College, a Christian college; Mr. Leon's School of Hair Design; and The Moscow School of Massage.

Health Care The 25-bed Gritman Medical Center is a critical access hospital that provides for most of the city's health care needs. The city also has two general medical clinics and an urgent care clinic. Moscow has several assisted-living facilities, two nursing homes – Good Samaritan Village and Aspen Park Healthcare – and a day use program, Gritman Adult Day Health.

Transportation The north-south U.S. Highway 95 and east-west State Highway 8 intersect the city.

Airline service is available at the 6,731-foot runway at Pullman-Moscow Regional Airport five miles west of town. The Lewiston Airport is 35 miles south and Spokane, Washington, International Airport is 89 miles north.

Railroad service is available for freight only, but even that use is coming to an end.

Utilities and Services Private companies provide electricity, telephone, gas and cable television services. The city provides general governmental services, such as police and fire protection, in addition to water, sewer and solid waste services. The city boasts a state-of-the-art working environment backed up by fiber optic cable and a sophisticated telecommunications infrastructure.

Vision for 2050

Over the past several years, Moscow's population has grown at a moderate rate, just over 1 percent annually. These trends will likely continue. However, even if the city's population exceeds 35,000 by 2050, the community is committed to maintaining its unique heritage. It will retain its compact, pedestrian-friendly form; distinct tree-lined neighborhoods; and historic small-town charm.

City Hall, circa 2010.

At the same time, advances in research, technology, computer science, broadband, fiber optics and other virtual amenities will keep Moscow's competitive edge in the ever-changing job market of the twenty-first century.

To keep up with demands of the modestly growing population, the city will have expanded its transportation network including extended bicycle-pedestrian pathways, enhanced local and regional bus and air service, flexible telecommuting opportunities and reduced reliance on petroleum fuels.

The University of Idaho and Washington State University will continue to influence the character of the community – attracting world-class speakers, entertainment, educators, students and researchers. One cannot imagine Moscow without the seasonal flux of student-inspired vitality balanced with calm summer days; the signature Farmers' Market in Friendship Square; and an abundance of community festivals, picnics, concerts and family-oriented recreational activities.

Discerning consumers made up of the so-called "creative class" associated with universities and a significant demographic influx of baby-boomers will demand high quality services, retail and clean light industry. In turn, providers of those services will be attracted by Moscow's highly marketable economic engine known as the "Palouse Knowledge Corridor." Residents attracted by the safe environment, four-season climate, walk-ability and stimulating social activities will also find quality healthcare, a variety of affordable housing choices and a strong sense of community.

In 2050 Moscow residents and visitors will appreciate the foresight of the community which recognizes the need to preserve parkland, plans for a sustainable water supply, provides opportunities for multi-modal transportation, maintains a healthy and inviting downtown core and supports an ethic of environmental sustainability. Moscow is sure to keep its reputation as being a leader in sustainability, historic preservation, art appreciation, academic excellence and quality of life.

Mayors

1887 William McConnell
1889 Lindel Smith
1891 W. B. Lyle
1892 W.T. Griffin
1892 E.C. Hall
1894 L.B. McCarter
1895 Frank White
1896 Frank Cornwall
1897 Alex Ryrie
1899 Bayard T. Byrne
1904 J.C. Wolfe
1905 William Morgan
1907 R.S. Mathews
1909 Bayard T. Byrne
1911 J.N. Clarke
1915 J.G. Gibson
1917 Warren Truitt
1919 J.G. Gibson
1921 Hawkin Melgard
1927 Harry J. Smith
1928 Ray Carter
1930 George S. Richardson

1931 J.E. Wilson
1934 Henry Rach
1935 Homer Estes
1939 Henry C. Hansen
1940 F.L. Kennard
1941 T.M. Wright
1941 William L. Anderson
1947 Robert K. Bonnett
1951 William L. Anderson
1953 Everett Will
1957 Spencer Lewis
1961 Fred Handel
1970 Larry Merk
1973 Paul Mann
1978 Don Mackin
1982 Dee Hager
1985 Gary Scott
1990 Paul Agidius
1998 Marshall Comstock
2006 Nancy Chaney
2014 Bill Lambert

Onaway.

Onaway

Statistical Data

Population: 189 *
Elevation: 2,640 feet
Precipitation: 24 inches **
Average Snowfall: 38 inches **
County: Latah

Temperature Range – Fahrenheit: **
Spring: 39 to 65
Summer: 43 to 82
Fall: 28 to 73
Winter: 22 to 42

* U.S. Census Bureau Estimates July 2015
**Historical averages

Onaway and the much larger city of Potlatch are of such close proximity, only their legal boundaries distinguish them as separate towns. Even though their origins are different, they have certain common histories and future prospects.

A century ago, white pine forests – Idaho's state tree – covered much of what is now Onaway. These giant trees rose to over 200 feet and had a butt-diameter of over 7 feet. As sawyers cut the trees for the mills, the forest products companies sold the cleared land to farmers. Today, fields of wheat, lentils, peas, oats and barley interspersed with wooded ravines and woodlots now surround the twin cities of Potlatch and Onaway.

The St. Joe National Forest lies a few miles to the north, east and south of the city. Moscow is about 12 miles south.

Pre-Incorporation Years

Around 1810 European and, later, American trappers/explorers began trapping beaver and establishing trading posts in the region. At that time, nomadic American Indians – principally of the Nez Perce and Palouse Tribes – frequented the area.

In the late 1850s John Grizwold and his Indian wife settled in the region. In 1860 Captain Elias Davidson Pierce and a party of 10 prospectors found large quantities of placer gold about 60 miles southeast of what is now Onaway. The ensuing gold rush attracted thousands of prospectors who scoured the region looking for gold.

They found gold in the area of the Hoodoo Mountains, about 15 miles northeast of what is now Onaway and formed the Hoodoo Mining District. Ed and Jerry Chambers ran a stage line from Walla Walla, Washington, to a roadhouse they built about four miles northeast of what is now Laird Park, named after a Potlatch Company officer. They named their stage stop Grizzle Camp after John Grizwold. The Boy Scouts of America now have a camp nearby named Camp Grizzly.

In the 1880s Wells Fargo either acquired the Chambers stage line or started another line that ran from Palouse, Washington, to Grizzle Camp. Between the two communities, Wells Fargo built a stage stop they named Bulltown after the Bull family who had settled in the area. The Bulltown stage station attracted several new settlers who changed the name of the community to Onaway, the name of the town that they had come from in New York.

Around 1900 Frederick Weyerhaeuser – from St. Paul Minnesota and one of Idaho's most influential figures in the wood products industry – began acquiring large tracts of Northern Idaho timberland.  In 1903 Weyerhaeuser formed he Potlatch Lumber Company, then a timber real estate holding company, with William Deary as general manager.

Deary continued to acquire timberland and in 1905 founded the town of Potlatch just southwest of Onaway. A year later, he completed construction of one of the then largest sawmills in the world and a company-owned town with over 275 buildings.

In 1907 Weyerhaeuser formed the Washington, Idaho and Montana Railway Company (WI&M). Deary extended the 45-mile-long railroad from Palouse, Washington, following the Palouse River on the south side of Potlatch to Bovill where it connected with the western terminus of the Milwaukee Road.

The WI&M and Potlatch Lumber Company founded the towns of Deary, Bovill, Yale, Harvard, Vassar and Elk River. Except for Elk River where the company also built a sawmill, these locations were log collection and loading points as well as depots providing freight, passenger and mail transportation services. As they cleared the timber, they sold the property for farmland.

Incorporation

On April 7, 1953, Onaway became an incorporated village.

Turning Points

Gold The discovery of gold in the Hoodoo Mining District served as the catalyst that brought the stage line between Palouse, Washington, and Grizzle Camp with a stop in between that became Onaway.

Sawmill Frederick Weyerhaeuser's decision to build a branch railroad and establish his premier sawmill on the bend of the Palouse River provided the underlying basis for making Potlatch a wholly-owned company town built around a single business. The mill also provided the economic basis for the future growth of Onaway, as many of the town's residents found employment at the mill.

Closure of the Mill Until its closure in 1981 the mill largely underpinned Onaway's economy. In 1981 the company closed the mill and the era of the "Potlatch Company Town" came to a close.

Onaway Today

Amenities and Attractions The 83-mile White Pine Scenic Byway passes through the largest stand of White Pine trees in North America, extending from Potlatch/Onaway on Idaho Highway 6, north to Idaho Highway 3 and then north on Highway 3 to Interstate 90 near Old Mission State Park at Cataldo.

Onaway is near Potlatch's three historic districts listed on the National Register of Historic Places. The Commercial District has 10 acres and seven buildings. The Workers Neighborhood District is a 30-acre parcel with 23 buildings. The Nob Hill District has 30 acres and 18 buildings.

The 5,300-acre Mary Minerva McCroskey Memorial State Park is located about 10 miles north of Onaway. The park offers an 18-mile skyline drive and 32 miles of multi-purpose trails, shelters, primitive camping and picnic areas. To the west are spectacular views of the rolling Palouse country.

Three other state parks – Heyburn, Winchester Lake and Old Mission – are located within an hour's drive of the city. The Latah County Museum is in Moscow.

Fishing and boating are available in the several lakes and rivers that lie within an hour's drive of the city. The 54-mile-long Dworshak Reservoir on the North

Fork of the Clearwater River is 35 miles across the mountains. Lake Coeur d'Alene lies 35 miles north.

Economy and Major Employers Onaway's business district consists primarily of convenience stores and restaurants along Onaway Road, which forms an irregular two-mile beltway from Idaho Highway 6 north of Potlatch, through Onaway then rejoining Highway 6 at the unincorporated town of Hampton.

Most of the city's workforce has jobs in Potlatch or other nearby cities.

Education The Potlatch School District operates elementary, junior and senior high schools in Potlatch.

The closest institution of higher learning is the University of Idaho in Moscow.

Health Care There is a general medical clinic in Potlatch. The closest hospital is Gritman Medical Center in Moscow.

Transportation Onaway Road intersects the city and connects with Idaho Highway 6 about a mile on either side of the city. U.S. Highway 95 is about two miles west of town.

Commercial airline service is available at the Pullman-Moscow Regional Airport located in Washington, five miles west of Moscow.

Rail service for freight is available in Potlatch.

Utilities and Services Private companies provide electricity, telephone, satellite and wireless services. The City provides water and sewer services and fire protection. Police protection is provided by the County Sheriff under contract with the City.

Vision for 2050

Onaway's population has remained around 200 for half a century. Historical trends will likely continue.

Potlatch historical marker.

Potlatch

Statistical Data
Population: 806 *
Elevation: 2,600 feet
Precipitation: 24 inches **
Average Snowfall: 38 inches **
County: Latah
Website: www.potlatchidaho.org

Temperature Range – Fahrenheit: **
Spring: 29 to 65
Summer: 43 to 82
Fall: 28 to 73
Winter: 22 to 42
* U.S. Census Bureau Estimates July 2015
**Historical averages

Potlatch is Idaho's Historic Company Town. It is the state's first completely planned community, designed and built by a single company to support a massive commercial operation, a distinct downtown and several hundred employees and their families.

A century ago before the Potlatch Lumber Company built its sawmill and the community it named Potlatch, vast tracts of white pine forests covered most of the region around the future mill. The white pine is Idaho's state tree. The trees can reach the astounding height of over 200 feet and a diameter of seven feet.

The city lies at the base of Idaho's Panhandle six miles east of the Idaho/Washington border. Fields of wheat, lentils, peas, oats, barley, timothy hay and bluegrass interspersed with wooded ravines and woodlots create a beautiful landscape of color and texture. The Palouse River adds to the picturesque setting as it wraps around the southern end of this heart-shaped city.

The St. Joe National Forest is a few miles to the north, east and south of the city. Moscow is 18 miles south.

Pre-Incorporation Years

The land around Potlatch was the exclusive domain of nomadic American Indians – principally of the Nez Perce and Palouse Tribes – until around 1810 when trappers and explorers came into the area. (*See The Region – American Indians; and Early Trappers/Explorers.*)

In the late 1850s John Grizwold and his Indian wife settled in the area. In 1860 Captain Elias Davidson Pierce and a small party of prospectors found large quantities of placer gold 60 miles southeast near what is now Pierce. The ensuing gold rush attracted thousands of prospectors, who scoured the region for gold. (*See The Region – Gold Mining.*)

The Potlatch Lumber Company sawmill in Potlatch, the reason the company town was established. Built in 1906, the mill was hailed as the largest white pine mill in the world. It closed in 1981 and was completely dismantled.

Some found gold in the area of the Hoodoo Mountains about 15 miles northeast of what is now Potlatch and formed the Hoodoo Mining District.

Capitalizing on this new demand for transportation, Ed and Jerry Chambers ran a stage line from Walla Walla, Washington, to a roadhouse they built about four miles northeast of what is now Laird Park – a prominent campground 11 miles east of Potlatch and named after a Potlatch Company officer. They named their stage stop Grizzle Camp after John Grizwold. The Boy Scouts of America now operate "Camp Grizzly" near that historic location.

In the 1880s Wells Fargo began its stage line from Palouse, Washington, to Grizzle Camp. Between Palouse and Grizzle Camp, Wells Fargo built a stage stop called Bulltown after the Bull family, who had settled in the area. The Bulltown stage station attracted several new settlers, who changed the name to Onaway in honor of the town in Michigan where they once lived.

At the turn of the century, timber baron Frederick Weyerhaeuser – of St. Paul, Minnesota, and one of the most influential figures in the wood products industry in Idaho and the Northwest – began acquiring large tracts of Northern Idaho timberland. In 1903 Weyerhaeuser and a conglomerate of associates formed the Potlatch Lumber Company that, at the time, was a timber real estate holding company with William Deary as general manager. Deary continued to acquire timberland and in 1905 founded the town of Potlatch. (*See The Region – Forest Products.*)

A year later, workers, under the supervision of architect C. Ferris White at the townsite and William A Wilkinson at the mill site, completed construction of what was then one of the largest lumber mills in the world and a town with over 275 buildings. The mill, using steam power and belt-driven

Potlatch Bridge, 1906.

saws and equipment, began operating on September 11, 1906.

Deary located the lumber mill on a flat area adjacent to the Palouse River with the town situated on elevated land overlooking the mill site. The town was pedestrian friendly – an elaborate network of boardwalks and bridges connected the mill to the town's commercial and residential districts.

In addition to the large mill site with its ponds and rail yard, the town included Nob Hill, a residential area where Deary and other company officials lived. The commercial district included a department store, an opera house, apartment buildings, a hotel, a bank, a post office, an athletic club with a gymnasium and boxing

Potlatch Mercantile, the company store in Potlatch. It carried everything from food and dry goods to farm implements, fine china and work clothes. "The Merc" was known for amazing sales that attracted hundreds of shoppers, with bargain hunters sometimes enticed by free stud service for horses and mules. The store burned in 1963.

ring, a confectionary, a creamery, churches and a train depot. The residential neighborhood contained a variety of worker housing, ranging from boarding houses and small homes at the bottom of the hill to more substantial family housing at the top. To help alleviate transiency, the company encouraged married men to work in the mill and reserved its houses for families.

The company added to the town's active social life with company picnics and garden parties for visiting officials. It provided schools, hiring the best teachers available and supporting school functions. The first church built was St. Mary's Catholic Church. The Union Church served the various Protestant denominations.

In 1905 Potlatch Lumber Company directors incorporated the Washington, Idaho and Montana Railway Company (WI&M). Deary was general manager of both companies. WI&M built a 45-mile-long railroad from Palouse, Washington, to Bovill, where it connected with the western terminus of the Milwaukee Road.

In addition to the Potlatch mill, the company also built a mill at Elk River. The WI&M and Potlatch Lumber Company also founded the towns of Harvard, Yale, Vassar and Deary. These locations were log collection and loading points as well as depots providing freight, passenger and mail transportation services.

In an effort to improve efficiency, the Potlatch mill joined the mills in Lewiston and Coeur d'Alene in 1931 to form a new entity, Potlatch Forests Incorporated.

The Union Church, built by Potlatch Lumber Company in Potlatch. The church seated 1,000 people and hosted many large community events including high school graduations. It burned in 1951.

A few years later, PFI began divesting itself of all of its Potlatch assets not directly related to the mill's operation. For example, in 1940 the company sold the bank and in 1948 the electrical power generation facility. It donated public facilities to the town and church-related real estate to the respective church organizations and sold company houses to the occupants at discounted prices. By late 1952 the town was largely independent, except PFI continued as the community's largest employer.

Incorporation

On December 1, 1952, the county approved the community's application to become an incorporated village. On September 12, 1960, the village changed its form of municipal government to an incorporated city.

Turning Points

Frederick Weyerhaeuser
Weyerhaeuser's decision to build a branch railroad and establish his premier sawmill on the bend of the Palouse River provided the underlying basis for making Potlatch a wholly-owned company town built around a single business.

Closure of the Mill
Through the period 1908 to

The Potlatcher, also called "the bug." The railcar ran the full WI&M line between Palouse and Bovill, delivering mail, passengers and freight.

1927 the mill produced 131 million board feet of lumber annually and had several hundred employees. During those years, the town's population was approximately 1,500. In 1981 the company closed the mill and the era of the "Potlatch Company Town" came to an end.

New Economy The city has initiated a variety of actions to make the town more attractive to new businesses and residents. In 1990 community leaders beautified the town by building "Scenic 6 Park" on part of the historic 16-acre mill site that had been donated to the city.

Recently, the city updated its water and municipal wastewater treatment facilities with capacity for growth. Annexation of adjoining lands will facilitate further growth as the city's economic base changes.

Original Potlatch depot.

Potlatch Today

Amenities and Attractions Potlatch has two city parks. Scenic 6 Park features a historic steam locomotive and the original Princeton Train Depot that the community moved and restored in the park. There is also a restored miner's cabin, two baseball fields, a volleyball court, two covered picnic shelters, children's playground areas, walking paths and a modern RV park. The five-acre Lions Club Park has a swimming

Restored Potlatch depot.

pool, a covered shelter, a kitchen and a picnic area. The day before Easter, the Parent Teacher Organization and Lions Club sponsor an annual Easter egg hunt and games.

On the second weekend in July, the Railroad Preservation Group sponsors a Speeder Car Event with speeder car rides between Princeton; Harvard; and Palouse, Washington. On the same day, the community sponsors the "Wooden Bat Tournament." Teams from Northern Idaho and eastern Washington compete in the three-day baseball event that also features bluegrass music and food booths.

On the third weekend of July, the city celebrates "Potlatch Community Days" with a breakfast at Lions Club Park and a parade through town to Scenic 6 Park where there are craft and food booths, kids' games,

Potlatch Library.

logging events, lawnmower races and volleyball 3-on-3 tournaments. The event concludes with a free Family Pool Party, barbeque and teen dance complete with a DJ and karaoke.

The community sponsors the "Potlatch Fiddle Show" on the first Saturday in August. Fiddlers come from all over the Northwest to participate in this event held in the Potlatch High School gymnasium.

On the third Saturday of August, the community sponsors "Potlatch Blues Fest" at Lions Club Park. Blues bands from the surrounding area come to perform.

Each September, the Potlatch Recreation District sponsors the annual "Pie in the Park" celebration as a thank you to the Recreation District's patrons. The event includes a guest singer or band along with hamburgers, sausages and pie.

In October, the "Lets Get it Started" youth group puts on a Halloween Party and Haunted House at the high school gymnasium. The Potlatch Recreation District finances the fun family event that includes pumpkin carving, costume contests and Halloween games.

Dale's Saturday Market at Junction Lumber in Potlatch offers locally-grown produce, crafts and fresh cinnamon rolls during the summer season. The market also features a petting zoo and a variety of community events during the months it is open.

On the first weekend in November, the Potlatch Christmas Committee begins the task of putting up over 75,000 Christmas lights and displays in Scenic 6 Park. On Thanksgiving, they turn on the lights. This light display gets larger every year, attracting families from all over the region.

On the first Saturday in December, the community follows the lighting of the park and the historic locomotive with the "Lighted Christmas Parade" followed by free chili, hotdogs, hot cider and chocolate and the "Largest Winter Fireworks Display in Latah County" sponsored by the Potlatch Recreation District.

There are walking tours through the city's three historic districts – each on the National Register of Historic Places. The Commercial District has 10 acres and seven buildings. The Workers Neighborhood District is a 30-acre parcel with 23 buildings. The Nob Hill District has 30 acres and 18 buildings. The Washington, Idaho & Montana Railway History Preservation Group, Inc. is completely restoring the historic

The historic Number One steam locomotive in Scenic Six Park in Potlatch.

1906 Potlatch Train Depot to its former grandeur. The depot – which currently houses a bus station, gift shop and artisan's studio – will soon house a museum of historic area artifacts and exhibits.

The 83-mile White Pine Scenic Byway passes through the largest stand of white pine trees in North America. The byway passes many public campsites as it extends north from Potlatch and Onaway on Idaho Highway 6 to Idaho Highway 3, then north to Interstate 90 near Old Mission State Park at Cataldo.

The 5,300-acre Mary Minerva McCroskey Memorial State Park is located about 10 miles north of Potlatch. The park offers an 18-mile skyline drive and 32 miles of multi-purpose trails, shelters, primitive camping and picnic areas. To the west are spectacular views of the rolling Palouse country.

Three other state parks – Heyburn, Winchester Lake and Old Mission – are within an hour's drive of the city. The Latah County Museum is in Moscow.

Fishing and boating are available in the several lakes and rivers that lie within an hour's drive of the city. The 54-mile Dworshak Reservoir on the North Fork of the Clearwater River is 35 miles across the mountains. Lake Coeur d'Alene is 35 miles north.

Economy and Major Employers Bennett Forest Products has about 150 employees and is the city's largest employer. Potlatch School District has about 90 employees. Washington State University and the University of Idaho have research operations in the city, and each has about 60 employees. D-8 Manufacturing, located on Highway 95 three miles north of Potlatch, makes aluminum molds and has about 50 employees. Several small businesses, retail establishments and the U.S. Forest Service District Office provide most of the other jobs in the city.

Education The Potlatch School District provides elementary, junior and senior high school education.

The closest institution of higher learning is the University of Idaho in Moscow.

Health Care The city has a general medical clinic. The closest hospital is Gritman Medical Center in Moscow.

Transportation Idaho Highway 6 intersects the city. U.S. Highway 95 is about two miles west of town.

Commercial airline service is available at the Pullman-Moscow Regional Airport in Washington, 30 miles southwest of Potlatch.

Rail service is available for freight. Commercial bus service is available for passengers.

Utilities and Services Private companies provide electricity, telephone, propane gas, cable, satellite, Internet and wireless services. The City provides water and sewer services. The Potlatch Rural Fire Department provides fire protection and ambulance service for all of the communities in the Potlatch area. When needed, Bennett Forest Products Wild Land Fire Team also provides fire protection services. The Latah County Sheriff's Office provides police protection under contract with the City.

Vision for 2050

Over the last eight years, the City has installed all new water and sewer lines. These improvements include updating all domestic wells and a new liner in the 1.2 million gallon water reservoir. The improved sewer system that includes an upgraded lift station, lagoon and land application systems is being completed.

The city is annexing 390 acres – 320 acres of which comprise the old mill site – along with 37 acres north of town and 25 acres on the east. In coordination with the development desires of the mill site owner, Potlatch Corporation, the city council will likely zone most of the mill site land residential with significant portions of the property zoned commercial including a manufacturing incubator, recreational area and a 9-hole golf course. On the east side, the owner plans to build an assisted living center.

Potlatch City Hall, originally constructed in 1917 as the headquarters for the Potlatch Lumber Company.

These and other economic development actions along with the city's attractive location – one mile off Highway 95, having the only rail line in the county and located only a few minutes away from the beautiful St. Joe National Forest – will have the probable effect of attracting expanded and new businesses as well as new residents to the city. With such a good location, quality schools and recreation, Potlatch is an attractive place for families and light manufacturing businesses to locate.

Because of the forgoing, in a few years, Potlatch's population will begin to grow by more than two percent annually. By 2050 the population will have likely doubled to around 1,500.

Mayors

1952 Richard Wallace *
1953 Milfred Jones *
1953 Dewey Lavoy *
1957 Wilburn Granlund *
1960 Ted Sadd
1964 Russell Bailey
1970 Paul Tobin

1978 Eugene Walters
1982 Neil Candler
1998 Scott Kammeyer
2001 Carol Pettibone
2002 David Brown
* Village Chairman

Troy

Statistical Data

Population: 881 *
Elevation: 2,487 feet
Precipitation: 25 inches **
Average Snowfall: 45 inches **
County: Latah
Website: www.troyidaho.net

Temperature Range – Fahrenheit: **
Spring: 31 to 66
Summer: 45 to 84
Fall: 30 to 74
Winter: 23 to 41
* U.S. Census Bureau Estimates July 2015
**Historical averages

Troy is nestled in a beautiful narrow valley surrounded by a patchwork of fertile fields of wheat, barley and peas interspersed by pine-covered ravines. The city's beautiful setting in a canyon with wooded slopes exudes a feeling of comfort and peace.

The Palouse Range, with Moscow Mountain rising to nearly 5,000 feet, lies a few miles north. The western edge of the St. Joe National Forest begins about 18 miles northeast. Dworshak State Park Recreation Area and the 53-mile-long Dworshak Reservoir in the Clearwater National Forest are accessible about 33 miles southeast. The city of Moscow lies 11 miles west.

Pre-Incorporation Years

For centuries, tribes of the nomadic Nez Perce Indians passed through and hunted in the forests that once covered the land surrounding what is now Troy. In fact, the city's Main Street follows an old Nez Perce trail. In the late 1980s construction workers building the city's wastewater treatment plant on the south edge of town, unearthed the remains of an old Nez Perce hunting camp.

Early settlers called the canyon where Troy is located "Huff's Gulch." At that time, the canyon was densely forested and marshy. Early histories described the canyon as "so thick with forest [tall pine and cedar trees] that birds could scarcely fly through."

In 1885 J. Wesley Seat filed a homestead claim for 160 acres in the heart of what is now downtown Troy. He built a portable sawmill that he moved as he harvested the timber. Other homesteaders were also moving into the area.

Many of these homesteaders held church services in homes until they could construct their church

Flood in Troy.

buildings. The United Methodist congregation built their first church in 1887; Trinity Lutheran (Norwegian) in 1897; and Troy Christian Church and the Scandinavian Methodist Church were constructed a few years later. The Swedish Evangelical Lutheran Westdala congregation built a 24 foot x 26 foot x 14 foot church in 1891. It had a tower that was "at least no lower than that of the Scandinavian Methodist Church." It still stands on Main Street and has been in continuous use since then. The Troy Christian Church also still stands, but it is in serious disrepair and is no longer usable.

Around 1891 the Northern Pacific Railroad completed a branch line from Spokane, Washington, to Lewiston, Idaho. The survey took the railroad through Huff's Gulch. The railroad's steam engines required constructing a stop about every 20 miles in order to take on water and fuel.

In anticipation of the rail line, a group of Moscow and other entrepreneurs that included Seat and John P.

Troy train station.

Vollmer – a Lewiston merchant, banker and agent for the railroad – sought to plat a new town on Seat's land. Vollmer used his influence with the railroad to insure the rail line between Moscow and Kendrick would pass through the new town that the founders would name Vollmer.

With the railroad assured, the founders sold building lots in the new community. John Vollmer built a general merchandise store and livery stable on two of the lots.

Vollmer used a similar business strategy of using his influence and insider information to establish, or try to establish, other Northern Idaho cities. (*See Craigmont, Ferdinand and Genesee.*)

Homesteaders cleared their land and planted grains, peas and fruit they planned to ship by rail to commercial markets. In addition, about five sawmills had set up in the canyon.

Idaho Fire Brick Company plant.

Many homesteaders cut and corded wood for sale to the railroad to fuel the trains. By that time, the town had two grocery confectionery stores; a general merchandise store; a hotel; and two newspapers, the *Alliance Ledger* and the *Vollmer Vidette.*

The January 1, 1892, edition of the *Moscow Mirror* quoted an article in the *Alliance Register* of Vollmer extolling the agricultural benefits of the area, the timber resources and the "very healthy climate." The same article lists the leading businessmen and their enterprises in glowing terms. Not surprisingly, all persons listed were advertisers in the newspaper.

The article continues with a section about the homes in Vollmer. "We are pleased to see so many neat and tasteful residences in Vollmer and that the work of building and improving still goes on. There certainly has been a great improvement since last year, when the town could boast of scarcely anything except shanties."

Troy Lumber Company.

The town's business buildings had storefronts equipped with canvas awnings. When the weather warranted, they would roll up or down the awnings with a metal hand crank.

In 1893 school patrons erected the town's first schoolhouse on North Main Street. It had over 100 students. They separated the students into three age groups, taught by three teachers. The first known graduation took place in 1905 and consisted of 11 students.

Incorporation

On April 19, 1892, the Nez Perce County Commissioners approved the town's application making Vollmer an incorporated village.

A few years later, wet fall weather crippled the agricultural economy. For three years, rain soaked the wheat standing in shocks in the fields. This caused the wheat to sprout making it almost worthless. Many farmers could not pay their mortgages and lost their farms to foreclosure. These economic problems in the farming community had a ripple adverse effect on the town's business community.

At this time, many citizens had also become upset with John Vollmer. He had promised to build a community center and failed to do so. They also resented having their town named after a man who had amassed over 32,000 acres of land, much of it obtained by acquiring foreclosed farmland – perceived as taking unfair advantage of farmers' misfortunes.

Troy, 1928.

On September 6, 1897, the village held an election to reconsider the name of the town. A Greek railroad worker suggested they name the town Troy, the name of "the most illustrious city in the world." He offered a drink of whisky to anyone who voted for "Troy." The vote was 29 for Troy and 9 for Vollmer. On September 16, 1897, the county commissioners officially changed the name of the village to Troy.

Turning Points

Railroad The coming of the railroad was the impetus for the founding of Troy. It transformed the town into a thriving business community. With the advent of competition from motor vehicles, the train ended its service to Troy.

Sawmills The wood products industry was a major Troy industry through most of the last century. In an indirect way, it also affected the layout of the city's Main Street. In the early years, the village had not totally cleared Main Street of trees and stumps. In addition, the naturally marshy land was often muddy. Sawmill operators filled the streets with waste sawdust and chips to absorb the moisture. Wagon masters drove around the patches of trees and stumps. Northbound traffic passed on one side of the obstacles and southbound traffic on the other; an early version of a divided highway. In later years when the town improved Main Street, they made a single road but retained the width created by the improvised one-way roads.

Brick Manufacturing In 1900 Per Johanson discovered his Troy homestead had deposits of high-grade clay and kaolin needed in the manufacture of good bricks and pottery. He started a brick-making company that became a major employer until 1990 when subsequent owners closed the plant.

Technological Innovation in Farming Early settlers farmed with horses and used threshing machines for harvesting their grain. As tractors, self-propelled combines and improved strains of grains came into use, small farms sold out to larger operators who spread the increasing cost of operation over larger acreages. To the extent this resulted in fewer farm families coming to town to shop, it had an adverse effect on the city's economy.

Troy EMS.

Municipal Water System and Timberland Investment In 1944 the City purchased land on Moscow Mountain and built a reservoir and domestic water system with water lines providing gravity flow water into town. In addition, the City owned a large tract of timber that the city managed to provide sustainable timber sales used to augment the need for tax revenues.

World War II The war had a profound effect on Troy. Not only did most of the city's youth serve in the military, many families moved out of town for high-paying defense jobs on the coast. When the veterans returned home, they had new skills and high hopes. Many started new businesses that added to the city's economy.

However, this period of a vibrant downtown business community was short lived as gasoline rationing ceased and motor vehicles became the preferred mode of travel. Many residents drove to larger nearby cities to do their shopping. Several local retailers gradually closed their doors.

Troy Today

Amenities and Attractions The city has two parks comprising nine acres. The largest park, Welna Park, has a tennis court, softball field and children's playground. It also has a covered gazebo that holds several picnic tables and a bandstand. A walking path circles through the grassy park.

On the third Saturday in July each year, the park is the site of Troy's biggest celebration. The celebration, put on by the Troy Lions Club, is variously called Troy Day, Community Day or Old Timer's Day and includes a "Buffalo Hunt Raffle" where tickets go on sale over the Internet several weeks in advance of the drawing.

Other Troy Day activities are a pancake breakfast, parade, car show, kid's races, buffalo burgers and other raffles. The parade and an exhibit depicting facets of Troy history, prepared by the Troy Historical Society, occur downtown. In recent years, a street dance has been held on Main Street in the evening. Everything else is at the City Park.

The Greymalkin Art Gallery features the work of local artists. The Troy Community Library is located in the Bohman Building financed with a community fundraising campaign that started with the 1992 Centennial celebration and was completed with the help of volunteer labor.

Troy is the terminus for a walking and bicycle trail that begins in Moscow and ends on the southern edge of the city.

The nearby forests and Spring Valley Lake provide outstanding outdoor recreation, including fishing and hunting.

Economy and Major Employers The Troy School District with about 125 employees is the city's largest employer. Several small businesses operate in the

Winter in the Troy area.

city – including two light manufacturing companies and an electrical contractor – that have fewer than 30 employees each.

The downtown business community includes a grocery store; a floral, gift and coffee shop; two restaurants; three bars; two beauty salons; a liquor store; a bank; a garden nursery; an upholstery shop; an antique shop; a used car lot; a gas station with Laundromat and convenience store; and a welding machine shop.

Education Troy School District is the principle source of K-12 education. Troy Elementary School serves students through grade six. Students in grades 7 through 12 attend Troy Jr-Sr High School. A private pre-school meets in the Lutheran Church.

The closest institution of higher learning is the University of Idaho in Moscow.

Health Care A medical clinic in Troy and The Gritman Medical Center in Moscow provide for most of the city's health care needs.

Transportation Idaho Highway 8 is the city's Main Street as it passes through town to Moscow and U.S. Highway 95 on the west and Deary to the east. Idaho Highway 99 to Kendrick begins on the south side of town.

The closest air service is the Pullman-Moscow Regional Airport located about five miles west of Moscow.

Utilities and Services Private companies provide electricity, telephone, Internet and cable services. The City provides water and sewer services and police protection. The Troy Volunteer Fire Department provides fire protection as well as EMT and ambulance services.

Vision for 2050

In 1960 Troy's population was 555. Beginning in the 1970s the population grew until in the 1980s it stabilized at around 800. Historical population trends will likely continue into the next decade. However, by that time, other factors will come into play that will return Troy to moderate growth.

Chief among these factors are the spillover effect of economic growth in Moscow and the University of Idaho. More young families will choose to purchase affordable homes and raise their families in the peaceful hometown of Troy and commute the short distance to work in the larger community.

The city's current infrastructure is adequate to accommodate moderate growth within the existing tax structure and without significant improvement in facilities.

Mayors

1889 Olaf Olson *
1904 T.H. Christie *
1905 W.M. Duthie *
1909 F.M. Green *
1915 W.M. Duthie *
1919 K.T. Myklebust *
1923 H.H. Christie *
1927 George Smith *
1933 Henry Kaaen *
1935 Ed Solberg *

1955 Willis Bohman *
1967 Eldon Strom
1972 Pat Nunan
1977 Ray Soderstrom
1982 Alvin Zeller
1984 Stan Workman
1988 Marie Vogel
1996 John Blom
2004 Kenneth Whitney, Jr.
* Village Chairman

Elk near Kamiah in winter.

LEWIS COUNTY

Craigmont
Kamiah
Nezperce (County Seat)
Reubens
Winchester

View of Craigmont, 1960s.

Craigmont

Statistical Data

Population: 503 *
Elevation: 3,760 feet
Precipitation: 24 inches **
Average Snowfall: 70 inches **
County: Lewis

Temperature Range – Fahrenheit: **
Spring: 26 to 60
Summer: 48 to 78
Fall: 26 to 69
Winter: 20 to 40
* U.S. Census Bureau Estimates July 2015
**Historical averages

Craigmont is a farming and tourist community that lies in the upper Camas Prairie. Fields of wheat, barley and peas growing on gentle rolling hills form a patchwork of color and texture around the city.

Most of the land around the city belongs to the Nez Perce Indian Reservation. The city of Cottonwood is 15 miles south.

Pre-Incorporation Years

Following the treaty of 1846 with England establishing the boundary between the United States and Canada at the 49th Parallel, the federal government created territories and took control of the land. The U.S. Army compelled American Indians to follow the dictates of Congress. The nomadic Nez Perce was the principal tribe of Indians that frequented the area of what is now Craigmont.

In 1855 the federal government entered into a treaty with the Nez Perce establishing a reservation that covered a large part of Northern Idaho and Western Washington. However, around 1860 numerous gold prospectors and settlers began moving onto reservation land.

In 1860 prospectors found gold at Pierce. A gold rush ensued with thousands coming into the region. Almost overnight, Lewiston became a tent city on reservation land as miners, traveling by boat up the Columbia and Snake Rivers to Lewiston, geared up before making their trek to the gold fields at Pierce and beyond.

In 1867 Congress, seeking to promote settlement and appease the demands of prospectors and settlers, ratified a new treaty crafted in 1863. As part of this treaty, Native Americans ceded significant portions of 1855 treaty reservation land, including land around Lewiston and the gold mining areas around Pierce, to the federal government.

Many of the Nez Perce never signed the treaty and were angry about the loss of reservation land. A military conflict ensued, resulting in the Nez Perce fully complying with congressional and military directives. (*See Northern Idaho, the Nez Perce War*.)

On February 8, 1887, the U.S. Congress passed the Dawes Severalty Act. The Act authorized Native American tribal lands to be surveyed and specific acreages allotted to tribal members. Congress deemed land not so allocated as surplus and available for settlement. In 1935

Vollmer, 1912. Picture courtesy of Michael Peterson.

Congress repealed the law; however, by that time ownership of most former reservation lands was in the hands of non-Indians. (*See Northern Idaho – Dawes Severalty Act*.)

On November 18, 1895, Nez Perce Reservation land became open for settlement by non-Indians. An estimated 5,000 people participated in the land rush.

Many of the settlers who claimed homesteads near what is now Craigmont came at that time. In 1898 a group of settlers established a community about a mile west of what is now Craigmont which they named Chicago.

Postal authorities approved the post office. However, even though there was only one Chicago in Idaho, the settlers experienced many problems with mail deliveries sent to the more famous city in Illinois. In 1902 the settlers renamed their community Ilo, the name of a local leader's daughter.

In the early 1900s railroad interests began planning service from Lewiston to Grangeville. John Vollmer, an officer of the Northern Pacific Railroad, planned to personally profit from the railroad by directing the position of the railroad slightly away from existing communities, purchasing land and platting towns next to the planned stops where the railroad would build depots. His apparent strategy was to get the local businesses and residents to buy his lots next to the railroad tracks.

One of train stops was a mile east of Ilo. Vollmer named the new community after himself and placed it on the northeast side of the tracks.

Vollmer used a similar business strategy of using his influence and insider information to establish or try to establish other Northern Idaho cities. (*See Genesee, Ferdinand and Troy.*)

In 1908 the difficult-to-build Camas Prairie Railroad with high trestles, tunnels and bridges – a joint venture between the Northern Pacific and Union Pacific Railroads – was completed.

Most of the Ilo residents were angry with Vollmer and refused to buy lots in his new town. Instead, they moved their businesses and homes to a newly platted Ilo location on the southwest side of the railroad tracks.

As both communities grew, the railroad track and the antagonism created by John Vollmer's early self-serving actions kept the communities apart. The acrimony between the two towns' citizens became so sharp that residents of one community refused to cross the railroad tracks into the other town.

This conflict played a role in the March 3, 1911, selection of a county seat. At the time, the combined population of Ilo and Vollmer was by far the largest in the newly created Lewis County. However, largely influenced by the acrimony between the two communities, the town of Nezperce received the majority of the vote.

A few years later, the residents' desire to fulfill the needs of their children brought the two communities together. School patrons in both communities voted to consolidate the two school systems. In 1920 largely influenced by the consolidation of the schools, the two towns agreed to merge.

They named their consolidated town Craigmont in honor of Colonel William Craig who was born in Virginia in 1807, later came west, married a Nez Perce woman and in 1841 settled on Lapwai Creek – eight miles from the failed mission started five years earlier by Henry Spalding. Craig was one of the first white men to settle in Idaho and was a respected mediator between the Nez Perce, white settlers and federal representatives.

Incorporation

On June 17, 1920, Craigmont became an incorporated village.

Turning Points

Railroad The railroad was the basis for the founding and development of the communities that became Craigmont. Ilo moved to be near the railroad and Vollmer came as a direct result of it. The railroad provided transportation of farm commodities and rapid movement of passengers and the mail.

School Consolidation The consolidation of the Ilo and Vollmer school systems was the catalyst causing the residents of the two communities to merge into the town they agreed to name Craigmont.

Craigmont Today

Amenities and Attractions Winchester Lake State Park in Winchester is eight miles west of Craigmont. The park offers campsites, yurts, canoeing, biking, cross-country skiing, snowshoeing and fishing on the lake as well as nearby streams.

Economy and Major Employers With over 40 employees, Highland School District is the city's largest employer. Lewiston Grain growers and U.S. Timber Company each have over 20 employees. Small businesses, retail shops and governmental agencies provide most of the city's other jobs.

Education Highland School District operates an elementary school and junior and senior high schools in the city.

Harvesting grain near Craigmont.

The closest institution of higher learning is Lewis-Clark State College 37 miles northwest in Lewiston.

Health Care St. Mary's Hospital in Cottonwood provides most of the city's medical care.

Transportation U.S. Highway 95 intersects the city.

The 2,800-foot runway of Craigmont Municipal Airport provides service to small private and charter aircraft. The closest certified carrier airport is the Lewiston-Nez Perce County Regional Airport.

Utilities and Services Private companies provide electricity, telephone and satellite services. The City provides water and sewer and has a volunteer fire department. The County Sheriff's Office provides police protection under contract with the City.

Vision for 2050

For the past several decades the city's population has ranged between 500 and 600. Historical trends are likely to continue for decades.

In 2050 Craigmont will continue as a small friendly, peaceful agricultural and tourist based community – a wonderful place to live and raise a family.

Looking down at Kamiah.

Kamiah

Statistical Data

Population: 1,297 *
Elevation: 1,263 feet
Precipitation: 23 inches **
Average Snowfall: 92 inches **
County: Lewis (& Idaho)
Website: www.kamiahchamber.com (Chamber of Commerce)

Temperature Range – Fahrenheit: **
Spring: 32 to 72
Summer: 50 to 90
Fall: 31 to 79
Winter: 25 to 46
* U.S. Census Bureau Estimates July 2015
**Historical averages

The city of Kamiah (pronounced Kam-ee-eye and meaning the place of "many rope litters") is on the banks of the beautiful Clearwater River at the eastern edge of the Camas Prairie. Scenic foothills interspersed with fields of hay surround the city. The Clearwater National Forest begins a few miles to the east.

The city is located within the Nez Perce Indian Reservation about 23 miles south of Orofino and 15 miles east of Nezperce.

Pre-Incorporation Years

Long before Euro Americans entered the land of the Clearwater River, the Nez Perce Indian Tribe, called by the Nez Perce "Nimiipuu" (pronounced Nee-Me-Poo), wintered in the Kamiah area, fishing for steelhead. They also harvested dogbane, or Indian hemp, that grew in the area, using the fiber to weave floor mats and a rope they called "Kamia," the derivation of Kamiah's name.

On the return trip from their expedition, the Lewis and Clark Corps of Discovery camped at what is now Kamiah from May 14 to June 9, 1806. They called it Camp Chopunnish, or Long Camp, where they waited for the heavy snows in the rugged Bitterroot Mountains to melt sufficiently for them to cross.

The Corps first encountered the Nez Perce eight months earlier when the Indians provided them with food as they emerged nearly starved onto the Weippe Prairie after crossing the snow-covered Bitterroot Mountains. (*See The Region, Lewis and Clark.*)

Within a few years, trappers and explorers began coming into the region followed by Christian missionaries. In 1838 Asa B. Smith, a Presbyterian clergyman, started a mission to the Nez Perce near Kamiah, which he abandoned two years later. (*See The Region – American Indians; Early Trappers/Explorers; and Early Christian Missionaries.*)

Kamiah, 1912. Courtesy of Michael Peterson.

Until the Treaty of 1846, which fixed the boundary between the U. S. and England (Canada) at the 49th parallel, what is now Idaho was part of Oregon Country, a region claimed by both countries. By 1846 thousands of U.S. citizens had already established settlements in the contested Oregon Country. Many Indians fought against this intrusion, raiding farms and settlements and capturing livestock. The U.S. Army and local militias, in turn, initiated military campaigns against the Indians.

To avoid further conflict, the Nez Perce signed a treaty with the federal government in 1855 to live peacefully on a reservation comprising over a million acres – land on which white settlers would not encroach. A large part of what is now Northern Idaho was included in the original reservation.

Elias Davidson Pierce and a small party of prospectors discovered gold on Nez Perce Reservation land in 1860 near what is now Pierce, about 22 miles due northeast of Kamiah. Within a year, thousands of prospectors flooded the region in what was Idaho's first gold rush. The outnumbered and outgunned Nez Perce were largely powerless to keep the prospectors off their reservation. Two years later, prospectors made other gold discoveries on reservation land. (*See The Region, Gold Mining.*)

First Presbyterian Church was constructed in 1871 on land belonging to Nez Perce Chief Lawyer and continues to be used weekly for worship services. The Nez Perce language is used in its hymns. The church is on the National Register of Historic Places.

With the flood of settlers and miners on reservation land, the federal government moved to appease them by negotiating the Treaty of 1863, which was ratified by Congress in 1867. The new treaty significantly reduced the size of the 1855 reservation. About half of the Nez Perce tribes refused to sign the new treaty.

The Rev. H.T. Crowley, a Congregational minister, opened a mission three miles southeast of Kamiah in 1871. With federal funds and labor provided by Nez Perce adherents to the faith, he constructed a church that still stands.

Six years later, the U.S. Bureau of Indian Affairs ordered the Nez Perce to move to the Lapwai Reservation as specified in the Treaty of 1863. Those who did not sign the treaty, including the famous Chief Joseph, refused to move to Lapwai. A conflict termed the Nez Perce War ensued. (*See The Region, American Indians – Nez Perce War.*)

The State Bank of Kamiah Building is on the National Register of Historic Places.

In one of the war's military engagements, the army attacked and destroyed the Nez Perce village of Chief Lookingglass. The village site five miles east of what is now Kooskia is today part of the Nez Perce National Historical Park.

At the time of the war, the village of Nez Perce Chief Lawyer was encamped near what is now Kamiah. He did not join with the other Nez Perce, preferring to keep his band out of the conflict.

On February 8, 1887, Congress passed the Dawes Severalty Act which authorized Indian reservation lands throughout the nation to be surveyed and specific acreages allotted to tribal members. Congress deemed land not so allocated as surplus and available for settlement. In 1935 Congress repealed the law, but by that time ownership of most former reservation lands was in the hands of non-Indians. (*See The Region, American Indians – Dawes Severalty Act.*)

Kamiah Main Street.

Nez Perce Reservation land became open for settlement by non-Indians on November 18, 1895. An estimated 5,000 people participated in the land rush that included several Camas Prairie communities. Many of the settlers who homesteaded near Kamiah came at that time. (*See The Region, Federal Lands – Private Ownership and Preservation Laws.*)

The Northern Pacific Railroad, now Camas Prairie Railroad, built a rail line from Orofino through Kamiah to Stites in 1900 and in 1905 surveyor James Carlisle platted the community he named Kamiah. (*See The Region, Railroads.*)

Incorporation

On October 19, 1909, Kamiah became an incorporated village. The 1910 census reported the town's population at 324.

In 1967 in accordance with a change in state municipal law, Kamiah became a city.

Turning Points

Railroad The railroad made a significant difference to Kamiah's economy. With the availability of the railroad to transport farm commodities and lumber to market, homesteading, farm production and sawmills flourished.

Sawmills Following the arrival of the railroad, entrepreneurs constructed sawmills that produced the jobs that would underpin the city's economy. (*See The Region, Forest Products.*)

Kamiah Community Library.

Kamiah Today

Amenities and Attractions The city has two parks on four acres. Riverfront Park, along the Clearwater River, has a log amphitheatre, covered picnic area, playground equipment, volleyball court, native plant garden, informational kiosk and murals depicting the city's historic Lewis and Clark and Nimiipuu village heritage. In addition, the park features tiled artwork of four native flora species – biscuit root, camas, clarkia and dogbane.

A boat ramp is located adjacent to Riverfront Park as well as a nature path along the bank of the Clearwater River to Lawyers Creek.

The community encourages public art. In addition to the artwork in Riverfront Park, several murals adorn the downtown area. A three-block area starting at the credit union building and ending at the public library is an art display called Kamiah's Western Victorian Main Street.

DuPont Park on Idaho Street features the Kamiah Community Swimming Pool, outdoor basketball court, playground equipment, picnic tables and skate park.

The Nez Perce Wa A'Yas Community Building has indoor and outdoor basketball courts and facilities for educational services. A softball field is adjacent to the building.

The Kamiah School District Gymnasium is open for youth activities, including basketball, baseball, softball, soccer, football and track.

Just outside of Kamiah is Tommy Robinson Pond, a commercial fishery catering to family fishing. Each year the business sponsors the Spring Youth Fishing Derby.

The Kamiah Welcome Center on Main Street is open from 10 a.m. to 2 p.m. Tuesday through Saturday. The Center houses the original work of John Seven Wilson, a Nez Perce artist. His paintings – Four Seasons of a Nimiipuu Village and a Lewis and Clark Corps of Discovery – are on display along with an historic handcrafted dugout canoe.

The Lewis Clark Historical Society Exhibit Hall on Main Street, is open 10 a.m. to 2 p.m. during the summer. Displays and exhibits include historic farming, medical and dental instruments; artifacts made by early Nez Perce Indians; bones and tusks of a mammoth excavated in Kamiah; and the trunk owned by the McBeth sisters, early Christian missionaries to the Nez Perce.

The historic home of Sue McBeth, the First Presbyterian Indian Church and the Nez Perce National Historical Park Site's "The Heart of the Monster" - an important legend in Nez Perce Indian lore – are in East Kamiah.

The City and community sponsor numerous events throughout the year. The largest annual events include the Save the Pool Crab Feed in January featuring food, a variety show and dancing.

In August, the community sponsors the Chief Lookingglass Powwow, celebrating Nez Perce culture and history, including historic dress and dancing.

The Thursday before Labor Day, the Kamiah Chamber BBQ Days features four days of family fun activities.

Beginning each Thanksgiving, the community celebrates the holiday season with the Festival of Trees, Christmas Light Parade and the Night Before Christmas Bed Race.

One of the city's principal attractions is its easy access to lush forests, quiet mountain streams and clear running rivers. Large numbers of elk, whitetail deer, moose, bighorn sheep, mountain goats, wild turkeys, cougar and black bears roam the vast nearby public lands. Eagles and osprey are common sights along the rivers. City residents and visitors enjoy hiking, sightseeing, white water rafting, horseback riding, backpacking, bicycling, skiing, snowmobiling, snowboarding and ATV riding on the many trails in the area.

U.S. Highway 12 and Idaho Highway 13 are part of the Northwest Passage Scenic Byway which commemorates and frequently parallels or crosses the trail followed in 1805 to 1806 by the Lewis and Clark Corps of Discovery.

The Idaho portion of the Northwest Passage Scenic Byway is 212 miles long. From the western edge of Idaho, the Byway begins at Lewiston and parallels the winding Clearwater River through Orofino and Kamiah to Kooskia where the Byway forks. The eastern fork continues on Highway 12 along the wild and scenic Middle Fork of the Clearwater and Lochsa Rivers before reaching Lolo Pass and the Lewis and Clark Interpretative Center on the Idaho/Montana border. The southern fork follows Highway 13 to Grangeville and the Camas Prairie.

Twelve miles southeast of Kamiah just off U.S. Highway 12 is Lookingglass Camp, one of 38 sites that comprise the Nez Perce National Historical Park. The National Park Service manages the system of parks that follow the trail the Nez

Perce took into four states before those who stopped in Montana fought and surrendered to the U.S. Army.

Economy and Major Employers With 90 employees, the Kamiah School District is the largest employer. Several small businesses, retail and professional establishments and government agencies make up the balance of the city's employment base.

Education The Kamiah School District provides most of the primary and secondary education to the city's children and operates elementary, middle and high schools in the city. There are two faith-based schools and a strong home-school association within the city.

The closest institution of higher learning, Lewis-Clark State College 69 miles northwest in Lewiston, offers workforce training in the city. North Indian College has a distance learning campus located in the Wa A'Yas Community Building. Through a partnership with Elk City, the communities offer training for business startups through Framing Our Community, Inc.

Health Care The closest hospital, Clearwater Valley Hospital in Orofino, has a physical therapy clinic in Kamiah. St. Mary's Hospital in Cottonwood 22 miles southwest also has a medical clinic in the city. Syringa General Hospital in Grangeville is 22 miles north. In addition, the city has a public health clinic and the Nez Perce Tribe operates the Nimiipuu Health Clinic. Private businesses provide assisted living and home health care services.

Transportation U.S. Highway 12 intersects the city. Idaho Highway 13 to Grangeville begins seven miles south at Kooskia. Idaho Highway 168, extending into the Camas Prairie, intersects the city on the west.

City Hall.

The Nez Perce Appaloosa Express offers transportation services between Kooskia, Kamiah, Orofino, Lewiston and Lapwai.

The 3,000-foot runway of Kamiah Municipal Airport provides service to light private and charter aircraft. The closest certified commercial airport is in Lewiston.

Utilities and Services Private companies provide electricity, telephone and satellite services. The City provides water and sewer services and fire and police protection.

Vision for 2050

In 1960 Kamiah's population was 1,245. Since 2000 the population has held at around 1,100. We expect recent population trends to continue for several years. By 2050 Kamiah's population will likely not exceed 1,500. However, the city will continue to honor its rich cultural heritage and be an attractive community nestled between the fertile Camas Prairie and the beautiful Clearwater River and National Forest – a peaceful place to live and raise a family.

Nezperce today.

Nezperce

Statistical Data

Population: 467 *
Elevation: 3,202 feet
Precipitation: 22 inches **
Average Snowfall: 45 inches **
County: Lewis
Website: www.cityofnezperce.com

Temperature Range – Fahrenheit: **
Spring: 29 to 63
Summer: 45 to 81
Fall: 28 to 71
Winter: 22 to 41
* U.S. Census Bureau Estimates July 2015
**Historical averages

Nezperce, the county seat, is located on the Nez Perce Prairie, a broad plateau in eastern Lewis County. The Clearwater River is located about 10 to 20 miles to the east and north. The Clearwater National Forest lies 26 miles northeast and the Nez Perce National Forest is 30 miles southeast.

Nearby cities include Orofino, 24 miles north; Grangeville, 24 miles south; and Kamiah, 16 miles east.

Nezperce is in the heart of the Nez Perce Prairie surrounded by fertile black-soil farms producing a variety of crops including wheat, barley, dry peas, grass, canola and garbanzos.

Extending beyond the city in all directions is the Nez Perce Indian Reservation. The city, named for the Nez Perce Indian Tribe, is French for "pierced nose," although they did not practice nose piercing. The Nez Perce name for themselves is Nimi'ipuu (pronounced Nee-Me-Poo), which means simply "the people" or "we the people."

Pre-Incorporation Years

For centuries, the Nez Perce Tribe of American Indians lived in the warmer river valleys, but passed through what is now Nezperce, hunting and gathering, on their way to their seasonal encampments.

In 1805 about 18 air miles northeast at what is now Weippe, the Nez Perce met and nurtured the starving Lewis and Clark Corps of Discovery as they emerged from making the extraordinarily difficult crossing of the rugged Bitterroot and Clearwater Mountains.

The Nez Perce accompanied the revived Lewis and Clark party to what is now Orofino and assisted them in making dugout canoes that would carry the expedition to the Columbia River and the Pacific Ocean. The Nez

Earliest known photo of Nezperce, circa 1897, looking northeast. Presbyterian Church, constructed in 1897, on left.

Perce provided Lewis and Clark further assistance on their return trip to St. Louis and Washington, D.C., the following year.

Within a few years, trappers and explorers began coming into the region followed two decades later by Christian missionary groups seeking to convert the Indians. In 1838 Asa B. Smith, a Presbyterian missionary, started a mission to the Nez Perce near Kamiah. The mission was not successful and soon closed. (*See Northern Idaho – Early Missionaries*.)

On February 8, 1887, the U.S. Congress passed the Dawes Severalty Act. The Act authorized Native American tribal lands to be surveyed and specific acreages allotted to tribal members with land not so allocated deemed surplus and available for settlement. In 1935 Congress repealed the law. However, by that time, ownership of most former reservation lands was in the hands of non-Indians. (*See Northern Idaho – Dawes Severalty Act.*)

The Felt Mercantile Co. is having a suit sale. Mismatched suit coats and pants were tossed from the roof and the recipients could buy them if they could find a match. Circa 1905.

On November 18, 1895, former Nez Perce Reservation land became open for settlement by non-Indians. An estimated 5,000 people participated in the land rush. One of the land rush participants, George W. Tamblin, selected and platted a townsite on his 160-acre homestead. He called the town "Nezperce City."

Frank Graham, a surveyor working for Tamblin, was quoted in an interview in the Nezperce Herald in 1951: "The year prior to the opening, I worked for a surveyor, George Tamblin, laying out the townsite of Nezperce – mark it off into lots, conceal the markings, which were called bench marks, underneath the tall bunch grass, which then covered the land. A sentinel kept watch and at the approach of meddlers a signal was given and work ceased. Finally, the job was finished and 160 acres of land looked just like the rest of the prairie." For his work, he collected a dollar a lot. There were 690 lots altogether, 526 of which were taken at opening. A block was set aside for a public school and 25 lots reserved as bonuses for the erection of business houses to cost not less than $500 each. Miss Margaret Simons was given two lots for being the first lady in the new town.

Opera House, 1911.

"On the evening of November 17," continued Mr. Graham, "I left Cottonwood in company with my father John Graham, Archie Lee, Ed Ellis and Dave Story. We were on horseback with one man driving a large load of hay and oats. Our job with this load was to block the traffic across Lawyers Canyon, so no one could be on the townsite before 12 o'clock noon – about half way up the grade a wagon wheel broke. Of course traffic was blocked – When the wagon was repaired, there were at least 500 wagons waiting – My job as leader was to keep the caravan from reaching the townsite before noon." It was still early, so Mr. Graham had to take a circuitous route to the townsite wandering around the prairie. He was the only one who knew the location of the townsite. "Finally we made a circle and saw that we had to cross our tracks and that meant the followers, when they discovered that I had been stalling, would be ready to hang me." Graham split off, leaving Nash Wayland to hold the wagons until he reached the northwest corner of town at five minutes of twelve. "Thirty minutes after the government lots in the townsite had been staked, the wagon train came in from Cottonwood, not in a walk, but on the run. By evening it was estimated that from five to ten thousand people were here to camp on the townsite."

The December 4, 1895, edition of the *Lewiston Tribune* reported that Nez Perce had a general store, town hall, barbershop, restaurant and hotel under construction and foundations for many others ready to build as soon as lumber arrived.

The early settlers were unprepared for the rapidly increasing need for public school classroom space. In the next decade, they would build three school buildings. Volunteers built the first schoolhouse in 1896 – a 12-foot-by-24-foot building that also served as a place for public gatherings. In 1898 volunteers replaced the old facility with a larger two-story school. In 1902 voters approved a $5,500 bond to build a larger two-story structure. By 1904 student enrollment reached 302 with larger facilities needed.

Incorporation

In July 1901 Nezperce became an incorporated village with an estimated population of 883 residents. At that time, it had a bustling retail district that served farm families and communities for over a 15 mile radius. Important municipal services became available around the same time.

One of the first projects initiated by the village trustees was to drill a public well. Their plans for a domestic water system took until 1905 to complete. They constructed the system's main waterline with wedge shaped strips of wood bound together with heavy wire. The water caused the wood to swell and kept it leak proof.

Nezperce Horse Racing Association—circa 1913. Horse races were held on the flat east of the 1912 school and the1897 Presbyterian Church. The airport, built in 1947, is now located here.

On March 15, 1901, the first telephone reached Nezperce with the telephone signal carried over barbwire mounted on insulators nailed to fence posts. In 1904 the newly organized "Barbed Wire Company" provided telephone service to Kamiah.

Electric power and streetlights came in 1903 from a privately owned hydroelectric dam on Lolo Creek.

Turning Points

Dawes Severalty Act The 1877 passage of the Dawes Severalty Act opened all Indian reservation lands for settlement. The Act became the legal basis leading to the founding of Nezperce as well as many other non-Indian settlements.

Railroad In 1910 the Nezperce & Idaho Railroad extended a rail line from what is now Craigmont to the city of Nezperce. The railroad that built its line to the Nezperce Roller

Nezperce, circa 1950. Courtesy of Mike Peterson.

Mills and Granaries, the newly erected stockyards and grain warehouse, had a major positive effect on the economy of the city and the agricultural community. Passengers could purchase round-trip fare to Vollmer for $1.00 and Lewiston for $2.40.

County Seat On March 20, 1911, the Legislature created Lewis County with Nezperce as the county seat. This event had an important stabilizing effect on the economy of the town. Largely due to becoming the county seat of government during the following decade, the population of Nezperce grew from 599 (1910 Census) to 677 (1920 Census).

The city's growing population, location and availability of railroad transportation were factors influencing voters to select Nezperce as the county seat. This selection provided a source of stable employment for public and private workers and gave prestige to the new county seat of government.

Nezperce Today

Nezperce downtown airport.

Amenities and Attractions Nezperce has three city parks. Nezperce Memorial Park lies along the banks of Long Hollow Creek. It has a large picnic pavilion, volleyball court and trees honoring departed citizens. There is a small park in the center of town and a few blocks south is a park featuring playground equipment and picnic and BBQ facilities.

The Nezperce Community Library is located in the historic bank building built in 1910. A new 4,200-square-foot library building is under construction.

The Nez Perce National Historical Park is a 38-site park managed by the National Park Service. The sites are in four states – Oregon, Washington, Idaho and Montana. Most of the sites follow the Lewis and Clark Trail and the Trail of the Nez Perce as they fought and fled from the U.S. Army in 1877.

Main Street.

Many of the Idaho sites are within an hour's drive of Nezperce. One of the sites is the park visitors' center near Spaulding, 44 miles northwest of Nezperce on U.S. Highway 95. About 16 miles east, near Kamiah, is Heart of the Monster National Monument – a rock formation that, according to Nez Perce legend, represents the source from which the Nez Perce sprang.

Two Idaho State Parks are near Nezperce. The 418-acre Winchester State Park has a 103-acre lake. It is 20 miles west near Winchester. The 850-acre Dworshak State Park lies about 30 miles north on the western shores of Dworshak Reservoir.

The Clearwater and Nez Perce National Forests nearby offer camping, hiking and backpacking trails, hunting and fishing opportunities.

Downhill skiing is available at Cottonwood Butte Ski Area located 25 miles southwest. Grangeville's Snowhaven is 35 miles south.

The four-day Lewis County Fair takes place the last weekend in September. In addition to usual county fair exhibits and events, the

Before road districts were established, car owners had to maintain and repair roads. This is a gathering circa 1915 preparing to go out to repair roads. Sign reads "Nezperce Road Improvement Club starting out for a day's work."

Nezperce Lions Club sponsors a combine demolition derby that has become an attraction that brings people from throughout the Northwest.

The annual Nez Perce Prairie Day celebration is held every second Saturday in July. This historic celebration of a parade, music, food, kids' events and high school reunions started in 1982.

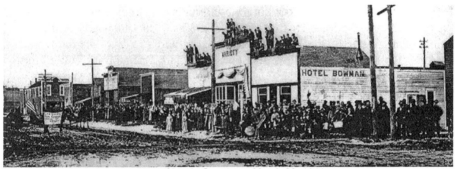

Nezperce celebrated the creation of Lewis County on March 20, 1911.

Economy and Major Employers The largest public employer, with 49 employees, is the Nezperce School District. Lewis County has 45 employees. The largest private employer, a light-equipment manufacturing company, has 30 employees. Other companies – with fewer than 20 employees each – are a grain warehouse, three fertilizer/chemical companies, a grass seed company and two farm equipment dealers.

The city's commercial area consists of a grocery store, two insurance companies, a title company, a barber/beauty shop, two farm implement dealers, a bar, two law offices, a weekly newspaper, a hotel, two restaurants, two crop dusters and a bank. Nezperce also has five churches, a public library and a visitors' center along with a very active and growing senior center.

Education The Nez Perce School District provides elementary and secondary education. Nezperce Elementary and Nezperce High School are both located in the city.

The nearest institution of higher learning is Lewis-Clark State College in Lewiston.

Health Care Nezperce has a general medical clinic. The nearest hospital is St. Mary's Hospital, 18 miles southwest in Cottonwood.

Transportation The north-south Idaho Highway 162 intersects the city. Also intersecting the city are the 15-mile-long Idaho Highway 64 to Kamiah and U.S. Highway 12. U.S. Highway 95 lies 16 miles west at Craigmont.

Airport service for light private and charter aircraft is available at the 2,000-foot runway at Nezperce Municipal Airport in Nezperce. The closest commercial carrier airport is Lewiston-Nez Perce County Airport, located 56 miles northwest in Lewiston.

Utilities and Services Private companies provide electricity, telephone, cable and satellite. The City provides water and sewer services and fire protection. The Lewis County Sheriff's Office provides police protection under contract with the City. The Nez Perce Volunteer Fire Department and EMT provide fire protection and ambulance services.

Vision for 2050

The city's population was 667 in 1960. In the past few decades, the population has stabilized at around 500.

The current downtown revitalization effort has broad-based community involvement.

In the next decade, Nezperce will be a growing, economically vibrant crossroads

Downtown Nezperce.

community at the heart of the Nezperce Prairie.

By 2050 Nezperce will have many of the same small-city characteristics it has today. Honoring its agricultural and family heritage, it will continue to have a peaceful hometown character and environment and be a wonderful place to work, live and raise a family.

Scenery near Reubens.

Reubens

Statistical Data

Population: 72 *
Elevation: 3,514 feet
Precipitation: 21 inches **
Average Snowfall: 67 inches **
County: Lewis
Temperature Range – Fahrenheit: **

Spring: 26 to 60
Summer: 42 to 78
Fall: 26 to 69
Winter: 20 to 40
* U.S. Census Bureau Estimates July 2015
**Historical averages

Reubens is located on the Camas Prairie at the northern edge of Lewis County. Rolling hills of farmland are interspersed with groves of pine and fir, mountain plateaus, ravines and creeks. Two rivers famous for steelhead fishing – the Clearwater and Snake Rivers – are 12 miles north and 23 miles west, respectively. Much of the land surrounding the city is part of the Nez Perce Indian Reservation.

Reubens is a quintessential bedroom community. Substantially all of the city's workforce commutes to other cities for work. Lewiston is about 30 miles west on U.S. Highway 95.

Pre-Incorporation Years

In 1805 Lewis, Clark and the Corps of Discovery first encountered the Nez Perce in the Weippe Prairie 30 miles northeast of what is now the city of Reubens. Prior to that time, the Nez Perce Indians had encampments throughout the region.

On February 8, 1887, the U.S. Congress passed the Dawes Severalty Act. The Act authorized Native American tribal lands to be surveyed and specific acreages allotted to tribal members with land not so allocated deemed surplus and available for settlement. (*See Northern Idaho – Dawes Severalty Act.*)

On November 18, 1895, former Nez Perce Reservation land became open for settlement by non-Indians.

Around 1906 the Camas Prairie Railroad planned to build a rail line between Sweetwater, 15 miles northwest, and Grangeville, 75 miles south. Residents in several scattered communities tried to persuade the railroad to build the line through their towns. The emotions of some of the competing interests reached fever pitch.

The railroad settled the matter by building its rail turnaround stop and depot in a location where a Yellow Pine forest once stood. The railroad named the depot Reubens after James Reubens, a Native American of the Nez Perce Tribe who fought with U.S. troops and served as a government interpreter.

Homesteaders moved in to file their claims. In 1908 the townspeople formed the First Presbyterian Church and built a facility that is still in use and continues to be part of the community's social fabric. In 2006 the city and the First Presbyterian Church celebrated their joint 100th anniversaries at the historic church building.

Incorporation

On January 12, 1912, ten months after the creation of Lewis County, the Lewis County Commissioners approved Reubens becoming an incorporated village.

Turning Points

Railroad The railroad opened the heavily forested land to logging. At its peak, 17 sawmills were located

Grain storage facility.

within four miles of town at which time Reubens had a population of 1,700. As long as the trees lasted, the city prospered. However, beginning in the mid-1900s, market forces and the availability of timber began to have an adverse effect on the area's timber industry. All of the 17 sawmills closed with a devastating effect on the city's economy.

Domestic Water System In 1932 the federal Works Progress Administration built a 30,000-gallon redwood water tank for the city. In 1970 the city replaced the old water tank with a 50,000-gallon metal water reservoir. This water reservoir continues to serve the city.

Fire In the 1950s a fire of unknown origin destroyed most of the city, including the small city hall. City records prior to that date are no longer available.

The town quickly rebuilt a new city hall; however, the facility was built out of white cement block. Unfortunately, the building was too cold, so on cooler days the village trustees held their council meetings in a home where it was warmer.

Reubens residents take pride in their community as they plant trees for Arbor Day 2012

School Consolidation In 1962 the patrons of Reubens, Craigmont and Winchester School Districts determined that their children would get a better education at less cost if they consolidated. They named the new consolidated school district Highland. In 1967 the district sold the school in Reubens.

Natural Disasters In 1962 a devastating hailstorm with hailstones two inches in diameter ruined crops and seriously damaged homes, gardens and roads.

In the late summer of 1973, a huge fire burned hundreds of acres of timber as well as the ripened grain crops that surrounded the town. This had a devastating effect on the Reubens' economy. In 1978 the town grocery store and cafe burned. This left a grain elevator as the town's only business.

Willson Ranch.

Beginning around 1980 smaller family farms began merging or were sold to larger agricultural ventures. Economies of scale and technological innovation allowed larger farmers to be more productive with substantially fewer employees. Bill Thomason, who served as mayor at the time, equated the loss of farm employment equivalent to farming the same amount of land with only one-fifth the previous labor force.

Movie Location In 1978 the city was the location for filming the movie "Breakheart Pass" starring James Bronson and his wife, Jill Ireland. One attraction that drew filmmakers was the Camas Prairie Railroad line on the grade from Lapwai Creek to Reubens. Over a seven-mile stretch, the railroad had seven tunnels and several high wooden trestles crossing deep canyons.

Reubens Today

Amenities and Attractions City residents view their rural setting as an asset. They live in a small peaceful community surrounded by fabulous natural beauty, yet within a short drive of urban shopping and medical services.

Three state parks with excellent fisheries and one national park unit are within a short drive of the city.

The 418-acre Winchester Lake State Park with its 103-acre lake is just 11 miles southwest of the city.

The 850-acre Dworshak State Park in the Clearwater National Forest is 15 miles northwest over the mountains. However, most travelers must drive 40 miles on highways 95 and 12 to get there. The park is at the western edge of the 53-mile-long, 16,000-acre Dworshak Reservoir. The hydroelectric Dworshak Dam, completed in 1973, is 717 feet high and 3,300 feet wide.

Hells Gate State Park is located south of Lewiston, 42 miles away. This 960-acre park is part of the 652,488-acre Hells Canyon National Recreation Area. The Area includes North America's deepest river gorge. This Snake River gorge lies more than a mile below Oregon's west rim and on the Idaho side, more than 8,000 feet below He Devil Peak of the Seven Devils Mountains.

The Nez Perce National Historic Park – managed by the National Parks Service and partially staffed by tribal members – is in Spaulding, 30 miles northwest.

The city and the First Presbyterian Church co-sponsor an annual "sausage feed." The sausage feed is now a regional attraction and an example of the city and the church working together for the betterment of the community.

Train entering town.

Economy and Major Employers Most of the city's workforce commute to their jobs in Lewiston and Craigmont. The only business in town is a grain growers – co-operative that employs two people. There are no other commercial buildings in Reubens – not even a U.S. Post Office.

Education The Highland School District provides elementary and secondary education. Students are bused to Craigmont to school.

Lewis-Clark State College, located in Lewiston, is the closest institution of higher learning.

Health Care The nearest health clinic is in Craigmont. Hospital services are available 30 miles away in either Orofino or Lewiston.

Transportation County Highway P3 intersects the city. Reubens is ten miles west of U.S. Highway 95.

The closest airline service is in Lewiston. Rail service is available for freight.

Utilities and Services Private companies provide electrical, telephone and satellite services. The City provides domestic water. A volunteer fire department provides fire protection. The county sheriff provides law enforcement services. The homes have individual septic systems. Ambulance service is available from Craigmont.

Vision for 2050

In 1960 the city's population was 116. By 1990 it had declined to 46. Subsequently, families seeking affordable housing in a small town with a beautiful natural setting and within a short commute to their jobs and shopping in larger cities have begun moving to Reubens.

In recent years, Reubens population has grown by less than one percent annually. These modest growth trends are likely to continue. By 2050 the city's population will likely exceed 100. This increased population will not cause a significant change in the municipal services needed in the city. The community will continue as a small, quiet, peaceful town in some of the most beautiful locations in Idaho.

Mayors

1953 William J Thomason **
Mid-1960s Bill Thomason
1995 Kathy Johnson
2003 Luke Lowe

* Early city leaders are unknown due to loss of records.
** Village Chairman

Winchester City Hall.

Winchester

Statistical Data

Population: 343 *
Elevation: 3,965 feet
Precipitation: 21.12 inches **
Average Snowfall: 59.4 inches **
County: Lewis

Temperature Range – Fahrenheit: **
Spring: 26 to 60
Summer: 42 to 78
Fall: 26 to 69
Winter: 20 to 40

* U.S. Census Bureau Estimates July 2015
**Historical averages

Winchester, a former sawmill town, lies at the northern edge of the beautiful 418-acre Winchester Lake State Park. The principal feature of the park is its 103-acre trout and bass stocked lake open to small non-motorized boats.

Forests of Ponderosa pine and Douglas fir interspersed by farmland surround the park and city. To the southwest, the Craig Mountains rise to over 6,600 feet.

Lewiston is 27 miles northwest on Highway 95.

Pre-Incorporation Years

Winchester lies within the Nez Perce Indian Reservation. On February 8, 1887, the U.S. Congress passed the Dawes Severalty Act. Under the Act, the federal government allocated acreages of American Indian Reservation lands to individual tribal families and members – generally 160 acres to each family. All land not allocated to tribal members was deemed surplus and available for settlement by non-Indians. (*See Northern Idaho – Dawes Severalty Act.*)

In 1862 Congress passed the Homestead Act. The Act authorized conversion of up to 160 acres of public land to private ownership if the homesteader improved the land and lived on it for five years.

On November 18, 1895, Nez Perce Reservation land was opened for settlement. At that time, homesteaders began filing claims on land in and around what is now Winchester.

Axel Kaline, an early settler, built a general store, planning for it to become the nucleus of the new town.

Residents generally attribute the origin of the town's name of Winchester to a meeting of the early settlers where they discussed potential names. In normal fashion, the

Main Street, circa 1911. Courtesy Museum of Winchester History

settlers carried their rifles to the meeting and leaned them against the inside wall of the building. During the discussion, one settler observed that, since the Winchester Company manufactured most of the settlers' guns, Winchester would be a good name for the town. In 1906 Kaline successfully applied to postal authorities for a post office named Winchester.

In 1909 Wisconsin investors formed the Craig Mountain Lumber Company and began construction of the then largest sawmill in Idaho about a mile from Kaline's store. In the same year, the company began building a six-mile railroad from the mill to the Camas Prairie Railroad at Craig

Winchester Main Street, 4th of July 1911. Courtesy Museum of Winchester History

Junction. In January 1911 freight and passenger service began.

The company also built a waterworks and a hydroelectric dam on Lapwai Creek. The dam created an over 100-acre lake, which also served as a millpond.

Around 1909 the lumber company formed the Winchester Townsite Company, which platted a new town near the mill and built homes for 270 new workers and their families. Kaline moved his store and the Winchester Post Office to the new town. On July 4, 1910, the sawmill cut its first log with state-of-the-art machinery that could cut up to 120,000 board feet of lumber every 10-hour shift.

The company's hydroelectric dam produced electricity for the mill and the city. However, the amount of electrical power generated did not meet all needs. Management devised an electricity rationing plan that generally stayed in effect until 1937 when Washington Water Power began providing service.

Under the rationing plan, the mill switched some of the power to the city in the early morning to facilitate preparation of breakfast and lunch. On Monday and Tuesday, they extended the electricity cutoff time until noon so families could do laundry. The city also received electricity from dark until 10 p.m. on weekdays and midnight on weekends.

Incorporation

On the January 18, 1911, Winchester became an incorporated village in Nezperce County. On March 3, 1911, Winchester became part of Lewis County when the Legislature divided Nez Perce County.

Winchester with mill. Courtesy Museum of Winchester History.

Turning Points

Sawmill The early settlers named the town and established the post office. However, for all practical purposes, Winchester was a company town developed for the sole purpose of meeting the needs of the Craig Mountain Lumber Company and its employees. The community's economy depended on this single business. Consequently, the cyclical fortunes of the mill directly affected the town's economy.

In 1919 following World War I, the lumber market collapsed and the mill shut down. At that time, the company had 30-million board feet of lumber in its yard and another million board feet in its millpond.

In 1922 the company reopened. In 1930 at the beginning of the Great Depression, the declining market forced the mill to close again.

On January 31, 1935, the company reopened the mill and operated it until 1950 when it was sold to Halleck and Holland Lumber Company. In 1960 Boise Cascade Corporation

Railroad trestle.

acquired the mill and operated it for five years before shutting it down for good. The available timber for cutting was too far distant and the lumber market too weak to make continued operation of the mill economically feasible.

Announcement of the mill closure stunned the community. Since the mill underpinned the city's economy, many people had to sell their homes at depressed prices and look for work elsewhere. By 1970 the city had lost nearly 40 percent of its population.

Winchester Lake State Park Governor Robert Smylie and Boise Cascade worked to ameliorate some of the job loss problems faced by city residents. In 1966 Governor Smylie came to town for its 60th anniversary and announced that the State would construct Winchester Lake State Park on the mill site property.

Under the plan, Boise Cascade would clean the site and then donate it to the State for a park. For its part, the company drained the lake and removed the sunken logs, auctioned off all the buildings, mill and railroad equipment it could and in 1967 razed the remaining structures.

To develop the park, the Legislature appropriated $175,000 and the federal government contributed $121,383. The Idaho Department of Parks and Recreation would oversee the development and continued maintenance of the park. The Idaho Department of Fish and Game would keep the lake stocked with rainbow trout and

Winchester Lake State Park.

bass. The project would take five years to complete.

Today, the old millpond – also known as Lapwai Lake – and the surrounding land is a beautiful, well-maintained, year-round modern campground with 69 campsites and four yurts. The State allows small boats on the lake but prohibits gasoline engines.

Fire Throughout its history, fires in commercial buildings posed serious threats to the town's economy. However, the owners or patrons of the buildings generally rebuilt their facilities. The first major fire was the 1910 fire that burned the Craig Mountain Lumber Company planing mill while it was under construction.

A few years later, the city's pool hall and opera house burned. In 1929 fire destroyed the elevator and warehouse. Fire destroyed the hospital in 1932. In 1933 the school burned down. In 1964 fire wiped out most of the city's business block including the post office and grocery store.

Visitors Center.

Highway 95 In 1961 federal and state transportation agencies realigned U.S. Highway 95. The realignment moved the road to the east, bypassing Winchester except for two access roads into the city. One road intersects Highway 95 about a mile to the north and the other road connects with the highway about two miles to the east. This road realignment had an adverse effect on traffic flow through town and the city's economy.

Winchester Today

Amenities and Attractions The city's greatest attraction is Winchester Lake State Park. In addition to the park's camp sites and yurts, visitors and residents enjoy canoeing, biking, cross-country skiing, snowshoeing, fishing in the lake and nearby streams and hunting.

Fire Station.

Many trails suitable for snowmobiling in the winter and ATV riding in the summer start near the city and lead into the Craig Mountains.

The Museum of Winchester History is a wonderful attraction that tells of the area's Nez Perce heritage and early pioneers. It has many photographs of the Craig Mountain Lumber Company mill, millpond, railroad and changes to the town including the fire loss of wooden structures and businesses. It also has displays of hand wrought tools, clothing, household items and fire-fighting equipment that document the struggle of life on the edge of the Camas Prairie.

The Museum has been located in the Community Hall since its beginning in 1965. Museum employees also record oral history stories and recollections from pioneers and their families.

The Greater Craigmont Chamber of Commerce sponsors the Winchester Visitor Center.

The center offers a slide presentation with information about the area. In addition, the city has a public library with computer access.

The nearby Wolf Education & Research Center (WERC) is located on 20 acres of Nez Perce Tribal land. The WERC runs three packs of wolves in its enclosure, the largest enclosures for captive wolves in North America. The WERC is open to the public from Memorial Weekend through Labor Day. Winter visits are by appointment only.

Winchester hosts seven Canadian Intercollegiate Rodeo Association (CIRA) rodeos each year. Winchester Open Rodeo takes place annually in early July. Summer Series Rodeos & Finals take place in June, July and August. Though you must be a member of CIRA to compete, the public is welcome to attend and admission is free.

The city also sponsors the "Bite the Bullet" Bike Race; a 4th of July Celebration on the first Saturday of July, with an open rodeo; Winchester Lake State Park "Paddlefest" in July; "Cadillac Ranch Car Show" in July; Winchester City Wide Yard sale; and Christmas in the Pines Craft Show in November.

Winchester is located on the northeast corner of the Craig Mountain Wildlife Management Area (WMA). This WMA comprises about 140,000 acres under the ownership of several state and federal agencies, the Nez Perce Tribe and the Nature Conservancy. Most of the WMA is open to the public for specified uses and provides habitat for a wide variety of wildlife. Much of the WMA is extremely rugged. The lower portion of the WMA includes the Hells Canyon Gorge on the Snake River, the deepest gorge in the United States.

The Soldier Meadow Lake and Camp area is a primitive campground located about three miles southwest of the city.

Economy and Major Employers Most residents of Winchester commute to Lewiston for work. Many retirees make their homes in the city. Other residents are employees of government agencies or one of several retail shops, stores and motels.

Hollywood movie studios have occasionally come to Winchester to film sequences that include railroad tunnels and tall wooden train trestles

Yurt in the forest.

that cross area gorges. When this has occurred, the studios have employed local residents as extras.

Education The Highland School District provides public education to students in Reubens, Winchester and Craigmont. Each city has an elementary school serving grades 1-6. Students in grades 7-12 ride the bus to Craigmont.

The closest institution of higher learning is Lewis-Clark State College in Lewiston.

Health Care A medical clinic is located in Craigmont. The closest hospitals are St. Mary's Hospital 22 miles south in Cottonwood and St. Joseph Regional Medical Center in Lewiston. Volunteer EMT services are available in the city.

Transportation Winchester is two miles west of U.S. Highway 95. Craigmont Municipal Airport provides service for light private and charter aircraft. Commercial aircraft services are available in Lewiston at Lewiston-Nez Perce County Airport.

Utilities and Services Private utilities provide electricity, telephone, cable and satellite services. The City provides water. Homes and businesses are on individual septic systems. The County Sheriff's Office provides police protection. Winchester's Fire Department has 12 volunteers and a Quick Response Team.

Vision for 2050

Since 1970, Winchester's population has remained somewhat constant at around 300. Existing municipal systems are generally adequate to support such population.

Should the city's population increase, it will likely be due to retirees or families with jobs in Lewiston seeking affordable housing in a forested land near a beautifully maintained lake and park.

Mayors

1911-? Unknown
? Steven Bly

2008 Roger Marks
2010 Randy Stewart

Peck, 1917.

NEZ PERCE COUNTY

- Culdesac
- Lapwai
- Lewiston (County Seat)
- Peck

Culdesac nestled in the valley.

Culdesac

Statistical Data

Population: 379 *
Elevation: 1,680 feet
Precipitation: 24 inches **
Average Snowfall: 52 inches **
County: Nez Perce

Temperature Range – Fahrenheit: **
Spring: 36 to 70
Summer: 54 to 88
Fall: 34 to 77
Winter: 28 to 46
* U.S. Census Bureau Estimates July 2015
**Historical averages

Culdesac is located on the northern Camas Prairie within the Nez Perce Indian Reservation about 20 miles east of Lewiston.

The foothills of the Craig Mountains interspersed with fields of wheat, barley and peas surround the city. Lapwai Creek flows through town.

Pre-Incorporation Years

In 1855 the federal government entered into a treaty with the Nez Perce Indians establishing a reservation that covered a large part of Northern Idaho and Western Washington. However, beginning around 1860 numerous gold prospectors and settlers began moving onto reservation land.

In 1860 prospectors found gold at Pierce. A gold rush ensued with thousands of fortune hunters coming into the region. Almost overnight, Lewiston became a tent city on reservation land as miners, traveling by boat up the Columbia and Snake Rivers to Lewiston, geared up before making their trek to the Pierce gold fields and beyond. (*See Northern Idaho – Mining, Placer Gold.*)

Around 1863 what is now Culdesac was an Outlaw Headquarters named "Shebeen," an Irish name often meaning an illicit bar or club selling alcoholic beverages. Legend has it that the infamous road agent and turncoat California sheriff, Henry Plummer, and his gang stayed there during the time that they were robbing miners working the Elk City and Florence goldfields.

In 1867 Congress, seeking to promote settlement and appease the demands of prospectors and settlers, ratified a new treaty crafted in 1863. As part of this treaty, Native Americans ceded significant portions of 1855 treaty reservation land, including land around Lewiston and the gold mining areas around Pierce, to the federal government.

Many of the Nez Perce never signed the treaty and were angry about the loss of reservation land. A military conflict ensued, resulting in the Nez Perce fully complying with congressional and military directives. (*See Northern Idaho, Nez Perce War*.)

On February 8, 1887, the U.S. Congress passed the Dawes Severalty Act. The Act authorized Native American tribal lands to be surveyed and specific acreages allotted to tribal members. Congress deemed land not so allocated as surplus and available for settlement. In 1935 Congress repealed the law. However, by that time, ownership of most former reservation land was in the hands of non-Indians. (*See Northern Idaho – Dawes Severalty Act*.)

On November 18, 1895, Nez Perce Reservation land became open for settlement by non-Indians. An estimated 5,000 people participated in the land rush.

One of those participating was John McKenzie. He filed his 160-acre homestead claim on land that, in part, would become the site of what is now Culdesac.

Most of the Camas Prairie settlements began around this time. Railroad interests, anticipating heavy freight demand from thousands of farms developing on the prairie, began planning rail service from Lewiston to Grangeville. Mr. Mellon, president of the Northern Pacific Railroad, toured the planned rail route. In 1889 when his party reached what is now Culdesac, he declared the place "a veritable culdesac."

In the fall of that year, the railroad built a train depot at that location and named it Culdesac. In most new towns started by the railroad, incoming mail generally bore the name of the train depot. However, in the case of Culdesac, town residents were not pleased with the name and tried to get it changed. In 1900 hoping postal authorities would see it their way, they applied for a post office named Mellon.

In rejecting their application, postal authorities apparently told them that the name of the train depot that received the mail and the name of the post office needed to be the same, because a year later community leaders made another application. However, this time, they showed their displeasure by keeping the pronunciation of the name but spelling it "Cul-de-sac."

Postal authorities apparently enjoying the "ping pong" game rejected the use of hyphenated words but granted the post office with the name of "Magnolia." In July 1902 community leaders, realizing they were not going to win the battle, made a successful application for a post office named "Culdesac," the same spelling used for the railroad station.

Incorporation

On January 1, 1903, Culdesac became an incorporated village. At that time, the community tapped the water from a large spring and installed a domestic water system.

Turning Points

Railroad Railroad interests established Culdesac in 1889. However, it would take nearly a decade before the difficult-to-build Camas Prairie Railroad with high trestles, tunnels and bridges – a joint venture between the Northern Pacific and Union Pacific Railroads – was completed. Culdesac became the principal shipping center for the hundreds of area farms as soon as the railroad reached the village in 1908.

Farm Consolidation In 1910, seven years after incorporation, the town had a population of 436. The agricultural-based economy grew rapidly until at its heyday in the early1990s it was a regional service and shopping center for hundreds of nearby farm families with a population of about 1,500. At that time, the city had multiple churches, a two-story opera house, bandstand, school, newspaper

Culdesac Main Street, June 27, 2004.

and several retail stores and shops. The town also had several service businesses including hotels, livery and blacksmith shops, banks, a flourmill, barbershops, a mortuary, a doctor, a dentist, a judge, two lawyers and a veterinarian.

In the mid 1900s farm consolidation began rapidly as technological innovation and economies of scale made large-scale farming more profitable. While farm productivity increased, it resulted in significantly fewer farm families and employees coming to town to shop. This decline in workforce has had a significant adverse effect on Culdesac's economy. (*See Northern Idaho – Agriculture.*)

Natural and Manmade Disasters Lapwai Creek has periodically overrun its banks causing significant damage. Culdesac has seen floods in 1904, 1905, 1965 and 1995. On March 20, 1961, the town's flourmill, constructed around 1917, burned to the ground.

Culdesac Today

Amenities and Attractions Culdesac City Park is adjacent to Culdesac School. The park has old-growth trees, children playgrounds, benches and picnic areas, basketball and tennis courts and a walking path that crosses Lapwai Creek. The park has a monument to local men and women who served in the military and a historic fire hose.

Separate from the park on the west side of town is a baseball field and the Culdesac Gun Club and Shooting Range that is often the location for local shooting contests.

Shebang Days, the two-day event named after Culdesac's history as an outlaw headquarters named "Shebeen," starts each year on the first Saturday of June. The event features a parade, breakfast, yard sale, food and craft vendors, games, auctions and street dancing after sundown.

Winchester Lake State Park in Winchester is 12 miles south of the city. The park offers campsites, yurts, canoeing, biking, cross-country skiing, snowshoeing and fishing on the lake as well as nearby streams.

The northeast border of the Craig Mountain Wildlife Management Area (WMA) begins about 15 miles southwest of Culdesac. This WMA comprises about 140,000 acres under the ownership of several state and federal agencies, the Nez Perce Tribe and the Nature Conservancy. Most of the WMA is open to the public for specified uses and provides habitat for a wide variety of wildlife. Much of the WMA is extremely rugged. The lower portion of the WMA includes the Hells Canyon Gorge on the Snake River, the deepest gorge in the United States.

Economy and Major Employers The Culdesac School District has 36 employees and is the city's largest employer. Several commercial businesses including a bank, a hardware store, a seed mill, a log-furniture manufacturer, a bar, a library, a grocery market, a post office and grain silos provide the balance of the jobs in the city. Some of the city's workforce commute to Lewiston for their employment.

Education The Culdesac School District provides most of the K-12 education. The district has a single complex that houses an elementary, middle and high school as well as the district offices.

The nearest institution of higher learning is Lewis-Clark State College in Lewiston.

Health Care The closest hospital is St. Joseph Regional Medical Center in Lewiston.

Transportation Culdesac lies on the northern edge of U.S. Highway 95. Airline service is available at the Lewiston-Nez Perce County Airport.

Utilities and Services Private companies provide electricity, telephone and satellite services. The City provides water and sewer services and fire protection through a volunteer fire department. The Nezperce County Sheriff's Office provides police protection.

Vision for 2050

In 1960 the city's population was 209. The 2000 census reported the city's population at 378. Since that time, the population has remained somewhat constant. Recent trends will likely continue, in which case by 2050 the city's population will approach 500.

Lapwai City Hall.

Lapwai

Statistical Data

Population: 1,149 *
Elevation: 940 feet
Precipitation: 18 inches **
Average Snowfall: 19 inches **
County: Nez Perce
Website: http://cityoflapwai.com

Temperature Range – Fahrenheit: **
Spring: 36 to 70
Summer: 54 to 88
Fall: 34 to 77
Winter: 28 to 46
* U.S. Census Bureau Estimates July 2015
**Historical averages

The city of Lapwai (pronounced Lap-way), the seat of government for the Nez Perce Indian Nation and the northern Idaho location of the federal Bureau of Indian Affairs, lies in the Lapwai Valley on the Nez Perce Indian Reservation. Gentle rolling hills overlook the valley through which Lapwai Creek flows.

Three miles north, Lapwai Creek combines with the Clearwater River. Lewiston is 12 miles west.

Pre-Incorporation Years

In 1805 assisted by Nez Perce Indians, the Lewis and Clark Corps of Discovery floated hewn canoes down the Clearwater River as they passed through the area on their quest to find a Northwest Passage to the Pacific Ocean. (*See Northern Idaho, Lewis and Clark*.)

In 1836 Henry and Eliza Spalding, Presbyterian missionaries, established a mission at this location that they named Lapwai, a Nez Perce word meaning "the place of butterflies." The Spalding's taught Christianity and farming principles to the Nez Perce and opened a school. Soon Nez Perce families began cultivating garden plots near the mission. (*See Northern Idaho, Early Christian Missionaries*.)

In 1841 the first overland migration of settlers came into what was then called Oregon Country, a territory claimed by tribes of American Indians, England and the United States.

Fort Lapwai.

Also in 1841 Colonel William Craig, a mountain man who had married a Nez Perce woman, settled on Lapwai Creek, eight miles from Spalding's mission. Craig befriended the Nez Perce and taught irrigation and farming skills. He was a respected mediator between the Nez Perce and federal representatives. He defended the Indians from Spalding's sometimes abusive treatment and protected Spalding when the Indians wanted to punish him. The Nez Perce Treaty of 1855 exempted Craig's property from Nez Perce reservation land, and in 1920 the citizens of Craigmont named their town after him.

In 1942 as part of its "Manifest Destiny" philosophy, Congress sponsored an exploration party led by Captain John C. Fremont to map trails and write physical descriptions of the land that pioneers could follow in settling the West. As soon as Congress published Fremont's maps and findings, tens of thousands of settlers began heading West on the Oregon Trail, many headed to the Willamette Valley in Oregon.

Teepees in the Lapwai area.

In the Treaty of 1846 between the U.S. and Great Britain, England released claims to Oregon Country below the 49th Parallel.

In 1847 when prospectors found rich deposits of placer gold in California, the ensuing gold rush brought an even larger migration. The California Gold Rush prompted a flow of fortune seekers scouring the mountains and streams throughout the West.

In 1855 the Nez Perce chiefs entered into a treaty with the federal government that included specifying Nez Perce reservation lands generally in Northern Idaho and western Washington.

However, in the ensuing years non-Indian gold prospectors and settlers moved onto reservation land. In 1860 prospectors found gold at Pierce. A gold rush ensued with thousands coming into the region. Almost overnight, Lewiston, which was then on reservation land, became a tent city as miners, traveling by boat up the Columbia and Snake Rivers to Lewiston geared up before making their trek to the Pierce gold fields and beyond.

In 1862 in response to Nez Perce complaints about non-Indians invading reservation land in violation of the 1855 Treaty, the U.S. Army built Fort Lapwai. However, the military's ability to stop and remove the thousands of prospectors from the reservation proved ineffective.

In 1867 Congress, seeking to promote settlement and appease the demands of prospectors and settlers, ratified a new treaty that had been crafted in 1863. In that treaty, the Nez Perce ceded significant portions of 1855 Treaty reservation land, including land around Lewiston and the gold mining areas around Pierce, to the federal government.

Lapwai, circa 1930. Courtesy Michael Peterson.

Some of the Nez Perce chiefs did not sign the treaty, and they were angry about the loss of reservation land. In 1877 a series of military battles ensued wherein the Nez Perce eventually surrendered to the U.S. Army and most of the surviving Nez Perce returned to live on their smaller Lapwai Reservation. (*See Northern Idaho, the Nez Perce War.*)

On February 8, 1887, the U.S. Congress passed the Dawes Severalty Act. The Act authorized Native American tribal reservation lands to be surveyed and specific acreages allotted to tribal members. Congress deemed land not so allocated as surplus and available for non-Indian

Lapwai Community Library.

settlement. In 1935 Congress repealed the law; however, by that time ownership of most former reservation lands was in the hands of non-Indians. (*See Northern Idaho – Dawes Severalty Act – Opening Reservation Land for Settlement.*)

In 1889 the Northern Pacific and Union Pacific Railroads formed a partnership called the Camas Prairie Railroad. It connected Lewiston with the agriculture and timber areas of the Palouse and the Camas Prairie. By stopping in Lapwai, the railroad had an important effect on the city's economy, providing transportation for the city's commerce and residents.

On November 18, 1895, Nez Perce Reservation land became open for settlement by non-Indians. An estimated 5,000 people participated in the land rush. Most of the Camas Prairie settlements began around this time.

Incorporation

On January 30, 1911, Nez Perce County Commissioners approved incorporation of Lapwai as a village.

Nimiipuu Health.

Turning Points

Treaty of 1863 Even though the treaty of 1863 was not signed by all of the Nez Perce chiefs, it established the Lapwai Reservation and led to the establishment of Lapwai, subsequently becoming the seat of government for the Nez Perce Nation and the Northern Idaho location for the federal Bureau of Indian Affairs.

Lapwai Today

Amenities and Attractions The Lapwai City Park is located next to City Hall and includes playground equipment, a sand pit, lighted horseshoe pits, picnic tables and a powered arbor for performances or concerts.

Post Office.

The 652,488-acre Hells Canyon National Recreation Area (HCNRA), including the 960-acre Hells Gate State Park, is located approximately 20 miles west of Lapwai. The HCNRA includes North America's deepest river gorge, which forms the Idaho/Oregon border. On the Oregon side, the gorge lies more than a mile below the rim. On the Idaho side, the gorge is more than 8,000 feet below He Devil Peak of the Seven Devils Mountains.

The HCNRA provides opportunities for hiking, camping, swimming, boating, horseback riding, hunting and fishing.

The Spalding Museum and Memorial Park are located four miles north on the Nez Perce Reservation in Spalding. The museum includes artifacts and exhibits of the historic Spalding mission to the Nez Perce tribe.

The Nez Perce National Historic Park is comprised of 38 sites scattered across Idaho, Oregon, Washington and Montana. Old Fort Lapwai, located in the city, is one of these sites; Spalding is another.

Economy and Major Employers With approximately 270 employees, the Nez Perce Tribe is the city's largest employer. Several small businesses, restaurants and retail shops provide most of the city's other employment. The Lapwai School District is also a major employer.

Education The Lapwai School District provides most of the K-12 education. The district operates an elementary school, middle school, high school and alternative school in the city.

The closest institutions for higher learning are the Lapwai Campus of the Northwest Indian College and Lewis-Clark State College in Lewiston.

Women's Shawl Dance.

Health Care The closest hospital is the St. Joseph Regional Medical Center in Lewiston.

Transportation U.S. Highway 95 intersects the city. Commercial air service is available at the Lewiston-Nez Perce County Airport. Railroad service is available in the city for freight.

Utilities and Services Private companies provide electricity, telephone and satellite services. The City provides water and sewer services and fire and police protection.

Vision for 2050

For more than a decade, the city's population has remained stable at just over 1,100. These historical population trends will likely continue into the foreseeable future.

Aerial view of Lewiston.

Lewiston

Statistical Data

Population: 32,482 *
Elevation: 738 feet
Precipitation: 12.8 inches **
Average Snowfall: 18 inches **
County: Nez Perce
Website: www.cityoflewiston.org

Temperature Range – Fahrenheit: **
Spring: 36 to 70
Summer: 54 to 93.3
Fall: 34 to 77
Winter: 28 to 40.4
* U.S. Census Bureau Estimates July 2015
**Historical averages

Lewiston lies at the confluence of the Snake and Clearwater Rivers on the Washington/Idaho Border. The city is an inland seaport to the Pacific Ocean. In 1861 steamers brought prospectors up the Columbia and Snake Rivers to Lewiston where they disembarked and made their way west for 60 miles to the goldfields at Pierce. Today, barges carry commodities of agricultural and wood products 465 miles from the Port of Lewiston to docks on the Pacific Coast.

To the north of the city are the high cliffs of the Palouse plateau and broad stretches of fertile farm land. To the east are farms, the Nez Perce Indian Reservation and the canyons and mountains through which the Clearwater River flows. To the south are the deep gorges of Hells Canyon cut by the Snake River. Across the Snake River to the west is Clarkston, Washington, and vast tracts of farm and public lands.

Pre-Incorporation Years

For millennia, Nez Perce American Indian tribes migrated seasonally throughout the Inland Northwest. In September 1805 Meriwether Lewis, William Clark and their Corps of Discovery emerged onto the Weippe Prairie, 50 miles west of what is now Lewiston, hungry and weak from crossing the rugged Bitterroot Mountains. There they met villages of Nez Perce Indians harvesting camas lily bulbs. The Nez Perce provided the Corps with food, directions and assistance in making dugout canoes.

On October 10, 1805, the Lewis and Clark expedition rode their newly built canoes down the Clearwater River to what is now Lewiston. There they traded with the Nez Perce for food and camped for the night.

Lewiston, circa 1862.

During the next five decades, explorers/trappers and Christian missionaries came into the area to establish trading posts and missions among the Nez Perce.

The most notable two missions in the Lewiston area were those begun in 1836 by the Presbyterian Church and led by Henry H. and Eliza Spalding and Dr. Marcus and Narcissa Whitman.

The Whitman mission was with the Cayuse Indians about 60 miles southwest of what is now Lewiston and near Walla Walla, Washington. Dr. Whitman provided medical care for both Indian and white patients alike. The whites generally recovered; however, many Indians died. In the winter of 1846 to 1847, the Cayuse attacked the mission, killing the Whitman's and many others.

The Spalding mission to the Nez Perce was located about 12 miles east of what is now Lewiston at Lapwai. One of Spalding's converts was Old Joseph – father to Chief Joseph, who was born in 1840 and became one of Idaho's famous Indian leaders.

Spalding successfully taught the Nez Perce how to farm and raise livestock. However, the Whitman massacre sent shockwaves through the area. Henry and Eliza abandoned their mission, leaving it in the hands of their Nez Perce converts.

In late 1860 Captain E.D. Pierce, who had previously scouted the area, led a band of gold prospectors onto the Nez Perce Reservation without permission.

Pierce's party discovered large quantities of placer gold near what is now Pierce. A major gold rush ensued with further discoveries at Elk City and Florence. At one time, over 10,000 fortune seekers were working in the mountains to the east and southeast of Lewiston. Except for their 1855 Treaty with the U.S. government that had practical enforcement limitations, the 2,000 Nez Perce were at a distinct disadvantage in terms of numbers.

Steamships began bringing prospectors and supplies up the Columbia and Snake Rivers to the confluence of the two rivers. The steam ships dropped off their cargo on Nez Perce Reservation land at what is now Lewiston.

Steamships came up the Columbia River to Idaho's only seaport at Lewiston.

In order to avert potential armed conflict, the Federal Bureau of Indian Affairs negotiated a modification to the 1855 Treaty. The modification allowed miners and prospectors the temporary use of reservation land, provided the U.S. troops stationed at Fort Lapwai would keep peace and order. The agreement excluded from mining activity specified areas used by the Nez Perce to camp and gather food. Further, when the mines played out, the visitors were to leave the reservation.

As the fortune hunters came through, they were astonished to see how many of the Nez Perce, under the former tutelage of the Spaldings, had adapted to cultivating the land. In 1861 Dr. G.A. Nobel reported to the Oregon City Argus that, "These Indians have some fine crops here, well-fenced and apparently well-cultivated both chickens and eggs [were for sale]."

In May 1861 the Oregon Steamship and Navigation Company established a settlement at the drop-off site named Lewiston after Meriwether Lewis. In October 1861 they contracted with Dr. J.B. Buker to plat the Lewiston townsite.

Under the agreement with the Bureau of Indian Affairs, the settlers could not construct permanent structures on reservation land. Therefore, Lewiston soon became a

Lewiston Main Street, 1907.

community of canvas tents nicknamed "Ragtown." By 1862 around 2,000 people lived in the town. Lewiston had a reputation as a wild, lawless town, with considerable gambling, robbery, prostitution, violence and murder.

A marker at the foot of 13th Street Grade illustrates the criminal element that existed at the time. The marker describes the events surrounding the first trial by an Idaho court. It began in 1863 and culminated with the March 1864 hanging of the three robbers and murderers of Lloyd Magruder, a prominent Northern Idaho packer and trader, and his four traveling companions.

This intriguing story combines criminal conspiracy with the alert and persistent work of Hill Beachy, a Lewiston hotelier and Magruder's friend. Beachy became a deputized sheriff, received gubernatorial cooperation between jurisdictions, led a criminal pursuit and capture of the murderers in San Francisco, returned them to Lewiston for trial and execution and retrieved stolen gold for return to the widow and children.

The story ends with the Idaho Territorial Legislature appropriating $6,244 to defray the costs incurred by Beachy in solving the case, pursuing the felons and bringing them to justice. (*See History of Idaho, Volume 1, Leonard J. Arrington, pages 217-220 for the full story.*)

Even though Lewiston residents lived on land owned by the Nez Perce, they bought and sold lots as though they had legal ownership – essentially forcing the Nez Perce off the land. Seeking to avoid armed conflict, town residents negotiated a lease with the Nez Perce for townsite land.

Lewiston Main Street, 1925.

On March 4, 1863, President Abraham Lincoln signed the Organic Act creating Idaho Territory. As sovereign nations, American Indian Reservation lands were not part of the territory.

On June 9, 1863, the Bureau of Indian Affairs reached agreement with about half of the Nez Perce Nation to reduce the size of the reservation. The Nez Perce Tribes – led by Old Joseph and, later, Chief Joseph – refused to sign the 1863 treaty. This was one of the factors contributing to the Nez Perce War of 1877.

The new boundaries of the 1863 treaty removed Lewiston from the reservation. However, Congress did not ratify the treaty until April 20, 1867, thus delaying the effective date of the treaty. Most non-Indians disregarded the legal timing of events and proceeded as though the 1863 treaty was immediately in effect.

Under the Organic Act, the territorial governor could designate the territory's temporary capital; however, establishing the permanent site required legislation. Idaho's first territorial governor, William H. Wallace, called the Legislature to convene its first session on December 7, 1863, in the more accessible town of Lewiston.

However, before the legislative session started, Wallace resigned as governor and left for Washington, D.C., as the territorial delegate to Congress, leaving the territorial secretary as acting governor. President Lincoln appointed Caleb Lyon as Wallace's successor. Lyon arrived in Lewiston in August 1864 in time to be present for the second legislative session in December.

Before Lyon arrived, the goldfields to the east of Lewiston were playing out. The population in the region had fallen by 90 percent. Lewiston's 1862 population had declined to 365.

By 1863 gold discoveries in the Boise Basin had attracted over 16,000 prospectors, miners and settlers. By the end of that year, the Boise Basin population was second only to Portland as the most populous area in the Northwest.

On December 7, 1864, the Second Territorial Legislature passed landmark legislation, signed by Governor Lyon, making Boise the state's first chartered city, creating Ada County and establishing Boise as the permanent territorial capital.

Citizens of Lewiston and Northern Idaho were outraged and filed suit alleging the law was invalid because the Legislature met six weeks before their official term of office began.

Lewiston Probate Judge John G. Berry sided with the plaintiffs. He issued an injunction against removal of the Territorial Seal and artifacts from Lewiston and summoned Governor Lyon to appear in court and answer the charges.

Under the guise of a duck hunting trip, Lyon crossed the river into Washington Territory. Unable to arrest Lyon,

Port of Lewiston, Idaho's only seaport.

the sheriff carried out the balance of the court order by locking the Great Territorial Seal of Idaho and the territorial archives in the Lewiston jail.

In Lyon's absence, the Territorial Secretary, Clinton DeWitt Smith, became acting governor with authority over federal personnel in the territory. On March 2, 1865, Smith dispatched federal troops to Lewiston to retrieve the Seal and artifacts from the jail and rendezvous with him outside the city.

On April 14, 1865, Smith entered Boise with the Seal and artifacts. However, that did not end the dispute. Lewiston officials appealed the matter to the territorial district judge who sustained the ruling of the lower court.

Smith appealed the case to the newly created Idaho Territorial Supreme Court in Boise. On June 14, 1866, the Supreme Court overturned the district court, thus establishing Boise as the legal capital of Idaho Territory.

With the mining traffic through Lewiston gone, agriculture and timber became Lewiston's economic base. During the 1870s farmers and ranchers began staking homestead claims and moving into the surrounding area. Wheat was the major crop.

In 1874 E.B. True prepared a plat of Lewiston and filed it with the County. A year later the city completed the Lewiston Ditch, that for over 15 years, flowed through the city providing water for lawns, gardens, flowers and domestic use.

In 1880 the Territorial Legislature made the Lewiston Independent School District Idaho's first chartered school district.

Incorporation

In 1881 the Territorial Legislature made Lewiston a chartered city. It was the second of Idaho's three chartered cities – Boise being first and Bellevue third.

In 1893 the Legislature amended the charter to allow the city to levy additional taxes and incur indebtedness for public works projects. In 1969 in order to allow the city to annex the "Orchards" area, Lewiston had to give up its historic charter. The annexation doubled Lewiston's population.

Turning Points

Territorial Boundary Disputes From 1864 when Boise became the territorial capital until statehood, the question of Northern Idaho's territorial boundary was a hotly debated issue, both locally and in Washington, D.C. One faction – initially led by Alonzo Leland, editor of The Lewiston Teller – sought annexation of Northern Idaho into Washington Territory. Later, the mining interests of the Silver Valley wanted to become part of Montana. Still others sought to put Southern Idaho into Nevada.

The annexation efforts culminated in 1887 with Congress passing a North Idaho annexation bill. However, Idaho Territorial Governor Edward A. Stevenson appealed to President Grover Cleveland to veto the bill, and President Cleveland complied. He vetoed the bill after Congress adjourned, thus eliminating any chance for an override election. Subsequent annexation attempts failed. Idaho's statehood in 1890 effectively put an end to further credible annexation attempts.

County Seat Idaho's first Territorial Legislature created Nez Perce County on February 4, 1864, with Lewiston as the county seat. Around 1883 Moscow and other residents north of the Clearwater River petitioned the Territorial Legislature to separate from Nez Perce County. The Legislature denied the petition, but passed a bill allowing county residents to vote on the location of their county seat. The county held an election with the majority voting to keep the county seat in Lewiston.

The Moscow and North Nez Perce County citizens lobbied the U.S. Congress. In 1888 Congress passed legislation splitting Nez Perce County and creating Latah County. Lewiston continued as county seat of a much smaller Nez Perce County.

Flood Control and Dworshak Dam Spring flooding was a constant threat. In the spring of 1894 the Clearwater dike broke and floodwaters wreaked havoc in the city. Lewiston quickly rebuilt. In 1971 the U.S. Army Corps of Engineers built Dworshak Dam on the North Fork of the Clearwater River near Orofino, substantially eliminating future flooding risks.

Lewis-Clark State College In 1893 the Idaho Legislature created the Idaho State Normal School, now Lewis-Clark State College (LCSC). The school has consistently had a major positive influence on the city's culture and quality of life.

Railroad In 1889 the Northern Pacific and Union Pacific Railroads formed a partnership called the Camas Prairie Railroad. It connected Lewiston with the agriculture and timber areas of the Palouse and the Camas Prairie.

The Camas Prairie Railroad received recognition as the "railroad on stilts" because of the high trestles required over the many mountainous ravines it crossed. For example, one five-mile stretch had a dozen trestles.

Potlatch Around 1927 Potlatch Corporation constructed a large sawmill in Lewiston. In 1950 Potlatch Forests, Inc., a merger of Potlatch Corporation and two other companies, built a paper mill in Lewiston that produced bleached pulp and paper, paperboard, milk cartons, paper plates and tissue paper. The paper mill still stands and is Lewiston's largest employer.

Idaho's Seaport In 1934 entrepreneurs formed the Inland Empire Waterways Association. The Association appealed to the Army Corps of Engineers (Corps) to assist in building an inland waterway that allowed commercial barge traffic. In 1938 the Corps submitted a report to Congress recommending a waterway to the Pacific Ocean, which included dredging and additional dams on the Clearwater, Snake and Columbia Rivers.

Congress approved the recommendations, and by 1975 the Corps completed the recommended work. The Corps also constructed dikes to protect the city from the rising slack waters produced by the dams and levees. The dykes became beautiful landscaped amenities including trees, shrubs, bike and pedestrian paths and picnic areas.

Entrepreneurs built the Port of Lewiston. Barges with drafts of up to 14 feet and load capacities of 12,000 tons now provide non-stop shipment of cargoes of grain and wood products between Lewiston and Coastal ports.

Lewiston City Hall.

Lewiston Today

Amenities and Attractions Lewiston is home to Lewis-Clark State College. The school has 3,500 students and is located on a 46-acre campus in a residential part of Lewiston. This four-year public institution is one of the city's prominent focal points. It is not only a major employer, but it is a workforce training center and a major contributor to the city's culture and way of life.

Lewiston has 368 acres dedicated to parks, cemetery, golf course and open spaces at 35 locations throughout the city.

Pioneer Park is the oldest park. It includes a band shell and statues of Lewis and Clark and Sacagawea. Kiwanis Park is located on the Snake River, with plenty of space for picnics. Sunset Park includes playground equipment, tennis courts and a softball field. Other park amenities include two swimming pools; 17 baseball/softball diamonds; 19 tennis courts; two basketball courts; a birling pond, a lumberjack competition consisting of walking on floating logs; a kids fishing pond; and a skateboard park. Locomotive Park is located at the southeast approach to Memorial Bridge. The park's primary exhibit is the last steam-powered logging locomotive used by Potlatch Corporation. The locomotive started service in June 1924 and retired in 1953.

There are four year-round 18-hole golf courses. Two are country clubs. Bryden Canyon and Quail Ridge are public links.

The levee system provides 27 miles of National Recreation Trail for walkers, runners and bikers.

Prominent annual events include the Dogwood Festival that takes place each April. The weeklong event takes place under the blossoms of the dogwood trees found throughout the valley. Activities include garden tours; sporting events; concerts; plays and "Art under the Elms," an arts and crafts fair on the LCSC campus.

Entertainment and opportunities for self-expression are available through the Lewiston Civic Theatre, chamber orchestras and the Washington Idaho Symphony.

The Center for the Arts in downtown Lewiston sponsors events and exhibitions showcasing local and regional artists and authors.

Each September, The Lewiston Roundup Association sponsors a signature rodeo, parade and other attractions. The event, which started in 1935, is the longest running community event in the Lewiston-Clarkston area.

During each Thanksgiving week, the Lewiston Chamber of Commerce sponsors the Snake Clearwater Steelhead Derby.

Boating and fishing enthusiasts enjoy the close proximity to the Snake and Clearwater Rivers. Numerous boat launches in Lewiston and nearby Clarkston provide easy access to the rivers. One popular sport is fishing from rafts, drift boats and jet boats for Steelhead, bass, white sturgeon, trout, Kokanee and Chinook salmon. Other anglers fish from the riverbanks.

The 652,488-acre Hells Canyon National Recreation Area (HCNRA), including the 960-acre Hells Gate State Park, is located three miles south of Lewiston. The HCNRA includes North America's deepest river gorge. The Snake River gorge forms the Idaho/Oregon border. On the Oregon side, the gorge lies more than a mile below the rim. On the Idaho side, the gorge is more than 8,000 feet below He Devil Peak of the Seven Devils Mountains.

The HCNRA provides opportunities for hiking, camping, swimming, boating, horseback riding, hunting and fishing.

The Nez Perce Indian Reservation is located at Lapwai, 14 miles southeast of Lewiston. Descendents of Chief Joseph's band live on the Reservation.

The Spaulding Museum and Memorial Park are located on the Clearwater River 11 miles east of Lewiston on the Nez Perce Reservation in Spalding. The museum includes artifacts and exhibits of the historic Spalding mission and the Nez Perce Tribe.

The Nez Perce National Historic Park is comprised of 38 sites scattered across Idaho, Oregon, Washington and Montana. One of these sites is at Spalding.

Clarkston, Washington, which is about half the size of Lewiston, lies immediately across the Snake River. From a practical standpoint, the legal boundary between the two cities is transparent. Residents of each city often patronize businesses and attractions of the other. One of Clarkston's prominent attractions is the Asotin County Aquatic Center, a family water park.

Economy and Major Employers Potlatch Corporation's paper mill employs over 2,000 and is the city's largest private employer. St. Joseph Regional Hospital; LCSC; and Alliant Techsystems, an aerospace and defense contractor, each have from 600 to over 800 employees and are the next largest employers.

Several other businesses support the operation of the Port of Lewiston. As a regional shopping, health care and business center, the city has several retail, hospitality and service businesses. Numerous light manufacturing businesses also operate in or near the city. The manufacture of welded aluminum jet boats has become one of Lewiston's signature industries. The nearby diversity of river experiences is excellent for testing the boats sold worldwide.

Education Lewiston School District provides most of the K-12 education for the Lewiston area. The district has a high school, two junior high schools and seven elementary schools operating in the city. In addition, four parochial schools are located in Lewiston.

Lewis-Clark State College offers technical, professional, arts and science baccalaureate degrees and vocational programs.

Health Care St. Joseph Regional Medical Center provides most of the health care needs of area residents. There are also several medical clinics and offices and six convalescent and assisted living centers in the city.

Transportation U.S. Highways 95 and 12 intersect the city. Highway 12 is a major part of Idaho's Northwest Passage Scenic Byway. For over 90 miles, the Byway parallels or follows the rugged and beautiful trail of the Lewis and Clark expedition from Lewiston east to Lolo Pass and the Idaho/Montana border.

Freight transportation is available for railroad, barge, truck or air. Luxury riverboats provide passenger service between Lewiston and Portland, Oregon.

Commercial and private airline service is available at the Lewiston-Nez Perce County Airport.

Utilities and Services Private companies provide electric, telephone, natural gas, cable and satellite services. The City provides police and fire protection, emergency medical services, water and sewer.

Vision for 2050

For the past several years, Lewiston's population has held somewhat steady at about 31,000. However, the city has adopted strategic plans to promote moderate growth of about one to two percent annually. In that event, by 2050 Lewiston's population could exceed 50,000.

These plans include supporting the city's existing economic base and encouraging more light manufacturing and hospitality businesses. Lewiston's strategic location as a regional business and educational center with numerous tourist attractions gives the city a valuable basis to promote this growth.

The city's existing municipal systems, with routine maintenance and improvements, should be adequate to meet the requirements for this moderate rate of growth.

Mayors

1862 Robert Dyson
1863 M.A. Kelly
1867 T.G. Wright
1871 Levi Ankeny
1874 Henry Stainton
1876 S.C. Hale
1877 N.B. Holbrook
1878 S.C. Hale
1879 A. Gillman
1880 T.S. Billings
1881 S.C. Hale
1882 Ezra Baird
1885 J.B. Menomy
1886 M.A. Kelly
1887 Lafayette Rowley
1887 J.M. Howe
1888 Jasper Rand
1889 D.M. White
1891 S.C. Hale
1892 Chas G. Kress
1894 S.C. Hale
1895 C.E. Monteith
1896 Geo. E. Erb
1897 Thomas Cooper
1899 Chris Weisgerber
1900 R.C. Beach
1901 W.H. Skinner
1903 Chas G. Kress
1905 Henry Heitfeld
1909 Ben F. Tweedy

1911 L.J. Perkins
1913 J.B. Morris
1915 L.J. Perkins
1917 C.F. Osmers
1921 Wm. Thomson
1925 E.G. Braddock
1931 Ray J. White
1937 Eugene J. Bauman
1941 R.R. McGregor
1943 Verner R. Clements
1945 Leo J. Morgan
1949 Ardie Gustafson
1951 D.KI. Worden
1959 Marvin Dean
1962 G.H. Williams
1964 Paul Wise
1970 Ronald Jones
1974 Leonard E. Williams
1976 Richard J. Adams
1978 Duane St. Marie
1980 Delitha Kilgore
1982 Gene Mueller
1987 Marion Shinn
1988 Delitha Kilgore
1992 Lovetta Eisele
1994 Gayle McGarry
1998 Jeffrey G. Nesset
2006 Doug Havens
2010 Kevin Poole
2014 James Kleeburg

Peck Community Library.

Peck

Statistical Data

Population: 201 *
Elevation: 1,089 feet
Precipitation: 25 inches **
Average Snowfall: 111 inches **
County: Nez Perce

Temperature Range – Fahrenheit: **
Spring: 34 to 72
Summer: 52 to 90
Fall: 33 to 80
Winter: 26 to 46
* U.S. Census Bureau Estimates July 2015
**Historical averages

Peck is located in narrow valley a mile and a half south of the Clearwater River. Forested hills, canyons and mountains surround most of the city and valley.

A high percentage of the surrounding land is part of the Nez Perce Indian Reservation. Orofino lies 11 miles east and Lewiston is 35 miles west.

Pre-Incorporation Years

Until 1805 when the Lewis and Clark Corps of Discovery came into the area, the nomadic Nez Perce American Indians were the principal inhabitants of the region. Lewis and Clark first encountered the Nez Perce as their expedition emerged cold and starving from their terrible ordeal crossing the deep snows of the rugged Bitterroot Mountains. The Nez Perce were gathering camas bulbs on the Weippe Prairie 25 miles southeast of what is now Peck.

Lewis and Clark stayed with the Nez Perce for several days to recuperate and complete construction of the canoes they made at their "Canoe Camp" on the banks of the Clearwater River, now a National Historic Site between Peck and Orofino.

They also stayed with the Nez Perce the following year on their return trip to St. Louis, Missouri, and Washington, D.C.

In 1811 European trappers/explorers began coming into the area. In 1836 Henry and Eliza Spaulding opened their mission to the Nez Perce near what is now Lapwai about 20 miles west of Peck.

In 1860 Elias Davidson Pierce and a small party of prospectors discovered gold on Nez Perce Reservation land 33 miles due east of what is now Peck. By 1861 about 3,000 prospectors converged on the area. Most of these fortune-seekers passed near what is now Peck as they came into Lewiston and traveled east to the gold fields.

In 1877 the U.S. Bureau of Indian Affairs ordered the Nez Perce – many of whom were at that time in the Wallowa Valley in Washington and friendly to the whites – to move to the Lapwai Reservation in Idaho. Several young Nez Perce warriors were incensed and went against the direction of their chiefs, attacking nearby white settlements and killing many settlers.

Hauling grain.

General O.O. Howard interpreted this action as a general revolt and ordered his military to attack the Nez Perce Tribes. What ensued was a running battle where the U.S. Army chased the Nez Perce bands of Chiefs Joseph and White Bird to Montana near the Canadian border. White Bird's band escaped across the border but the army captured Joseph's band before they could follow. Several years later, the federal government allowed the remaining Nez Perce to return to their reservation. (*See Northern Idaho – Nez Perce War.*)

On February 8, 1887, Congress passed the Dawes Severalty Act in an attempt to mainstream Indians into American society. The Act authorized the survey of Native American Reservation lands and allotting of specific acreages, generally 160 acres per head of household, to tribal members. The Act deemed land not so allocated as surplus and available for homesteading by non-Indians. Under this Act, a large part of former reservation lands came under cultivation. (*See Northern Idaho – Dawes Severalty Act.*) Congress repealed the Act in 1935.

On November 18, 1895, former Nez Perce Reservation land became open for settlement. At that time, an estimated 5,000 settlers were poised to participate in the land rush allowed by the Dawes Act.

In 1896 two brothers, Ike and Marion Radcliffe, homesteaded on a flat area in the valley created by Canyon Creek about a mile above the creek's confluence with the Clearwater River. The settlers built a wagon road through the canyon that connected the Camas Prairie farmland to the south with the roads bordering the Clearwater River.

John Herres built a ferry across the Clearwater River near the confluence of the two streams and opened a small general store. Tom Kirby, a merchant from

Kendrick, Idaho, opted to purchase a parcel of land from the Radcliffe brothers to build his store.

In 1898 the Northern Pacific Railroad completed its rail line from Lewiston to Orofino. Jacob Peck, the railroad's engineer, conducted a survey of Big Canyon for a possible railroad branch line through the village and south to the new homesteaded farms developing on the Camas Prairie.

In 1899 the Radcliffe brothers platted the balance of the land near Kirby's store and named the new town Peck in honor of Jacob Peck. The town soon began to grow; however, a railroad line through town never materialized.

Incorporation

On January 14, 1905, the Nez Perce County Commissioners approved incorporating Peck as a village.

Turning Points

Strategic Site The Radcliff brothers' decision to establish Peck near the intersection of the roads from Lewiston to Orofino and to the Camas Prairie was critical to the continued existence of the village.

In 1905 the wagon road west to Lewiston was over 50 miles of steep, winding grades; dropping down into canyons and climbing out again; and crossing through farmland and forests. It took a strong team of horses and a good reason and buggy to make the journey from Peck to Lewiston in a day. The road to Orofino on the east climbed over Bobbitt Bench and took three hours.

Peck was a natural stopping-off point and trading center for a large geographical area. Farmers sold their produce in Peck and purchased "store bought" necessities. Often they stayed to join in the town's activities and entertainment. Peck had a reputation as a "wild little town."

By 1910 the town's population was 236; however, on any given day, the population swelled with travelers and people coming to do business. At that time, the village had a post office, bank, three hotels, a livery stable, a blacksmith shop, several general stores, a newspaper, a furniture store and undertaker's parlor, a drug store, a doctor's office, a barber shop, a butcher shop, a creamery and several small sawmills which produced lumber for the growing community. By 1918 the town's population was estimated at 400.

The town itself had wooden sidewalks lining both sides of Main Street. Four flights of stairs went to the homes built on the upper benches of the canyon.

Orchards grew on Peck's sun-warmed benches. Many of these fruit farmers shipped their produce to markets outside the area.

Motor Vehicles and Improved Roads By the 1920s the use of motor vehicles and the construction of improved roads began to diminish the need for the Peck business center. With the improvement of U.S. Highway 12, people began driving their motor vehicles to larger towns to shop and do business.

In 1925 the bank in Peck closed and many Peck residents began commuting to other cities for work.

School Consolidation Peck's first school was a small log building. Residents soon replaced it with a larger wood-frame schoolhouse. In 1910 patrons built a two-storied school building on the north end of town overlooking Bear Creek. This schoolhouse served as a high school on the upper floor and a grade school downstairs. At one time, the school had an enrollment of 100.

The social life of the community centered on the school and its activities. There were programs and plays, dinners and dances. The high school, "Peck Pirates," won many basketball games with enthusiastic supporters filling the gym to overflowing.

In 1942 to reduce costs and improve the education program, the Peck School District merged into the Orofino School District.

Peck Today

Amenities and Attractions The Peck City Park has picnic and children's play areas, a covered shelter and an athletic field. The Peck Post Office and Library serve residents of the city, as well as those living on the ranchettes and farms that surround the city.

Peck, 1976.

The Peck Community Club – founded in 1927 by a group of women promoting the social, spiritual and financial interests of the community – sponsors several fund-raising and cultural events throughout the year.

The 850-acre Dworshak State Park in the Clearwater National Forest is about 14 miles northeast on the shores of Dworshak Reservoir. The reservoir is a 16,000-acre body of water in the Clearwater National Forest that is 53 miles long. The hydroelectric Dworshak Dam, completed in 1973, is 717 feet high and 3,300 feet wide.

The 418-acre Winchester Lake State Park with its 103-acre lake lies 25 miles southwest of the city.

Hells Gate State Park is located 40 miles away just south of Lewiston. This 960-acre park is part of the 652,488-acre Hells Canyon National Recreation Area. The Area includes North America's deepest river gorge. This Snake River gorge lies more than a mile below Oregon's west rim and, on the Idaho side, more than 8,000 feet below He Devil Peak of the Seven Devils Mountains.

The Nez Perce National Historic Park, managed by the National Parks Service and partially staffed by tribal members, is 25 miles west in Spaulding.

The Idaho Transportation Department's Northwest Passage Scenic Byway – Highway 12 – passes near the city.

The nearby national forest, lakes and streams are an outdoor paradise. Boating, fishing, hunting, hiking, cross-country skiing and other outdoor activities are popular.

Economy and Major Employers Most of Peck's residents are retired or commute to Orofino and Lewiston for work. A few small retail establishments comprise the city's business district.

Education The Orofino School District provides elementary and secondary education. There are 15 to 20 students in the first through fifth grades. They attend Peck Elementary a three-room brick school built in 1954. Middle and high school students ride the school bus to Orofino.

The closest institution of higher learning is Lewis-Clark State College in Lewiston.

Peck Hill.

Health Care The closest hospital is the 17-bed Clearwater Valley Hospital in Orofino. The 167-bed St. Joseph Regional Hospital is in Lewiston.

Transportation U.S. Highway 12 passes one and a half miles north of the city. Improved county roads connect the city with communities to the south and west.

The closest air service for small private and charter aircraft is the 2,500-foot runway at Orofino Municipal Airport. The closest commercial airfield is the Lewiston-Nez Perce County Airport.

Utilities and Services Private companies provide electricity, telephone and satellite services. The City provides domestic water. The homes and businesses have individual septic systems. Peck has a rural fire department. The Nezperce County Sheriff's Office provides police protection. The City of Orofino provides EMT and ambulance services.

Vision for 2050

For the past five decades, the population of Peck has generally remained just under 200. The city's historical population trends will likely continue until the economies of Orofino or Lewiston grow. Then more people with jobs in those cities or retirees will seek the more affordable housing and the slower pace of life in the surrounding fabulous natural beauty available in Peck.

Mayors

1961 C. Dee Greene *
1963 Harvey Smith *
1964 Bill Deyo *
1966 Edwin Blake
1971 Jens Jacobsen
1972 William La Rue
1974 Raymond Klaudt

1978 Mary Lou Deyo
1981 Roy Irey
1990 Delbert Walker
1998 Randy Olson
2002 Sarah Walz
2006 Nancy Greene
* Village Chairman

Kellogg postcard.

SHOSHONE COUNTY

- Kellogg
- Mullan
- Osburn
- Pinehurst
- Smelterville
- Wallace (*County Seat*)
- Wardner

Kellogg from mountain.

Kellogg

Statistical Data

Population: 2,063 *
Elevation: 2,310 feet
Precipitation: 30 inches **
Average Snowfall: 59 inches **
County: Shoshone
Website: www.kellogg-idaho.com

Temperature Range – Fahrenheit: **
Spring: 30 to 60
Summer: 55 to 85
Fall: 35 to 55
Winter: 0 to 30
* U.S. Census Bureau Estimates July 2015
**Historical averages

Kellogg lies near the center of the legendary Coeur d'Alene Mining District, generally known as the Silver Valley. The city lies in the beautiful and rugged Bitterroot Mountains. The Coeur d'Alene River passes through the city. Two components of the Panhandle National Forest border the city – the Coeur d'Alene National Forest to the north and the St. Joe National Forest to the south.

Through most of the twentieth century, the name Kellogg was synonymous with deep-shaft, hard-rock lead, zinc, silver and gold mining – the home of the famed Bunker Hill Mine. The mine closed in 1981 with devastating effects on the city and its residents.

Today that has all changed. Kellogg has a new direction and business community. The fabulous outdoor amenities of the

Miners.

surrounding national forest are now the foundation of the city's new economy. Recreation, Internet marketing, service and tourism are leading the way. A growing retirement community is adding economic strength and diversity.

Pre-Incorporation Years

Around 1860 prospectors began looking for placer gold along the Coeur d'Alene River and its tributaries. In November 1878 gold prospector A.J. Prichard was working in the streambeds of what is now Prichard Creek about 10 miles northeast of what is now Kellogg. There he discovered a lead quartz outcropping and, in the stream, promising quantities of gold. Encouraged by his find, he quietly built a cabin and returned to his claim each summer to successfully pan for gold. His secret got out, however, and in 1882 several prospectors showed up at his cabin insisting that he show them his claim. The following year, 10,000 prospectors descended on the region, creating the mining town of Murray – not only finding gold but lead-silver ore as well.

Kellogg train depot, 1895.

In 1885 Jonathan F. Ingalls laid claim to a level area of land at the base of the Milo Creek gorge, later to become the Kellogg townsite. He planned to establish a cattle ranch and sell beef to the miners.

That fall, Noah S. Kellogg, an unemployed carpenter turned prospector, was working off a grubstake. Along with his jackass, Kellogg discovered a lead-silver-zinc ore outcropping two miles up the mountain gulch from Ingalls' ranch.

Kellogg did not record just how he made the discovery. However, the stories he told became the core of the colorful folklore that developed. One of these accounts was a description written by James Wardner, one of Kellogg's associates in the mine.

Kellogg and his jackass were on opposite sides of Milo Creek, Wardner wrote, when Kellogg saw the animal intently looking at an object. He investigated and found the burro staring at a vein of lead and silver ore sparkling in the sun.

Since those metals oxidize into a dark color when exposed to the air, others theorized that if the jackass was indeed mesmerized by the gleaming metal ore, it was a rock dislodged by the donkey's hoof.

Others dispelled that version of the story and speculated the jackass was just eating bunch grass near the ore outcropping when Kellogg found him.

In any case, the story of Kellogg's incredible jackass became a legend that spread throughout the mining community.

Kellogg returned to Murray to notify his grubstake partners so they could come and stake additional claims. Wardner, hearing of Kellogg's success, followed along. However, while the others were staking their mine claims, Wardner marked a large section of the gulch and filed on the water rights that included Milo Creek and

10,000 miners' inches of the South Fork of the Coeur d'Alene River, making him a lead partner in the discovery. Later, Kellogg's first two grubstake partners sued and won a combined 25 percent interest in the mines.

All of partners had to work together to develop the mine. The closest smelter was Selby Smelting Company in San Francisco. Wardner took ore samples to the smelter and sealed a sales contract. The first ore shipments were loaded on wagons, transported west to the railhead at Rathdrum, then by rail to Portland and by boat south to San Francisco.

A tent city developed in Milo Gulch. In October 1885 Kellogg and his partners named the new community "Kentuck" and applied for a post office location. When postal authorities rejected the name, the miners chose Wardner in recognition of James Wardner's efforts in promoting the mine. Postal authorities approved the Wardner Post Office and the partners named their mine the

Getting around in Kellogg was not only slow, but rough, in the early days as this scene from the uptown area shows.

Bunker Hill and Sullivan Mining Company (Bunker Hill).

In 1886 Ingalls, observing all of this activity, dropped the ranching idea. He determined that a more profitable use of the land would be for a town. He surveyed the property and created a township that he named Milo after the nearby creek and gorge. By the end of 1886 the community of Milo had a general merchandise store, one saloon, two log cabins and several tents.

In 1887 Ingalls realized that if the town was to grow, it needed a name that better reflected its mining image. He decided to capitalize on Noah Kellogg's notoriety and changed the name of his town to Kellogg.

By 1890 all of the original partners in Kellogg's discovery had sold their claims. The new owners of the Bunker Hill Mine built an ore-processing mill in Kellogg. While the main entrance to the mine was two miles up the mountain near Wardner, the valley floor at Kellogg was a more suitable location for the mill. To get the ore down to the concentrator and processing mill, the miners sent it down the mountain on tramcars.

To improve productivity and reduce costs, the entrance to the mine and tram were replaced in 1892 by a two-mile tunnel and light rail line cut laterally into the mountain from the Kellogg mill site to the main shaft.

Moving the mine entrance had an almost immediate effect on both towns. Workers and many businesses moved in whole or in part from Wardner to Kellogg.

The history of Kellogg is pivotal to the Silver Valley. Kellogg was at the center of the sharp conflicts between the mine owners and labor that burst into armed conflict across the valley in 1892 and again in 1899. (*See Northern Idaho, The Region, Silver Valley Mines.*)

The railroad built the first rail line into the valley in 1887, a narrow gauge 44-inch-wide line at a time when national standards were changing. In 1889 the Oregon-Washington Railroad and Navigation Company replaced the line with a 56.5-inch-wide track, connecting its rail system in Spokane to Kellogg and Wallace.

In his two-volume book History of Idaho, Gem of the Mountains, James H. Hawley wrote that by 1913 the city had "two banks, two newspapers, a commercial club, a smelter, electric light and waterworks, churches of several leading denominations, hotels, stores and large mining interests."

Incorporation

On July 7, 1893, community leaders joined Ingalls to complete the work he started and filed the original plat with the county. Eight men, including founder Jonathan Ingalls, signed the plat. Kellogg became an incorporated village on October 22, 1907.

The 1910 U.S. Census reported Kellogg had a

Street in Kellogg, circa 1940s or 1950s.

population of 1,273. It had more than enough population to qualify for a change in municipal legal status from a village to a "city of the second class," which it did in May 1913. While creation of the city achieved many objectives, it is clear that the principal purpose was to support the interests of the Bunker Hill Mine.

Turning Points

Bunker Hill Mine When Noah Kellogg made his lead-silver ore discovery, he knew he had a major find. What he could not have known was that over the next century his find would produce prodigious quantities of lead, zinc, silver and gold that fueled the Silver Valley economy and contributed greatly to Idaho history and ranking as among the top silver producing mining districts in the world. (See Northern Idaho, The Region, Silver Valley Mines – Historical Mine Production and Ranking.)

Kellogg essentially became a company town when the Bunker Hill Mine owners built their processing mill there, even more so when management moved the mine entrance to Kellogg and most of Wardner's residents and businesses moved with it.

Bunker Hill management sought to improve the quality of life of Kellogg residents, most of whom were company employees and their families, by making several community improvements. The company built a three-story medical building in 1908 and leased it to several doctors. Four years later it constructed a three-story YMCA building with a gymnasium, locker rooms, swimming pool, boxing ring, game room, reading rooms and a four-lane bowling alley. The facility became the social center of town. In the same year, Wardner's weekly newspaper moved to Kellogg and added the Kellogg name to its masthead.

From inception, ownership of the company that now comprises over 500 patented mining claims and 6,500 acres has changed hands multiple times. While most of the surface structures have been razed, the present owner, the New Bunker Hill Mining Company, has placed the property in a care and maintenance mode.

Miner statue.

Lead Smelter Kellogg's economy got a boost when Bunker Hill added a lead smelter to its mill complex in 1917. The addition increased the company's payroll from 800 to 1,100. For many years, the 715-foot-high smokestack at the lead smelter and the 615-foot-high stack at the zinc plant were beacons of prosperity and jobs. However, by the 1970s the lead and acid forming chemicals emitted from the stacks were becoming a regional focal point for the campaign against air pollution.

Electrolyte-Sulfuric Acid Processing Plant Employment again expanded when the Bunker Hill and Hecla Mining Companies constructed a state-of-the-art electrolytic zinc processing plant just outside the city in 1928. In the electrolytic process, concentrated zinc ore is introduced into an electrolyte-sulfuric acid solution and circulated around silver grids to which the zinc adheres.

Escaping the Economic Problems of the Great Depression Because of Bunker Hill, the city avoided many problems associated with the Great Depression of the 1930s. Metal prices held up sufficiently that the company kept most of its employees working, albeit at reduced hours.

Acquisition of Bunker Hill Gulf Resources and Chemical Corporation acquired Bunker Hill in a tender offer to shareholders in 1968, ushering in an era of increased production from the aging plant. At that time, Bunker Hill had over 1,700 workers. Under the initial years of GRC management, the number of workers increased and the mine grew to over 150 miles of lateral tunnels with the main shaft penetrating more than a mile below the earth's surface.

In 1973 the smelter facility, which already needed to reduce dust emissions, was partially burned. During the six months it took to repair, the company continued operations, greatly increasing the amount of lead and other pollutants coming from the tall smokestack and falling on the countryside.

Most of Kellogg's residents supported the company and its actions. However, beginning in the 1960s national attitudes about protecting the environment brought a wave of federal environmental, health and safety and other laws, including creation of new federal agencies such as the Environmental Protection Agency (EPA) in 1970. These national laws and regulations would impose environmental protection and health and safety requirements that forced significant changes in the way Bunker Hill had historically operated. (*See Northern Idaho, The Region, Mining and Forest Products, the Decline of Idaho's Signature Industries.*)

Closure of the Bunker Hill Mine The most devastating blow to the citizens of Kellogg came in August 1981 when GRC made the shocking announcement that it would gradually shut down Bunker Hill after 94 years of operation. The closure eliminated nearly 2,100 jobs with an annual payroll of over $50 million. The population of the city and nearby communities plunged by more than a third. Property values collapsed. Residents who could find work elsewhere commuted long distances. Many businesses downsized or closed.

Other economic losses included the sharp decline of the company's property taxes of $1.5 million that supported many local government jobs. "Uncle Bunker" also paid Union Pacific Railroad $13 million annually in freight bills and spent another $2 million a year for electricity and natural gas from Washington Water Power Company.

A street in Kellogg in the winter.

GRC blamed their closure decision on punishing losses due to the ailing metals market, the prohibitive cost of federal regulations and inflexible labor contracts.

In November 1982 three private investors announced they had acquired Bunker Hill from GRC for an undisclosed sum and that mine operations would not resume until "metals prices increased drastically."

Sunshine Mine Eight miles southwest of Kellogg is the world famous Sunshine Mine, recognized as one of the most productive silver mines in the world with historic production of around 400 million tr. oz. of silver, more than double that produced by Nevada's famous Comstock Lode.

In addition, the mine is the scene of a devastating fire in which 91 of 174 miners working thousands of feet below the earth's surface died of smoke and carbon monoxide inhalation on the morning of May 2, 1972. On the day of the fire, 81 workers were rescued, a week later, two more were found alive. After the fire, the mine closed for seven months.

Today a 12-foot-high statue of a solitary miner with his drill pointing skyward stands as a memorial to those who lost their lives. The memorial is located three and a half miles east of Kellogg on Interstate 90 at the Big Creek exit.

Following the tragedy, national mine safety policies were significantly strengthened. Today, every miner in the U.S. is required to carry a self-rescue breathing device to increase the chances of surviving carbon monoxide poisoning in the event of fire.

Environmental Protection Agency Rulings In 1998 the Environmental Protection Agency placed a large area around Kellogg and Wardner on its Superfund list of hazardous waste sites requiring cleanup. Over the intervening years, accumulations of lead and other contaminants in the soils and streams that had occurred over a century of environmentally insensitive mining and smelting activities had to be removed and remediated. In Kellogg, EPA contractors replaced contaminated soil with clean soil and new sod. Many city residents were among those hired to do the remediation work.

Today more than 1,400 residential properties have been remediated and over 200 acres of hillsides re-vegetated. Once contaminated streams now boast sustainable populations of fish.

Building a New Economy
Through years of economic turmoil, the citizens of Kellogg showed uncommon resilience. Community leaders objectively evaluated their options and embarked on a campaign to attract environmentally clean businesses and build a tourist and hospitality economy based on the area's beautiful natural resources.

Kellogg Alpine village.

Dave Smith Motors was the first to expand operations. He started his innovative Internet nationwide sales business in 1982 after Bunker Hill closed. In 2004 the Silver Mountain Resort broke ground for its Gondola Village and condominiums, and, less than a year later, the Shoshone Medical Center opened its new facility.

These progressive, environmentally clean businesses are leading the way in returning Kellogg and the Silver Valley to a more prosperous course.

Kellogg Today

Amenities and Attractions The city has four municipal parks on 3.5 acres, a library and a golf course.

The historic Bunker Hill Mine "Staff House," a former company-owned hotel used to house mine visitors, is now a mining museum that displays Kellogg's mining history.

On the last weekend in July, the Silver Valley Chamber of Commerce hosts the Silver Hoops 3 on 3 Basketball Tournament and family festival. One hundred twenty teams participated in 2006.

The city celebrates Independence Day each July 4 with a parade, games for kids, food and fireworks.

The Silver Mountain Resort, part of a chain of destination resorts in the Northwest, offers year-round outdoor activities and sponsors concerts and other community events.

Starting at Gondola Village in Kellogg, the Silver Mountain Gondola – the world's longest – takes patrons 3.1 miles, rising 3,400 feet to the ski lodge, village and condominiums at the Mountain Haus terminal on Kellogg Peak. The resort also includes Wardner Mountain. These mountain peak elevations are 6,300 and 6,200 feet, respectively. Additionally, the resort has 67 named ski runs and trails and six ski lifts.

The 18-acre Old Mission State Park is located 15 miles west. It features the old Cataldo Mission of the Sacred Heart, built around 1850 by Roman Catholic missionaries and the American Indians they taught. The historic mission building is Idaho's oldest building.

The Route of the Hiawatha, a scenic 30-mile round trip on a paved non-motorized path built on the rail bed of the old Milwaukee Railroad, is headquartered 10 miles southwest in Wallace.

The Trail of the Coeur d'Alenes, a Rails to Trails Conservancy project, is a paved 72-mile non-motorized trail built on the old Union Pacific rail bed from Mullan, near the Montana border, to Plummer, near the Washington border. The section of the trail running directly through Kellogg is surrounded by grass and trees with a restroom and picnic facilities installed by the city to enhance the trail and add to the beauty of the community.

In addition to nearby trails and resorts, the surrounding forest, mountains and the Coeur d'Alene River and its tributaries offer fabulous opportunities for camping, hunting, fishing, hiking, biking, cross-country skiing and other outdoor recreation and activities.

Street in Kellogg.

Economy and Major Employers Kellogg has a vibrant downtown with several retail, financial and service businesses. The Shoshone Medical Center and the Kellogg School District each employ about 160.

Dave Smith Motors has about 100 employees. This auto dealer has successfully developed a national Internet marketing system. The company is one of the largest automobile dealers in the nation with car and truck sales often exceeding 1,000 per month.

The Silver Mountain Resort has about 80 full-time and seasonal employees.

Education The Kellogg School District provides most of the elementary and secondary education. The school district operates a high school, alternative high school, middle and elementary schools. A private school provides education up through the sixth grade.

The nearest institution of higher learning is North Idaho College in Coeur d'Alene. North Idaho College also has a satellite location in Kellogg.

Health Care The 25-bed Shoshone Medical Center, other medical clinics and a nursing home meet most of the city's medical care needs.

Transportation Interstate 90 runs through the city.

The 5,500-foot runway at Shoshone County Airport, located three miles away, provides service for light private and charter aircraft. The closest air terminal for heavier commercial aircraft is 51 miles east in Coeur d'Alene.

Utilities and Services Private companies provide electricity, gas, ambulance and EMT services. Central Shoshone County Water District in Kellogg provides water services. South Fork Sewer District in Osburn provides regional municipal wastewater treatment services. The Kellogg Police Department provides law enforcement. Fire District 2, headquartered in Kellogg, provides fire protection. The fire district also serves Smelterville, Pinehurst, the west end of Shoshone County and parts of Kootenai County.

Vision for 2050

Over the past several years, Kellogg's resident population has remained somewhat constant at around 2,300. However, its visitor and tourist populations surge during the skiing and summer seasons. The increased tourist traffic is having a positive effect on many of the city's businesses. This

Kellogg and the freeway.

trend will likely continue with other businesses coming to Kellogg.

The combined economic development efforts taken by Silver Valley cities are paying off. Now that the area's environment is healing from the abuses of the past, more people are looking to move their homes and businesses to this beautiful part of Idaho and the nation. Several Silver Valley mines are growing in response to increasing metal prices with technological innovation providing a dramatic positive effect on the mining industry. Today, mines operate with fewer employees in an environmentally friendly manner under strict federal and state laws. The abuses of the past will not recur.

The combined effect of increased tourism and a healthy and gradual resurgence of the mining industry will likely cause the city to resume a growth rate of around 1 percent annually. By 2050 the city's resident population should be around 4,000.

The tax revenues and impact fees will be adequate to pay the additional costs associated with this growth.

Mayors

1913 C.W. Simmons	1961 Dr. Robert Cordwell
1917 Dr. T.R. Mason	1963 Roger Fulton
1921 Burke A. McIntosh	1974 R.C. Lyons
1923 Dr. T.R. Mason	1975 Ford Hoback
1929 J.W. McCrane	1982 Jim Vergobbi
1939 J. Burmeister	1985 Mervin Hill
1941 H.C. Seeber	1995 Mac Pooler
1942 E.P. Biotti	1998 Roger Mangum
1947 H.C. Seeber	2002 Mac Pooler

View of Earle Street in Mullan, looking toward new (1985) city hall and fire station.

Mullan

Statistical Data

Population: 673 *
Elevation: 3,277 feet
Precipitation: 38 inches **
Average Snowfall: 53 inches **
County: Shoshone

Temperature Range – Fahrenheit: **
Spring: 27 to 63
Summer: 45 to 79
Fall: 28 to 70
Winter: 20 to 39
* U.S. Census Bureau Estimates July 2013
**Historical averages

Mullan is nestled in the beautiful and rugged Bitterroot Mountain range. National forests surround the city. The Coeur d'Alene National Forest is on the north and west, the St. Joe lies to the south and the Kaniksu National Forest on the east in Montana. One of the highest mountains in the area is the 6,625-foot Tiger Peak, five miles due north at the head of Gorge Gulch above Burke.

Mullan is the easternmost city of the 40-mile-long valley gorge cut by the Coeur d'Alene River. Designated for a century as the Coeur d'Alene Mining District, it now has the distinctive name of the Silver Valley.

Over the past century, mining interests have extracted massive quantities of silver, lead, zinc and gold from ore deposits that extend over a mile below the earth's surface. (*See The Region, Silver Valley Mines, Mining – Historic Mine Production and Ranking.*)

A few mines still operate in the valley, and rich ore reserves remain. However, environmental concerns and costs, along with cyclical markets, have left the mining industry in the Silver Valley a shadow of its previous economic dominance.

Today, tourism and outdoor recreation play prominent roles in the valley's economy. (*See The Region, The Region's Economic Base, Historically and Today.*)

Pre-Incorporation Years

Until 1859 the mountainous terrain around what is now Mullan was largely the sole domain of the American Indians who passed through the area. (*See The Region, American Indians.*)

That year, U.S. Army Captain John Mullan – then a lieutenant and a topographical engineer – and a crew of over 200 began construction of a 624-mile military wagon road between Fort Walla Walla, Washington, and

"Morning Mill" Federal Mine and Milling Cos' Mill. Photo by V.A. Slocum, 1924.

Fort Benton, Montana. The road passed near what is now Mullan and Interstate 90.

Mullan said that while the road was under construction, he would lie night after night on the ground with his men with nothing but pine needles for a bed and a saddle for a pillow. "In my imagination I heard the whistle of the engine," he said, "I saw the country thickly populated, thousands pouring over the borders to make homes in this far western land."

Even though Mullan Road was a military road, it was primarily used by prospectors, miners and settlers. (*See The Region, Mullan Road – The Military Wagon Road That Opened the Region.*)

Andrew J. Prichard discovered placer gold in November 1878 about 13 miles north of what is now Mullan. Word of his discovery got out, and in 1883 a gold rush brought 10,000 fortune seekers into the region. They not only discovered more gold but also rich deposits of lead, zinc and silver ore. (*See The Region, Gold Mining.*)

In May 1884 G.J. Hunter and C.W. Moore, prospectors working the area, discovered a silver-lead lode that became the Gold Hunter Mine. They found the Morning Mine claims in July. News of the discovery incited a rush of fortune seekers into the area and a boomtown emerged. Many of the first mineworkers and their families were living in tents. There was a pressing need for a municipal government, fire brigade, school and churches. (*See The Region, Silver Valley Mines – Hard Rock Mines – Silver, Lead and Zinc.*)

Business leaders proposed a 19-acre plat for a townsite. However, they could not agree on specifics and the attempt failed.

Charles J. Best, George S. Good, A.J. Betaque, C.C. Earle and another man formed a company that platted a townsite in 1885 and named it Mullan, after Captain John Mullan.

Old-timers in Mullan, 1889.

They filed their plat as an unincorporated community on August 4, 1888. At that time, the town had 20 log and 15 frame houses, a sawmill, two hotels, several saloons and a population of 150.

The town's first school was a log cabin on Hunter Street. However, school patrons soon began constructing a new school on Knob Hill.

As the town's population grew, the residents constructed new and better buildings on Earle Street including a larger brick school. By 1889 Earle Street had displaced Hunter Street as the city's principal thoroughfare. The old school building on Knob Hill became St. Andrew's Episcopal Church.

That year was also momentous in other regards. Residents greeted completion of the Northern Pacific Railroad from Wallace to Mullan with great celebration. They celebrated again when they heard that congressional leaders had told Idaho delegates to proceed with the state's constitutional convention, even though Idaho would have to wait until the next year for statehood. Idaho became the nation's 43rd state on July 3, 1890.

These exciting events only briefly overshadowed the dark and brewing labor union/mine owner disputes taking place at the mines throughout the district.

The first of several disputes between miners and mine owners erupted in 1889. Having their demands rebuffed by management, the workers at the various mines began to unionize. On November 3, 1890, the Mullan mine workers organized under the Knights of Labor. Four months later, the owners of the mines near Mullan responded by joining the Silver Valley's Mine Owners' Association.

The differences between the two sides became so acute that in 1892 and again in 1899 the governor declared Mullan and much of Shoshone County "in a state of insurrection" and placed the area under martial law. (*See The Region, Silver Valley Mines, Labor Union/Mine Owner Conflicts.*)

In January 1891 six years after community leaders proposed the first fire brigade, the Mullan Volunteer Fire Department was finally organized.

Incorporation

In August 1892 Mullan business leaders filed for a U.S. townsite patent at the Coeur d'Alene Land Office. However, authorities rejected the filing because it included only the business portion of town and not the entire settlement.

On July 15, 1904, a group of Mullan leaders established the town boundaries, appointed officers and trustees, drew up ordinances, defined crimes, set fines and petitioned the Shoshone County Commission to incorporate as a village.

However, the Federal Mining Company claimed survey errors and, specifically, referenced the cemetery and "Village Park" land as being improperly included in the plat. Once again, authorities denied the petition.

The 1910 U.S. Census reported the Mullan population at 1,667. In September 1910 community leaders again applied, unsuccessfully, for incorporation as a village.

It was not until March 13, 1912, after an appeal to Idaho Senator William Borah and other elected officials, that Mullan became an incorporated village. In 1967 Mullan become an incorporated city in accordance with a new state law.

Plaque at John Mullan Centennial Park, 2004.

Turning Points

Mining Mullan is a mining town, owing its existence to the 1884 silver-lead ore discoveries that led to development of the Gold Hunter and Morning Mines. The Lucky Friday and Gold Hunter Mines still produce most of the jobs for city residents.

Forest Fire Because of good fortune and innovative fire fighting work, Mullan largely survived the massive forest fire of August 1910 that ravaged Wallace and other towns and forests in Idaho and Montana. Heavy winds pushed the fire toward Mullan. The Mullan Volunteer Fire Department worked to save the city as smoke and falling ash swirled all about them. At the last minute, the wind shifted away from the city's core, missing all but 10 tent homes on the edge of town. (*See The Region, Forest Products – Great Fire of 1910.*)

Environmental Laws and Market Forces Mullan's 1960 population was 1,477 – almost twice what it is today. Beginning in the 1970s Congress passed several environmental protection and workplace health and safety laws. These laws not only brought many mining practices and processes into question but also created and expanded the powers of certain regulatory agencies. Compliance with these new pollutant discharge or emissions laws was costly to implement.

At the same time, world demand for many precious and industrial metals was in decline. Mine closures and long unemployment lines were common.

However, the mines in Mullan were able to comply with the new regulatory laws and weather the economic challenges. The Mullan mines emerged from the mining problems of the twentieth century more technologically advanced and less labor intensive. (*See The Region, Mining and Forest Products – Leading Causes for Loss of Economic Dominance.*)

Interstate 90 Construction of Interstate 90 in the 1970s opened the valley to increased traffic. However, the freeway allowed traffic to bypass the town, causing the city's downtown businesses to lose customers. The freeway corridor passed through a residential part of town, requiring development of a subdivision for affected homeowners.

Mullan Today

Amenities and Attractions The city's downtown center includes a beautiful park with flowers, shrubs, trees, gazebo, playground equipment and a historical museum with an eclectic collection of artifacts and memorabilia of Mullan's past. A commemorative statue of Captain John Mullan stands in front of the city's fire station and city hall, facing the old Mullan Road.

Emmanuel Lutheran Church, 2004.

The Lookout Pass Ski Area, six miles east, is a popular family-oriented ski area featuring a free ski school. Snowboarding and snowcatting are also popular.

The Trail of the Coeur d'Alenes is a 72-mile paved public trail connecting cities from Mullan to Plummer, opening up a cross-section of the natural beauties of Northern Idaho's magnificent national forests and wildlife to walkers, hikers and bikers.

The Route of the Hiawatha is a non-motorized rail-to-trail mountain path. It follows the old Milwaukee Road rail bed between Pearson, eight miles southeast of Mullan, and St. Regis, Montana. This area has some of the most spectacular scenery in the nation. Today, only a sign remains to designate the location of the old town of Pearson.

1967 Mullan Athletic Pavilion.

Mullan has many attractive homes built at the turn of the twentieth century. These historic buildings give a nostalgic sense of the bygone days when hundreds of miners inhabited the town.

Economy and Major Employers Even though many of the mines in the region have closed, the Mullan mines provide most of the city's employment. Just outside the city limits, Hecla Mining Corporation, the city's largest employer with about 250 employees, operates the Lucky Friday Mine and adjoining Hunter ore body. The mine is a deep-shaft hard-rock silver, lead, zinc and gold mine. Hecla concentrates the ore at the site and ships it out of state for refining.

Many residents commute a few miles west to work in the Galena and Coeur Mines near Wallace. Lookout Pass Ski Area and the Mullan School District each have about 45 employees and are the city's next largest employers. Other residents either own or work in local businesses or are retired.

Education The Mullan School District provides most of the primary and secondary education. The Mullan Junior-Senior High School and the John Mullan Elementary School operate in the city. In 1984 Mullan High School received an award for excellence from the U.S. Department of Education.

During the winter, school buses drive students to Lookout Pass Ski Resort where they receive free ski lessons. The school district also owns an athletic pavilion donated by Hecla

John Mullan Centennial Park, 2004.

Mining Company. The facility includes an Olympic-size swimming pool, regulation basketball court, weight room, bus storage area and other amenities.

The closest institution of higher learning is North Idaho College, about 55 miles west in Coeur d'Alene.

Health Care The closest hospital is the Shoshone Medical Center, about 17 miles west in Kellogg.

Transportation Mullan is located just off Interstate 90 between the Idaho/Montana border and the base of Lookout Pass.

Shoshone County Airport in Kellogg provides service for small private and charter aircraft. Coeur d'Alene Airport is available for larger commercial aircraft.

Utilities and Services Private companies provide electricity, gas, telephone and satellite and cable services. East Shoshone County Water District provides water. The City provides sewer services as well as fire protection with a volunteer fire department. The County Sheriff's Office provides police protection under contract with the City.

Vision for 2050

For more than two decades, Mullan's population has remained somewhat constant at about 800. However, by 2050 the city's population will likely have doubled. This population growth will come from greater employment in tourist-related businesses, expanded mining activity and an increased number of retirees and second homeowners choosing to live in Mullan to be near the stunning outdoor beauty of the forests and nearby amenities.

Higher metal prices and improved environmentally friendly ore-processing technologies and equipment will drive expanded mining activity. An increased number of hospitality businesses will come to handle the increased number of tourists that come year round to use the beautiful rails-to-trails systems and the resort at Lookout Pass.

Existing municipal systems will be adequate to handle the early stages of this growth. City officials will manage the need for expanded municipal systems in such a manner that growth will largely pay for itself.

Mayors

1904 Fred L. Taft **
1905 John A. "Gus" Glowe **
1907 William Flood **
1909 William Coumerilh **
1911 Archie Gillis **
1912 Archie Gillis *
1913 B.F. Tolbert *
1915 A.P. McRae *
1917 A.A. Heltness *
1919 R.J. McLeod *
1921 A.P. McRae *
1923 R.J. McLeod *
1923 D.F. Clark *
1925 C.B. Johnson *
1927 A.J. Harwood *
1930 Stalker Clubb *
1931 C.W. Bentley *
1934 Geo S. Price *
1941 Belden Brewer *
1943 Chas J. Bloom *
1945 John F. Posnick *

1947 Harold H. Hultner *
1949 Floyd Jacobson *
1951 John Prescott *
1951 Dan Colahan *
1952 Ralph Stoker *
1953 John Posnick *
1957 Dave Elder *
1959 John Krulitz *
1961 Walter Smith *
1962 Luke Tallent *
1964 Glen McRae *
1966 Lonnie Greer
1968 Blair Gosline
1972 Lonnie Greer
1980 Wayne Koski
1986 Blair Gosline
1989 Gary Pemble
1998 Michael Dunnigan
2014 Donald Kotschevar
* Village Chairman

** Village Chairman before Incorporation

Birds' eye view of Osburn.

Osburn

Statistical Data

Population: 1,504 *
Elevation: 2,520 feet
Precipitation: 38 inches **
Average Snowfall: 53 inches **
County: Shoshone

Temperature Range – Fahrenheit: **
Spring: 27 to 63
Summer: 45 to 79
Fall: 28 to 70
Winter: 20 to 39
* U.S. Census Bureau Estimates July 2015
**Historical averages

Osburn lies at the center of the historic and beautiful Silver Valley. The city of Wallace is six miles southeast on Interstate 90 and Kellogg nine miles northwest. The rugged and heavily timbered Bitterroot Mountains of the Coeur d'Alene National Forest surround the city. The St. Joe National Forest begins three miles south.

Pre-Incorporation Years

In August 1860 U.S. Army Captain John Mullan, then a lieutenant – a topographical engineer with a crew of around 200 – completed construction of a 624-mile military wagon road between Fort Benton, Montana, and Fort Walla

Walla, Washington. Interstate 90 generally follows the old Mullan Road. (*See Northern Idaho – Mullan Road.*)

On September 30, 1860, a band of prospectors found placer gold about 70 miles south at what is now Pierce. The discovery started Idaho's first gold rush, which on February 4, 1864, led to the establishment of Shoshone County with Pierce as the county seat. Pierce is now located in Clearwater County.

In 1877 reacting to concerns about Indian conflicts in the West, General William Tecumseh Sherman, the Union Civil War hero, made an inspection tour of military forts in the Northwest. While traveling over Mullan Road, Sherman passed along the northern shore of Lake Coeur d'Alene. He was so impressed with the setting that he made a recommendation to Congress that they authorize construction of a new military post on the north shore of the lake.

Congress approved Sherman's recommendation and in 1878 authorized construction of Fort Coeur d'Alene in what is now the city of Coeur d'Alene. The name of the fort was later changed to Fort Sherman.

With the establishment of Fort Coeur d'Alene, the military strung a telegraph

Circa 1891, Court House in the center. Race track at the bottom right.

line along Mullan Road. They built a maintenance way station they named Evolution about a mile west of what is now the city of Osburn. Travelers on Mullan Road often camped at Evolution.

In 1881 A.J. Prichard, who had prospected in the Silver Valley area for years, found placer gold on the North Fork of the Coeur d'Alene River near what would become the town of Murray, about 10 miles north of what is now Osburn. His discovery prompted a gold rush that brought about 10,000 people into the Silver Valley. (*See Northern Idaho, Mining – the Silver Valley.*) In 1885 Murray would become the Shoshone County seat.

In 1884 W.B. Heyburn discovered silver ore, the Polaris Mine, near what is now Osburn. A small mining community named Polaris grew up around the mine.

On September 10, 1887, the Spokane Falls and Idaho Railroad, later Northern Pacific Railroad, extended a rail line from Coeur d'Alene to Wallace.

The railroad generally paralleled Mullan Road. However, when the surveyors reached the intersection of Two Mile Gulch Road and Mullan Road, they preferred that location to Evolution for the place to plat a townsite, which they named Georgetown.

In 1885 Seth McFarren and Samuel Norman acquired a 160-acre ranch near the south boundary of Georgetown and erected a house and out buildings. In March 1886 they sold the ranch to S.V. William Osburn for $2,000.

Osburn built a hotel, barn, stables, icehouse, cellars and fences and cultivated 60 acres. He called his property Buckhorn Ranch. However, others called it the Osburn Ranch.

In 1887 the Georgetown/Osburn community had grown to over 60 residents. "Billy" Osburn applied for a post office to be located in his hotel with him as postmaster. Postal authorities approved his application but spelled his name "Osborn."

In 1890 Osburn became the Shoshone County Seat. In the fall of 1890 with the population at 260 people, the Idaho Supreme Court established a District Court in Osburn. A new courthouse and a 20-room hotel were added to the town site. In 1893 the District Court and the county seat were moved to Wallace.

During the 1890s major conflicts arose between mine owners and labor. Virtually every Silver Valley community was affected. (*See Northern Idaho – Mining – the Silver Valley, Mining – Labor/ Mine Owner Conflicts and Murder of Idaho's Governor, Mining and Forest Products.*)

Polaris Mine.

On May 10, 1915, following a one year closure, postal authorities re-established a post office for the residents of Osburn Ranch and Georgetown. However this time, they spelled the name "Osborne." On January 31, 1920, postal authorities closed the Osborne post office. On

Day's Market & Hotel. Courtesy Nila Jurkovich; taken by Rieske's Studio in Kellogg.

February 3, 1922, postal authorities re-established the post office. This time, they properly spelled the name of the re-opened post office "Osburn."

In 1940 the town's population exceeded 1,400. Shortly after the 1941 U.S. declaration of war against Japan, the community formed the Osburn Civil Defense Administration. Among its first actions was to have a fundraising campaign to buy a large air-raid siren to warn the people if there was an impending Japanese bombing raid. After Pearl Harbor, there was general concern in the U.S. that Japan planned a follow-up attack on Western Coastal cities.

The fundraiser netted $618. However, with the money in the bank they decided the siren was not a high priority after all, so they left the money in the bank.

On March 8, 1949, Civilian Defense Administrator Ralph Neyman gave a speech wherein he said that since it was a unanimous opinion of the people that the money was the property of the community, it was an opportune time to incorporate as a village and let elected officers spend the money on behalf of the community.

Incorporation

On July 17, 1950, with a population of 1,850, Osburn became an incorporated village with Neyman as Village Chairman. The money for the air-raid siren was the first deposit into the village's treasury.

In April 1958 the town of Polaris requested annexation into the Village of Osburn which took place on May 1, 1958.

Circa 1930s: Radio station tower is on the left. Cameron Apartments are on the right. Myle's Motel is on the far right. Courtesy Clarence "Butch" Jacobson.

On April 12, 1967, in accordance with new Idaho law, Osburn, with a population of around 1,850, became an incorporated city.

Turning Points

Railroad The railroad established the framework that encouraged entrepreneur Billy Osburn to acquire land south of the platted town of Georgetown and build a business infrastructure that became the city of Osburn.

Mining While the city did not grow up around a particular mine as was common in other cities of the Silver Valley, the mining industry had a direct effect on its economy.

Osburn Today

Amenities and Attractions There are two parks in the city. Gene Day Park has three covered kitchens, picnic areas, a pond, a baseball field, basketball and tennis courts, children's playground equipment and bathrooms.

Osburn Lion's City Park has a covered picnic area with children's playground equipment.

A Loyalty Day Parade, sponsored by the Veterans of Foreign Wars, is held on the first Saturday in May. Prizes are awarded and hamburgers and hotdogs are sold.

The Coeur d'Alene District Mining Contest takes place the first Saturday in August at Gene Day Park. The event includes many mining activities with prizes given for the winners of each contest.

Nearby activities include those offered in neighboring cities such as the Silver Mountain Water Park in Kellogg. Outdoor enthusiasts have an abundance of other available activities including ATV, motorbike and snowmobile trails, hunting, fishing on the North Fork River less than a mile away and boating 45 minutes away on Coeur d'Alene Lake.

The "Trail of the Coeur d'Alenes," a 72-mile paved public trail connecting cities from Mullan to Plummer, runs through the city. This wonderful amenity opens up a cross section of the natural beauties of Northern Idaho's magnificent national forests and wildlife to walkers, hikers and bikers. It is one of the most spectacular paved non-motorized trails in the Western U. S.

Gene Day Park.

The Route of the Hiawatha is a non-motorized rail-to-trail mountain path. When complete, it will follow the old Milwaukee Road rail bed between Pearson, Idaho, about 10 miles south of Osburn, and St. Regis, Montana. It has some of the most spectacular scenery in the nation.

Downhill skiing is available at Lookout Pass Ski Area, located about 16 miles east on the Idaho/Montana border. The resort receives up to 400 inches of snow each year and has several ski runs and lifts – a popular, family-oriented ski area.

The 18-acre Old Mission State Park, home to the oldest building in Idaho, is located 17 miles west at Cataldo.

Osburn Drug.

Economy and Major Employers Several small businesses – including an excavation, concrete and gravel contractor, home health care provider, grocery store, two banks, several other retail and professional establishments and the Shoshone School District – form the Osburn employment base.

Many of the city's residents commute to jobs in nearby cities.

Education The Wallace School District 393, with district offices in Wallace, provides K-12 education. Elementary students attend Osburn Elementary School. Junior and senior high students attend school in Wallace.

The nearest institution of higher learning is North Idaho College, located in Coeur d'Alene. North Idaho College also has a satellite location in Kellogg.

Health Care Shoshone Medical Center in Kellogg is the nearest hospital. There is a doctor's office in Osburn.

Transportation Interstate 90 intersects Osburn.

Shoshone County Airport in Kellogg has a 5,500-foot runway available for light private and charter aircraft. The Coeur d'Alene Air Terminal, 59 miles west, offers service for larger aircraft. The nearest international airport is 97 miles west in Spokane, Washington.

Utilities and Services Private companies provide solid waste services, electricity, telephone, cable, television, satellite, internet and natural gas. The City provides police protection. Shoshone County Fire Protection District #1 provides fire and EMT protection and is located in the city of Osburn. Local taxing districts provide sewer and water.

Vision for 2050

In 1960 Osburn had a population of 1,788. In the 1970s to 1980s when the mining industry was still a major employer in the Silver Valley, the population swelled to over 2,200. In recent years, the population has stabilized at around 1,400.

Recent historical population trends will likely continue for several years. There are two factors that could change these trends.

The natural rugged beauty and outdoor amenities of the nearby national forests are becoming an increasing attraction for retirees and outdoor enthusiasts. Tourism and recreation businesses are finding increased opportunity in the city. Increasing metal prices are encouraging expansion of certain underground mines.

Regardless of whether these phenomena significantly change the city's economic base or not, community leaders are committed to insuring that Osburn will continue as a beautiful and peaceful place to live and raise a family.

Mayors

1950 Ralph Neyman *
1967 Harvey J. Curtis
1972 Wes Mason
1976 Charles Mooney
1980 Ben Haskell

1984 Emil Wurst
1988 Dennis Doney
1995 Robert McPhail
2012 Kim R. McGillivray
* Village Chairman

Pinehurst

Statistical Data

Population: 1,575 *
Elevation: 2,220 feet
Precipitation: 30 inches **
Average Snowfall: 59 inches **
County: Shoshone

Temperature Range – Fahrenheit: **
Spring: 29 to 68
Summer: 47 to 83
Fall: 28 to 72
Winter: 21 to 42
* U.S. Census Bureau Estimates July 2015
**Historical averages

Pinehurst lies near the confluence of the main Coeur d'Alene River and the South Fork of the Coeur d'Alene River, whose headwaters are near the Idaho/Montana border and which flows through the heart of the Silver Valley. The narrow valley of the South Fork broadens as it reaches Smelterville and Pinehurst.

The fabulous Coeur d'Alene National Forest – with its heavily wooded Bitterroot, Coeur d'Alene and St. Joe Mountains – surround the city. Kellogg is six miles east and the city of Coeur d'Alene is 29 miles west.

Pre-Incorporation Years

Before the early 1800s when the first explorers/trappers came into the area of the Coeur d'Alenes, American Indians – principally of the Coeur d'Alene Tribe – inhabited the region around what is now Pinehurst.

In 1841 Roman Catholic missionaries, led by Father Pierre Jean de Smet, came to teach the Indians their religion and culture.

In 1860 Captain John Mullan led 230 soldiers and civilian workers in the construction of a 624-mile military wagon road from Fort Benton, Montana; through what are now the Silver Valley; Pinehurst; and the city of Coeur d'Alene to Fort Walla Walla, Washington. It was the first engineered road in the Inland Northwest. Interstate 90 generally follows Mullan Road.

In 1877 reacting to concerns about Indian conflicts in the West, General William Tecumseh Sherman, the Union Civil War hero, made an inspection tour of military forts in the Northwest. While traveling over Mullan Road, Sherman passed along the northern shore of Lake Coeur d'Alene. He made a recommendation to Congress that they authorize construction of a new military post on the north shore of the lake.

Congress approved Sherman's recommendation and in 1878 authorized construction of Fort Coeur d'Alene on 999 acres of land at the headwaters of the Spokane River. The name of the fort was later changed to Fort Sherman. The military also commissioned Captain C.P. Sorensen, a boat builder from Portland, to build a steamboat to patrol the 30-mile-long lake.

Civilians employed to build the fort and other settlers started a small tent and log cabin village, which they called Coeur d'Alene City, near the fort.

At this same time, a prospector named A.J. Prichard made a significant placer gold discovery about 20 miles northeast of what is now Pinehurst.

In 1883 Prichard made disclosure of his discoveries, setting off a major gold rush. Ten thousand people had converged on Shoshone County by the end of 1885, scouring the mountains and streams in search of precious metals.

One of these prospectors was an unemployed carpenter named Noah Kellogg. Kellogg secured grubstakes and began prospecting several locations including Milo Gulch and Creek at what is now Wardner. There he discovered a rich outcropping of lead, zinc and silver ore.

Colorful folklore stories developed around how Kellogg actually discovered the ore body. The stories are hearsay, as Kellogg did not record the events. However, Kellogg told others who wrote and told various accounts making Kellogg and his fabled jackass a legend.

Kellogg and his partners worked together to develop the mine. The closest smelter was in San Francisco. James Wardner, one of Kellogg's partners, took ore samples to Selby Smelting Company to seal a sales contract for the ore. The first shipments of ore were loaded on wagons, transported through what are now Pinehurst and Coeur d'Alene to the railhead at Rathdrum, then by rail to Portland and by boat to San Francisco.

Atent city developed in Milo Gulch. In October 1885 Kellogg and his partners named the new community Wardner and the mine the Bunker Hill and Sullivan (Bunker Hill Mine). By 1890 all of the original partners in the discovery had sold their claims to investors who, in a few years, moved the entrance of the mine down the mountain to Kellogg and built a new concentrator and smelter.

The Bunker Hill Mine played a pivotal role in the early history of Pinehurst and the Silver Valley.

In the 1880s prospectors made lead, zinc and silver ore discoveries just south of Pinehurst on Pine Creek – later named the Pine Creek Mining District. It was at this time that retail business entrepreneurs established their businesses on the broader Coeur d'Alene River Valley and platted a town they named Pinehurst.

In 1887 railroad interests built the Silver Valley's first rail line, a narrow gauge 44-inch track. Shortly thereafter, national standards changed and in 1889 other railroad interests replaced the line with a wider 56.5-inch-wide track that extended from Spokane, Washington, to Wallace, Idaho.

By 1892 the Bunker Hill Mine was the largest mine operation in the 40-mile-long Silver Valley that extended from Pinehurst to Mullan. In 1892 and again in 1899 the Bunker Hill Mine became the center of sharp conflicts between the mine owners and labor unions. These conflicts quickly spread affecting mines and towns across the valley as they turned violent, resulting in loss of life, dynamiting the Bunker Hill facilities and, later, the murder of Idaho's governor. (*See Northern Idaho, Mining – the Silver Valley and Mining – Labor/Mine Owner Conflicts and Murder of Idaho's Governor.*)

Incorporation

On February 10, 1970, Pinehurst became an incorporated city.

Turning Points

Mines The 1883 discovery of gold and subsequent discovery of massive lead, zinc and silver ore bodies in the valley led to the creation of Pinehurst, as well as several other Silver Valley communities.

Railroad Beginning in 1887 the railroad played a critical role in the successful development of the mines and cities of the Silver Valley.

Superfund Site In 1998 the federal Environmental Protection Agency (EPA) declared most of the Silver Valley a Superfund Site. Over the intervening years, there has been massive removal of soils contaminated by lead and other heavy metals to landfills. They then hauled in clean soils, restored streams and replanted the land with native species of vegetation. In Pinehurst homes and businesses, EPA contractors have replaced contaminated soil with clean soil topped with new sod and replaced certain road drains and other infrastructure.

Pinehurst Today

Amenities and Attractions The 18-hole Pinehurst Golf Course draws patrons from throughout the western part of the Silver Valley.

The Silver Mountain Resort, part of a chain of destination resorts in the

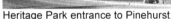

Heritage Park entrance to Pinehurst.

Northwest, is located in Kellogg and is one of the largest private businesses in the valley.

The resort complex starts at Gondola Village in Kellogg and takes patrons for a 3.1-mile gondola ride that passes over Wardner as it rises 3,400 feet to the ski lodge, village and condominiums.

The expanding resort includes two mountains – Kellogg and Wardner Peaks at 6,300 and 6,200 foot elevations, respectively. Additionally, the resort has six ski lifts and 67 named ski trails and runs.The resort sponsors year-round outdoor activities including concerts.

Pinehurst is close to other outstanding attractions. Old Mission State Park is located four miles west of the city. It is the location of the old Cataldo Mission of the Sacred Heart, Idaho's oldest standing building.

The Route of the Hiawatha is a scenic 30 mile round trip on a paved, non-motorized path built on the rail bed of the old Milwaukee Railroad. It is headquartered 19 miles southwest in Wallace. The path is also part of the Lookout Pass Ski and Recreation Area located east of Wallace on the Montana border.

The Trail of the Coeur d'Alenes is a "Rails to Trails Conservancy," a national organization, project. It is a paved 72-mile-long trail built on the old Union Pacific rail bed between Mullan and Plummer.

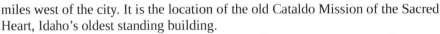

In addition to nearby trails and resorts, the surrounding forest, mountains, streams and the Coeur d'Alene River and its tributaries offer fabulous opportunities for camping, hunting, fishing, hiking, biking, cross-country skiing and other outdoor recreation and activities.

Economy and Major Employers With about 40 employees, Kellogg School District is the city's largest employer. Several small businesses, retail stores, shops and service businesses provide most of the jobs in Pinehurst.

Education Kellogg School District provides elementary and secondary education. Children in grades K-5 attend Pinehurst Elementary. Middle and high school students attend school in Kellogg.

The nearest institution of higher learning is North Idaho College in Coeur d'Alene. North Idaho College also has a satellite location in Kellogg.

Health Care The closest hospital is the 56-bed Shoshone Medical Center in Kellogg.

Transportation Interstate 90 passes on the northern edge of the city.

The 5,500-foot runway at Shoshone County Airport, located across I-90 at Smelterville, provides service for light private and charter aircraft. Larger facilities are available at Coeur d'Alene Airport.

Utilities and Services Private companies provide electricity, telephone and satellite services. The City provides police protection. Fire District 2, headquartered in Kellogg, provides fire protection. Central Shoshone Water in Kellogg provides water. The South Fork Sewer District in Osburn provides municipal wastewater treatment

Pinehurst City Hall and Police Department.

services for the cities in the region.

Vision for 2050

In 1970 the city's population was 1,934. Between 1970 and 1990, the population decreased slowly to 1,722, an average of about a half percent annually. Since 2000 the population has stabilized at around 1,600.

Recent historical trends will likely continue for several years before turning to manageable slow growth.

By 2050 Pinehurst will likely have a population of around 2,000 and will continue to be a quiet, peaceful community in a beautiful mountain setting – a great place to live and raise a family.

Entering Smelterville.

Smelterville

Statistical Data

Population: 603 *
Elevation: 2,234 feet
Precipitation: 30 inches **
Average Snowfall: 59 inches **
County: Shoshone

Temperature Range – Fahrenheit: **
Spring: 29 to 68
Summer: 47 to 83
Fall: 28 to 72
Winter: 21 to 42
* U.S. Census Bureau Estimates July 2015
**Historical averages

Smelterville lies on the western end of the historic, 40-mile-long Silver Valley as it begins to open up into a broader plain. The heavily wooded Coeur d'Alene National Forest surrounds the city. The South Fork of the Coeur d'Alene River flows north of the city.

The city of Kellogg is three miles east and the cities of Pinehurst and Coeur d'Alene are four and 33 miles west, respectively.

Pre-Incorporation Years

American Indians – principally of the Coeur d'Alene Tribe – inhabited the region around what is now Smelterville in the early 1800s when the first explorers/trappers came into the region.

In 1841 Roman Catholic missionaries led by Father Pierre Jean de Smet came to teach the Indians their religion and culture.

In 1860 Captain John Mullan led 230 soldiers and civilian workers in the construction of a 624-mile military wagon road from Fort Benton, Montana, through what are now the Silver Valley and the cities of Smelterville and Coeur d'Alene to Fort Walla Walla, Washington. It was the first engineered road in the inland Northwest. Interstate 90 generally follows Mullan Road.

In 1877 reacting to concerns about Indian conflicts in the West, General William Tecumseh Sherman – the Union Civil War hero – made an inspection tour of military forts in the Northwest. While traveling over Mullan Road, Sherman passed along the northern shore of Lake Coeur d'Alene. He made a recommendation to Congress that they authorize construction of a new military post on the north shore of the lake.

A.J. Prichard.

Congress approved Sherman's recommendation and in 1878 authorized construction of Fort Coeur d'Alene on 999 acres of land at the headwaters of the Spokane River. The name of the fort was later changed to Fort Sherman. The military also commissioned Captain C.P. Sorensen, a boat builder from Portland, to build a steamboat to patrol the 30-mile-long lake.

Civilians employed to build the fort and others started a tent and log cabin village, which they called Coeur d'Alene City, near the fort.

At the same time, A.J. Prichard made a significant placer gold discovery about 17 miles northeast of what is now Smelterville.

Noah Kellogg.

In 1883 Prichard made disclosure of his discoveries, setting off a major gold rush. Ten thousand people converged on what is now Shoshone County by the end of 1885, scouring the mountains and streams in search of precious metals.

One of these prospectors was an unemployed carpenter named Noah Kellogg. Kellogg secured grubstakes and began prospecting several locations including Milo Gulch and Creek at what is now Wardner. There he discovered a rich outcropping of lead, zinc and silver ore.

Colorful folklore stories developed around how Kellogg actually discovered the ore body. The stories are hearsay, as Kellogg did not record the events. However, Kellogg told others who wrote and told various accounts making Kellogg and his fabled jackass a legend.

Kellogg and his partners worked together to develop the mine. However, the closest smelter was in San Francisco. James Wardner, one of Kellogg's partners, took ore samples to Selby Smelting Company in San Francisco to seal a sales contract for the ore. The first shipments of ore were loaded on wagons, transported through what are now Smelterville and Coeur d'Alene to the railhead at Rathdrum, then by rail to Portland and by boat to San Francisco.

In October 1885 Kellogg and his partners named the new community that grew up around the mine Wardner and the mine Bunker Hill and Sullivan (Bunker Hill Mine). By 1890 all of the original partners in the discovery had sold their claims to investors who, a few years later, moved the entrance of the mine down the mountain to Kellogg and built a new concentrator and smelter.

The Bunker Hill Mine played a pivotal role in the early history of Smelterville and the Silver Valley. Tailings from the Bunker Hill Mine were deposited along the South Fork of the Coeur d'Alene River on what was then called Smelterville Flats.

In 1887 railroad interests built the Silver Valley's first rail line, a narrow gauge 44-inch track. Soon thereafter, national standards changed and in 1889 other railroad interests replaced the line with a wider 56.5-inch-wide track that extended from Spokane to Wallace.

By 1892 the Bunker Hill Mine was the largest mine operation in the Silver Valley – a valley that extended from Pinehurst to Mullan. In 1892 and again in 1899 the Bunker Hill Mine became the center of sharp conflicts between the mine owners and labor unions. These conflicts quickly spread affecting mines and towns across the Silver Valley as they turned violent – resulting in loss of life, dynamiting the Bunker Hill facilities and, later, the murder of Idaho's governor who was in office at the time of the conflict. (*See Northern Idaho, Mining – The Silver Valley and Mining – Labor/Mine Owner Conflicts and Murder of Idaho's Governor*.)

Incorporation

On October 2, 1947, Smelterville became an incorporated village.

Turning Points

Bunker Hill Mine

Noah Kellogg's 1885 discovery of the lead-zinc-silver ore deposits that led to the formation of the Bunker Hill Mine underlies the founding of Smelterville. Smelterville Flats was the depository for tailings produced by the Bunker Hill smelter.

Railroad Beginning in 1887 the railroad played a critical role in the development of the mines and cities of the Silver Valley.

Superfund Site In 1998 the federal Environmental Protection Agency (EPA) declared most of the Silver Valley a Superfund Site. Over the intervening years, there has been massive removal of soils contaminated by lead and other heavy metals to landfills and temporary realignment of the river. They then brought in clean soils, restored streams and replanted the land with native species of trees, shrubs and grasses. In Smelterville, EPA contractors removed millions of cubic yards of mine tailings to restore the land and the river to as near to its pre-mining condition as possible. A large Wal-Mart store now sets on the land once covered with mine tailings.

Smelterville Today

Amenities and Attractions The Silver Mountain Resort, part of a chain of destination resorts in the Northwest, is located in Kellogg and is one of the largest private businesses in the valley.

The resort complex starts at Gondola Village in Kellogg and takes patrons for a 3.1-mile gondola ride that passes over Wardner as it rises 3,400 feet to the ski lodge, village and condominiums.

The expanding resort includes two mountains – Kellogg and Wardner Peaks at 6,300 and 6,200 foot elevations, respectively. Additionally, the resort has six ski lifts and 67 named ski trails and runs. The resort sponsors year-round outdoor activities including concerts.

Aerial view of Smelterville.

Old Mission State Park is located eight miles west of the city. It is the location of the old Cataldo Mission of the Sacred Heart, Idaho's oldest standing building.

The Route of the Hiawatha is a scenic 30-mile round trip on a paved, non-motorized path built on the rail bed of the old Milwaukee Railroad. It is headquartered 16 miles southwest in Wallace. The path is also part of the Lookout Pass Ski and Recreation Area located east of Wallace on the Montana Border.

The Trail of the Coeur d'Alenes is a "Rails to Trails Conservancy," a national organization, project. It is a paved 72-mile-long trail built on the old Union Pacific rail bed between Mullan and Plummer.

In addition to nearby trails and resorts, the surrounding forest, mountains, streams and the Coeur d'Alene River and its tributaries offer fabulous opportunities for camping, hunting, fishing, hiking, biking, cross-country skiing and other outdoor recreation and activities.

Economy and Major Employers Wal-Mart is the city's largest employer. Several small businesses, retail stores, shops and service businesses also provide jobs for Smelterville residents.

Education Kellogg School District provides elementary and secondary education. Smelterville children attend school in Kellogg.

The nearest institution of higher learning is North Idaho College in Coeur d'Alene. North Idaho College also has a satellite location in Kellogg.

Health Care The closest hospital is the 56-bed Shoshone Medical Center in Kellogg.

Transportation Interstate 90 passes on the northern edge of the city.

The 5,500-foot runway at Shoshone County Airport, located across I-90, provides service for light private and charter aircraft. Larger facilities are available at Coeur d'Alene Airport.

Utilities and Services Private companies provide electricity, telephone and satellite services. Central Shoshone County Water District in Kellogg provides water services. South Fork Sewer District in Osburn provides regional municipal wastewater treatment services. The Kellogg Police Department provides law enforcement under contract with the City. Fire District 2, headquartered in Kellogg, provides fire protection. The fire district serves Kellogg, Smelterville, Pinehurst, the west end of Shoshone County and parts of Kootenai County.

Vision for 2050

Smelterville City Hall.

In 1960 Smelterville had a population of 1,127. Within two decades, environmental problems led to the federal government shutting down the Bunker Hill Mine and other mining operations in the Silver Valley and declaring the area a Superfund Site. By 1990 the city's population had fallen to 464. To the extent possible, EPA contractors hired local workers to clean up the Site. By 2000 the city's population had increased to 651. Since that time, Smelterville's population has stabilized at around 600.

Recent historical population trends will likely continue with modest increases in population as the valley's economy grows. In 2050 Smelterville's population will likely not exceed 800.

Rainbows over Bank Street, Wallace. Courtesy Dean Cooper.

Wallace

Statistical Data

Population: 760 *
Elevation: 2,744 feet
Precipitation: 38 inches **
Average Snowfall: 53 inches **
County: Shoshone

Temperature Range – Fahrenheit: **
Spring: 27 to 63
Summer: 45 to 79
Fall: 28 to 70
Winter: 20 to 39
* U.S. Census Bureau Estimates July 2015
**Historical averages

Wallace lies in the beautiful Silver Valley at the confluence of three creeks and the South Fork of the Coeur d'Alene River. The rugged Bitterroot Mountains of the Coeur d'Alene National Forest tower over the city. The St. Joe National Forest begins three miles south. Ten miles west on Interstate 90 is the Idaho/Montana border.

Wallace played a prominent role in the historic Coeur d'Alene Mining District, more commonly known as the Silver Valley. The entire downtown is listed on the National Register of Historic Places. Many of these buildings date back to 1890, the year Idaho became a state.

The architecture of the historic buildings gives residents and visitors alike a nostalgic sense that they are walking the streets of a late nineteenth century mining town. The city's success in preserving its historic past makes Wallace an exceptionally interesting and memorable city.

Pre-Incorporation Years

After the 1848 California Gold Rush began to subside, prospectors spread throughout the Western United States. In 1860 a party led by Elias Davidson Pierce made Idaho's first gold discovery near what is now Pierce about 70 miles due south of Wallace. A gold rush ensued the following year – an event that prompted the creation of Shoshone County, then in Washington Territory with Pierce as the county seat. (*See The Region, Gold Mining*.)

Wallace circa 1900, looking west.

On March 4, 1863, President Abraham Lincoln signed the Organic Act, creating the Idaho Territory which included part of western Montana and Wyoming. By the time Idaho became a state 27 years later, the territorial boundaries would have changed three times. (*See The Region, Idaho Territory*.)

In 1881 A.J. Prichard discovered placer gold along the tributaries of the North Fork of the Coeur d'Alene River. The ensuing gold rush that started in 1883 created the town of Murray, located about seven miles north of what is now Wallace.

The city of Wallace was the vision of William R. Wallace, the nephew of Idaho's first territorial governor, William W. Wallace. W.R., as he was known, had been a colonel in the U.S. Army and served in the Civil War. He

NP Depot, circa 1998, moved with I-90 in background, late winter.

was one of the early participants in the Prichard Creek gold rush, panning and sluicing for gold on the Canyon Creek drainage of the South Fork of the Coeur d'Alene River in 1883. The early snows drove him from that unsuccessful effort.

In that same year, W.R. filed a homestead claim and built a cabin in a valley basin of the South Fork of the Coeur d'Alene River. The next spring he and several associates surveyed the future townsite of Wallace on his homestead. They named the town Placer Center because W.R. believed it would become the commercial center for the increasing number of prospectors and miners moving into the area.

His forecast proved accurate. Within a few years, prospectors made several discoveries of precious and industrial metal ore deposits in the nearby mountains. One, made in 1885 near Placer Center, was named the Galena Silver Mine. The population of the area soared, and the town of Placer Center prospered. (*See The Region, Silver Valley Mines – Hard Rock Mines – Silver, Lead and Zinc.*)

In early 1886 town leaders applied for a post office and named W.R.'s wife, Lucy, as the postmistress. However, postal authorities objected to the name "Placer Center," so Lucy resubmitted the application with the name of Wallace. On August 17, 1886, postal authorities approved the Wallace Post Office, effectively renaming the town.

On September 10, 1887, the town's economy received another boost when the Spokane Falls and Idaho Railroad extended a narrow gauge line from Coeur d'Alene to Wallace. (*See The Region, Railroads.*)

A year later, the Northern Pacific Railroad acquired all of the valley's railroad properties. It replaced the narrow gauge line with standard gauge and built a beautiful train depot that now houses the Northern Pacific Depot Railroad Museum.

Incorporation

On May 3, 1888, the Shoshone County Commission approved incorporation of the village of Wallace. The commissioners appointed five village trustees with W.R. Wallace as chairman to serve until the next election.

Citizens were excited about their future, but it would soon be clouded as clear title to their property came into question.

When W.R. filed his homestead claim in 1883, he

Wallace 1905, looking south, Sixth Street, photograph by Arthur Fay.

used Sioux script to pay the filing fee. Federal officials later determined that the foreign script violated the requirement for the fee to be paid in U.S. legal tender. W.R. had been notified in 1887 that his homestead had been canceled.

At that point, neither he nor those who bought lots from him had clear title to their property, but W.R. kept the facts quiet.

Word finally leaked out in 1889. What ensued was chaotic. People began "property-jumping," filing property claims on platted lots and posting claim notices all over town.

The village trustees immediately called the citizens together and established rules that recognized existing streets as public property and honored property ownership rights acquired in good faith.

W.R. filed suit in district court but lost on grounds that he failed to appeal the homestead cancellation within the statutory period. The townsite patent was issued in 1892 generally in accordance with the rules established by the citizens committee. Devastated, W.R. and his family moved away from the city he founded.

Bank Street, circa 1918, looking east in winter.

A year later, Wallace became an incorporated city. At about the same time, the town installed a waterworks system and a nearby hydroelectric plant began providing electricity to the city.

Turning Points

Mines The histories of Wallace and hard rock mining in the Silver Valley are intertwined. Since the late 1800s, hard-rock mining and the Galena Silver Mine have underpinned the city's economic base. As Shoshone County's seat of government, Wallace has been at the center of many Silver Valley mine-related legal conflicts. (*See The Region, Silver Valley Mines.*)

Railroad The advent of the railroad in 1887 allowed the economies of the Silver Valley and Wallace to swell. Mining equipment and workers could be brought in more efficiently and mine production could be promptly shipped to distant markets. It also sharply improved the quality of life, making goods more accessible, mail more timely and passenger travel easier.

Fires Several months after incorporation of the village of Wallace in 1889, Idaho Territorial Governor Edward A. Stevenson said that the city of 1,000 in the beautiful basin of the South Fork of the Coeur d'Alene River at the junction of Nine Mile, Placer and Canyon Creeks, was "the supply depot of the great mining interests in these gulches. It is the railway transfer point of all the tributaries of the Upper South Fork and has many well supplied and substantial businesses housed in every branch of trade."

The downtown buildings Governor Stevenson saw were wood structures. The following year, a fire started in one of the hotels and spread, destroying the entire downtown area. It could have destroyed the economic vitality of the city, but merchants immediately moved their businesses into tent shelters and began rebuilding – this time, brick was a major building material. Many of these historic buildings still stand.

Fire had another devastating impact on the city in 1910. In August of that year, following a summer of drought and high temperatures, fierce winds accompanying a cold front whipped smaller fires into raging infernos that in two terrifying days burned across Northern Idaho and western Montana, killing eighty-five firefighters and civilians and destroying three million acres of forest – an equivalent of six billion board feet of lumber. It was the largest fire in U.S. history.

Wallace was in the fire's path. The heroic efforts of local residents and firefighters and, more importantly, a favorable shift in wind currents saved two-thirds of the city from the flames. (*See The Region, Forest Products – The Great Fire of 1910.*)

County Seat Voters made Wallace the county seat of Shoshone County in 1893, eight years after prospectors discovered the Galena Silver Mine and five years after the railroad came into the Silver Valley. Voters in Shoshone County frequently moved their county seat as the population shifted, generally as old mines played out and new ones came on line. Pierce, now in Clearwater County, was first in 1864. County voters moved the seat of government to Murray in 1885 and chose Osburn five years later.

When Wallace became the county seat, Shoshone County was in the early stages of becoming one of the richest mining districts in the world. Almost overnight, Wallace became the focal point of many of the dynamic events and conflicts that brought national and international recognition to the Silver Valley and the prodigious quantities of silver, lead, zinc and copper produced from its mines. (*See The Region, Silver Valley Mines.*)

Trolley. Courtesy Dean Cooper.

Federal Environmental Laws and the Closure of Mines In the latter half of the twentieth century, many people across the nation became concerned about the declining quality of air in cities and industrial areas as well as ground and surface waters, wildlife and habitat and general lack of care government agencies had given to the nation's public lands, environment and worker safety. This motivated Congress to enact numerous laws including creation of the Environmental Protection Agency (EPA) and the Occupational Health and Safety Administration (OSHA) in 1970 and the Clean Water Act in 1973. Environmental groups filed numerous lawsuits that effectively delayed or stopped most mining and timber harvests on federal land.

Within two decades, legal conflicts, market forces and restrictive environmental laws caused many of the Silver Valley mines to close, eliminating thousands of high-paying jobs. During that time, nearly 60 percent of Wallace's population moved away. (*See The Region, Mining and Forest Products – Leading Causes for Loss of Economic Dominance; and Silver Valley Mines – Superfund and Aftermath.*)

Wallace Today

Amenities and Attractions The city has two parks totaling five acres and offering picnic facilities, children's playground areas and athletic fields.

Four museums add to the town's ambiance and offer exhibits and memorabilia from the valley's historic mining days – the Wallace District Mining Museum, the Oasis Bordello Museum, the

A crowded street in Wallace. Courtesy Dean Cooper.

Northern Pacific Depot Railroad Museum and the Sierra Silver Mine Tour & Museum.

The Railroad Museum is located in the historic Wallace Train Depot, a center of activity when railroads dominated valley transportation.

Wallace is also home to the Northern Pacific Depot Days celebration and classic car show the Saturday before Mother's Day.

Gyro Days-Lead Creek Derby is a three-day event in mid-June, featuring a downtown carnival and the Lead Creek Derby, where event organizers drop a large decorated medicine ball into the river in Mullan and follow it to Wallace.

Mid-July is the time for the ATV Jamboree that features a parade and ATV rodeo.

In mid-August, the city holds the Wallace Heritage-Huckleberry Festival with walking tours of the city's many historic buildings and museums.

Downhill skiing is available at Lookout Pass Ski Area 10 miles east on the Idaho/Montana border. The family-oriented resort receives up to 400 inches of snow each year and has 34 ski runs and three lifts. The Silver Mountain Resort in Kellogg, 12 miles northwest, has six lifts including a single stage gondola and 73 trails. It gets more than 300 inches of snow a year.

The 18-acre Old Mission State Park, home to the oldest building in Idaho, is 25 miles west at Cataldo.

The 72-mile-long Trail of the Coeur d'Alenes is one of the most spectacular paved non-motorized trails in the Western U. S. It begins at Mullan and extends east through Wallace, ending at Plummer. The trail is an abandoned railroad line that passes over high railroad trestles and through railroad tunnels, national forests and old mining towns.

The natural rugged beauty and outdoor amenities of the national forests are becoming an increasing attraction for retirees and outdoor enthusiasts. Tourism and recreation businesses are finding increased opportunity in the city.

Economy and Major Employers Many of the mines in the region have closed; however, the Galena Silver Mine – presently owned by U.S. Silver Corporation – continues to operate. The mine's main shaft is a mile below the surface. Its lateral tunnels extend for miles and connect with other mines. Recent improvements have dramatically increased the mine's proven silver and copper ore reserves. The mine employs approximately 200 and is the city's largest employer.

With over 80 employees, Magnuson Hospitality-Wallace Inn is the city's second largest employer.

The city's other employers include several retail stores, light manufacturing and service businesses.

Education The Wallace School District provides most primary and secondary education. In 2003 the district built a new high school. Pre-kindergarten through sixth grade students attend classes in Osburn. The Wallace Junior/Senior High School is in Wallace.

The nearest institution of higher learning is North Idaho College (NIC), about 60 miles northwest in Coeur d'Alene. NIC also has a satellite location in Kellogg.

Health Care A general clinic located in the city and the 25-bed Shoshone Medical Center 13 miles west in Kellogg provide for most of the city's medical needs.

Transportation Interstate 90 intersects the city.

The 5,500-foot runway at Shoshone County Airport, near Kellogg, provides service for light private and charter aircraft.

Wallace summer view. Courtesy Dean Cooper.

Air terminals for commercial aircraft are in Coeur d'Alene and at Pullman/Moscow Regional Airport, 87 miles southwest.

Utilities and Services Private companies provide electricity, gas, satellite, ambulance and emergency medical services. The City provides domestic water. The South Fork Sewer District in Osburn provides wastewater treatment services for the region. The Wallace Police Department provides law enforcement. Fire District 2, headquartered in Kellogg, provides fire protection for Wallace and western Shoshone County.

Vision for 2050

In 1960 Wallace's population was 2,413. By 1990, largely due to federal environmental laws and market forces that led to the reduced operation or closure of mines, the city's population had fallen by more than half. Since 1990 the city's population has continued to decline at an average rate of under 1 percent annually.

Improved metal prices and mining technologies will likely allow mine owners in and around Wallace to expand their operations. However, today's mining technologies provide greater productivity with a much smaller, but highly paid, labor force. Improvement in mining activity should be a future source of new employment.

The city's retail economy is transitioning to meet the increasing tourist trade. The preservation of Wallace's historic buildings, colorful history, numerous museums and annual events are key elements promoting growing tourism. Summer attractions and four-season recreational opportunities have helped stabilize the economy that historically fluctuated widely with changing metal prices, federal policy and laws affecting the mining industry.

Building upon its past while expecting an improving industrial base, Wallace entered the twenty-first century with optimism. Its location on Interstate 90 and status as the Shoshone County seat will continue to draw attention to one of Idaho's more famous cities.

Mayors

1888 W.R. Wallace *
1893 W.D. Haskins
1894 O.B. Wallace
1895 Jacob Lockman
1897 Herman J. Rossi
1898 Thomas N. Barnard
1899 P.F. Smith
1902 T. Don Coner
1904 Herman J. Rossi
1907 Hugh L. Toole
1909 Walter H. Hanson
1911 James H. Taylor
1915 Charles R. Mowery
1917 Hormer G. Brown
1919 Hugh Toole
1927 W.H. Herrick
1929 Herman J. Rossi
1930 Ray Williams
1930 J.H. Munson
1931 Emil Pfister

1935 Herman J. Rossi
1937 L.E. Worstell
1943 John Batts
1949 R.G. Binyon
1951 C.A. Magnuson
1957 George Albertini
1957 Fred Leverling
1957 Clyde Murray
1959 Arnold Keller
1973 Herbert Wellman
1980 Paul A. DeCelle
1981 Frank Morbeck
1985 Maurice Pellissier
1991 Greg Kimberling
1992 Debbie Mikesell-Chavez
1996 Archie Hulsizer
1997 Ronald G. Garitone
2010 Dr. Dick Vester
* Village Chairman

Wardner City Hall.

Wardner

Statistical Data

Population: 185 *
Elevation: 3,065 feet
Precipitation: 30 inches **
Average Snowfall: 59 inches **
County: Shoshone

Temperature Range – Fahrenheit: **
Spring: 29 to 68
Summer: 47 to 85
Fall: 28 to 72
Winter: 19 to 42
* U.S. Census Bureau Estimates July 2015
**Historical averages

Wardner is one of the historic cities of the Panhandle's Silver Valley. It is nestled in a mile-long draw rising to the south of Kellogg in the scenic Bitterroot Mountain Range of the Coeur d'Alene National Forest.

Today, Wardner is a quiet, peaceful community in a beautiful mountain setting whose northern boundary abuts Kellogg. Its residents are a blend of retirees, families who commute to work and school and second homeowners who come a few weeks each year to relax and recreate in the mountains.

Pre-Incorporation Years

In November 1882 several prospectors, in company with A. J. Prichard who had been successfully working the area for four years, discovered large quantities of placer gold about 15 miles northeast of what would become Wardner. Their largest discoveries were along Prichard Creek near Murray. (*See Northern Idaho, The Region, Gold Mining.*)

What followed was another western gold rush. Within three years, 10,000 prospectors and miners flooded the Coeur d'Alene Mining District, later known as the Silver Valley.

One of these newcomers was an unemployed carpenter turned prospector named Noah Kellogg. Kellogg secured a grubstake from two partners. It consisted of about $18 of assorted food and supplies purchased from a store in Murray operated by James F. Wardner.

Kellogg loaded his burro with supplies and began prospecting several locations including what is called Milo Gulch and Creek. Milo was the name of Noah Kellogg's departed brother whose spirit, Noah said, directed him to his ore discovery. A month later, with his grubstake gone, Noah returned to Murray for more supplies.

The original tunnel founded by Noah Kellogg in 1885.

However, Kellogg's first investors apparently were not interested so he found new partners to finance his expedition. Newly supplied, he returned with his burro to Milo Gulch where he discovered a rich outcropping of lead, zinc and silver ore.

Colorful folklore stories developed around how Kellogg actually discovered the ore body. The stories are hearsay since Kellogg did not record the events.

However, Kellogg told others who provided various accounts. One of these accounts was a fanciful description written by James Wardner. He said that Kellogg and his jackass were on opposite sides of Milo Creek. Kellogg saw the jackass was intently looking at an object so he went over to investigate. He found the burro was staring at a vein of bright shiny lead and silver ore sparkling in the sun.

Since lead, zinc and silver oxidize and turn a dark color when exposed to the air, some have modified the story. If the jackass was indeed mesmerized by the gleaming metal ore, it was rock dislodged by the burro's hoof.

Some dispel that version of the story and speculate the jackass was just eating bunch grass near the ore outcropping when Noah found him.

Whatever the true story, Kellogg knew he had a major find but could not know that his find would ultimately produce prodigious quantities of lead, zinc, silver and gold and play a major role in the Silver Valley economy and Idaho history.

Kellogg returned to Murray to notify his grubstake partners so they could come and stake additional claims. James Wardner, hearing of Kellogg's success, followed along. However, while the others were staking their claims, Wardner marked a large section of the gulch and filed on the water rights that included Milo Creek and 10,000 miner's inches of the South Fork of the Coeur d'Alene River. (Miner's inches are measured by flow of water, and in Idaho, one miner's inch equals 1.2 cubic feet of water per minute.) As such, he became a lead partner in the discovery. Later, Kellogg's first two grubstake partners filed suit and received a 25 percent interest in the mines.

This assorted group of partners had to work together to develop the mine. The closest smelter was in San Francisco. Wardner took ore samples to Selby Smelting Company to seal a sales contract for the ore. The first shipments of ore were loaded on wagons, transported to the railhead at Rathdrum, then by rail to Portland and by boat to San Francisco.

A tent city developed in Milo Gulch. In October 1885 Kellogg and his partners named the new community "Kentuck" and applied for a post office location. However, postal authorities rejected the name. The miners then chose the name of Wardner in recognition of James Wardner's efforts in promoting the mine. The postal authorities approved the Wardner Post Office. The partners named their mine the Bunker Hill and Sullivan (Bunker Hill).

By 1890 all of the original partners in the discovery had sold their claims. The new investors built a concentrator at Wardner near the mine's main entrance. The concentrate was loaded on tramcars and sent down the mountain to Kellogg for transport to the smelter. Wardner became the entrance to the mine and the home to businesses and thousands of miners and their families who crowded into the gulch.

However, the entrance to the mine only stayed at Wardner for seven years. To improve productivity and reduce costs, the company made a lateral cut two miles long into the mountain in 1892. The tunnel's entrance at Kellogg connected the new plant site with the main mineshaft. (*See Northern Idaho, The Region, Silver Valley Mines.*)

Incorporation

When the mine entrance and ore concentrator moved down the mountain in 1892, the town's businesses and residents also began their move to Kellogg. Vacant lots began to dot the streets where homes once stood.

By the time of incorporation on June 17, 1902, the city still had a viable business district. However, that soon changed as the bank, school, post office and last grocery store either relocated to Kellogg or closed.

Turning Points

Bunker Hill Mine Noah Kellogg's ore discovery near Wardner in 1885 and the subsequent development of the mother lode that became the Bunker Hill Mine created the town of Wardner.

However, seven years later when the mine entrance and concentrator moved two miles down Milo Gulch to Kellogg, Wardner almost dried up. The city's businesses, school and most

Wardner in the valley.

of its population relocated to Kellogg.

Superfund Site In 1998 following a century of mining practices that allowed and caused massive environmental damage, the federal Environmental Protection Agency (EPA) declared a large area around Kellogg and Wardner a Superfund Site. (*See Northern Idaho, The Region, Mining and Forest Products, the Decline of Two of Idaho's Signature Industries.*)

Over the next decade EPA conducted a major clean up of lead and other contaminants in the soils and streams. Federal contractors moved the course of Milo Creek away from Wardner homes and yards or buried it in two 54 inch pipes. They also replaced contaminated soil with clean soil and topped it with new sod. The city now has new curbs and gutters, storm drains, blacktop and fresh beautiful yards.

The New Economy In March 2004 the Silver Mountain Resort broke ground at its Gondola Village and condominiums in Kellogg. Once this occurred, Wardner's vacant lots were in great demand. Real estate prices and property taxes soared. Developers raced in and started building expensive homes and condominiums. Almost overnight, instead of urban blight problems, city officials had to deal with traffic management and street widening.

Wardner is now a residential community where most residents drive the short distance to Kellogg for shopping and services. (*See Northern Idaho, The Region, The Region's Economic Base – Historically and Today*)

Wardner Today

Amenities and Attractions The city has a privately owned museum with considerable memorabilia of historic Wardner.

There are two parks. Mayor's Park, directly behind city hall has a picnic table, swings for the children and a plaque with the names and terms of all mayors.

Councilman's Park contains an impressive amount of playground equipment, all purchased with donations made in memory of current and former Wardner residents. The park will soon have a half basketball court and benches.

Most amenities and attractions in Kellogg are also available to Wardner residents, including the Kellogg Public Library and golf courses.

Silver Mountain Resort gondola.

The Silver Mountain Resort, one of a number of destination resorts in the Northwest, is Kellogg's largest private business. Originally, the resort lodge was in Wardner's city limits. Today the lodge has moved up the mountain to the 5,700-foot elevation.

The resort complex starts at Gondola Village in Kellogg and takes patrons for a 3.1-mile gondola ride that passes over Wardner as it rises 3,400 feet to the ski lodge, village and condominiums.

The expanding resort includes two mountains, Kellogg and Wardner Peaks at 6,300 and 6,200 feet, respectively. The resort has six ski lifts and 67 named ski trails and runs. It also sponsors year-round outdoor activities including concerts.

Wardner is close to other outstanding attractions. The old Cataldo Mission of the Sacred Heart, which is Idaho's oldest standing building, is located 15 miles west of the city.

The Route of the Hiawatha is a scenic 30-mile round trip on a compacted gravel, non-motorized path built on the bed of the old Milwaukee Railroad. The path, which lies 15 miles southwest, is part of the Lookout Pass Ski and Recreation Area.

The Trail of the Coeur d'Alenes is a project of the national Rails to Trails Conservancy. It is a paved 72-mile trail on the old Union Pacific rail bed between Mullan, near the Montana border, and Plummer, near the Washington border.

Each August the city celebrates Wardner Days with a picnic. Approximately 100 people attend the event. Every Christmas, Santa visits the city, riding down

Main Street and stopping to hand out candy and stuffed toys to the children who flock to see the jolly old elf.

In addition to nearby trails and resorts, the surrounding forest, mountains, streams and the Coeur d'Alene River and its tributaries offer fabulous opportunities for camping, hunting, fishing, hiking, biking, cross-country skiing and other outdoor recreation and activities.

Economy and Major Employers Wardner has no business district. Residents commute the short distance to Kellogg or other nearby cities for work or shopping.

Education The children of Wardner attend elementary, junior and high school in Kellogg.

The nearest institution of higher learning is North Idaho College, located in Coeur d'Alene. North Idaho College also has a satellite location in Kellogg.

Health Care The 56-bed Shoshone Medical Center and medical clinics in Kellogg provide most of the city's medical care.

Transportation Interstate 90 intersects Kellogg two miles north.

The 5,500-foot runway at Shoshone County Airport near Kellogg provides service for light private and charter aircraft. Heavier commercial aircraft serve Coeur d'Alene 51 miles west and Pullman/Moscow Regional Airport 87 miles southwest. Spokane International Airport is 97 miles west.

Utilities and Services Private companies provide electricity, gas, ambulance and EMT services. Central Shoshone Water in Kellogg provides water. South Fork Sewer District in Osburn provides municipal wastewater treatment services. The Kellogg Police Department provides law enforcement. Fire District 2, located in Kellogg, provides fire protection.

Vision for 2050

For two decades, the population of Wardner has ranged from 200 to 250. Since Wardner lies in a dead-end draw with steep mountains on both sides and Kellogg at the mouth, the city's ability to grow is restricted. Complicating projection of future growth is the fact that many homeowners are not residents. Other than property taxes, they are not particularly beneficial to the city or its economy.

The city's history is also its future. What happens in Wardner is often dependant on what happens in Kellogg. By 2050 Wardner's population may not be much different from historical trends. However, citizens will continue to cherish and preserve the city's beauty, charm and heritage.

Mayors

1902 Hugh France	1943 L.R. Stebbins
1905 W.F. Goddard	1955 Woodrow Grant
1907 Hugh France	1972 Art Roose
1908 H.W. Van Warren	1974 C.R. Peterson
1909 E.L. Brown	1986 Jo Ann Groves
1911 D.W. Pupler	1990 C.R. Peterson
1913 B. Flaig	1998 Jo Ann Groves
1917 Earl R. Redding	2014 Joseph A. Guardipee
1942 Herman Carlson	

BIBLIOGRAPHY

The 2000 Comprehensive Plan: City of Eagle, Idaho. Eagle: Eagle City Council, 1999.

2005-2006 Teton Valley Visitors Guide. Idaho Falls: Canyon Media for the Teton Valley Chamber of Commerce, 2004.

The 2007-2008 Teton Valley Activity Guide. Idaho Falls: Canyon Media for the Teton Valley Chamber of Commerce, 2006.

2009 and 2010 Answer Book. Coeur d'Alene: Coeur d'Alene Press (supplemental publication), March 31, 2009, and April 28, 2010.

Abramson, Ruby. Spanning the Century: The Life of W. Averell Harriman, 1891-1986. New York: William Morrow & Co., 1992.

Aiken, Katherine G. Idaho's Bunker Hill: The Rise and Fall of a Great Mining Company, 18851981. Norman: University of Oklahoma Press, 2005.

Alt, David, and Donald W. Hyndman. Roadside Geology of Idaho. Missoula: Mountain Press Publishing Company, 1989.

---Roadside Geology of the Northern Rockies. Missoula: Mountain Press, 1972.

Anderson, Abraham C. Trails of Early Idaho. Caldwell: Caxton Printers, Ltd., 1940.

Anderson, Alfred Leonard. Detailed Geology of the Minnie Moor and Queen of the Hills Mining Property. Moscow: University of Idaho, 1950.

---, et al. Detailed Geology of Certain Areas in the Mineral Hills and Warm Springs Mining District. Moscow: University of Idaho, 1950.

---, and Warren Richard Wagner. A Geological Reconnaissance of the Hailey Gold Belt (Camas District) Blaine County, Idaho. Moscow: University of Idaho, 1946.

Arrington, Leonard J. History of Idaho. Moscow: University of Idaho Press, 1994.

Atteberry, Jennifer. "Domestic and Commercial Architecture in Caldwell." Idaho Yesterdays, Winter 1980, pp. 2-17.

Baker, Bessie's Meadows Valley High School English Class. History of Meadows Valley. 1945.

Basalt Centennial Committee, Verlyn Dye Outcelt, Chairman. Basalt Idaho Centennial. Idaho Falls, Idaho: Valley Litho., 1985.

Beal, Merrill D., and Merle W. Wells. History of Idaho. New York: Lewis Historical Publishing Company, 1959.

Beierle, Amber. "Boise's Birthday." Office of the City Historian <http://www.boisehistory.com> 2004.

Benedict, Hope A. "A Common Heritage: A Promise of Abundance: Cow Camps, Mining, and Timber Operations of Lemhi County." Salmon: Salmon National Forest, 1994.

Bingham County History. Written and compiled by the people of Bingham County, Idaho. Blackfoot: Bingham County Centennial Book Committee, 1985.

Bingham, Randy E. Burley Irrigation District History: The First 100 Years. Burley: Burley Irrigation District, nd.

Bird, Annie Laurie. Boise, the Peace Valley. Caldwell: Canyon County Historical Society, 1975, c1934.

---My Home Town. Caldwell: Caxton Printers, 1968.

---Old Fort Boise. Parma: Old Fort Boise Historical Society, 1971.

Blase, Fred W. "Political History of Idaho Territory 1863-1890." Master's Thesis, University of California, 1924.

Boone, Lalia Phipps. From A to Z in Latah County, Idaho: A Place Name Dictionary. Moscow: Latah County Historical Society, 1983.

Bottolfsen, C.A. Author and editor. Articles about the early history of the Lost River from the files of the South Custer County Historical Society.

Bourasaw, Noel V. "James Frederick Wardner Series." Skagit River Journal of History and Folklore. <http://www.skagitriverjournal.com/WA/Whatcom/FairhavenSth/Pioneers/Pre1900/Wardner/Wardner01-JamesBioPortal.html> August 2010.

Bowen, A.W. Progressive Men of Southern Idaho. Chicago: A.W. Bowen & Co., 1904.

Brainard, Wendell. Golden History Tales from Idaho's Coeur d'Alene Mining District. Ray Chapman, ed. Kellogg: Wendell Brainard, 1990.

Brock, Eugene Linda, et al. Pioneer Settlers and Pioneer Ranches of Valley County. A Valley County History Project. Grand Junction: Action Services, 2002.

Brosnan, Cornelius James. History of the State of Idaho. Idaho: Charles Scribner's Sons, 1918.

Buckway, JaNene Johnson. Wendell: Hub City of Magic Valley. Shoshone: Wendell 75th Anniversary Committee, 1984.

Burg, Thomas E. White Pine Route: The History of the Washington, Idaho and Montana Railway Company. Coeur d'Alene: Museum of North Idaho Publications, 2003.

Caldwell Centennial Calendar 1883-1983: 100 Years of Documentary in Words and Pictures. Caldwell: Caldwell Historic Preservation Commission, 1982.

Each day of this 1983 calendar contains an historic note. It is indexed.

Caldwell Public Library. Oral History Committee. Voices from the Past. Caldwell: Caldwell Public Library.

A series of slide-tape programs about early Caldwell including businesses, music, women, architecture and irrigation.

"Caldwell Revisited 1883-1923." News Tribune. July 4, 1976. A special edition printed during the U.S. bicentennial year.

Carlson, Jimmie I. "Remaking Idaho's Capitol City: A Case Study in Urban Renewal." Masters Thesis, Boise State University, 1996.

Carney, Ellen. Historic Soda Springs: Oasis on the Oregon Trail. Wayan: Traildust Publishing, 1998.

Carns, Iva Hollingsworth. Steamboats and Memories. Coeur d'Alene: Iva Carns, 1990.

Casner, Nick, and Valerie Kiesig. Trolley: Boise Valley's Electric Road, 1891-1928. Boise: Black Canyon Communications, 2002.

"Cavalcade Issues." Idaho Press Tribune.

The Idaho Press Tribune publishes a special series in the spring of each year, which often includes historical articles. Some have been indexed.

Chapman, Ray. Uncle Bunker. Kellogg: Chapman Publishing, 1994.

---. History of Idaho's Silver Valley: 1878-2000. Kellogg: Chapman Publishing, 2000.

---. History of Kellogg, Idaho, 1885-2002. Kellogg: Chapman Publishing, 2002. Chedsey, Zona, and Carolyn Frei, eds. Idaho County Voices: A People's History From the Pioneers to the Present. Grangeville: Idaho County Centennial Committee, 1990.

Clanton, Dorothy M. The Georgie Oakes: The Lady of the Lake.

---Bringing the Iron Horse to the Coeur d'Alenes.

Clark, Lynda Campbell. Nampa, Idaho, 1885-1985: A Journey of Discovery. Nampa: Pacific Press, 1985.

Clements, Louis J., and Harold S. Forbush. Pioneering the Snake River Fork Country. Rexburg: Eastern Idaho Publishers, 1972.

A Completed Century 1888-1988. Caldwell: Centennial Committee Boone Presbyterian Church, 1987.

Conley, Cort. Idaho for the Curious: A Guide. Cambridge: Beckeddy Books, 1982.

Cox, Cheryl A., and Lexie Ann French. Second Stories: Historical Narratives of Idaho Falls Women. Idaho Falls: The Graphic Experience, 1986.

Crosby, Mike. "A Common Heritage: Lemhi County, the Salmon National Forest, and the Civilian Conservation Corps." Salmon: Salmon National Forest, 1994.

Crow, Donna Fletcher. Kathryn: Days of Struggle and Triumph. Chicago: Moody Press, 1992.

---Elizabeth: Days of Loss and Hope. Chicago: Moody Press, 1993.

---Stephanie: Days of Turmoil and Victory. Chicago: Moody Press, 1993.

Crowder, David Lester. Rexburg, Idaho: The First One Hundred Years 1883-1983. Rexburg: D.L. Crowder, 1983.

Culdesac Idaho Centennial 1903-2003: 100 Years of Memories. Culdesac: Culdesac Gem Committee, 2003.

Davis, Belinda. A Study of Irrigation and the Development of Ada County. Boise: Ada County Historical Preservation Council, 1990.

Davis, L.J. "Tearing Down Boise." Harpers. November 1974.

Declo History Committee and Declo Alumni Association, contributors. Declo, My Town, My People. Burley: Burley Reminder, Incorporated, 1974.

DeVoto, Bernard, ed. The Journals of Lewis and Clark. Boston: Houghton Mifflin Company, 1953.

Dillion, Wilda Collier. Deaths and Burials: Boise Barracks Military Reserve, Idaho, 1863-1913.

Boise: W.C. Dillion, 2003.

Downing, James L. History of Teton City, Idaho: 1833-1900. Rexburg: Ricks College, 1971.

Driggs, B.W. History of Teton Valley, Idaho. Louis J. Clements and Harold S. Forbush, ed.

Rexburg: Arnold Agency, 1926, revised 1970, copyright 1970 by Louis J. Clements, Rexburg: Eastern Idaho Publishing Company.

Driggs Idaho Stake: Diamond Jubilee 1901-1981. Rexburg: Ricks College Press, 1982.

Driscoll, Ann Nilsson. They Came to a Ridge. Moscow: News Review Pub. Co., 1970.

Druss, Claudia, et al, eds. Patterns of the Past: The Ada County Historic Sites Inventory. Boise: The Arrowrock Group, 2001.

Eagle Island State Park Master Plan. Boise: Beck & Baird, 2000.

Elsensohn, Sister M. Alfreda. Pioneer Days in Idaho County, Volume 2. Cottonwood: Caxton Printers, 1971.

Etulain, Richard W., and Bert W. Marley, eds. The Idaho Heritage: A Collection of Historical Essays. Pocatello: Idaho State University Press, 1974.

Fanselow, Julie. Idaho Off the Beaten Path: A Guide to Unique Places. Guilford: Globe Pequot Press, 2010.

--- What a Democracy Looks Like, Kuna, Idaho: Where a Community Pulls Together to Face Growth." Study Circle Resource Center, 2004.

Feser, Bonnie Jean Bacon. Georgetown, ID (Twin Creeks), 1869-1950. Georgetown: Bonnie Jean Bacon Feser, 2006.

Fick, Bob. "Idaho Governor Awards $2.1 Million in Community Grants." Gem County Chamber of Commerce. OpenPotion. 7 July 2006. <www.emmettidaho.com> August 2010.

Fisher, Vardis. Idaho Encyclopedia. Federal Writers" Project. Caldwell: Caxton Printers, Ltd. 1938.

Fisk, Dale, and Don Dopf. The P&IN to the Golden Heart of Idaho: The Story of the Pacific & Idaho Northern Railway. Boise: Writers Press, 2001.

Flanders, Robert Bruce. Nauvoo: Kingdom on the Mississippi. Urbana: University of Illinois Press, 1965.

Fogg, P.M. A History of the Minidoka Project, Idaho, to 1912 Inclusive. Boise: Bureau of Reclamation, 1915.

Frandsen, Rebecca, and Ruth Ann Olson. The Best Trader on the Emigrant Road: The Life and Adventures of Bob Dempsey, Mountaineer. Lava Hot Springs: Greater Lava Hot Springs Chamber of Commerce, 1979.

---Lava Hot Springs. For City of Lava Hot Springs Tourist Information Center

Franzen, John G. Southeastern Idaho Cultural Resources Overview, Burley and Idaho Falls Districts: Final Report R-2196. Jackson: Commonwealth Associates, 1981. Pp 115-191.

French, Hiram T. History of Idaho: a narrative account of its historical progress, its people and its principal interests. Chicago: Lewis Publishing Co., 1914.

Fritzen, Mary Jane, ed. Idaho Falls, City of Destiny. Idaho Falls: Bonneville County Historical Society, 1991.

---Bonneville County: Its Formation and Description. Idaho Falls: Bonneville County Heritage Association, 2006.

Gentry, James R., et al. A Centennial History of Bliss, Idaho: 1883-1983. Gooding: Pilot Press, 1983.

---In the Middle and on the Edge: The Twin Falls Region of Idaho. Twin Falls: College of Southern Idaho, 2003.

Gidley, J.W. Hunting Fossils on the Old Oregon Trail. Smithsonian Institution, 1930.

Gilbert, Millie. "Emmett: Spotlight City." Idaho Magazine. March 2005. 33-40.

Gittins, H. Leigh. Pocatello Portrait: the early years, 1878 to 1928. Moscow: The University Press of Idaho, 1983.

Gooding County History Book Committee. Gooding County Roots and Branches, 1989. Gooding: Taylor Publishing Company, 1989.

Graff, Leo W. Jr. "Fred T. Dubois-Biographical Sketch." Idaho State University: Eli M. Oboler Library. Idaho State University. n.d. <http://www2.isu.edu/library/special/mc004b.htm> 12 Jan 2007.

Gray, Dale M. "Moved Properties in American Falls, Idaho." National Register of Historic Places. Nomination 2005.

Groefsema, Olive. Elmore County: Its Historical Gleanings " A collection of pioneer narratives, treasured family pictures, and early clippings about the settling of Elmore County, Idaho. Caldwell: Caxton Printers, Ltd., 1949.

Hafen, LeRoy R., ed. Trappers of the Far West: Sixteen Biographical Sketches. Lincoln: University of Nebraska Press, 1965.

Hailey, Leona Cartee. "Boise in the Seventies." Cartee Collection, Idaho State Historical Society MS 376.

Haines, Aubrey L. Historic Resource Study: Historic Sites Along the Oregon Trail. Denver: Denver Service Center, Historic Preservation Team, National Park Service, 1973.

Haines, Jr., Francis D., ed. The Snake Country Expedition 1830-1831: John Work's Field Journal. Norman: University of Oklahoma Press, 1971.

Hall, Jory. Kuna Civil War to Chauatuqua: Thumbprints Across the Pages of History. Kuna: Thumbprints, 1997.

Hart, Alfred B. "History of Bloomington, Idaho." compiled May 12, 1933.

Hart, Arthur A. Wings over Idaho: An Aviation History. Caldwell: Caxton Press, 1991.

Hartkopf, Frank. History of Bingham County, Idaho. Laramie: University of Wyoming, 1942.

Hartman, Hugh H. The Founding Fathers of Boise. Boise: Hugh H. Hartman, 1989.

Hawkes, Blaine. (Uncopyrighted local history book, used with permission of the author.)

Hawley, James H. History of Idaho, the Gem of the Mountains. Chicago: The S.J. Clarke Publishing Co., 1920.

Hay, O.P. "The Pleistocene of the Western Region of North America and Its Vertebrate Animals." Washington: Carnegie Institution of Washington Publication N. 322B:1-346, 1927.

Hine, Robert. Community on the American Frontier. Norman: University of Oklahoma Press, 1980.

History of Arimo: Including Arkansas, Hawkins Basin, Marsh Center, and Robin. Compiled by the Arimo Centennial History Committee for the Idaho Centennial. Arimo: Arimo Centennial History Committee, 1991.

History of the Brick Plant at Troy, Idaho. Troy: Troy Historical Society.

History of Cassia County and Burley Idaho. 1952.

History of North Idaho. or An Illustrated History of North Idaho: Embracing Nez Perce, Idaho, Kootenai and Shoshone Counties, State of Idaho. Spokane: Western Historical Publishing Company, 1903.

Holladay Engineering Company. "Wastewater System Preliminary Engineering Report " 6/1/051-12."

Holland, Wendolyn. Sun Valley: An Extraordinary History. Ketchum: The Idaho Press, 1998.

Holm, Debra Nelson, et al. Nampa's People, 1886-1986: Discovering Our Heritage. Nampa: Nampa Centennial Committee, 1986.

Horton, Alice, et al., eds. Beautiful Bonneville. Logan: Herff Jones, 1989.

House, Connie. Firestorm! Big Blowup II in North Idaho. Coeur d'Alene: Listos Publications, 1992.

Hult, Ruby El. Steamboats in the Timber. Coeur d'Alene: Caxton Printers, 1952.

---Northwest Disaster: Avalanche and Fire. Portland: Binford & Mort, 1960.

Idaho Poets and Writers Guild. These to Remember. S.L.: The Guild, 1962.

Idaho Power Company. "Early History of the Idaho Power Company." 1929.

Idaho State Historical Society. Emigrant Trails of Southern Idaho. (Idaho Cultural Resource Series Number 1). Boise: U.S. Bureau of Land Management, 1993.

---. "Goodale's Cutoff from Boise Valley to Powder River." (Reference Series Number 1048). Boise: Idaho State Historical Society, 1994.

--- "Massacre Rocks." (Reference Series Number 234). Boise: Idaho State Historical Society, 1971.

---"Route of Alexander Ross, 1824." Idaho State Historical Society Reference Series, Number 86. July 1990. <http://history.idaho.gov/sites/default/files/uploads/reference-series/0086.pdf> April 2016.

---Postmarked Idaho: A List of Idaho Post Offices. Boise: Idaho State Historical Society, 1975.

---"Weldon Brinton Heyburn: May 25, 1852 " October 18, 1912. (Reference Series Number 544). Boise: Idaho State Historical Society, 1971.

---"The Beginning of the New York Canal." Idaho State Historical Society Reference Series, Number 190. March 1972.

---"Packer John's Cabin." Idaho State Historical Society Reference Series, Number 292. 1996.

---"Seven Devils." Idaho State Historical Society Reference Series, Number 116. 1981.

---"Gilmore and Pittsburgh Railroad." Idaho State Historical Society Reference Series, Number 215. 1976.

---"Salmon Falls and Thousand Springs." Idaho State Historical Society Reference Series, Number 184. 1987.

---"Oregon Trail Routes in and around Boise." Idaho State Historical Society Reference Series, Number 921. 1989.

Idaho State Transportation Department. Idaho Highway Historical Marker Guide. Boise: Idaho State Transportation Department, 2010.

Idaho Travel Council. Idaho: Official State Travel Guide. Boise: Idaho Department of Commerce, nd.

Idaho: Where the Past Comes Alive. Idaho City: Idaho City Chamber of Commerce.

Inman, Mary J. Twin Falls Centurybook: 1904-2004. Twin Falls: Hosteler Press, 2003.

International Daughters of the Utah Pioneers. Pioneer Women of Faith & Fortitude. Salt Lake City: Daughters of the Utah Pioneers, 1998.

Iona Centennial History Book 1883-1983: A Centennial History Book, Containing Historical Material and Personal Histories, Submitted by the Residents and Previous Residents of Iona, Bonneville County, Idaho. Rexburg: Ricks College Press, 1983.

Irving, Washington. Astoria or Anecdotes of an Enterprise Beyond the Rocky Mountains. Philadelphia: Carey, Lea & Blanchard, 1836.

Johnson, Stella E. History of Troy 1892-1992. Troy: Stella E. Johnson, 1992.

Jordan, Grace Edgington. The King's Pines of Idaho: A Story of the Browns of McCall. Pontiac: Kirkwood Pub. Co., 1998.

Klenck, Dee. A Jewel Between Two Rivers: the History of Fruitland, Idaho. Fruitland: Gem Publishing Company, 1990.

Kunkler, Lois Roark. "A Brief History of the Eagle High School Broncs." The Eagle Express, Jan. 13, 1995, p. 1.

Kuna Chamber of Commerce. Gateway to the Birds of Prey: Kuna, Idaho. Kuna: Economic Development Committee, Kuna Chamber of Commerce, 1999.

Layton, Stanford J., ed. Utah's Lawless Fringe: Stories of True Crime. Salt Lake City: Signature Books, 2001.

Lee, William H. "A History of Phosphate Mining in Southeast Idaho." U.S. Geological Survey, U.S. Department of Interior, Open File Report #00-425, Version 1.0. <http://geopubs.wr.usgs.gov/open-file/of))-425> September 2010.

Lemhi County History Book Committee. Centennial History of Lemhi County, Vol. I. Salmon: Lemhi County History Book Committee, 1992.

Leppert, Elaine and Lorene Thurston. Early Caldwell Through Photographs. Caldwell, Idaho: Caldwell Committee for the Idaho State Centennial, 1990.

Link, Paul Karl, and E. Chilton Phoenix. Rocks, Rails & Trails, 2nd Edition. Pocatello: Idaho Museum of Natural History, 1996.

Lohrey, Dana, et al. The Elk City Wagon Road. Centennial Edition. Grangeville: Dana Lohrey, 1995.

Longley, C.L. "Assay Office in Boise Holds Venerable Place in Story of Yellow Dust." Boise: Idaho Statesman, January 19, 1930.

Longteig, Margaret Nell, and Rheba Miller. Remember When. 1976.

Lorenzen, Marilyn. Personal knowledge and writings.

Lovell, Edith Haroldsen. Captain Bonneville's County. Idaho Falls: The Eastern Idaho Farmer, 1963.

Lowell, Helen, and Lucile Peterson. Our First Hundred Years: A Biography of Lower Boise Valley 1814-1914. Caldwell: Caxton Printers, 1976.

Lucas, F.A. The Fossil Bison of North America. Washington: Smithson.Proceed.v.21, 1899.

Lukas, J. Anthony. Big Trouble. New York: Simon and Schuster, 1997.

Lyon, Ruth B. The Village that Grew: Emmettsville, Martinsville, Emmett. Lithocraft for R.B. Lyon, 1979

MacGregor, Carol. "The Founding Community in Boise Idaho: 1882-1910. Ph.D. Diss., University of New Mexico, 1999.

Madsen, Brigham D. The Shoshoni Frontier and the Bear River Massacre. Salt Lake City, Utah: University of Utah Press, 1985.

"Magic Valley Region Wildlife Management Areas." Idaho Fish and Game. <www.fishandgame.idaho.gov/cms/wildlife/wma/carey> April 2016.

Marker, Joe L. Eagle Rock, U.S.A. (now Idaho Falls, Idaho). Idaho Falls: Roboco Printing, 1980.

Market Lake Centennial Committee, ed. Market Lake Centennial (1867-1967). Roberts: Market Lake Centennial Committee, 1967.

McConnell, W.J. Early History of Idaho. Glendale: The Arthur H. Clark Company, 1913.

McDevitt, Thomas. Idaho's Malad Valley: A History. Pocatello: Little Red Hen, Incorporated, 2001.

McGonigal, Mary Brown. Spring of Gladness: Reminiscences of Pioneer Life in the Wood River Valley. Ketchum: McGonigal, 1976.

McLeod, Geo A. History of Alturas and Blaine Counties Idaho. Hailey: The Hailey Times, 1930.

Mendiola, Judy. "A History of Eagle, Idaho." Eagle: The Author, 1998.

Meyers, Rex. "The Implausible Gilmore and Pittsburgh." The Colorado Rail Annual, No. 15. Golden: Colorado Railroad Museum, 1981.

Miller, John B. The Trees Grew Tall. Moscow: The News Review Publishing Company, 1972.

Mills, Nellie Ireton. All Along the River: Territorial and Pioneer Days on the Payette. Montreal: Payette Radio Limited, 1963

Mini-Cassia Chamber of Commerce & Visitor Center. <http://www.minicassiachamber.com/> April 2016.

Mitchell, Victoria E. History of Selected Mines in the Alder Creek Mining District, Custer County Idaho. Special Staff Report. Moscow: Idaho Geological Survey, University of Idaho, 1997.

Monroe, Julie R. Moscow: Living and Learning on the Palouse. Charleston: Arcadia Publishing, 2003.

---et al. Rekindled Spirit. Moscow: Idaho State Historical Society, 2009

Neilsen, Judith. "A Brief History of the Washington, Idaho & Montana Railway Company." University of Idaho Special Collections & Archives, Manuscript Group 139, 1982.

Okelberry-Jones, Sharon. History of Oakley, Idaho. Unspecified Publisher, 1990.

Oppenheimer, Doug. Sun Valley: A Biography. Boise: Beatty Books, 1976.

Otness, Lillian Woodworth. A Great Good Country: A Guide to Historic Moscow and Latah County, Idaho. Moscow: Latah County Historical Society, 1983.

Parker, Karen, et al. Teton Centennial: 100 Years of Progress, 1883-1983. Teton: Teton Centennial Committee, 1983.

Petersen, Keith. Company Town: Potlatch, Idaho, and the Potlatch Lumber Company. Pullman: Washington State University Press, 1987.

Pettite, William Stibal. Memories of Market Lake, Vol. II. Roberts: William Pettite, 1977.

Pfeifer, Friedl. The Sun Valley Ski Book. New York: A.S. Barnes & Company, 1939.

Plastino, Ben J. Coming of Age: Idaho Falls and the Idaho National Engineering Laboratory 1949-1990. Ed. Diane Plastino Graves. Chelsea: Bookcrafters, 1998.

"Portrait of a Small City: Eagle, Idaho." Boise: Journal of Commerce, 1979, no paging.

Postmarked Idaho: List of Idaho Post Offices. Boise: Idaho State Historical Society, 1975.

Quinn, Larry. A History of Magic Valley. Twin Falls: Publishing West Associates, 1996.

Ransel, Sandra, and Charles Durand. Crossroads: A History of the Elmore County Area. Mountain Home: Elmore County Historical Research Team, 1985

Rasker, Ray, and Ben Alexander. Working Around the White Clouds. Bozeman: Sonoran Institute, 2003.

Records and minutes of the various cities in Idaho.

Reed, Mary. "Latah Legacy" articles published by Latah County Historical Society

Reid, Wallace and Bates. Blackfoot Historic Homes and Buildings. 1996.

The Renaissance: a Book of Historical Nature and Especially a Record of Past Year's Events at the College of Idaho. Caldwell: Associated Body of the College of Idaho, 1908.

Rexburg Community Review. Boise: Idaho Rural Partnership, 2004.

Ricketts, Virginia. Then and Now in Southern Idaho. Jerome: Falls City Publishing, 1998.

Roberts, Edwards. Shoshone and Other Western Wonders. New York: Harper & Brothers, 1888.

Robertson, Donald B. Encyclopedia of Western Railroad History; Volume II: The Mountain States. Dallas: Taylor Publishing Co., 1991.

Rockwood, Craig, et al. Iona History Book, Vol. II. Iona: Iona Historical Committee, 2005.

Ronda, James P. Lewis and Clark among the Indians. Lincoln: University of Nebraska Press, 1984.

Route of the Oregon Trail in Idaho. Boise: Idaho Department of Highways, 1963.

Rowland, Frank P. Founding of McCall, Idaho. Caldwell: Caxton Printers, 1960.

Russell, Osborne. Journal of a Trapper: Nine Years in the Rocky Mountains, 1834-1843. Edited from original manuscript by L.A. York. Boise: Syms-York, 1914.

Salant, Priscilla, et al. Profile of Rural Idaho. Boise: Idaho Commerce & Labor, nd.

Scharnhorst, Marie H. "Genesee, 100 Years." Latah Legacy (Spring, 1989, V. 18 No. 1). Moscow: Latah County Historical Society, 1989. Pp 3-36.

Scott, Donna. A ribute to the Past, a Legacy for the Future. Miriam Booth Breckenridge, et al, eds. Twin Falls: Twin Falls County Business History, 1990.

Scott, Orland A. Pioneer Days on the Shadowy St. Joe. Coeur d'Alene: Caxton Printers Ltd, 1968.

The Settlement of the Kuna Region, 1900-1925. Caldwell, Caxton Printers, 1983.

"Seventieth Anniversary and 'Days of '83' edition." Caldwell News Tribune. May 6, 1953. An excellent special edition of the newspaper describing Caldwell's early days; the advertisements are histories of many local businesses.

Shadduck, Marvin E. The Dalton Story. Coeur d'Alene: Museum of North Idaho, 2003.

Shallat, Todd, and Johnny Hester. "Trails and Rails: Boise as a Transportation Hub." Office of the Boise City Historian. <http://www.boisehistory.com/> 2005.

Shoup, George E. History of Lemhi County. Reprint. Salmon: Salmon Public Library Association, 1992.

Sims, Robert C., and Hope Ann Benedict, eds. Idaho Governors: Historical Essays on Their Administrations. Boise: Boise State University Press, 1992.

Singletary, Robert. Kootenai Chronicles. Coeur d'Alene: Century Publishing, 1995.

Slavik, Walter K.M. "Pioneering Public Power: Minidoka Project, Idaho." The Reclamation Era. Boise: Bureau of Reclamation, 1941.

Smith, Evelyn L. A Century of Progress, Evolution to Excellence, 1889-1989: A History of the Schools of Mullan, Idaho. Mullan: Mullan Education Foundation, 1989.

Smith, Robert Wayne. The Coeur d'Alene Mining War of 1892: A Case Study of an Industrial Dispute. Corvallis: Oregon State University Press, 1961.

Smythe, Rachel. Entertaining Strangers. Salt Lake City: Amber Pen, 2005.

Solum, Romola Hansen. History of Georgetown. Lola Hoskins, researcher.

South Custer County Historical Society, Inc. photograph collection.

Spence, Clark C. For Wood River or Bust: Idaho's Silver Boom of the 1880s. Moscow: University of Idaho Press, 1999.

Stacy, Susan M. Proving the Principle: A History of the Idaho National Engineering and Environmental Laboratory, 1949-1999. Washington: United States Government Printing, 2000.

---Legacy of Light: A History of the Idaho Power Company. Boise: Idaho Power Company, 1991.

Stapilus, Randy. It Happened in Idaho. Guilford: Globe Pequot Press, 2002.

Stearns, H.T., Lynn Crandall, and Willard G. Steward. Geology and Ground-water Resources of the Snake River Plain in Southeastern Idaho: Water Supply Paper 774. Boise: U.S. Government Print Office, 1938.

Stene, Eric A. The Minidoka Project. Denver: Bureau of Reclamation History Program, 1993.

Stoll, William T., and H.W. Whicker. Silver Strike: the True Story of Silver Mining in the Coeur d'Alenes. Boston: Little, Brown, and Co., 1932.

Stoddard, Bonnie J., researcher and compiler. History of Dubois.

Strahorn, Carrie Adell. Fifteen Thousand Miles by Stage. New York: Putnam's, 1911. Two chapters tell of the establishment of Caldwell, "City Building-Caldwell, and other Towns on the Frontier" and "Pot-Pourii." The University of Nebraska published a two-volume edition in 1988.

Tacke, Kathryn. Regional Economist. "Idaho County Workforce Trends." Boise: Idaho Department of Labor, January 2010

Taking the Scenic Route: A Guide to Idaho Scenic Byways. Boise: Idaho Transportation Department, 2000.

Taylor, Dorice. Sun Valley. Sun Valley: Ex Libris Press, 1980.

Tollefson, Gene. BPA and the Struggle for Power at Cost. Portland: Bonneville Power Administration, 1987.

Toponce, Alexander. Reminiscences of Alexander Toponce. Norman: University of Oklahoma Press, 1971.

Travel the Oregon Trail in Caribou County: A Self-guided Tour of Sites Documented in Emigrant Diaries & Journals of Early Explorers. Soda Springs: Soda Springs Chamber of Commerce, 2004.

Trego, Byrd. Author, editor, and newspaper publisher. Articles about the history of the Lost River from the files of the South Custer County Historical Society.

Trent, Geneva. History of Eagle Fire Department. Eagle: Eagle Historic Preservation Commission, 1997.

Tweedy, Doug. Clearwater County Profile. Orofino: Idaho Department of Commerce and Labor, 2006.

Twin Falls Historical Society. Twin Falls County Territorial Centennial 1863-1963: A Folk History of Twin Falls County, Idaho. Twin Falls: Standard Printing Company, 1963.

Walgamott, Charles S. Reminiscences of Early Days: a Series of Historical Sketches and Happenings in the Early Days of Snake River Valley. Twin Falls: Idaho Citizen, 1926.

---Six Decades Back. Moscow: University of Idaho Press, 1936

Walker, Deward E., Jr. Indians of Idaho. Moscow: University of Idaho Press, 1978.

Walker, Lola, Lula Barnard, and Faunda Bybee. Tosoiba: Sparkling Waters. Soda Springs: Daughters of the Utah Pioneers, 1958.

Wells, Merle. Gold Camps and Silver Cities: Nineteenth Century Mining in Central and Southern Idaho, 2nd edition. Moscow: Idaho Department of Lands, Bureau of Mines and Geology, 1983.

Wells, Merle, and Arthur Hart. Boise: An Illustrated History. Sun Valley: American Historical Press, 2000.

Whitlock, Flint, and Bob Bishop. Soldiers on Skis: A Pictorial Memoir of the 10th Mountain Division. Boulder: Paladin Press, 1992.

Whitman, Narcissa Prentiss. My Journal 1836. Edited and with introduction by Lawrence L. Dodd. Fairfield: Ye Galleon Press, 1994.

Winslow, Dilla Tucker. From Sagebrush to Green Fields: A History of Greenleaf Idaho. Private Printing, 1984. (Permission to re-publish granted to the City of Greenleaf by the heirs of Dilla Tucker Winslow.)

Witherell, Jim. "History Along the Greenbelt." Boise: Ada County Centennial Committee, 1990.

Woods, Shelton, ed. Valley County Idaho Prehistory to 1920. A Valley County History Project. Grand Junction: Action Publishing, 2002.

Wright, Patricia, and Lisa B. Reitzes. Tourtellotte & Hummel of Idaho: The Standard Practice of Architecture. Logan: Utah State University Press, 1987.

Young, Virgil M. The Story of Idaho. Moscow: University of Idaho Press, 1990.

Yorgason, Blaine and Brenton. Roger and Sybil Ferguson History. Unknown.

Unpublished works:
Adkinson, Virginia, local White Bird resident and historian. Research and writings.

Asker, Bonita, local White Bird resident and historian. Research and writings.

Baker, Ronald J. "Chronology of Eagle, Idaho" Unpublished manuscript on file at Eagle Public Library Reference Dept., 2005.

Benedict, Hope Ann. "Place and Community in the Mining West: Lemhi County, Idaho, 1866-1929" Ph.D. diss., University of Oregon, 1996.

Bennett, E.H. "Genesee Timeline." Unpublished history and notes about Genesee, Idaho.

Benton, Jon. "Thirsty for a Water System."

Benton, Josh. "Telephone Troubles."

Brown, Kimberly Rice, unpublished files.

Burtenshaw, Frances D. Compiled writings of George F. Shelley, Theodocia M. Dana, and Mary S. Davis. "Eagle Public Library History." Unpublished manuscript on file at Eagle Public Library Reference Dept., 1984.

Hale, Kent. "Oakley Has Magnificent Homes." (Information sheet provided by the City.)

Hansen, Hortense. History of the City of Shelley.

Kreiman, Marilyn. "Biography of Pear Lucile Small Lewis."

"A history of the Kuna Grange," unpublished manuscript, 2005. Compiled by Sharon Fisher, Lecturer, Kuna Grange, 2005, from information originally written by Mrs. Laura Rea (originally made available by Mrs. Ben Aylsworth of Nampa, and compiled from old record books and data

collected by E. G. May and B. Mathews), Lois Dustman, and Ruth Burningham. Help also
provided by Wayne and Blanche Kuhlman and Florence Chaney.

Miller, John B. Unpublished articles.
Peterson, Lynn. Research paper: History of St. Charles, Idaho.
Sleeper, Richard. "Biography of Richard Crampton Sleeper."
Smith, Elizabeth. "History of the Salmon National Forest," ca. 1970.
Strong, Sam. Unpublished recollections.
Thomason, William J. "Reubens History." 1990.
Wilde, J.P., Journal Correspondent. "Story of Georgetown."

Newspapers and Magazines:
American Falls Press. "Tragedy Brought Moral Uplift, Recollections of W.T. Oliver."
February 25, 1915.
--- "American Falls Townsite Jumped, Recollections of W.T. Oliver." March 11, 1915.
---"Untold Wealth Within Reach, Recollections of W.T. Oliver." March 18, 1915.
American Whitewater Journal. Issue 4, July/August 1997.
The Arco Advertiser. Bound files.
Better Roads Magazine. November 1952.
Blackfoot Magazine. By the Greater Blackfoot Area Chamber of Commerce, 2005-2006.
The Blackfoot News.
Bonner County Daily Bee. <www.bonnercountydailybee.com>
Bovill Herald. 1911-1912.
Bovill Record. 1913.
Buhl Herald. April 1941.
Burley Bulletin.
Burley Herald.
Burley Herald-Bulletin.
Caldwell Daily News.
Caldwell News.
Caldwell News Weekly.
Caldwell News Tribune.
Caldwell Press Tribune.
Caldwell Progress Bulletin.
Caldwell Times.
Caldwell Tribune.
Daily Idahonian.
Family Circle Magazine. August 2010.
Forbes Magazine. March 2008.
Gem State Rural. Sept 15, 1895-May, 1916.
Genesee News. 1888-1968.
The Harrison Searchlight. June 2005 and June 2006 issues.
Hoot Owl. On microfilm at the Salmon Public Library.
Hub City Irrigationist.
Idaho County Voices.
The Idaho Enterprise.
Idaho Farm Journal. Black Canyon Edition, September 29, 1949.
The Idaho News.
Idaho Press-Tribune.
Idaho Recorder. On microfilm at the Salmon Public Library.
Idaho State Journal. "Malad's Early History Was Replete with Color." By Mary Matthews,
November 25, 1982.
Idaho Statesman.
Idaho's Yesterdays. Vol. 7 No. 4.
Inc. Magazine. 2008.

Independent Enterprise.
Irrigation Age. September 1980.
Kiplinger. 2008.
The Kooskia Mountaineer. 1927.
Latah County Press. 1944-46.
Lemhi Herald. On microfilm at the Salmon Public Library.
Lewiston Morning Tribune. "Town sprouts out of nowhere." By Jodi Walker, April 27, 2006.
Mackay Miner Newspaper. Microfilm and hard copy newspaper issues 1907-1975.
McCall Magazine.
Money Magazine. June 2010.
The Morning News.
Moscow Mirror. January 1, 1892. (Article on Vollmer first published in the Alliance Ledger.)
Mountain Home News.
Mullan News Bulletin. Summer Edition.
Mullan Progress. 1912-1918.
Mullan Tribune.
News Review. 1934.
News Tribune. Nov 16, 1966 " June 30, 1981.
North Side News. Bicentennial Edition, July 1, 1976.
---October 22, 1981.
North Side News: 75th Anniversary Edition. August 5, 1982.
Northern Idaho News. September 22, 1908.
---1908-1910.
Outdoor Life Magazine. June/July 2009.
Parma Review. "Our Yesterdays from 1910 to 1980, a historical record published December 1980 in celebration of its 70th anniversary.
Pierce city ordinances.
The Recorder Herald. July 2010.
Rupert Pioneer Record. August 22, 1907.
Sandpoint Online. <www.sandpointonline.com>
Semi-Weekly Mining News. On microfilm at the Salmon Public Library.
Snake River Echoes.
South Idaho Press. July 6, 1970. (Article by Al Dawson)
---March 11, 2004. (Article by Renee Wells)
Spokesman Review.
Star Mirror. 1934.
The Star-News.
The Times News. June 24, 1987.
Twin Falls News.
Twin Falls Weekly. 1904-1906.
United States Department of Agriculture, Issue 12-06. "Agriculture In Idaho." June 28, 2006.
US News and World Report. November 29, 2007.
The Warren Times.
Wendell Irrigationist.

Documents and Records:
1888 Polk Directory for Shoshone County.
1981-92 Polk Directory.
2000, 2008 and 2010 Census.
2005-06 Emmett Area Telephone Book.
2005-2006 Idaho Blue Book.

2006-2020 City of Driggs Comprehensive Plan. Adopted November 2, 2006, by the Driggs City Council.

A Pause for Reflection. Estes.

Ada County Historic Preservation Council 2006 Preservation Plan for Cultural and Historic Resources.

Adams County historical records.

Bloomington Comprehensive Plan. November 2008.

Boise Basin Museum.

Bonner County Historical Society.

Books of Deeds filed in Valley County Courthouse, Cascade, Idaho.

Boundary County Museum.

Bruneau-Grand View School District Records.

"Cassia County Agent Annual Report for 1923."

City of Dubois records.

City of Mountain Home records.

City of Orofino records.

City of Post Falls records.

City of Roberts Comprehensive Plan Revised. 2007.

City of Stites archives of meeting minutes and published ordinances.

City of Teton Comprehensive Plan, 2004.

City of Wendell Gem Community Update. "A Peek Into the Past." 2003-2008.

Clark County Historical Society.

Clearwater County Guide for Newcomers brochure.

Clearwater Historical Museum.

Coeur d'Alene Tribe official website. <http://www.cdatribe-nsn.gov/> 2016.

Comprehensive Plan for the cities of Juliaetta and Kendrick.

Craig Mountain Lumber Company papers, University of Idaho, September 1980.

Downtown Rexburg Revitalization Blueprint.

Elmore County Historical Foundation.

Excerpts taken from paper written by JaNene Buckway, chair, Lincoln County Centennial Committee, 1995.

Excerpts taken from Shoshone Historic Walking Tour, written by Christy Pyles, chair, Gem Community Committee and the residents of Shoshone, 1995.

Explorations and Fieldwork of the Smithsonian Institution in 1929, Publication 3060:31-36.

"Final Environmental Impact Statement." U.S.D.A. Forest Service, Salmon National Forest, June 1991.

Fremont and Clark County courthouse records.

Grand View City records.

Grand View Water and Sewer Association, Inc., records.

Historic Opera Theatre brochure, Glenns Ferry Opera Theatre.

Historic Oakley brochure.

Idaho Atlas and Gazetteer. DeLorme, 2002.

Idaho Historical Society archives and public records.

Idaho Parks and Recreation records.

Idaho State Archives/Historic Records. Collection AR202: "Bridge and Highway Contracts."

Idaho State Mining Records.

Idaho State Veterans" Cemetery: Cultural Resource "Inventory and Assessment, Ada County, Idaho." Grand View: Frontier Historical Consultants, 2002.

J.R. Simplot Company records.

Jerome Jt. School District No. 261 Physical Plant Inventory.

Jerome School District records.

Jobs Plus records.

Johnson Flying Service records, Missoula, MT.

Larsen Farms.

Latah County Courthouse Records and Documents.

Latah County Historical Society Archives.

Latah County Historical Society Research Library. Moscow, Idaho.

Lemhi County Commissioners Records.

Madison Economic Partners. 2008-2009 Community Profile. "Sugar City: Sweetest Town Around."

--Sugar City Business Park: a Great Place to Build a Business. 2009.

McCall Area Comprehensive Plan.

Meadows Valley School District records.

Minutes and Ordinances from the City of Bovill Archives.

Minute books for the City of Cambridge.

Minutes of past meetings of the Horseshoe Bend City Council.

Minutes of stockholders of Georgetown Reservoir Company held April 27, 193.

Minutes of the Salmon City Council.

Mountain Home Economic Development records.

Mountain Home Historical Museum pamphlet.

National Weather Service.

New Meadows City and Village records.

New Meadows Master Plan & Revitalization.

North Central Idaho Travel Association. Discover North Central Idaho. 2004-2006.

Personal records and pictures of Iona Residents.

Post Falls Chamber of Commerce.

Post Falls High School documents and records.

Post Falls Historical Society files.

Post Falls School District records.

Recreation Features Report.

The Rexburg Civic Life and Community Involvement Focus Team.

Richards, Bob, Economic Development, History of Spears Mfg. Jerome Idaho: Historical timeline from Spears purchase of Tupperware Plant to 2003.

Riverbed Commerce Park records.

Salmon Historical Society records.

Sanborn Fire Insurance Maps: Caldwell. New York: Sanborn Map Company. The Caldwell Public Library has mounted photocopies of the maps for 1888, 1890, 1892, 1900, 1908, 1911 and 1921.

Sandpoint Experiment Station 1910-2004.

Scenic Payette River Historical Society records.

Sugar City 2008 Comprehensive Plan.

Teton Scenic Byway Corridor Management Plan. Teton Scenic Byway Committee, Planmakers Planning & Urban Design, 2008.

The Twin Falls North Side Land and Water Company records. August 31, 1909.

University of Idaho Library Archives.

Upper Snake River Historical Society records and archives.

U.S. Forest Service records.

Valley County Comprehensive Plan.

Village of Notus Ordinance book dated 1921-1988.

Wastewater Status Update for the City of Greenleaf. April 28, 2009.

Wikipedia. "Skaggs Family."

Welcome to Oakley brochure.

Websites:

About the University of Idaho. <http://www.ucm.uidaho.edu/default.aspx?pid=86023> November 2005.

Ada County Development Services. "A Brief History of the Kuna Area." (PowerPoint Presentation.) <https://adacounty.id.gov/Portals/0/HisPreServ/Doc/ABriefHistoryoftheKunaAreaforweb.pdf> May 2016.

--- "Ada County Chronicles: An Overview of the Development of Ada County." (PowerPoint Presentation.) <https://adacounty.id.gov/Portals/0/HisPreServ/Doc/AdaCountyChroniclesHandout6perpage.pdf> May 2016.

Ada County Historic Preservation Council. "A Walking Tour of Kuna's Beginnings." <https://adacounty.id.gov/Portals/0/HisPreServ/Doc/kuna_Walking_Tour_Brochure201 2.pdf> May 2016.

AirNav.com <http://www.airnav.com> 2005.

America's Promise Alliance for Youth. "100 Best Communities for Youth: Meridian, Idaho." May 2016.

Bannock Development Corporation. <www.bannockdevelopment.org> July 2010.

Bonner County History Museum. <http://www.bonnercountyhistory.org> August 2010.

Cassia County. "Cassia County History." <http://www.cassiacounty.org/about-cassiacounty/history.htm> 2005.

Cinema Treasurers "Howells Opera House." <http://cinematreasurers.org/theaters/4167>

City Data. <www.citydata.com>

City of Ashton. "Whistles and Smoke: Ashton's Railroad Legacy." <www.cityofashton.com/whistles-and-smoke> April 2016.

City of Dalton Gardens. <www.daltongardens.govoffice.com> 2005.

City of Dover. <www.doveridaho.org> 2016.

City of Eagle. "Official web site of the City of Eagle, Idaho." <http://www.cityofeagle.org> September 2010.

City of Fairfield, Idaho. <www.fairfieldidaho.us> 2016.

City of Hayden. <www.cityofhaydenid.us> 2005.

City of Heyburn. <www.heyburnidaho.org> May 2016.

City of Kooskia. <www.kooskia.com> 2016.

The City of Lewiston: Idaho's Only Seaport. <http://www.cityoflewiston.org/> May 2016.

City of Moscow. <http://www.ci.moscow.id.us> 2005.

---Peterson, Jon R., et al. "Growth in Moscow: A Study of Modest Population Growth and Rising Economic Prosperity." <http://www.ci.moscow.id.us/records/City20Reports/Why_is20_Moscow_Growing_06.pdf#search=Growth%20in%20moscow%3A%20a%20study%20of%20modest%20population%20growth%20and%20rising%20economic%20prosperity> 2006.

The City of Mountain Home. <www.mountain-home.us> May 2016.

City of Pocatello. <www.pocatello.us> August 2010.

City of Rigby. <www.cityofrigby.com> 2016.

CityTownInfo.com. <http://www.citytowninfo.com> May 2016.

Community Library. <http://leadore.lili.org> May 2016.

"Dam Details: Little Wood River Dam." Bureau of Reclamation. <http://www.usbr.gov/projects/Facility.jsp?fac_Name=Little+Wood+River+Dam&groupName=General> April 2016.

Drive the Top Ten. <www.drivethetop10.com> 2005. (May 2016, no longer a viable site.)

Elk River Lodge & General Store. <www.elkriverlodge.net> 2006.

Ellersick, Steven Donald. White Pine Savages: Ellersicks in the Lumber Industry. <http://myplace.frontier.com/~sde22ssw/Eller5-sde.html> May 2016.

Epodunk. <http://epodunk.com> 2005.

Farnovision. <http://www.farnovision.com/> 2016.

Felton, Ann. "Airport Expansion, 1929." Office of the Boise City Historian. <http://www.boisestate.edu/history/cityhistorian/3workpapers_pdf/airport_expands.pdf> 2004.

Fremont County Idaho. <www.co.fremont.id/us> 2016.

Full text of History of Custer County, Idaho. <http://www.archive.org/stream/historyofcusterc00blac/historyofcusterc00blac_djvu.txt> 2016

Gem County Historical Society and Village Museum. <www.gemcountymuseum.org> August 2010.

Grand Targhee Resort. <www.grandtarghee.com> 2016.

Greater American Falls Area Chamber of Commerce <http://www.amfallschamber.com/> May 2016.

Greater Newport Area Chamber of Commerce. <http://newportareachamber.com/> 2016.

Greater Pocatello Chamber of Commerce. <www.pocatelloidaho.com> July 2010.

Greater Yellowstone Resource Guide. <http://www.free-press.biz/> 2005.

Handy, J.A. Heyburn " Its Origin and Early History. 1959. <http://heyburn.id.gov/index.asp?SEC=59AED487-1297-4A0D-B5FB6B8A80C30AB0&DE=8A62CC31-8BB8-4F3C-9E05D99AB627AC01&Type=B_PR> May 2016.

Hayden Chamber of Commerce. <www.haydenchamber.org> 2016.

Hester, Johnny. "Subdivisions of Boise." Office of the Boise City Historian. <http://www.boisestate.edu/history/cityhistorian/2atlas_subdivisions/index_subdivisions.html> 2005.

History of Kootenai County. <www.kcgov.us/community/history>

History of Latah County: Moscow. <http://users.moscow.com/lchs/history.html#moscow> November 2005.

Howell, Thomas. Snake River 4x4. "History of Warm River, Idaho." <http://www.snakeriver4x4.com/warmriver.php> 2005.

Idaho Chapter Oregon California Trail Association. <www.idahoocta.org> August 2010.

Idaho City Chamber of Commerce. <www.idahocitychamber.org> May 2016.

Idaho Community Profiles. <http://www.epodunk.com/communities_id.html> May 2016.

Idaho Department of Commerce. <http://commerce.idaho.gov/> 2016.

Idaho Fish and Game. <http://www.fishandgame.idaho.gov> 2005.

Idaho Fish and Wildlife Service. <www.fws.gov> 2016.

Idaho Rural Partnership. March 2005 Community Review. Kuna: A World of Potential. <http://www.irp.idaho.gov/Documents20and20Settings/14/Site20Documents/Site20Media/Community20Review/Kuna20Community20Review%20Report.pdf> May 2016.

Idaho State Parks. <http://www.stateparks.com/idaho_parks_and_recreation_destinations.html> May 2016.

Idaho State University. <http://www.isu.edu> 2005.

Idaho Wool Growers Association. <http://www.idahowool.org/> August 2010.

inidaho.com. "Plan Your Trip to Donnelly Idaho." <http://www.inidaho.com/City.asp?City=Donnelly> 2016.

Jackson Hole. <http://www.jacksonhole.com/> 2006.

Kiplinger. <http://www.kiplinger.com> September 2010.

"Lake Pend Oreille History." Sandpoint Online.com: Lake Guide. <http://www.sandpointonline.com/rec/lakeguide/history.html> August 2010.

Lava Hot Springs Area History. <http://lavahotsprings.com/info/history.html> May 2016.

Los Angeles Times. "Regional Report: Vanishing Railroads." <http://articles.latimes.com/1990-06-20/news/mn-226_1_union-pacific> 2005.

Miners Inch. <http://sizes.com/units/miners_inch.htm> August 2010.

Minidoka County Idaho. "Minidoka County History." <http://www.minidoka.id.us/general/history.htm> May 2016.

Moscow Chamber of Commerce. <http://www.moscowchamber.com> March 2007.

National Park Service. <https://www.nps.gov> May 2016.

--- "National Register of Historic Places. <https://www.nps.gov/nr> May 2016.

National Weather Service. <www.weather.gov> 2016.

Nez Perce Tribal Web Site. <www.nezperce.org> 2016.

Northwest Nazarene University. <www.nnu.edu> 2016.

OVAC Oakley Valley Arts Council. <http://oakleyvalleyartscouncil.org/>

Palouse Country. "Moscow's Unique Beginning." <http://the.palouse.net/Moscow/history/history_beginnings.htm> November 10, 2005. (No longer a viable site in May 2016.)

Pocatello Marathon. <www.Pocatellomarathon.com> August 2010.

Portneuf Greenway Foundation. <www.pgfweb.com> August 2010.

Portneuf Medical Center. <www.portmed.org> August 2010.

Roots Web. "Coeur d'Alene Tribe History."
<http://www.rootsweb.ancestry.com/~idreserv/cdhist.html> 2016

Rupert's Wilson Theatre. www.ruperttheatre.com

Rural Northwest.com. "Kootenai History: Hayden was booming at turn of century."
<http://www.ruralnorthwest.com/artman/publish/printer_4478.shtml> 2005.

Sangres. <http://www.sangres.com> August 2016.

School District #25. <www.d25.k12.id.us> August 2010.

Schwantes, Carlos. "A Brief History of the University of Idaho."
<www.ucm.uidaho.edu/default.aspx?pid=86022> November 2005.

"Silver Creek Preserve." The Nature Conservancy in Idaho.
<http://www.nature.org/ourinitiatives/regions/northamerica/unitedstates/idaho/placesweprotect/si
lver-creek-preserve.xml> April 2016.

Smith, Jerry E. A History of "Rancharrah". <http://www.jerryesmith.com/index.php/42>
2016.

Snake River Stampede. <www.snakeriverstampede.com> 2016.

Southeast Idaho: Be Here! <www.seidaho.org/grace.htm> April 2016.

South Lemhi School District. <www.leadoreschool.org> May 2016.

St. Luke's Jerome Medical Center. <https://www.stlukesonline.org/communities-
andlocations/facilities/hospitals-and-medical-centers/st-lukes-jerome-medical-center> 2016.

Stanley: Trailhead to Idaho Adventure. <http://stanleycc.org/> 2016.

Star Idaho. <http://staridaho.us/> 2016.

Steppe, Kali. "Clang, Clang, Clang Went the Trollies." Office of the Boise City Historian,
<http://www.boisehistory.com/> 2004.

Swan Valley Elementary School. <http://sd92.k12.id.us> 2006.

Tamarack Resort. <http://www.tamarackidaho.com> 2005.

Teton Valley Trails and Pathways. <http://tvtap.org> 2016.

Three Rivers Ranch: for the discriminating flyfisher. <http://www.threeriversranch.com>
May 2016.

Time. "Electrical Engineer Philo Farnsworth."
<http://content.time.com/time/magazine/article/0,9171,990620,00.html> 2016.

Topozone. <www.topozone.com> 2016.

Troy, Idaho USA. <http://www.troyidaho.net> May 2016.

Twin Lakes Canal Company history <http://www.twinlakescanalcompany.com/history.html>
2006.

Uhlenkott, Dale "Popeye." "Ferdinand, Idaho: Memoirs of Frank M. Bieker."
<http://idaho.idgenweb.org/PDF/Ferdinand%20Story%20Aug%2013%202004.pdf> April 2016.

Ultimate Idaho.com. <www.ultimateidaho.com> 2016.

United States Census Bureau. <http://www.census.gov/> 2016.

United States Geological Survey. <https://www.usgs.gov> 2016.

Upper Lemhi Valley Chamber of Commerce. <www.leadorechamber.com> May 2016.

U.S. Bureau of Reclamation. <www.usbr.gov> May 2016.

U.S. Forest Service. <www.fs.fed.us> May 2016.

U.S. Parks. <http://www.us-parks.com/> 2016.

Utah Power in the Gem Valley and Grace.
<http://www.graceidaho.com/html/utahpower.html> April 2016.

Visit Idaho. <https://visitidaho.org/> 2016.

"The War Mothers' Organization in Elmore County." Elmore County, Idaho: a proud part of
the ID GenWeb Project. <http://elmore.idgenweb.org/Military/Mothers.html> April 2016.

Warner, Eva. Historical Sketch of Heyburn, Idaho: The Town that Refused to Die. Written
March 1970. <http://heyburn.id.gov/index.asp?SEC=59AED487-1297-4A0D-
B5FB6B8A80C30AB0&DE=5E77EFFE-88FA-4D41-AD99034E9E5D0C36&Type=B_PR>
May 2016.

Washington County: The Heart of Idaho. "History of the County." <http://co.washington.id.us/about-washington-county/> May 2016.

Water Archives. <http://www.waterarchives.org> August 2016.

The Weather Channel. <https://weather.com/> May 2016.

Weather Today. <www.weathertoday.net> July 2010.

Welcome to Glenns Ferry, Idaho: A Community of Opportunity! <http://glennsferryidaho.org> April 2016.

Welcome to Grace & Gem Valley: Grace Chamber of Commerce. <http://www.graceidaho.com> April 2016.

Wendell Chamber of Commerce: Hub City of Magic Valley. <http://www.wendellchamberofcommerce.org/> May 2016.

Western Regional Climate Center data <http://www.wrcc.dri.edu/> 2016.

Wheels That Won the West. <www.wheelsthatwonthewest.com> April 2016.

Wikipedia: the Free Encyclopedia. "Teton Dam." <http://en.wikipedia.org/wiki/Teton_Dam> December 12, 2005.

---"Fort Hall" <https://en.wikipedia.org/wiki/Fort_Hall,_Idaho> 2005.

---"Notus, Idaho." <https://en.wikipedia.org/wiki/Notus,_Idaho> 2016.

---"Oregon Shortline Railroad." <https://en.wikipedia.org/wiki/Oregon_Short_Line_Railroad> 2016.

---"Pend Oreille County, Washington." <https://en.wikipedia.org/wiki/Pend_Oreille_County%2C_Washington> August 2010.

Wolf Education & Research Center. <http://wolfcenter.org/> 2016.

Interviews:
Baker, Laurie, Eagle Historical Museum.
Bath, Teri, Eagle Chamber of Commerce.
Banner, Kent.
Bentz, Laurice.
Bergmann, Sharon, City of Eagle City Clerk.
Blanchard, Tom.
Brown, David.
Buster, Dick, Environmental Protection Specialist. September 2005.
Cada, Dave.
Carnegie, Amy.
Clark, Walter E., history of Georgetown, Idaho.
Collard, Mark.
Coyner, Barbara.
Crosby, Wayne.
Dahl, Melanie.
Everett, Kelly.
Fiori, Frank A.
Fisher, Betty.
Friend Dan, City of Eagle Fire Chief.
Gibson, Mike, Business Manager, Jerome School District.
Gillerman, Dr. Virginia, Economic Geologist/Associate Research Geologist, Idaho Geological Survey.
Good, Austin. Oral History.
Goodman, Don. Oral History.
Guerber, Steve, Former Eagle City Councilmember.
Hart, Arthur A., historian.
Hatzenbuhler, Ron, ISU Professor.
Hays, Sam H. Oral History.
Henderson, Ray, Minerals Specialist, U.S. Forest Service. September 2005.
Hiller, John.

Hopkins, Terry, First American Title.
House, Rod, Idaho State Archives/Historic Records Center.
Hatzenbuhler, Ron, ISU Professor.
Jackson, Kathy, Reubens City Clerk.
Jatkevicius, Jim. Boise Public Library.
Kenyon, Dale.
Kesler, Kelly.
Kunau, Lex.
Lierman, Amy. Public Relations, Idaho Transportation Dept. "History of I-84 US93 and Hwy 25." April 26, 2006.
Marshall, Ron.
Matheson, John.
Mendiola, Judy.
Merrill, Nancy, Former Eagle Mayor.
Miller, Amy.
Miller, Wendy.
Moldenhauer, Rocky and Dawn.
Moser, Lynn, Eagle Sewer District.
Ogden, Jerry.
Parrish-Manwaring, Angelyn.
Peak, Clifford.
Porath, Mrs.
Pruett, Jimmy J.
Richardson, Greg.
Rupe, Kevin.
Sales, Dorothy.
Scott, Diane, Eagle Historical Preservation Commission.
Sims, Larry, Hauser Fire Chief.
Standley, Carla, a historian writing a book about the PI&N Railroad and a general historian and researcher of Meadows Valley.
Stephens, Dick, 1964.
Stevens, Louise Powers, September 29, 1994.
Thomasen, Everta. February 26, 2007.
Trent, Geneva, Eagle Historical Museum.
Urquidi, Richard.
Utt, Edith.
Valantine, Virgil.
Wallace, Doris, EISF Manager, 2005.
Ward, Opal.
Wiggers, Gene, Chief Pocatello Project. 2008.

Made in the USA
Middletown, DE
19 February 2021